THE VISION OF HELL

Satan in Hell (cf. *Vision of Tundal*). Miniature by the Limbourg brothers in *Les Très riches Heures du duc de Berry*. Chantilly, Musée Condé MS 65. 1413–1416. (Photo Giraudon.)

THE VISION OF HELL

Infernal Journeys in
Medieval French Literature

D. D. R. OWEN

1970
SCOTTISH ACADEMIC PRESS
EDINBURGH & LONDON

Published by
Scottish Academic Press Ltd.
25 Perth Street, Edinburgh 3

Distributed by
Chatto and Windus Ltd.
40 William IV Street
London WC2

ISBN 0 7011 1677 3

Printed in Great Britain by
R. & R. Clark, Ltd., Edinburgh

ACKNOWLEDGEMENTS

This work began life as a Ph.D. thesis (*The Visit to Hell*, Cambridge, 1955), and since then it has spent a secluded if not entirely private existence. From time to time I have been urged to put it into print; so it now appears in a completely recast form and, there being new fashions and discoveries even in infernal matters, brought as far as possible up to date. If it has any merit or usefulness, this is due less to diabolic inspiration than to the unstinting help, criticism and advice of more friends and colleagues than I can hope to name. It was the late Reverend H. J. Chaytor who put the subject into my mind; and my early studies were guided principally by Dr S. C. Aston, M. F. Lecoy and Professor R. C. Johnston. In the past year I have had good counsel and assistance from Dr A. R. Pacheco and Mr A. B. Hunt, while my wife has grappled patiently with the drafting of Bibliography and Index. The kindness and tolerance of the staff of the St Andrews University Library and of the members of the Scottish Academic Press must also be recorded. To all who have helped me in those first and these latter stages my thanks is as sincere as to the many unnamed who offered guidance and encouragement in the intervening years. But the road to Hell is paved with gold as well as good intentions; and I owe an especial debt of gratitude to those who have provided generous financial assistance: to the Carnegie Trust for the Universities of Scotland for subsidising the book's publication, and to the Marc Fitch Fund for their grant towards the cost of its illustration.

D. D. R. O.

St Andrews
October 1970

v

CONTENTS

LIST OF ILLUSTRATIONS

INTRODUCTION

IN the Middle Ages Hell was considered a grim reality, not merely a matter for pious conjecture. So real was it that in special circumstances it was accessible to living human beings, who might visit it in spirit or even in the flesh—a somewhat academic distinction, this, since the journeying soul is normally described as having a corporeal existence. And those who returned from the infernal regions were not sparing of vivid detail in their accounts of the horrors they had witnessed. So with each succeeding description, the topography of the place became more precise and the activities of the demons more familiar, to the extent that Hell might almost be said to have been fashioned in the course of the Middle Ages by the hands of the people who claimed to have visited it. It was not, however, created from the void.

In his attempts to solve the riddle of life and death, of good and ill fortune, primitive man has readily accepted the existence of supernatural powers which consciously work for or against his welfare. These spirits might be elemental, personifying nature's own forces, or they might be more intimately associated with the individual as in an ancestor-worshipping society. Just as they preside over a man's life, so they might also exert some influence upon that part of him which survives after death; but in primitive religions a man's fate in the after-life is seldom connected with his moral conduct when on earth. The idea of retribution after death may have been a relatively late arrival in the history of religion; but before the Christian era it can be traced in Egyptian, Greek, Indian and Persian religious systems. Indeed, its introduction into the Hebrew religion after the Babylonian captivity was probably conditioned by contact with Mazdaism and Greek eschatological conceptions.[1] A natural corollary to the belief in physical punishment for the wicked after death is the assumption that retribution was exacted in specific places of torment.

Several factors helped to encourage the notion that these fearsome regions were situated beneath the crust of the earth. Firstly, the custom of burial led to the supposition that the soul as well as the body was committed to a subterranean dwelling-place.[2] Hence we find deep caverns and grottoes treated with superstitious awe as being entrances to the Underworld. The souls of the Baperi in South Africa go down through the cavern of Marimatlé;[3] the Samoan Islanders believe that two holes in the earth are used by departing souls—a smaller one for those of the commoners and a larger one for the souls of their chiefs;[4] the entrance to the Virgilian Hades is of the same nature, as is that to St Patrick's Purgatory in Ireland; and in our own days tradition places an entrance to Hell in Paris, not a mile from the Sorbonne.[5] Natural phenomena, then, contribute to the conception of a subterranean Otherworld, and many other instances could be quoted.[6] The setting of the sun was held by several races to be the occasion for its nocturnal passage through the nether regions. Indeed it is natural enough that primitive folk should think of a gloomy Otherworld as existing beneath the ground in the depths of black caverns far from the radiance of the sky. For the early Christians, believing as they did in a Hell of fire, volcanoes had a special significance:[7] Gregory the Great tells of a hermit seeing the soul of King Theodoric hurled into the crater of a volcano on Lipari; and Mount Etna was commonly considered to be a chimney of Hell.[8]

The idea that the places of retribution have a more or less precise geographical location encouraged the belief that they could be visited on occasion not only by divine or semi-divine personages but even by especially privileged mortals. In the Ancient World this supposed possibility was exploited to the advantage of diverse religions and mythologies; and so the theme of the infernal descent came into being.[9] It was to remain popular in Western Europe until the end of the Middle Ages, although with a more mystical approach to the Deity and the world beyond the grave the emphasis tended to shift towards the spiritual, as opposed to the physical, aspect of the descent. This accounts for the pre-eminence of the "vision" type of account in the Middle Ages, catering as it did both for the public craving for sensationalism and for the clerical desire to moralise and instruct in matters concerning the after-life. Not that vision literature was absent in ancient times (we shall see that some of it even influenced medieval accounts), but it was left to the Middle Ages to exploit it to the full.

Only a small number of the pre-Christian descent stories were known to medieval Europe. The Persian legend of Ishtar's descent, the nocturnal journey of the Egyptian sun-god Ra, the mysteries of the Orphic cult,[10] Indian mythology—these have no direct link with medieval eschatological theory and description, although striking analogies may sometimes be found there which hint at a venerable ancestry for certain later motifs.[11] In any case, medieval writers were not concerned with the ultimate origin of their theme (what a shock it would have been to many of them to learn of it!). The furthest they ventured was to refer now and then to some widely known and respected source such as holy writ, the Christian Fathers, or perhaps an honest pagan like Virgil. Nevertheless, the ancestry of most of their texts is clear or can be deduced with reasonable certainty; and among the forebears a few Classical and early Christian works are of particular importance, since the line between them and the medieval texts is unbroken. Of the Ancients, Virgil and Ovid call for special mention, the former principally because of his account in the *Aeneid*, Book VI, of the hero's descent into Hades, and Ovid for his description of the adventures of Orpheus in the Underworld.[12] Both were known in Western Europe throughout the Middle Ages and were widely popular from the twelfth century onwards. And though no more than adaptations of the story in the *Metamorphoses* have come down to us in French literature, which is my particular field of study in this book, the Virgilian legend has survived, as we shall see, in reasonably faithful translation. Of the early Christian works I shall speak in my first chapter.

It is not my intention merely to present in these pages a descriptive catalogue of medieval French accounts of Hell and its visitors. I shall try as well to suggest how in their treatments the authors disclose something of their own attitudes towards the Christian Otherworld, and in doing so give us a curious insight into the general medieval conscience.

NOTES

1. See, e.g., J. Monnier's Introduction to *La Descente aux enfers* (Paris, 1904); E. O. James, *Comparative Religion: An Introductory and Historical Study* (London, 1938), Chs. IX & XII; A. Lods, *De quelques récits de voyage au pays des morts* (Mâcon, 1940); S. G. F. Brandon, *Man and his Destiny in the Great Religions* (Manchester, 1962); idem, *The Judgment of the Dead* (London, 1967).

2. F. B. Jevons, *An Introduction to the History of Religion* (London, 1896), pp. 299 ff.; F. Bar, *Les Routes de l'Autre Monde* (Paris, 1946), p. 8; E. O. James, *Prehistoric Religion* (London, 1957), pp. 132–3.

3. Jevons, op. cit., p. 305.

4. E. B. Tylor, *Primitive Culture* (4th edn., London, 1903), II, p. 66. See also Rosalind Moss, *The Life after Death in Oceania and the Malay Archipelago* (Oxford, 1925), especially Chs. V and VI.

5. G. Cohen, *Histoire de la chevalerie en France au moyen âge* (Paris, 1949), p. 84, n. 1.

6. See, e.g., J. Hastings, *Encyclopaedia of Religion and Ethics*, IV (New York, 1911), p. 648; A. van Gennep, *Les Rites de passage* (Paris, 1909), pp. 215 ff.

7. W. E. H. Lecky, *History of European Morals from Augustus to Charlemagne*, II (3rd edn., London, 1877), p. 221; Tylor, op. cit., II, p. 69; Bar, op. cit., p. 8.

8. Th. de Cauzons, *La Magie et la sorcellerie en France* (Paris, n.d.), II, p. 110; A. Graf, *The Story of the Devil* (tr. E. N. Stone, London, 1931), p. 168; H. R. Patch, *The Other World, According to Descriptions in Medieval Literature* (Harvard, 1950), p. 236. See Gregory's *Dialogues* IV, 30, 35 (J. P. Migne, *Patrologia Latina*, Vol. 77, cols. 368–9, 380).

9. See O. Delepierre, *L'Enfer décrit par ceux qui l'ont vu. Essai philosophique et littéraire* (in *Miscellanies of the Philobiblion Society* VIII and IX, London, 1863–6), i, pp. 13 ff; Hastings, op. cit., IV, pp. 648–54; H. Diels, "Himmels- und Höllenfahrten von Homer bis Dante", *Neue Jahrbücher für das klassische Altertum, Geschichte und deutsche Literatur* 49 (1922), pp. 239 ff.; J. Kroll, *Gott und Hölle: der Mythos vom Descensuskampfe* (Leipzig & Berlin, 1932).

10. For the eschatological aspect of the cult see J. R. Watmough, *Orphism* (Cambridge, 1934).

11. For instance, the Bridge of Dread seems to have been taken over from Persian religious ideas embodied in the *Avesta* (see Patch, op. cit., pp. 8–10, 95–7, *et passim*); E. J. Becker and A. B. van Os have noted features from Buddhist eschatology which correspond with others in the medieval texts (see especially Appendix IV to van Os's *Religious Visions: The Development of the Eschatological Elements in Medieval English Religious Literature* [Amsterdam, 1932]); the weighing of a soul's good and bad actions at the hour of death, often depicted in medieval literature and art, was known to Mazdaism and Egyptian mythology alike (Bar, op. cit., p. 23; Lods, op. cit., p. 19; Brandon, *The Judgment of the Dead*, pp. 23 ff. *et passim*).

12. *Metamorphoses* X, ll. 1–77; the legend is also treated by Virgil in his *Georgicon* IV, ll. 453–527. For other references see Hastings, op. cit., IV, p. 651. On Aeneas' descent see August Rüegg, *Die Jenseitsvorstellungen vor Dante und die übrigen Voraussetzungen der "Divina Commedia"* (2 vols., Einsiedeln/Köln, 1945), I, pp. 131–67.

CHAPTER I

THE CHURCH'S WITNESSES:
THE LATIN ACCOUNTS

WHILE for the early Christians the Bible was the pure fount of all authority, it was not long before the scriptural stream was fed by apocryphal tributaries whose waters too were found sweet by all but the most discriminating. The canonical books themselves contain no descriptions of the infernal journey; but they do offer a few ambiguous or cryptic texts such as invite elaboration. The tradition of Christ's own descent, derived from, among other passages, *Matthew* xxvii. 52–3, *Luke* xxiii. 43, and *1 Peter* iii. 18–20, seems to have been current in the East by the second century; and as an article of faith it is found in certain fourth-century Arian formularies before appearing in the Aquileian Creed of Rufinus and spreading gradually throughout the West.[1]

An intriguing hint of a visit to the blessed realms is given by Paul in *2 Corinthians* xii. 1–5, another text to set the imagination running:

Si gloriari oportet (non expedit quidem), veniam autem ad visiones et revelationes Domini.

Scio hominem in Christo ante annos quatuordecim (sive in corpore, nescio, sive extra corpus, nescio, Deus scit), raptum hujusmodi usque ad tertium caelum;

Et scio hujusmodi hominem (sive in corpore, sive extra corpus, nescio, Deus scit);

Quoniam raptus est in Paradisum, et audivit arcana verba, quae non licet homini loqui.

Pro hujusmodi gloriabor; pro me autem nihil gloriabor nisi in infirmitatibus meis.

(It is not expedient for me doubtless to glory. I will come to visions and revelations of the Lord.

I knew a man in Christ above fourteen years ago, (whether
in the body, I cannot tell; or whether out of the body, I
cannot tell: God knoweth;) such an one caught up to the
third heaven.

And I knew such a man, (whether in the body, or out of
the body, I cannot tell: God knoweth;)

How that he was caught up into paradise, and heard un-
speakable words, which it is not lawful for a man to utter.

Of such an one will I glory: yet of myself I will not glory,
but in mine infirmities.)

Despite their reference only to Paradise, these verses were to
have dramatic consequences for the development of our theme
throughout the Middle Ages.

The pagan peoples of the East had traced their own paths to
the Otherworld and told in their legends of the heroes who
trod them and glimpsed the life beyond the grave. As well as
the Persian Ishtar and the Egyptian god Ra, we think of Greek
heroes like Orpheus, Hercules, Theseus and Pirithoüs, or
Homer's Odysseus; and in a less epic vein, Plato tells in his
Republic of the wanderings of the soul of Er the Pamphylian.
Hebrew lore embodied in various Old Testament apocrypha
knew and used the theme. An account of Enoch's visit to the
further realms antedates the Christian era, at least in part.
So it is small wonder that the writers of the New Religion
adopted the old, graphic ways of exploring man's future state
and were very ready to credit the Christian heroes with ex-
cursions beyond the bounds of the mortal world.

The earliest such apocalyptic account that we possess (and
this only in fragmentary form) is the *Revelation of Peter*, which
may date from the early second century.[2] It soon achieved wide
popularity. Purporting to tell through Peter how Christ led his
twelve disciples to see the joys of Heaven and the torments of
the damned, it retails with apparent relish the punishment of
different categories of evildoers, in a manner with which the
reader will become all too familiar in the course of this study.
But he shall have a brief respite: the *Revelation* influenced only
indirectly the vernacular accounts that come within our pur-
view, so a summary can be dispensed with now.

The *Vision of St Paul* is another matter.[3] Inspired by the
verses from *Corinthians* quoted above, and amplified with
material from sundry early apocalypses and above all from the
Revelation of Peter, it was responsible more than any other
single work for fixing the horrific detail of Hell in the medieval
eye. The original *Vision* was written in Greek, probably in the
third century A.D., although a spurious preface appended later
tells how it was discovered in Tarsus in A.D. 388. This version
we know only through subsequent recensions in Greek, Syriac,
Coptic, Arabic, Armenian, Slavonic and Latin. The oldest
Latin form[4] dates from the eighth century and is one of the so-
called Long texts. But by the twelfth century, when the French
vernacular versions began to appear, a number of abbreviated
redactions existed and, to judge from the distribution of the
manuscripts as well as various literary references, had achieved
considerable popularity, especially in England.

H. Brandes evolved a system of classification for the Latin
redactions, and this was later developed by H. T. Silverstein,
who supposed that they numbered at least ten, of which seven
have survived. But while such a system is useful in so far as it
helps us to grapple with the problems of transmission, it is
doomed to incompleteness, as a close study of the vernacular
versions shows.[5] From the number of extant manuscripts it
seems that the redaction numbered IV by Brandes and Silverstein was the most common; and certainly more vernacular
versions were based on it than on any other. So it is a summary
of this redaction that can most usefully be given here.[6]

Sunday is a day of great joy, and on this day the souls in
Hell enjoy a respite from their pains, a privilege obtained for
them by the Apostle Paul and the Archangel Michael when
they visited Hell at God's behest so that Paul might see the
torments.

Before the gates of Hell were fiery trees where damned
souls hung by their feet, hands, tongues, hair, ears and arms.

Paul next saw a multi-coloured furnace with seven separate
flames, and sinners punished within it. Around the furnace
were seven torments: snow, ice, fire, blood, serpents,
thunderbolt, stench. That was the torment for the non-

penitent, who are punished according to their works and long
for a death that cannot come.

We should fear the dolorous realms of Hell, where there is
a fiery wheel with a thousand spokes. It is struck a thousand
times a day by a Tartarean angel, and at each turn a thousand
souls are tortured.

Then Paul beheld a foul river in which swam many
infernal creatures like fish in the sea, devouring sinners as
wolves devour sheep. The river is spanned by a bridge
which the righteous cross with ease; but the sinful are immersed in the water according to their deserts and are
grouped according to the nature of their crime. For thus
said the Lord: "Bind them in bundles to burn them"
(*Matthew* xiii. 30). Paul saw some souls immersed to the
knees, others to the navel, lips or eyebrows, all in perpetual
torment. He asked Michael who these wretches were and was
told that immersion to the knees was for the slanderers, to the
navel for non-repentant fornicators and adulterers, to the
lips for those who quarrelled in church, to the eyebrows for
those who delighted in others' misfortunes. Paul wept at
their plight.

In a dark place he saw men and women chewing their
tongues. They were the merciless usurers. And elsewhere,
enduring all the torments, were black girls clad in black
raiment and covered with pitch and sulphur. Round their
necks were dragons and fire and serpents. Four evil angels
with fiery horns beat them and called upon them to recognise
the Son of God. Paul was told that these unchaste creatures
slew their illicit offspring and gave them as food to pigs or
dogs, or else drowned them: for these crimes they remained
impenitent.

Next Paul saw men and women in a place of ice, part of
which was bitterly cold and part full of fire. These were they
who harmed widows and orphans. The next torment was
for the fast-breakers, who were beside a stream with fruit
just out of their reach; but they were allowed neither to eat
nor to drink. Further on was an old man, weeping and
groaning as he was beset by four demons. Michael said that
he was a wicked bishop who, because of his lack of chastity,

PLATE I. The infernal wheel. Oxford, Bodleian MS Douce 134. French, 15th century.

his avarice, his deceit and his pride, would suffer thus until the Judgment Day. Paul wept, but his guide told him that he had not yet seen the greatest of the infernal torments.

He showed him a pit sealed with seven seals and told him to stand far off because of the stench of the place. The pit was opened, and the stench surpassed all the other torments in its vileness. And the angel said : "God will never more be mindful of those who are placed in this pit." They were those who did not believe in Christ. Yet another place of torture was as deep as the distance from earth to Heaven. It was packed with sinners like sheep in a fold. They were being gnawed by snakes and reptiles, and their groans were like thunder.

Paul then saw seven devils fly into the air carrying the soul of a sinner who had died that very day. God's angels upbraided him, and he read from a scroll whereon were recorded all his sins ; after that, the devils cast him into outer darkness. On the other hand, a good soul was greeted by a thousand angels before reading the record of his good deeds and being placed by Michael in Paradise amid great rejoicing.

The suffering sinners then cried out to Michael and Paul, beseeching them to intercede on their behalf. This they did, while the sinners themselves and a million angels joined in their pleas ; whereupon Christ Himself descended from Heaven with a diadem upon His head. He blamed the sinners for their wicked and unrepentant lives, but decreed, after further supplication, that on account of Michael and Paul and the angels, and also on account of His own great goodness, the sinners should have respite from the hour of none on Saturday until prime on Monday.

But Cerberus, the door-keeper of Hell, raised his heads in grief over all the pains of Hell, whereas those who suffered them praised Christ for his clemency. And Paul asked Michael the number of torments. There are 144,000 ; and a hundred men, each having a hundred iron tongues, could not enumerate them, even if they had been speaking from the beginning of the world. Therefore let us follow the Lord, that we may dwell with Him for ever.

VH B

The Long version is far more wordy and diffuse than this redaction. Opening with the seminal verses from *Corinthians*, it proceeds to tell how the text of the *Vision* was discovered in the foundations of Paul's house in Tarsus. Paul's account is then presented in the first person. He tells how he received the word of God regarding the sinful state of mankind, and how he himself was caught up into Heaven and witnessed the fate of worthy and sinful souls as they departed their earthly life. In the Third Heaven he encountered Enoch and Eljah and heard and saw things which it is not lawful for a man to reveal. The Land of Promise was shown to him with its rivers, and the city of Christ; and there he saw the prophets, the Innocents and the patriarchs, with David singing praises in Jerusalem. Only then was he conducted through Hell to view its torments, not all of them the same as those in the Fourth Redaction. Finally he was led through the Earthly Paradise, seeing the Virgin Mary and other saintly personages before returning to the everyday world, recording his experiences and seeing to the concealment of the text.

Here, then, was an early Christian legend inspired by a passage from the scriptures and leaning heavily on other apocryphal works as well as the canonical *Book of Revelation*.[8] From the beginning, there may have been some Classical reminiscence, for the Long Latin version already contained the clearly recognisable "Tantalus torment", applied to those sinners unable to drink the water or eat the fruit that they see just out of reach. Other apparent gleanings from pagan literature are drawn into the redactions and especially Redaction IV: an echo of Virgil, perhaps, in the fiery trees of Hell, the blazing wheel, the figure of Cerberus, and the reference to the iron-tongued men.[9]

We can see a morbid process at work. As the centuries passed, the men of God who handled this material grew less interested in the lengthy moralisings of the early *Vision*; and they turned from the blessed sights of Paradise and the saints to concentrate their gaze ever more intently on Hell, as if hypnotised by all its horrors. With their interpolations it was the pain and misery that they intensified, not the joys of the righteous or men's hope of salvation. Did they do it out of sheer masochism (for they must have trembled at their own imaginings)? Or were they persuaded that their only hope of bringing their contemporaries to heel was by terrorising them through this grisly form of spiritual shock treatment? Certainly, the shorter redactions and particularly the fourth were well suited for use as admonitory sermons, and this at a period which saw an intensification of preaching activities.[10]

From at least the second century it was supposed that Christ's purpose in visiting Hell was to rescue the souls of the righteous fathers. Here is a theme, the dramatic potentialities of which were not lost on the early weavers of Christian legend. The *Gospel of Nicodemus* or *Acts of Pilate* was composed, perhaps in the fourth century, to illustrate the story of Christ's Passion and Resurrection. Within a hundred years or so a second part was added, which presented an epic account of His Harrowing of Hell. This exists in two Latin versions, designated A and B by C. Tischendorff, and one Greek recension. I summarise from the Latin Version A.[11]

The two sons of Simeon, Karinus and Leucius, have been raised from the dead and are living in Arimathaea. They make separate written depositions to Annas, Caiaphas, Nicodemus, Joseph and Gamaliel about their strange experiences.

They were in the abyss with all those who had died since the beginning of the world, when suddenly the darkness was dispelled by a golden glow and a purple, royal light. Adam, the patriarchs and the prophets rejoiced greatly, and Isaiah and Simeon recalled their prophecies. Then John the Baptist arrived to herald the coming of Christ.

At Adam's bidding, his son Seth told of his journey to the gates of Paradise to seek from God the sacred oil for his father's healing. Michael had appeared to him and told him that after 5,500 years God's Son would appear on earth to anoint all believers with such oil.

When all the saints were exulting at the news, Satan bade Inferus to prepare to receive Jesus, who had opposed him in many things and done him much mischief, even raising the dead to life. Inferus doubted if Satan had the strength to resist Christ, but Satan tried to reassure him: he had just engineered Christ's death through the Jews. "But", said Inferus, "perhaps it was he who recently resurrected Lazarus, whom I had held dead for four days." Satan said that it was indeed Jesus; whereupon Inferus begged Satan not to bring Him here, for it was His intention to deprive Hell of its dead.

While Satan and Inferus were talking thus, there came a voice as of thunder: "Remove, O princes, your gates, and be ye lift up ye everlasting doors, and the King of glory shall come in!"[12] Hearing this, Inferus commanded Satan to depart and resist the intruder, and then called upon his demons to secure the brazen gates and iron bolts and bars of Hell. The patriarchs reproached Inferus for his action, and David and Isaiah recalled their prophecies.

Again a thunderous voice was heard uttering the same summons, and Inferus asked: "Who is the King of glory?" David answered: "The Lord strong and mighty, the Lord mighty in battle", and he bade Inferus open the gates. Immediately Christ entered in the form of a man, illuminating the eternal darkness, and broke the bonds that could not be loosed.

Inferus and Death and their legions trembled with fear and admitted their defeat, asking who was this man who could accomplish such wonders. Christ then trampled upon Death and, seizing Satan the prince, delivered him into the power of Inferus and drew Adam into His glory. (The Greek text is rather fuller here: Christ seized Satan by the head and delivered him to the angels, instructing them to bind with irons his hands and feet and neck and mouth. Then He handed him over to Hades, i.e. Inferus, to be kept safely until His second coming.) Inferus ranted at Satan for having secured Christ's death, and threatened him with dire torments. Christ then promised Inferus that he would have Satan in his power in place of Adam and his progeny.

Christ stretched out His hand to Adam to deliver him and the saints, whereupon they all fell at His feet and proclaimed their gratitude. Making the sign of the cross upon them, He

took Adam by the right hand and led them from Hell, whilst
David, Habakkuk and Micah sang the praises of the Lord.
When they came to Paradise, they were delivered to the
Archangel Michael and met by Enoch and Elijah. There-
after they saw the good robber, who recounted his story.

Karinus and Leucius record that they may only abide in
Jerusalem for three days. Karinus entrusts his account to
Annas, Caiaphas and Gamaliel, and Leucius gives his to
Nicodemus and Joseph. Then suddenly they are trans-
figured and vanish.

This legend, despite its obviously apocryphal origin, won
great popularity in medieval Europe and is found from the
seventh century onwards in many Latin manuscripts. At least
part of the *Gospel* was known to Gregory of Tours in the sixth
century,[13] though we have no proof that it circulated widely in
Western Europe at that time. It was well loved because it gave
animation and colour to a doctrine which might otherwise have
remained simply an article of belief in the Christian Creed. It
was loved because the author, by amplifying the dogmatic
statement of the descent tradition, had created a short Christian
epic showing the divine conquest of the powers of darkness, and
the release of the righteous souls from their imprisonment.
The pattern is age-old, and many pagan mythologies have
stories of a hero visiting the world beyond the grave and returning to earth with his spoils.[14] It is more than likely, for
instance, that the Eastern author of *Nicodemus* knew the legend
of Orpheus, or of the last labour of Hercules when he visited the
Underworld in order to capture the infernal hound Cerberus—
it may even have been this latter exploit that inspired him to
illustrate the descent of the "Christian Hercules". In any case,
the result is a mixture of reminiscences of the Old and New
Testaments and of pagan myth.[15] In this it follows the same
tradition as the *Vision of St Paul*; and with these two texts
the medieval Church has been provided with its most important
and well-documented eye-witness accounts of Hell and its
denizens.

Western Christendom was not slow to produce its own vision-
aries, and their warning voices echo down the ages. For among

their literate brethren ("literate", that is, in the sense of being able to read and write Latin) there were always a few whose piety went hand in hand with what we would today call journalistic flair, and who were ever ready to record or pass on a sensational story of things seen beyond this planet. Of the many medieval Latin visions that have come down,[16] I shall mention here only a representative few of which we happen to have versions in French. They may themselves have played no very significant part in creating the concept of Hell, but along with all the others that had some currency they helped to keep it burning in the mind of clergy and laity alike.

The *Dialogues* of Pope Gregory the Great did, to be sure, make a considerable impact on later generations, and perhaps in certain respects exerted some formative influence on our theme. Living in the latter part of the sixth century, Gregory was much concerned with visions and accounts of the other life. In Rome he had the opportunity to read widely not only in the literature of the early Church but also in that of Classical Antiquity, and his own writings bear the mark of this two-fold influence. The *Dialogues* contain one of the first known references in Christian literature to the bridge that links the realms of Hell and Paradise;[17] and one feels that Gregory's eschatological conceptions themselves form a bridge, spanning the gulf between the old world and the new. Through his anecdotes he betrays just such a concrete attitude to the life after death as we find in later exponents of the same *genre*, masters of the devout macabre like Ralph Glaber or Caesarius of Heisterbach. The favour in which his works were held is shown by the way in which medieval vision literature is strewn with quotations or unacknowledged borrowings from them.

Another feature which Gregory was probably the first to introduce into Western pious legend was what we may call the "apparent death theme". A man loses all, or almost all, appearance of life, but returns to his senses after a certain period (often three days) and tells of his experiences in the abodes of the dead. This means of achieving communication with the Otherworld no more originated with Christianity than did the divinely appointed vision or other concepts that we shall come across—the voyage over the sea, or the physical descent beneath the earth's crust. It is already found in Plato's tale of Er the Pamphylian and Plutarch's *Vision of Thespesios*.[18] Indeed one form of the theme as found in Gregory poses sharp problems for the Christian. But let us look now at those of his stories that are pertinent to our study. They are all found in Book IV of the *Dialogues*.[19]

A man called Reparatus dies to all outward appearances and is mourned by his family and friends. Suddenly he regains consciousness and demands news of a certain loose-living priest, Tiburtius. A messenger is despatched to obtain information, whereupon Reparatus tells of his own alarming experience. He has been to a place where a great pyre was prepared and Tiburtius burnt upon it. Then another fire was made ready, so high that it reached from earth to Heaven. Reparatus is asked for whom it was prepared, but before he can say, he dies. The messenger returns with the news that Tiburtius is already dead, which proves that Reparatus has indeed visited Hell.

(IV, 31)[20]

IV, 36[21] deals with those who have seen the Otherworld through an apparent mistake by supernatural powers. Gregory explains, however, that there has been no mistake : the incidents are, in fact, deliberate warnings. The title of the dialogue is : "De his qui quasi per errorem educi videntur e corpore, et de vocatione et revocatione Petri monachi, et de morte et resuscitatione Stephani, ac de visione cujusdam militis".

Peter, a Spanish hermit, dies ; but straightway his soul returns to the body having beheld the torments of Hell. He tells how he has seen some of those who were powerful in this life hanging in the infernal flames. He would himself have been cast into the fire had not an angel in shining raiment forbidden it and, after administering a warning to Peter, sent him back to the earth. Henceforth he leads a godly life.

Stephen, a well-known contemporary of Gregory, personally recounted to him the following story. He, Stephen, had died in Constantinople some time previously. When the surgeon and the embalmer were sought to attend to the body, they could not be found that day; so Stephen lay unburied throughout the night. Meanwhile his soul was led to see the torments of Hell. But when he was brought before the judge who presided there, he would not receive him, saying that he had commanded that not this man be brought, but Stephen the smith. So Gregory's friend returned to his body, and at the same instant the blacksmith died.

Three years before Gregory was writing,[22] Rome was ravaged by a plague; and among its victims, he tells us, was this same Stephen. A certain soldier was also brought by it to the point of death, and his soul left his body. But it soon returned, and the soldier was able to tell what had happened. He had seen a bridge spanning a black, smoking river, which had a foul and intolerable smell. But beyond it was a delightful place where white-garbed men walked in flowery meadows. Fine mansions were there too, and one of them seemed built of gold. On the river bank were other houses, some reached by a stinking mist from the river, but others quite clear of it. The nature of the bridge was that any wicked person attempting to cross fell off into the river, but the just passed easily to the pleasant place beyond.

The soldier continued that he had seen one Peter, a church dignitary who had died four years previously, loaded with a great weight of iron bonds in the foulest place. He had asked the reason for the cleric's punishment and had been told that in his life he had been a most cruel and merciless person. But the soldier had seen another priest pass easily over the bridge because of his good life. Stephen was there too. As he tried to cross, his foot slipped, and loathsome men rose from the river to try to drag him down, while white and beautiful persons attempted to raise him up. At this point the visionary returned to his body and was unable to tell the result of the struggle between the good and bad spirits for the soul of Stephen, whose plight was due to the fact that after his previous sight of Hell he had not completely mended his ways.

In the following dialogue, Gregory states his opinion that the riverside houses reached by the stinking mist were those of people who, despite their fundamental goodness, had sinned in the flesh.[23]

Each of these tales has the "apparent death theme" as its point of departure. But those in Dialogue IV, 36 contain an element which Gregory himself found rather troubling and for which he felt obliged to offer an explanation. This is the element of what may be called "divine error", because of which the wrong person dies and is subsequently sent back to earth. It is plainly more appropriate to a mythology in which the gods are seen as subject to human aberrations than to a system over which a divine omniscience presides. Certainly, St Augustine had already told of another smith, Curina, who had left the world under similar circumstances, had been shown the joys of Heaven, and had then returned to his body;[24] but ultimately the feature can be traced back to non-Christian sources. In Lucian, for example, we find accounts of visits to Hades.[25] One visitor, a certain Kleodomos, was led there in mistake for Demylos, a sick coppersmith. An even more striking parallel to Gregory's story of Stephen occurs in Plutarch.[26] A person called Antyllos was desperately ill and seemed to the doctors to retain no sign of life. Yet he awoke to declare that he had indeed been dead, but was ordered back to life; and those who had brought him had been severely chidden by their lord, who sent them to fetch Nikander instead, a well-known currier. Nikander was accordingly taken with a fever and died on the third day.

Similar mistaken summonings are found in Hindu and Chinese lore.[27] So for all the circumstantial detail, we must take Gregory's testimony with more than a grain of salt. Significantly enough, the lord of Hell in Stephen's account is not Satan, but simply the infernal judge, *praesidens judici*, more reminiscent of Minos than of any figure in Christian tradition. Gregory here had gone rather too far; and despite the reverence in which he was held by the later writers, they fought shy of using this awkward motif of divine error, whereas others they seized upon with alacrity.

Gregory's anecdotes lack the strong scriptural flavour of the other legends we have looked at so far. The same is true of most of the *exempla* that were collected into so many medieval compendia and used as a favourite vehicle for pious instruction. If some features of Gregory's tales probably originated in the East, this seems to have been the birthplace of many of the complete stories that were to enliven the sermons of western Christendom. This is especially true of the *Vitae Patrum*, a repertory of anecdotes by divers hands concerning the early monks and saints in Egypt. It has come down in a large number of manuscripts, the earliest dating from the sixth century, and must have been a splendid standby for generations of medieval preachers. Some of the stories catch more than a whiff of brimstone; and we shall meet in a later chapter one of them as it was taken over into an imitative French collection.

Moving on in time, we find Germany offering, from the pen of one Hetto, a vision that was vouchsafed in the year 824 to a monk named Wettin.[28] During a severe illness, he saw demons clustered menacingly about; but there appeared angels to protect him. In a subsequent vision he was guided by an angel through the places of torment, where he recognised many sinners, including none other than the Emperor Charlemagne. Afterwards he was conducted to Heaven. In the first half of the twelfth century this vision was adapted by the worthy scholar William of Malmesbury, so that it might stand as a miracle of the Virgin in his collection *Miracula Dei genetricis*. Here the repentant Wettin, who had previously fallen into sinful ways, saw the saints and the Virgin Mary intercede on his behalf before God with the result that he gained complete forgiveness. But William, explaining that Wettin's vision of Hell was of no consequence for his purpose, omitted it: a rare act of self-denial indeed for a writer of his period.

England was especially rich in this branch of literature;[29] and as well as adaptations of foreign material, a number of native visions were contributed. Bede, for instance, tells in his *Historia Ecclesiastica* of the terrifying experiences of Drycthelm, a Northumbrian man, who returned from death with eyes full of the infernal as well as blessed sights he had been shown.[30] This, to my knowledge, did not pass into French, though it influenced other accounts which did. One English text that was once known in France, in a translation now lost, was the *Vision of the Monk of Eynsham*. Written in Latin in the early years of the thirteenth century, it records a supposedly true event which occurred in the year 1196. The monk of Eynsham, in Oxfordshire, is said to have had his vision during a trance that lasted two days, from Good Friday to Easter Eve. He was led by St Nicholas to see the punishments inflicted in Hell before witnessing the joys of the Earthly Paradise. That a French rhymed version of this lively tale had existed is confirmed by the scribe of a thirteenth-century Latin manuscript, who says that his own rendering was taken over from such a poem: "De gallica edicione rithmice composita in latinam transtuli . . ."[31]

Two other English visions found their way into the *Speculum historiale* of Vincent de Beauvais. Vincent, who died in 1264, was a Dominican monk of Beauvais who enjoyed some measure of royal patronage under Saint Louis and was at one time lector in the Cistercian abbey of Royaumont.[32] In his *Speculum*, a veritable encyclopedia in thirty-two books, he retails numerous pious legends. Two of them, the *Vision of Tundal* and the *Vision of Charles le Gros*, I shall consider elsewhere. Suffice it here to look at two others, which originated on English soil.

We read the *Vision of the Boy William* in Book XXVIII, Ch. 84:

William, a fifteen-year-old boy, sees in his sleep a radiant man who bids him follow where he leads. To the left he sees a black shadow, but is comforted by the presence of his guide. He finds himself in a valley, on one side of which there is very cold water and on the other side fire. Then he sees many blazing seats filled with sinners, into whose mouths devils cram burning coins; and these pass out of their cheeks and throats only to be put back by the devils. Other souls are flung into boiling cauldrons, where they look like new-born babes. They are pulled out with iron forks and then become as before, but are immediately cast back into the cauldrons, and their torment is repeated. Next William sees men having all their joints broken before being cast into a fire whence they emerge ready to be "remade" and suffer the torture again. Further on are swiftly-turning wheels to which sinners are attached by their genitals. More souls are fixed to burning forks, head downwards; others are dying of cold, with clothes just too far away to grasp; and yet others are dying of hunger, with food just out of reach.

Not far away, the boy sees the pit of Hell open, and it is as deep as the distance from Dover to London. In the midst of the flames sprawls the Old Enemy. Suddenly a black spirit comes to accuse William of many sins—it is the black shadow which he had seen at the beginning of his vision. But on his guide's advice he crosses himself, and the devil departs. So does the angel, leaving William trembling with fear; but he soon returns and leads the boy to a wall beyond which lies Paradise. After a brief sight of the blessed regions, William returns to his body, which his soul has left for three days, from Monday until Thursday.

Chapters 6–10 of Book XXX contain the *Vision of Gunthelm, a Cistercian Novice*:

An English novice wishes to take the cross and go to Jerusalem instead of entering the Cistercian order as his abbot advises. When he does enter the order, he is persuaded by a devil to return to his first intention. The following night, he falls into a trance, which lasts for three days. While he is in this condition, St Benedict appears to him and leads him up a flight of stairs, where he is beaten by demons as he proceeds. However, St Benedict comforts him and grants him the privilege of seeing the Virgin Mary in Heaven.

Then the angel Raphael shows him the Earthly Paradise and afterwards leads him into the realm of the shadow of death, where he sees flaming, smoking towers that are none other than the chimneys of Hell. Further on is a man sitting on a blazing throne, where beautiful women thrust brands in his face and through his entrails. During his life he had loved the delights of the flesh and neglected his soul. Because he had loved women, he was tormented by demons in this form. Another man is flayed by devils, who then rub salt into his body. He had been a powerful tyrant, cruel towards his own subjects. Next the novice sees a man seated upon a fiery steed and carrying a blazing buckler. On the neck of his mount is a goat, and at its tail it trails a monk's habit. This sinner had robbed a poor woman of her goat, and at the end of his life he took the habit, not from penitence but from shame. Hence he trails the garment as something he despises. Passing on, the visionary is shown servants of the Church, of all ages and both sexes, who are pulling wry faces and insulting one another, while others are trying to glut their stomachs or their passions. But they are unable to do so, being restrained by devils, who beat their heads cruelly with great sticks.

The novice is then led by Raphael to the very depths of Hell, where there is a turning wheel with a man stretched upon it. The wheel is not fixed, and Gunthelm, for this is the novice's name, sees it dashed down with great clamour. The man on it is Judas the traitor; and he is attacked and reviled by all the devils and wretched souls in Hell.

Then Gunthelm is told to return to his body and to say nothing of his vision except in confession to his abbot. But when he regains consciousness, he cannot refrain from telling of his experiences, whereupon he receives a sharp reminder from St Benedict and has to stay speechless for nine days as a punishment. At the end of this period he makes a full confession to his abbot.

These two legends are rather more than simple *exempla*, although they plainly have some of the *exemplum*'s qualities. They may not be great works of literature, but they are more fully developed than the anecdote and do show quite an imaginative handling of the pains of Hell. The English authors seem to have tried to create something new from the eschatological material at their disposal, or at least to have selected the more striking images from other legends in order to combine them into a well-told narrative. For they are not at all what they purport to be: straightforward accounts of the mystical experiences of two young men.

The reader will no doubt have noticed some reminiscence of the *Vision of St Paul* in the story of William: the description of the pit of Hell, for instance, shows local colour oddly injected into a feature borrowed from that source. William's experience can, in fact, be shown to have been largely inspired

by one of the redactions of the *Vision of St Paul* and very
probably by the *Vision of Tundal*, an Irish legend that we shall
study in the next chapter. Analogies with Bede's story of
Drycthelm could, of course, be the result of direct use of
Bede's text; but they may be acounted for by the fact that this
was one of *Tundal*'s sources. On the other hand, whilst *Tundal*
was written in 1149, the *Vision of the Boy William* was first told
some time after 1144; and it has been suggested that the borrowing was in the other direction.[33]

The *Vision of Gunthelm*, which had been related by Helinand
of Froidmont a few years before Vincent de Beauvais added it to
his collection, is likewise heavily in the debt of earlier legends,
and possibly of *Tundal* also.[34] A curious feature of its family
tree is that it has clearly been influenced by a vernacular poem—
an early Anglo-Norman version of another Irish account that
we shall examine, the *Voyage of St Brendan*.[35] It is rare enough
to find the *litterati* stooping to make use of material in the
vulgar tongue; so it is even more remarkable to find the same
Anglo-Norman text being later turned into Latin verse, some
time in the fourteenth century.[36]

The Church's witnesses, it can be seen, were not entirely
reliable in their testimony, since they did not confine themselves
to recounting their own experiences or those of reliable infor-
mants. They were tellers of tales, more or less gifted, more or
less imaginative, more or less original, but no more scrupulous
in their adherence to cold fact than were the minstrels who
hawked their pseudo-historical chansons de geste round noble
court and market-place. In treating the theme of the infernal
journey, they were working within a particular literary tradition and with material much of which was not even Christian
in origin. And it was this literary tradition far more than any
Christian dogmatics that called up the most fearful incubus of
medieval times, the vision of Hell.

NOTES

1. *The Oxford Dictionary of the Christian Church*, ed. F. L. Cross (London,
O.U.P., 1958), pp. 391–2.
2. I use the translations from the Greek Akhmim fragment and the
Ethiopic text given by M. R. James in *The Apocryphal New Testament*

(Oxford, 1924), pp. 504–21. See also A. Rüegg, *Die Jenseitsvorstellungen vor Dante*, I, pp. 238–50.

3. H. Brandes, *Visio S. Pauli. Ein Beitrag zur Visionslitteratur, mit einem deutschen u. zwei lateinischen Texten* (Halle, 1885); H. T. Silverstein, *Visio Sancti Pauli. The History of the Apocalypse in Latin, together with nine texts* (London, 1935). See also Rüegg, op. cit., I, pp. 255–91; D. D. R. Owen, "The *Vision of St Paul*: The French and Provençal Versions and their Sources", *Romance Philology* XII (1958), pp. 33–51; Théodore Silverstein, "The Vision of St. Paul: New Links and Patterns in the Western Tradition", *Archives d'histoire doctrinale et littéraire du moyen âge*, 34e année (Paris, 1960), pp. 199–248.

4. Paris, B.N., MS n.a.lat. 1631 : published by M. R. James in *Apocrypha anecdota* (Cambridge, 1893), pp. 11–42, and, in English translation, in *The Apocryphal N.T.*, pp. 525–55. A St Gall MS of the ninth century contains a similar version (published by Silverstein, *Visio Sancti Pauli*, pp. 131–47).

5. This is the conclusion I reach, art. cit.

6. I summarise from the text published by Paul Meyer in *Romania* XXIV (1895), pp. 365–75.

7. The reference to Cerberus is confused in many Fourth Redaction MSS. Thus Paris, B.N., MS lat. 5266 reads : "Et hostarius inferni, qui vocatur Acharon, et canis eius, qui vocatur Cherberus, exultaverunt capita sua super omnes penas . . ." (fol. 23ʳ). The name of the second door-keeper, when it appears, varies from manuscript to manuscript, appearing as, e.g., Eternalis, Hestronel, Erner (see H. L. D. Ward, *Catalogue of Romances in the Department of Manuscripts in the British Museum*, II [London, 1893], pp. 397 ff.), Tenal (Silverstein, *Visio Sancti Pauli*, p. 192). It seems likely that these names are corruptions of the word *eternalis* except Acharon, which would be a substitution. See further Silverstein, ibid., p. 115, n. 59.

8. For the extent of the borrowing from *Revelation*, see my comments in art, cit., p. 34, n. 5.

9. For these and references to the rivers of the Classical Hades see Silverstein, *Visio Sancti Pauli*, pp. 65 ff.

10. Cf. R. Foreville in A. Fliche, etc., *Histoire de l'Église depuis les origines jusqu'à nos jours*, IX.2 (Paris, 1953), pp. 352–3.

11. See C. Tischendorf, *Evangelia Apocrypha* (Leipzig, 1853); R. A. Lipsius, *Die Pilatus-Acten kritisch untersucht* (2nd edn., Kiel, 1886); and, for dating, J. Quasten, *Patrology* (Utrecht, 1950–3), I, p. 116. Translations by B. H. Cowper, *The Apocryphal Gospels* (London, 1867), pp. 347 ff., and by M. R. James, *The Apocryphal N.T.*, pp. 117–46.

12. *Psalm* xxiv. 7.

13. R. P. Wülcker, *Das Evangelium Nicodemi in der abendländischen Literatur* (Paderborn, 1872), pp. 23–4. See also Albert Siegmund, *Die Überlieferung der griechischen christlichen Literatur* (München, 1949), pp. 35–6.

14. J. Hastings quotes a number of legends of this nature in *Encyclopaedia of Religion and Ethics*, IV, pp. 650–3. See also J. Kroll, *Gott und Hölle : der Mythos vom Descensuskampfe* (Leipzig & Berlin, 1932), *passim*, and especially Ch. I.

15. Apart from the idea of the descent itself, derived as we saw from certain scriptural texts, Christ's binding of Satan is a direct borrowing from *Revelation* xx. 1–3. The bursting of the gates of Hell may perhaps owe

its imagery to *Matthew* xvi. 18, where Christ tells Peter that the gates of
Hell shall not prevail against His Church; but certainly *Psalm* xxiv
had more direct influence, for here we find the very words used by
Christ when He comes before Hell's defences. Traces of Greek mythology appear in the personification of Hades (Inferus in the Latin
version), who is not merely shown as an equal companion of Satan, but
even placed in charge of him before Christ ascends to Paradise.

16. See C. Fritzsche, "Die lateinischen Visionen des Mittelalters bis zur
Mitte des 12. Jahrhunderts", *Romanische Forschungen* 2 (1886), pp.
247–79, and 3 (1887), pp. 337–69.

17. See Silverstein, *Visio Sancti Pauli*, p. 78, and Patch, *The Other World*,
pp. 95–7. Gregory of Tours had a few years earlier reported a vision of
Abbot Sunniulf, who saw people immersed to different degrees in a
fiery river spanned by a bridge that was scarcely a pace in width. Only
zealous clerics might pass over safely. (*Historia Francorum* IV, 33: in
J. P. Migne, *Patrologia Latina*, Vol. 71, col. 296.)

18. Plato, *Republic*, X, 614a–621b; Plutarch, *De sera numinis vindicta*, xxii.
I shall have further cause to refer to Plutarch's story.

19. Ed. W. Foerster, *Li Dialoge Grégoire lo Pape: Altfranzösische Übersetzung des XII. Jahrhunderts, mit dem lateinischen Original* (Halle & Paris,
1876); and in Migne, *Patrologia Latina*, Vol. 77, cols. 149–430 (to
which my column references relate). English translation in E. G.
Gardner, *The Dialogues of Saint Gregory* (London, 1911).

20. Cols. 369–72. This is IV, 32 in Foerster's edition.

21. Cols. 381–8. Foerster's IV, 37.

22. I.e. in 590.

23. Cols. 388–9.

24. See C. S. Boswell, *An Irish Precursor of Dante* (London, 1908), pp.
110–1 for mention of this motif, with particular reference to Gregory
and Augustine.

25. *Philopseudes*, Ch. 17–28.

26. Reported by Eusebius, *Evangelica Praeparatio*, XI. 36.

27. See F. Bar, *Les Routes de l'Autre Monde*, p. 11; E. B. Tylor, *Primitive
Culture*, II, p. 54.

28. Hetto (Heito), *Visio Wettini*, in *Monumenta Germaniae Historica:
Poetarum Latinorum Medii Aevi*, ed. E. Dümmler (Berlin, 1884), Vol. II,
pp. 267–75. Walafrid Strabo's metrical version is published on pp. 301–
33.

29. See A. B. van Os, *Religious Visions*.

30. Bede, *Historia Ecclesiastica*, V, xii; ed. with English translation by
J. E. King in *Baedae opera historica* (London, 1930), II, pp. 252–65.

31. See van Os, op. cit., pp. 68–74 (the vision is wrongly ascribed to the
monk of Evesham); Ward, *Catalogue of Romances*..., II, pp. 493 ff.;
Rüegg, op. cit., I, pp. 297–308; Patch, *The Other World*, pp. 118–9.

32. See the article on Vincent by H. Peltier in *Dictionnaire de théologie
catholique*, XV (Paris, 1950), cols. 3026–33.

33. St J. D. Seymour, *Irish Visions of the Other World* (London, 1930),
pp. 159–60. See also van Os, op. cit., pp. 67–8; Patch, op. cit., p. 112.

34. See later, pp. 27–33. It seems the author may have known the *Vision
of Tundal*, since the idea of a sinner carrying objects representing his
crimes (and in particular his thefts) appears there. The blazing throne
is slightly reminiscent of the punishment of King Cormachus in *Tundal*;

but we are more forcibly reminded of the episode in the *Vision of the Boy William* and of its parallel in the *Vision of Thurcill*, reported by Roger of Wendover (see van Os, op. cit., p. 77) ; and cf. Herod's appearance on a fiery throne in the *Vision of Esdras* (in A. Mussafia, *Sulla Visione di Tundalo* [Vienna, 1871], pp. 202–6). In *Thurcill* there also appears a sinner riding through Hell on a blazing steed (van Os, op. cit., pp. 76–7), apparently a popular feature in English visions of this period, for it also occurs in that of the monk of Eynsham (Ward, op. cit., II, p. 494).

35. See later, pp. 22–4 and pp. 57–62. The Anglo-Norman poem, by Benedeit, is the only other legend where we find an infernal wheel free to move from place to place in Hell; and the fact that Judas is seen attached to it is added confirmation of the borrowing. Moreover, the flaying and salting of a sinner has its corresponding torment in a neighbouring passage of the *Brendan*.

36. See E. G. R. Waters, *The Anglo-Norman Voyage of St Brendan by Benedeit, a poem of the early twelfth century* (Oxford, 1928), pp. cxv–cxxv.

CHAPTER II

TESTIMONY FROM IRELAND

WE have seen how certain pagan concepts filtered from the East and the Classical world into the general traditions of Western Christendom. The Irish Church was further prepared by its situation and history to assimilate into its teachings some elements of early Celtic mythology; and this process is particularly well illustrated in the first of three Irish works which contain our theme, and which make a distinctive and important contribution to this branch of literature. They are the *Voyage of St Brendan*, the *Vision of Tundal* and *St Patrick's Purgatory*.

The *Navigatio Sancti Brendani*[1] is found in manuscripts dating from the tenth century, although it is not improbable that it was composed even earlier. St Brendan himself was a historical personage, a Kerry man born, perhaps, in 484. After what seems to have been a life of travel in Britain and possibly beyond the Channel in Brittany, he died in about 577 and was buried in Clonfert. It may have been his roving life that caused the legend of his fabulous voyage to take shape around his memory; but whatever the reason, there are mentions of it in the *Book of Leinster* and in other texts that may go back to the ninth century. Once embodied by an unknown writer in the *Navigatio*, its fortune was assured; and over a hundred manuscripts scattered throughout Europe give ample evidence of the favour it enjoyed in the Middle Ages. The summary that follows is taken from the Latin compromise text published by C. Wahlund.

The wise and holy Brendan decides to set out over the sea in search of the Earthly Paradise, of which he has received a first-hand account. He is about to depart with fourteen chosen monks, when three others beg to be allowed to join him on his quest. He grants their wish, but warns them of a

dire fate that will be theirs. On the first of the islands to
which their vessel is guided by God one of the supernumer-
aries commits a theft at the instigation of a demon. St
Brendan causes the demon which possessed him to leave his
body in the sight of all; and when the monk dies immediately afterwards, his soul is received by angels. The companions voyage for many months, seeing strange islands and
stranger creatures. (§ 1–19)

One day the wind drives their vessel towards a rugged and
barren island covered with slag and full of smithies. The
saint expresses his fear of this place, from which comes the
thunderous sound of hammers beating upon anvils, and he
asks God for deliverance. One of the inhabitants of the island
emerges. He is shaggy, fiery, and dark in appearance, and
when he sees the pilgrims he returns into his forge. Brendan
orders his crew to try to flee the island; but the "barbarian"
runs to the shore bearing a huge, blazing mass of slag, which
he holds with a pair of tongs. He hurls it at the vessel, but
misses; and the sea boils where it falls, and smoke rises as if
from an oven. As the voyagers withdraw, all the inhabitants
of the isle rush to the shore and cast similar masses at the
ship and even at each other, then return to their forges and
light them, so that the island looks like a globe of fire. The
sea boils like a pot, and even when the fleeing pilgrims can no
longer see the island, they can hear the wailing of its inhabitants and smell the stench of the place. Then St Brendan
tells his companions that they have been close to Hell. (§ 20)

On another day they see towards the north a high, smoking
mountain, apparently covered by clouds. A wind blows them
towards that island, the coal-black cliffs of which rise sheer.
The second of the supernumerary travellers jumps out of the
ship, then cries that he cannot return. The monks rapidly
withdraw in their vessel and implore God's mercy. The
saint sees the unfortunate man led off by a crowd of demons
to be burnt. Then the company look back and see that the
smoke has dispersed, and fire is spewed forth by the mountain
and falls back into it. (§ 21)

The pilgrims sail south for seven days and then see what
appears to be a man sitting on a rock in the sea, with a veil

like a sack hanging before him from two iron forks, so that one might think that it was a storm-tossed ship. Indeed, some of the monks think it to be a bird, others a ship. Brendan commands that they steer towards the spot, and they find a misshapen, shaggy man sitting upon a rock and buffeted by the waves while the cloth whips his face. Questioned by St Brendan, the wretch replies that he is Judas; but his present condition is not to be counted as a torment, since this is Sunday, and at other times he burns, like a mass of liquid lead in a pot, in the midst of that mountain which the pilgrims have seen. There dwells Leviathan with his satellites, and there Judas was when the monks' comrade was received with joy into Hell. Judas enjoys his respite on Sundays, at Christmas, Easter, and on the feasts of the Purification and Assumption of the Virgin; but on other days he is tormented in the depths of Hell along with Herod, Pilate, Annas and Caiaphas. He begs the monks to intercede for him so that his respite on this occasion may be prolonged from the Sunday evening to the following morning. St Brendan promises that the demons shall leave him alone for that period. Judas explains that the cloth before his face has been given to him because in his life he gave it to a leper; but since it was not his own, it affords him no relief, but rather increases his pains. The forks he presented to priests in the temple so that they could hang their cauldrons from them. With the stone he once filled a hole in a public path. When evening arrives, many demons come to carry off the hapless Judas and call upon Brendan to let them deliver him to their prince; but the saint forbids it in God's name. In the morning they reappear, complaining that they have suffered many stripes for not having returned their prisoner, and threatening him with redoubled torment. This too St Brendan forbids in Christ's name; and after the demons have carried Judas off, the companions sail on. (§ 22)

After further adventures, the pilgrims see the Earthly Paradise and its delights, then return to their own country. (§ 23-5)

The *Voyage of St Brendan* as a whole (my summary has

concentrated on the passages concerning the sight of Hell) incorporates a good deal of Celtic mythological material.[2] Its main theme, that of the marvellous voyage, is found in many religions and mythologies. As the Egyptians watched the sun sink beneath the earth's rim at evening, they thought of their god Ra embarking for his nightly voyage through the lands of the dead. The thoughts of the Greeks turned towards the Blessed Isles, the lands of gold that lie to the westward beyond the setting sun. And in the same way the early Irish looked beyond the misty western horizon for their own strange islands, their own Hesperides which, in Christian mythology, became the Earthly Paradise. So from an early period they composed their own *Odysseys*, their own *Aeneids*, telling how one or another of their folk heroes set forth in a skiff in quest of these fabulous lands. Such are the Irish *imrama*, or tales of marvellous sea-voyages, a *genre* that had come into existence by the eighth century at the latest.[3]

The *imrama* seem originally, then, to have sprung from pagan myths; and one of them, the *Voyage of Bran*,[4] which was perhaps first committed to writing in the seventh century and then re-written in the tenth, is completely pagan in inspiration. Of the substratum of Celtic mythology in the *Voyage of St Brendan*, some may have been culled from the *Voyage of Bran* itself. Indeed, the very name of the god Bran may have influenced the choice of Brendan or "Brandan" as the hero. But a more immediate source for the legend of St Brendan is the *Voyage of Maelduin's Curach*, probably composed in the eighth century.[5] Whether or not H. Zimmer's theory that the Brendan story was inspired by the mention of a person of like name in *Maelduin* is well founded,[6] it is clear that our text does owe a great deal to *Maelduin*, provided always that this view of the relative chronology is reliable.[7] The island of smiths (tantalisingly reminiscent of Odysseus' adventure with the Cyclops as found in Homer and in Book III of the *Aeneid*) is a feature of both; and the sight of Judas in the *Voyage of St Brendan* has a significant counterpart in the other *imram* which may throw some light on the origin of the Brendan legend. Maelduin and his crew saw something like a white bird far off on the waves. As they approached they saw that it was a man,

covered only with his own white hair, who was kneeling
on a rock. They learned that he was a thief, who was sailing
one day in his boat when he was surrounded by demons;
and a strange man who had appeared on the waves told
him to throw his ill-gotten gains into the sea and then
let the boat take its own course. Where it stopped the
thief was to stay, under pain of suffering the torments of
Hell. He had been there for seven years, but without
enduring any torment, even from the inclemencies of the
weather.

Maelduin, though it shows some Christian influence, has
retained more pagan elements than *Brendan*; and this seems to
be one of them, since the strange man who appeared to the
thief bears a striking resemblance to the old Irish sea-god
Manannan as he is seen in the *Voyage of Bran*, a text to which
Maelduin was indebted for more than one feature. Although
this instance does not prove the mythological character of the
whole episode, and the figure does not appear at all in *Brendan*,
it does illustrate the way in which elements of the Christianised
imrama can be traced back to earlier, pagan stories of the same
type.

If today we can take a detached view of the processes both
literary and mythological which culminated in the gripping
account of St Brendan's exploits, this was not possible in the
Middle Ages themselves. And so people readily came to believe
in the actual existence of the island that had been the object of
the saint's quest, and governments even vied for its possession.
That privilege was at one time held by the King of Portugal;
and at the beginning of the sixteenth century one of his subjects, Luis Perdigon, states that the king had ceded the island
to his (Luis') father, should he succeed in discovering it. But
in the Treaty of Evora, by which Portugal ceded to Castille its
right to the Canary Islands, the still undiscovered Island of St
Brendan was included in the deal. Between 1526 and 1721 no
fewer than four Spanish expeditions set out to look for it.[8] So
though it may be idle to surmise whether the legend carries
some faint recollections of new lands seen by mariners beyond
the western sea, or whether it may have played a part itself in
luring men on to the discovery of the Americas, it can at least

be shown to have had some direct if modest influence on the course of history.

The *Vision of Tundal*, or at any rate that part of it which concerns us, shows no clear example of reminiscence from Celtic mythology. Although the *Visio Tnugdali*, the Latin original,[9] was written in Germany, both the author Marcus and the hero are Irishmen. Marcus tells us in his long Prologue that the vision was seen in the year 1149 (though 1148 has been suggested as a more likely date); and he states that he was translating "de barbarico in latinum ... eloquium". This presumably means no more than that he had heard the account from Tundal himself ("nobis postmodum narravit") in the Irish tongue and subsequently wrote it down in Latin. His Prologue is addressed to an Abbess G.; and since a Middle High German poem on Tundal by a Bavarian priest called Alber tells how the story was taken to Regensburg (Ratisbon) by a certain monk who wrote it down in the convent of St Paul there,[10] it has been deduced that the G. stands for Gisel, a one-time abbess of the convent. The rule observed there was that of St Benedict, and it appears from three references to it in the text that Marcus was himself a Benedictine monk. A native of Munster and probably of the town of Cashel, he may well have journeyed to Ratisbon by way of Clairvaux and there have met the illustrious St Bernard.[11] I summarise from the Latin text published by A. Wagner.

The long Prologue addressed to the Abbess G. is followed by a brief description of Ireland. From the metropolitan city of Cashel came a young nobleman, Tundal, who did not lack culture or pleasantness of character, but who neglected the Church and his religious duties, giving his wealth to mimes, jesters and minstrels. His experiences are recounted by the natives of Cork. A certain man owed him three horses and, receiving a visit from Tundal, invited him to dinner. At the meal, Tundal was seized by a sudden paralysis and lay with all the signs of death upon him from about the tenth hour on Wednesday until the same hour on Saturday. His grieving host sent for the clergy but refrained from burying him, since

there was still some warmth in the left side of his breast. On
Saturday Tundal recovered consciousness, took communion,
and related his experiences after professing repentance and
making over his wealth to the poor.

Tundal's soul had left his body and then begun to weep and
tremble when he saw a great crowd of devils filling the whole
house and indeed the entire town. With hideous chanting,
they said that he would burn in Hell for his sins. But a light
like a star appeared: it was Tundal's guardian angel, who
greeted him with reproach for not having listened to his
advice in the past. The angel pointed out one particular
demon as being he whose counsel Tundal had followed.
However, God has had pity on him, and he will return to the
body; but first he must follow the angel. The devils are
furious to see their prey escape them and set upon one
another with such rage that Tundal is fearful lest they turn
their attentions to him as he walks behind his guide.

Comforted by the angel, who is now his only light, he is
led to a deep valley full of burning coals and covered by a lid
six cubits thick. The stench of the place is more noxious
than anything Tundal has so far experienced. Sinners are
falling upon the lid, where they burn like bacon in a pan until
they melt like wax and pass through into the fire beneath, to
be renewed for further torments. The angel explains that
they are homicides, parricides and fratricides, and that after
this torment they will suffer a greater. But Tundal will be
spared, although he has richly deserved such punishment.

They come to a huge mountain burning with sulphurous,
dark fire on one side, and with the other side bitterly cold,
with wind and snow. Devils with blazing iron forks toss
sinners from one side to the other and back. This is the torment of the treacherous.

Next, Tundal sees a very deep valley, dark and reeking,
where there flows a sulphurous river full of shrieking souls.
A stench of putrid corpses adds to the horror of the valley,
which is crossed by a bridge a thousand paces long but only a
foot wide. None but the chosen of God may pass over without falling; and the travellers see a priest with a palm
branch in his hand make the crossing in safety. The angel

leads Tundal over; but though he escapes this evil, he must suffer another later. Here the sinners are the proud.

In the path followed by Tundal and his companion is a terrible beast greater than any mountain that he has ever seen. It has huge, burning eyes, and a gaping mouth so vast that nine thousand armed men could pass through it together. In this maw, which is belching fire and stench, stand two figures like columns, dividing it into three. One stands upright, the other is upside down. Sinners are terribly beaten by demons, who then drive them into the belly of the monster. The angel tells Tundal that its name is Acheron, and that this is a torment which he himself must suffer. It is the punishment for the greedy. The two figures he sees are giants and were righteous according to their own faith. Their names are Fergusius and Conallus. Left alone by his guide, Tundal is dragged through the beast by demons; and inside it he is tortured by dogs, bears, lions, serpents and many other creatures, as well as by more demons, violent fire and cold, and by his own burning tears and gnashing teeth. He even rends his own cheeks. At last he finds himself outside without knowing how, and the angel is there to comfort and revive him.

He is then led to a great, storm-tossed lake, whose waves blot out the sky. In it are many terrible, roaring beasts which devour sinners; and it is spanned by a bridge about two thousand paces long and of only a palm's width. The bridge is studded with iron spikes to lacerate the feet of those who pass there. If any fall off, they are devoured by the beasts, which are as huge as towers and breathe out fire so that the lake appears to boil. Tundal sees on the bridge a weeping soul carrying a heavy load of grain and suffering great torment. This is the punishment for thieves, who suffer according to the gravity of their crime. Tundal is especially deserving of this torment; and, because he once stole a cow which he only returned because he could not conceal it, he must lead a wild cow across the bridge. Tundal and the animal fall off the structure alternately, so that each in turn almost becomes the prey of the beasts in the lake. Half way across they are met by the soul bearing the grain. They cannot pass, nor can they retreat. But suddenly, without knowing how it happened, Tundal finds himself beyond the bridge, where the angel waits to heal his torn feet. His torments are not yet over, for the house of Phristinus awaits him.

With his guide he proceeds through a dark and arid place and comes to an immense, round building like a bakehouse, from whose thousand windows come fire and a great heat. Tundal cannot approach for the heat, but though he will be delivered from this, he must pass through the house. Seeing many demons waiting at the doors with hatchets, cleavers, and all manner of sharp implements with which to attack the sinners, he asks to be spared; but he is told that still greater torments await him. He is seized by the demons, and undergoes torture in this place of fire, where he sees many souls, of both laymen and clerics. There follows a homily by the angel, who explains how some good souls are shown Hell so that their joy may be greater in Paradise, and some sinners are shown Paradise to exacerbate their misery. Those who suffer the pains of this house are the gluttons and fornicators.

The next horror that awaits Tundal is in the form of a huge, long-necked beast with two wings and two feet armed with claws of iron; it breathes fire from its iron beak. It is on an ice-bound lake and is continually swallowing sinners, who are reduced as if to nothing before the beast gives birth to them so that they again find themselves on the lake, renewed for further torment. Then both men and women become pregnant with venomous serpents which finally issue forth from all their members, lacerating them with blazing, iron beaks and nails as they do so. The tongues of the serpents pierce the souls to their very nerves, bones and lungs. There are groans and wailings fit to move the very devils if they had a scrap of pity. Here are punished false ecclesiastics and all those guilty of lewdness. Tundal himself undergoes the torment and is afterwards healed by the angel.

They next pass along a dark way; and the further they go, the less the soul of Tundal hopes to return to his body. The angel tells him that this path leads to death. They come to a valley with many forges whence comes a sound of wailing. The angel says that the torturer is called Vulcanus, and he inflicts pains on the many souls who pass there. Tundal is to suffer this punishment. He is seized by demons with iron implements, flung into a brazier, and blown with bellows. When the souls are reduced almost to nothing, they are taken with iron forks and, in batches of up to a hundred, are beaten with hammers on an anvil. They are then tossed to other demons in other forges, who receive them with iron forks, tossing them up and down, and torture them as before. They long for a death which cannot come. Tundal is rescued by the angel, who says that all the sinners he has seen up to now are awaiting God's final judgment; but now he is to see the torments of Hell, the abode of the eternally damned. The punishment just witnessed is for those who heap sin upon sin.

Tundal is led along a cold, stinking, dark path, and it seems that the ground trembles beneath his feet. He stops and can go no further. Left alone by the angel, he hears a terrible clamour and thundering and sees the source of the great stench: a square pit like a cistern, from which pour forth flames and smoke, reaching to the sky. In the flames he sees devils and sinners flying like sparks, reduced to practically nothing, and falling back into the pit. Tundal cannot withdraw and calls for death; but he is surrounded by coal-black devils with eyes like lamps, teeth white as snow, scorpions' tails, iron claws and vultures' wings. They threaten to give him to Lucifer, who will devour him; but the angel reappears, puts them to flight, and promises to show Tundal the Great Enemy. He leads him to the gates of Hell.

The visionary is shown the Prince of Darkness. If he had a hundred heads and a hundred tongues in each, he could not tell everything. Lucifer is bigger than any beast ever seen, as black as a crow, formed like a man but having not less than a thousand hands, each a hundred cubits long and ten wide. There are twenty fingers to either hand, each a hundred palms long and ten thick. Iron nails, longer than lances, grow on hands and feet; and Lucifer has a long beak and a tail full of goads. He lies on a grill over coals blown by devils, and around him is gathered a vast multitude of the damned. Burning iron and brass fetters bind all his members at every joint, and he writhes in pain from one side to the other. As he does so, he grasps souls and squeezes them in his hands like a rustic squeezing grapes, before puffing them with his breath all over Hell. At this, a fetid flame erupts from the pit. Then Lucifer inhales the souls, striking with his tail those who escape his mouth. With their prince are the fallen angels; and here are those, already damned, who utterly failed to recognise Christ and keep His law. Some are prelates and the powerful of this world, for "potentes potenter tormenta patiuntur". Some moralising enters into the conversation between Tundal and the angel. Tundal sees many of his friends and acquaintances here; but the angel promises that he will suffer no further unless he so merit. Now he will see the glory of the blessed.

Tundal experiences growing happiness as he is led along another path. The angel takes him through a gate in a high wall to where there are many sad souls, hungry and thirsty and exposed to wind and rain; but there is light and no stench. These are the "mali, sed non valde": they were honest, but not generous to the poor. Beyond, they come through a gate to a flowery plain with a fountain of living water where it is never night. This is where the "boni non valde" remain until they are worthy to be with the elect. Those who drink of the fountain will have everlasting life and never thirst more. Tundal recognises two kings, Conchober and Donacus, whom he had seen on earth. They had been enemies, but had repented before death.

In a resplendent house sits King Cormachus, Tundal's erstwhile lord, on a golden throne, richly vested, and attended by those to whom he had shown generosity in life. Tundal asks if his late master suffers torments. With his guide he waits, and they see the house grow dark and its inhabitants become sad. King Cormachus leaves the hall, and Tundal sees him in fire up to his waist, and with a hair shirt upon his shoulders. This is his fate for three hours each day. His servants pray meanwhile for his pardon, since the fire torment is for his having broken his marriage vows, and the hair shirt punishes him for having slain a count "juxta sanctum Patricium".

There follows an elaborate description of Paradise, and

Tundal is allowed to see all but the Trinity. From one place he can see the glory of Paradise, the torments of Hell, and all the earth. The angel, despite Tundal's tears, informs him that he must return to the earth, but that he will remain with him as counsellor and guide. Tundal then feels himself back in his body, wakes, and takes the sacrament. He gives all he has to the poor and takes the sign of the cross upon his apparel. "Everything that he had seen he afterwards related to us, warning us to lead a good life; and with great devotion, humility and wisdom he preached the word of God, which earlier had been unknown to him."

There follows a short Epilogue addressed to the Abbess G.

Once again, for all the display of seemingly authentic detail, we are dealing with a piece of adroit literary fiction. Just how adroit would be revealed by a complete study of the *Vision*'s sources, a task which has not yet been systematically undertaken. To begin with, we are surprised to find that Marcus (or could it have been Tundal himself?) appears to have had some knowledge of Plutarch. In the last chapter I mentioned the occurrence of the "apparent death theme" in Plutarch's *Vision of Thespesios*, which was composed in about A.D. 81.[12] It concerns a man (a friend of a friend, says Plutarch) who had led a dissolute youth, spending his wealth and then winning it back in dishonest ways. Then he had an accident: falling on his neck from a height, he lay as if dead for three days. But at the very time of his funeral, he suddenly revived and later told his story. Thereafter he was a reformed character. Now although *Tundal* shows unmistakable use of Bede's *Vision of Drycthelm*,[13] and Bede's own story may in some way have been influenced by *Thespesios*, the Irish vision has close similarities of detail with the Greek such as it is difficult to explain by reference to an intermediary. Thus, when Thespesios' soul left his body, it was as a pilot fallen overboard into the sea. But soon it grew aware of huge stars, and also bubbles of fire that were released souls. One, a relative of the visionary who had died during his youth, became his guide to the Otherworld. Again, the germ of the torment meted out by the beast and serpents on the frozen lake is found in Plutarch's account. There, Nero's soul was pierced with incandescent rivets before being given the form of a viper, which ate its way out of its pregnant mother.

The tortures in the forges of Vulcanus may be compared with those that Thespesios saw inflicted in three lakes, one of boiling gold, another of exceedingly cold lead, and a third of iron. Demons seize the avaricious with their tongs and, like smiths, plunge them into the gold until they grow red-hot. They then immerse them in the lead until they become chilled and hard like hailstones, whereupon they cast them into the iron to become brittle. When they are crushed, they are flung back into the gold to begin again their round of suffering. Unlike Tundal, Thespesios does not have to undergo any of the tortures he sees ; but he, too, is abandoned by his guide and left in the hands of evil spirits. In his case, however, the guide does not return.

Did Marcus know and borrow from Moslem tradition ? It is a fascinating possibility. And although M. Asín Palacios went rather too far in his study of *Tundal*,[14] there are certainly remarkable parallels to be drawn. In Moslem literature, for instance, souls are to be found in the next world carrying burdens across the Azirat bridge (a feature also appearing in one of the vernacular versions of the *Vision of St Paul*).[15] And the most striking similarity I have noted to the form of the bridge itself occurs in a Moslem *hadith* found by the thirteenth century in French translation.[16] There we see the extreme narrowness as well as the iron spikes of Marcus' account ; so we are entitled to wonder if both descriptions do not ultimately stem from a single source, in either pagan or Christian literature. Again, in the episode of the serpents there are features surprisingly close to details in Moslem tradition concerning the Miraj, or ascension of the Prophet. Serpents and scorpions are both capable of reducing the sinner to nothing by injecting their venom into or over him. Then the wretch is re-created so that his punishment may be repeated indefinitely. Or else the evil creatures may be imprisoned within his body beneath seventy different skins, and there they wreak the same torments. The souls wish to die, but cannot.[17]

What may be thought an even more exotic parallel, this time with the "bakehouse" torment, is to be found in ancient Egyptian mythology. In a text describing the sun's passage through the Underworld,[18] details are given of various punishments meted out there. Swords and knives are used as instruments of divine vengeance on more than one occasion. But in the redness of the dawn at the sun's return to earth the Egyptians saw the flame of five vaulted furnaces, where female spirits armed with knives and spitting out fire put to death the enemies of the god Ra. So, as in *Tundal*, we find the linking of two punishments—by the fire of a great furnace and by attacks with knives and sharp instruments. If we knew the full significance of the name Phristinus (apparently cognate with Latin *pistor*, *pistrinum*: "baker", "bakehouse"), we might have a clue to the source of the passage.

It would be fanciful, of course, to think of Marcus not only poring over his Plutarch, but turning up Islamic writings and consulting rare repositories of Egyptian lore as well. While the borrowing from *Thespesios* may have been direct, any influence from Moslem or Egyptian sources, if influence there be, would probably have been picked up from oral tradition, or possibly from some compendium of knowledge found in the monastery library. Similarly a subsidiary source for the serpent episode could have been the venerable tradition regarding the birth of vipers as found in various Ancient writers, taken over by Pliny into his *Natural History*, and repeated in the seventh century by Isidore of Seville in his *Etymologiae*.[19] The main point I wish to make here is that *Tundal* is compounded of a remarkably cosmopolitan variety of material.

Other elements lie more squarely in the Christian tradition. The Bible supplies some of the illustrative detail. Despite its Classical name, the beast Acheron is a synthesis of the Leviathan and Behemoth of *Job* xl and xli, with the strange feature of the giants standing like pillars between its jaws probably suggested by the beast of *Daniel* vii. 5 ; and other of the monsters described in the same chapter of *Daniel* may have contributed to the loathsome image of the beast on the ice-bound lake. But Marcus seems not to have confined his reading to the approved text of the Vulgate, for reminiscences from the apocrypha may be detected in the description of Lucifer sprawling in the pit of Hell.

The opening figure could be a borrowing from the *Vision of St Paul*, or it may have been taken direct from Virgil's

Non, mihi si linguae centum sint oraque centum,
ferrea vox, omnis scelerum comprendere formas,
omnia poenarum percurrere nomina possim.

(*Aeneid* VI, 625-7)

The idea of Satan, or Lucifer, being cast into the bottomless pit
and fettered there certainly derives from *Revelation* xx. 1-3.
But the Greek text of the *Gospel of Nicodemus* elaborates a little,
making Christ tell the angels to bind with irons Satan's hands,
feet, neck and mouth. The manner of Lucifer's binding in
Tundal might well be an elaboration of this. And for the way
in which he inhales the damned souls, H. T. Silverstein has seen
a model in the depiction of Antichrist found in the *Vision of
Esdras*:

> ... in obscuro loco vermem inextinguibilem; eius magni-
> tudinem dinumerare nemo potuit, et ante os eius stabant
> multi peccatores; et cum duxit flatum ingrediebant in os
> eius quasi muscae, cum autem respiravit exibant omnes alio
> colore.[20]

For Lucifer's appearance, the picture of the fourth beast in
Daniel vii. 19-20, possibly suggested at least the detail of the
lance-like nails. An even more tempting parallel is, however,
found in an Irish homily, *Scél Lai Brátha* ("Tidings of Doomsday"), dating from the eleventh century at the latest. There the
"Piast", the infernal serpent, is shown as having a hundred
necks with a hundred heads on each and five hundred teeth in
every mouth, and a hundred arms each with a hundred hands
and a hundred claws on every hand.[21] From each source
Marcus may have drawn a detail or two; but it was his own
vivid imagination that welded them so successfully together in
this striking scene.

My summary of the *Vision of Tundal* could not convey any
idea of Marcus' literary style. He was a very competent writer
of some learning and a fondness for biblical quotation, who put
his reading to effective use. There is no abuse of the rhetorical
flourish, but the text is consciously, almost self-consciously
literary. The structure is well balanced, with a nice blending of
narrative and dialogue. And Marcus has succeeded in rising

PLATE 2. St Brendan and his companions. Oxford, Queen's College MS 30
French, late 15th century.

above the conventional to give his story colour, dramatic effect and a fierce realism which, to the modern reader, lend it an appeal unmatched in the *genre* before Dante. Indeed Dante himself would appear to have recognised its qualities to the extent of gleaning a feature or two for his *Inferno*.[22] For the artist with brush and pen its grotesque, contorted movement seems to have held a particular attraction.[23] Yet, as we shall see, it was never properly appreciated by writers in the French vernacular. Their purposes were better served by renderings of the *Vision of St Paul* or even of the third great Irish eschatological legend, *St Patrick's Purgatory*.

If the *Vision of St Paul* was in essence an extended pious homily illustrated by lively scenes of Hell, *St Patrick's Purgatory*, though it contains some homiletic material, is rather, like the *Voyage of St Brendan*, a sensational story of Christian adventure. Combining the adventurous element with the miraculous, it appealed to a wide section of the medieval community and is pervaded rather less by the atmosphere of church and cloister than is the *Vision*. The importance of this is seen particularly in the later fortunes of the story. Not that its presentation and message is anything less than thoroughly and indeed energetically Christian in character. In the *Voyage of St Brendan* one sees the Christian content disguising, but not entirely hiding, a basically pagan Celtic scheme. But in *St Patrick's Purgatory* all the essentials are Christian, even though Celtic myth and legend was the ground in which the story first germinated.[24]

By the middle of the twelfth century, it seems, certain pagan and Christian traditions had become fused, with the result that a spirit-haunted island, Station Island in Lough Derg, County Donegal, had come to be considered as a place where penitent Christians might be purged of their sin through the visitation of demons. Lough Derg, the Red Lake, is said to have taken its name from the blood of a dragon slain by Fingal on its shores. The blood tinged for all time its waters with red, which was the colour of death according to the pagan Irish. But Fingal was not the only legendary figure linked with the lough and its surrounding hills. Places nearby bear names that

VH C

preserve the memory of the Tuatha Dé Danann, a race of immortals forced to take refuge in underground palaces, one of which was traditionally situated under Station Island, one of the lake's scattered islets. Celtic mythology was rich in tales of enchanted islands; and these superstitions linger long in the minds of the country folk, who are more ready to see them transformed than uprooted.

The idea of purgation already existed in early Celtic beliefs regarding the Otherworld,[25] and a seemingly half-Christianised tradition of this kind was attached to a nearby mountain before the *Tractatus*, the legend of the Purgatory as we know it, was composed. The mountain was Cruachan Aigle, where St Patrick was supposed to have routed evil spirits in the guise of black birds. Jocelin of Furness, writing his *Vita Sancti Patricii* in about 1183, says that people who spend a night on the mountain are tormented and in the morning feel themselves purged of their sin.[26] Giraldus Cambrensis, who completed his *Topographia Hibernica* five or six years later, does not appear to know the *Tractatus* when he connects the trials of purgation with Station Island, the home of the Tuatha Dé Danann. The island is divided, he says, into two parts : one is delightful and fertile, the other rocky and barren. In the latter part are nine pits ; and anybody who spends a night in one of these is seized and tormented by evil spirits, an experience which exempts him from punishment after death.[27]

The *Tractatus* of which I speak is the Latin account of a certain knight's experiences in the Purgatory, and it forms the base of all the vernacular versions of the legend.[28] As far as we can tell, it is with this text that the conception of an actual entrance into the Otherworld was introduced.[29] A monk whom we know as Henry, or Hugh (he signed with a simple H.), of Saltrey, a Cistercian abbey in Huntingdonshire, wrote down the story with a dedication to the Abbot H. of Sartis (Warden in Bedfordshire) at a date difficult to determine, but usually supposed to be about 1190.[30] It is not unlikely, however, that Henry, to use his more commonly accepted name, did no more than put into its final, elaborate form a pious legend evolved by the Irish monks at the Augustinian abbey of Reglis on Insula Sanctorum, a neighbouring island in Lough Derg. Their immediate stimulus for the composition of the legend may have been the supposed discovery, in 1185, of the relics of the saint who was traditionally connected with their island and was in fact presumed to have founded the original monastery there. But Henry's account of how he came upon the story is quite different. He learned it from Gilbert, the Cistercian abbot of Basingwerk, who had himself heard it often from the very man, Owein, who had made the perilous journey into the Purgatory. Gilbert, at the time when he was still a monk at Louth, had been sent to Ireland to found a Cistercian house; and, not knowing the Irish language, he had availed himself of the services of Owein, who accompanied him as interpreter. So the *Tractatus* was composed in a completely Cistercian milieu and, moreover, bears unmistakeable signs of the white monks' propaganda.[31] Towards the end of the twelfth century, the order had some reputation for unscrupulousness, and it is by no means impossible that they borrowed an Augustinian legend for their own ends. It may even be that Henry was spurred on by a desire to compete in this field with the Benedictine Marcus, who had produced the *Vision of Tundal* some years earlier. At all events, the *Tractatus* is far removed from the mythology and pagan lore from which it ultimately derived. It is now a work of Christian propaganda with a slight sectarian bias.

In my summary, based on K. Warnke's edition of Text α, I treat Owein's sight of the places of torment more fully than the other episodes.

In the Dedication and Prologue, brother H. makes it clear that he is writing at the behest of the Abbot of Sartis. He continues by referring to Gregory the Great and to the information given in his writings concerning the soul's fate after death and the sight of the Otherworld by living persons. The remainder of the Prologue is devoted to a discussion of the nature of infernal and purgatorial torments, with arguments drawn mainly from Gregory and St Augustine. With the suggestion that the spiritual torments are represented in physical form so as to be understandable to those who witness them, Henry passes to his main narrative.

St Patrick preached to the pagan Irish (one old man did

not even know it was wrong to kill) and prayed for their salvation. Christ appeared to him and gave him a staff and a copy of the Gospels, then led him to a desert place and showed him a round pit. If a faithful and contrite person remained there for a day and a night, he would be purged of his misdeeds and behold the punishment of sinners and the joy of the righteous. St Patrick built a church on the spot and placed it in the care of canons regular. In his time it was visited by many pilgrims who saw the torments and joys of the next life. The pit is called St Patrick's Purgatory, and the name of the church is Reglis. There follows the story of one of its priors who was playfully taunted by the monks but blessed by the angels.

In and after St Patrick's day many have visited the Purgatory and returned, but many have perished there. The procedure for the pilgrim is first to obtain permission from his bishop, who should try to dissuade him; but if the pilgrim insists, he is to be sent with a letter to the prior of Reglis, who will also exhort him to forgo his enterprise. If he still cannot be dissuaded, the pilgrim has to fast and pray in the church for fifteen days and then take communion, with the people and clergy of the district assembled. Afterwards he is taken in procession to the door of the Purgatory and reminded of the dangers. Finally, if his determination is not shaken, he is shut in the Purgatory by the prior, and the clergy retreat to pray for his soul. If he is found alive in the morning, he is received with joy; otherwise all know he is lost.

In the time of King Stephen[32] a knight (*miles*) named Owein came to confess his sins to the bishop of the see in which the Purgatory is situated. The bishop wished to impose a penance, but Owein decided instead to visit the Purgatory. He goes through the ritual already described. The prior tells him that he will come to a great field and then to a fine hall, where God's messengers will advise him on what he must do. Then, according to previous pilgrims, demons will come to tempt him. Owein is of good courage, armed as he is with faith, hope and justice; he asks all to pray for him and enters the pit. The prior closes the door, and the procession moves back to the monastery to pray.

Owein walks on in the Purgatory. It grows darker and
darker, but when all daylight has gone, another feeble light
appears; so he comes to the field and the hall, lit as if by
winter twilight. The hall is very beautiful. It is not enclosed
all round, but has arches supported by pillars, like a cloister.
Owein sits down; and soon fifteen persons enter, tonsured
and white-robed.[33] They welcome him in God's name and
sit round him. One, who resembles a prior, speaks and warns
him of the devils who will shortly come with threats and
promises to lead him safely back to the entrance. But he
must be on his guard and invoke Christ's name to ward them
off. The fifteen men then depart with a blessing. Owein
waits, girt with the spiritual armour of the Christian.

He hears a terrible noise so that only God's power prevents
him from going mad. Many hideous demons arrive with a
mocking greeting. They say that others of their servants
have only come after death; so they are grateful to Owein,
who deserves a reward. They therefore promise to lead him
back to the entrance and the joys of the outer world. But
promises and threats are of no avail, so the demons tie Owein
hand and foot and cast him onto a huge fire they have built,
dragging him through it with iron hooks. He calls upon the
name of Jesus and is delivered from the fire, which is ex-
tinguished.

The demons drag him away to a black, barren place; and
in the darkness he can see naught but them. There is a hot
and piercing but almost silent wind. Owein is taken to where
the sun rises in summer, seemingly to the end of the world,
and then southwards through a wide valley to where it rises
in winter. He hears cries of anguish that grow louder, until
at last he is hauled into a great plain (*campus*) where people of
both sexes and diverse ages lie naked, face downwards upon
the earth. Red-hot nails pierce their hands and feet and pin
them to the earth, which they gnaw in their anguish, crying
for mercy. They are scourged by demons; and those who
accompany Owein warn him that he will be similarly punished if he does not follow their advice. He ignores them;
and when they attempt to implement their threats, he is
delivered as before.

The demons next drag him to a place of even greater grief,
where further sinners are pinned to the earth, but face up-
wards. Upon some sit blazing dragons, devouring them with
fiery teeth. Others have fiery serpents coiled about them,
piercing their hearts with tongues of fire. And there are huge
toads, all ablaze, which try to pull out their hearts with their
hideous beaks. The sinners here never cease to weep.
Demons run over them, whipping them. Owein cannot see
the confines of this vast plain. When he is menaced by his
escort, he calls on Jesus and is saved.

The third plain is full of woe, for it is full of naked sinners
lying fixed to the earth by so many red-hot nails that not so
much as a finger's space could be found between them on the
sinner's whole body. The souls cry like people on the point
of death. They are further tormented by a cold and burning
wind and are beaten by demons. Owein is threatened and
delivered as before.

In the fourth plain, which is full of fire and all manner of
torments, there are sinners hanging by burning chains from
their feet, hands, hair, arms, or from their shins with their
heads dangling in sulphurous flames. Others hang in fire,
with iron hooks piercing their eyes, ears, noses, throats,
breasts, or genitals. Yet others burn in sulphurous furnaces,
roast on grills or on spits, or are basted with molten metals.
Demons scourge them all. Owein sees some sinners whom he
recognises. When the escorting demons attempt to torture
him, he escapes as previously.

He is led on; and they come to a great, blazing wheel of
iron. The spokes end in hooks, on which hang sinners. Half
of the wheel is in the air and half in the earth, and foul,
sulphurous flames leap out of the earth around it. Demons
turn it so swiftly with iron levers that it is impossible to see
the sinners: only the fire is visible. Owein is cast onto the
wheel and is raised up into the air, but as he comes down he
calls on Christ and is delivered.

He is next conducted towards a vast, smoking house, which
gives off such great heat that he stops, unable to go further.
But the demons force him on, explaining that this is a bath
which he must enter. He is then taken into the house, from

which comes a great wailing. The floor has many round pits, set close together and full of different boiling metals and liquids. Many people are immersed in them, some to the eyebrows, others to the eyes, lips, neck, breast, navel, thighs, knees, or shins; and others have one foot or one or both hands in the liquid. All cry aloud for pain or grief. Owein is saved by the name of Christ from being forced to join them.

The hero is then taken to a mountain where there is a vast number of naked people crouching on tiptoe. They are facing the north and look like people awaiting death. A demon asks Owein why he wonders at their pitiful attitude; and he is being threatened with the same fate when a mighty wind from the north seizes the wretches and casts them, together with the knight and his attendant demons, into a stinking, icy river. As they try to climb out, other demons are waiting to push them back with iron hooks. Owein is delivered as before and finds himself on the opposite bank.

Now he is dragged to the south until he sees a dark, stinking, sulphurous flame issuing as from a pit. In it are naked sinners, thrown up like sparks, only to fall back into the fire. The demons tell Owein that this is the entrance to the pit of Hell, where they themselves dwell, and whither he must go for all time unless he consent to follow them back to the gate of the Purgatory. They pull him with them into the fire. As he descends into the pit, he is so terrified as almost to forget to call upon Christ; but when he does so, he is carried aloft in the flame and then cast down beside the pit, alone. Further demons come from the pit, saying that the others had lied in telling him that this was the entrance to Hell. They will show him the true Hell.

The new band of devils takes the knight to a wide, stinking river, blazing with sulphurous fire and swarming with more demons. He is told that below this river lies Hell. It is spanned by a bridge which he must cross; but they will cause a wind to blow him off into the river, where their companions wait to take him to Hell. He is placed on the bridge, which has three perilous qualities: it is slippery, it is so narrow that no one may stand upon it, and it is terrifyingly high. The demons once more offer to conduct him back to the gate, but he invokes the name of Christ and starts to cross. The further he goes, the wider and more easy to traverse the bridge becomes. Soon, a loaded cart would pass over; and eventually it is so broad that two carts could pass. The watching demons raise such a cry that Owein is more afraid than at the previous torments. Those in the river hurl their hooks at him; but he passes over unscathed.

A homily on the pains of Hell and the intercession of the living for the dead links the episode of the Purgatory with that of the Earthly Paradise, into which Owein now passes through a gateway set in a lofty wall. Two archbishops guide him through its delectable regions; and he is privileged to witness celestial manna descending from Heaven. Now he must return to earth, though a good life will earn him a place here. He wishes to stay, but his guides insist that he must return the same way as he came, although this time the demons will have no power to harm him. In fact, they flee as he passes. In the hall where he had first met the fifteen messengers of God he again sees them and is given their blessing. At the gate of the Purgatory the prior awaits him and conducts him to the church, where he spends fifteen days in prayer. Afterwards he takes the cross and leaves for Jerusalem. Upon his return, he asks the king to advise him as to which religious order it is best for him to enter.

There follows the account of how Owein served the monk Gilbert as his interpreter in Ireland. He did not himself take the habit, though he said he was very pleased to serve the Cistercians, for in Paradise no other order enjoyed as much glory as they. Gilbert often told the story, saying that for as long as he knew Owein, the knight led a holy life. Gilbert further insisted that Owein saw real, corporal punishments. He himself knew a monk who was one night carried from his bed by spiteful devils, who kept him for three days and nights. When he returned he was covered with deep, terrible wounds. After a brief epilogue by Henry,[34] there follow other narratives all intended to substantiate the legend of the Purgatory or the real, physical existence of devils.

I do not intend to probe all the possible sources of this text, for they have already been discussed at length by Warnke and other scholars.[35] Suffice it to say that the author seems well versed in the *Vision of St Paul* and the *Vision of Tundal*, and possibly also in a vision in the Irish tongue, the *Fis Adamnáin*.[36] He was very familiar too with the writings of St Augustine and Gregory the Great, as well as holy writ. Once again we are in the presence of a fiction that is essentially literary, though inspired by a local superstition, and which is brazenly passed off as authentic fact. Was there ever a knight Owein who visited Lough Derg in the reign of King Stephen? We have only Henry of Saltrey's word for it; and I am inclined to think that the worthy hero is himself just one more fiction. Some have seen him as a figure from Irish mythology: the Yvain of romance, or the pagan god Oengus, prince of the Tuatha, or else the legendary King Echu, whom tradition says St Patrick raised from the dead. I prefer to take as his prototype the soldier whose soul visited Hell in Gregory's *Dialogue* IV, 36, and who was a contemporary of the Stephen spoken of by Gregory.

Versions of or allusions to the legend of St Patrick's Purgatory proliferated throughout the Middle Ages and beyond, testifying to its wide appeal as an adventure story, whether presented in didactic wrappings or not. It attracted the preacher and reformer in search of an *exemplum*; and the idea of a human being making a real, physical journey through the realms of torment and then returning unscathed caught the imagination of all classes of the laity. The nobility in particular were gratified to find in Owein a hero of rank, with whom they could identify themselves. So the popularity of the legend had a broader base than that of the more homiletic *Vision of St Paul*; and this, together with a general faith in the truth of the facts narrated, had a marked influence on the later history of the Purgatory as a place of pilgrimage. A number of men, mainly knights and noblemen, have left records of their visits.[37] They came from the four corners of Europe: the Flemish Sire de Beaujeu, two Hungarians (George, son of the Count of Krisszafán, and Laurentius Ratholdi de Pászthó), the Catalan Ramon de Perelhos, William Staunton of Durham, Antonio Mannini from Italy, and a monk from Heemstade in northern Holland. Mannini's account is of special interest as it contains a hint of the pre-Christian lore associated with the district. As he approached the Purgatory, a hideous black bird rose into the air and flew off. This was the bird Cornu, which must leave when a Christian comes to the island. The story was that it had been a demon, but had been turned into this shape by St Patrick. The monk of Heemstade was not favoured with any such dramatic sight. Deceived and indignant to find that nothing happened during the night he spent in the damp grotto, he went so far as to complain to the Pope. The upshot was that on St Patrick's Day, 1497, the Purgatory was closed.

The closure did not deter would-be pilgrims for long. At one time there were even two Purgatories, one for men and one for women, so that no time should be lost because of the rule forbidding the simultaneous entry into the cavern of both sexes. Once more the pilgrimage was forbidden and the Purgatory enclosure destroyed. This was in 1632; but in 1704 the government still found it necessary to prohibit visits on pain of a fine of ten shillings or a public whipping. Perhaps the punishment seemed trivial to the pilgrims compared with the torments they hoped to witness and thereby avoid themselves. At all events they continued to turn up in their masses, and in the middle of the nineteenth century twelve or fourteen hundred a day might be seen at the Purgatory at the height of the season. It has still not lost its reputation of sanctity; and in recent times pilgrims have been able to spend the night in a new church erected on the site of the Caverna. So despite the Church's active disapproval, the legend has been long a-dying; and certainly in the Middle Ages there was little public scepticism.

The popularity of the Purgatory was, of course, fostered by the various literary accounts that were circulated from the twelfth century. G. P. Krapp gave a long list of those who related the original legend or referred to it in their works.[38] It includes such familiar names as Roger of Wendover, Matthew Paris and Vincent de Beauvais. Late in the fourteenth century, as we shall see in another chapter, Andrea da Barberino borrowed liberally from the story in composing his *Guerino il Meschino*. Then in 1569 a Toulouse professor of law, Étienne Forcadel, gave it a strange twist by making King Arthur visit the

Purgatory along with Gawain: Arthur, we are told, was only with difficulty prevented from entering. The story's success in Spain has not been confined to the adaptation by Ramon de Perelhos (we shall hear more of him), and in the seventeenth century alone it was called into service by writers as distinguished as Pérez de Montalván, Lope de Vega and Calderón. Montalván called his hero Ludovico Enio, and oddly enough it was through him that the legend returned into a Celtic tongue when a Breton mystery play was composed at about the time of the Revolution under the title of *Louis Eunius*.

The universal appreciation and love of the tale of Owein's adventures could not have been justified on purely literary grounds. Certainly it is well constructed as we find it in the *Tractatus* and most of the vernacular versions; indeed the description of the layout of the infernal parts is more precise than we find it in any other text before Dante, who may himself show its influence at times.[39] But the orderly sequence of events detracts from any suspense which we might otherwise feel; and there is not the compensating colour and liveliness that we detected in the *Vision of Tundal*. On the other hand, it had more impact on the credulous mind because of the fact that the journey was made by a mortal in the flesh. Moreover, a vital factor in the legend's success, the Purgatory had a real geographical existence. Reputable people were continually visiting it and returning with their impressions; and the reader or listener might have pictured himself as one day journeying to the hallowed grotto on the island in Lough Derg and, by submitting himself to the terrors of a single night, ensuring that he would not linger on the later road to Paradise.

The *Voyage of St Brendan*, the *Vision of Tundal*, *St Patrick's Purgatory*: the testimony of the pious witnesses from Ireland is as impressive as any available to those vernacular writers who considered it their duty to pass on to the unlettered public in England and France the awful evidence of Hell.

NOTES

1. For the Latin text see C. Wahlund, *Die altfranzösische Prosaübersetzung von Brendans Meerfahrt* (Uppsala, 1900); C. Selmer, *Navigatio Sancti Brendani abbatis* (Notre Dame, 1959). See also the Introduction to E. G. R. Waters, *The Anglo-Norman Voyage of St Brendan*; M.

Esposito, "Sur la *Navigatio Sancti Brendani* et sur ses versions italiennes", *Romania* LXIV (1938), pp. 328–46; and, for the legend in
general, Geoffrey Ashe, *Land to the West* (London, 1962). Further
bibliography in K. V. Sinclair, "Anglo-Norman Studies: The Last
Twenty Tears", *Australian Journal of French Studies* II (1965), pp.
132–3; James F. Kenney, *The Sources for the Early History of Ireland:
Ecclesiastical*, 1966 reprint (Irish U.P. & Columbia U.P., 1968), pp.
406–17.

2. This has been widely recognised. As well as the works already mentioned, see G. Schirmer, *Zur Brendanus-Legende* (Leipzig, 1888);
H. Zimmer, "Keltische Beiträge II. Brendans Meerfahrt", *Zeitschrift
für deutsches Alterthum und deutsche Litteratur* 33 (1889), pp. 129–220,
257–338; M. J. De Goeje, *La Légende de saint Brandan* (Leiden, 1890);
A. Schulze, "Zur Brendanlegende", *Zeitschrift für Romanische Philologie* 30 (1906), pp. 257–79; St J. D. Seymour, *Irish Visions of the Other
World*, pp. 83 ff.; F. Bar, *Les Routes de l'Autre Monde*, pp. 85–93;
H. R. Patch, *The Other World*, pp. 38 ff., where there are further
references.

3. Zimmer, op. cit., p. 331, suggests the seventh or eighth centuries, in
imitation of the voyage of Aeneas. A. G. van Hamel prints a number of
Irish texts, including *Bran* and *Maelduin* in his *Immrama* (Dublin,
1941).

4. K. Meyer & A. Nutt, *The Voyage of Bran Son of Febal to the Land of
the Living* (London, 1895). See also Patch, op. cit., pp. 30–1.

5. English translation by Whitley Stokes in *Revue Celtique* 9 (1888), pp.
447–95, and 10 (1889), pp. 50–95. French translation by H. d'Arbois
de Jubainville, *L'Épopée celtique en Irlande*, I (Paris, 1892), Ch. XVII.
Patch, op. cit., p. 31, gives further references. For a detailed comparison of the two texts see Wahlund, op. cit., pp. xxiv–xxvi.

6. Op. cit., pp. 288 ff.

7. Jubainville, Stokes and Esposito held that *Brendan* is the earlier text.
Zimmer was of the opposite opinion; and R. S. Loomis, in *Romania*
LIX (1933), p. 561, placed *Maelduin* in the eighth century. Selmer concludes that "a conclusive answer respecting the age, precedence, and
interrelation of these stories is still to be given" (op. cit., p. xxii).

8. See Jubinal, op. cit., pp. xv–xix; also Kenney's list of geographical
treatises bearing on St Brendan's island (op. cit., p. 408).

9. Ed. O. Schade, *Visio Tnugdali* (Halle, 1869); A. Wagner, *Visio Tnugdali:
lateinisch und altdeutsch* (Erlangen, 1882). For the circumstances of
composition see especially the Introduction to V. H. Friedel & K. Meyer,
La Vision de Tondale (Tnugdal) (Paris, 1907); and Seymour, op. cit.,
Chs. V and VI. For the literary tradition in Latin and the vernacular
see R. Verdeyen & J. Endepols, *Tondalus' Visioen en St Patricius'
Vagevuur* (Ghent & The Hague, 1914), Vol. I, Part II. Further bibliography in Kenney, op. cit., pp. 741–2; and see A. Rüegg, *Die Jenseitsvorstellungen vor Dante*, I, pp. 352–94.

10   *Sît brâht es ein münich guot
ze Regensburc in die stat.
Dô wîsete in daz phat
ze einer samenungen,
dâ sint vrouwen nunnen,
von sante Paul ist ez genant:*

dâ schreip erz mit sîner hant.
Offen er ez begunde
als erz vernam von enes munde.
(Wagner, op. cit., p. 122, ll. 44–52)

11. Cf. Seymour, op. cit., pp. 142–4.
12. Greek text, with English translation by Ph. H. De Lacy & B. Einarson, in *Plutarch's "Moralia"*, VII (London & Cambridge, Mass., 1959), pp. 269–99. The question of the relationship between *Tundal* and *Thespesios* has not received adequate attention, though E. J. Becker admitted "undoubted borrowings" (*A Contribution to the Comparative Study of the Medieval Visions of Heaven and Hell* [Baltimore, 1899], p. 85; some parallels are given on pp. 28–9, 85–7). A. B. van Os suggested one similarity of detail (*Religious Visions*, p. 56, n. 2); so too Bar (op. cit., p. 108, n. 2).
13. See above, p. 14.
14. *Islam and the Divine Comedy* (London, 1926), Part III, Ch. 3.
15. Ibid., pp. 115 ff. In the French Alexandrine version (see below, pp. 87–9) thieves carry their burden of sin on the infernal bridge.
16. The *Livre de l'Eschiele Mahomet*, which will be discussed in Ch. V.
17. See later, pp. 151–2.
18. Translated by G. Maspéro as *Le Livre de savoir ce qu'il y a dans l'autre monde*, and summarised by Bar, op. cit., pp. 16–20.
19. Book XII, Ch. 4 (J. P. Migne, *Patrologia Latina*, Vol. 82, col. 443).
20. A. Mussafia, *Sulla Visione di Tundalo* (Vienna, 1871: first published in *Sitzungsberichte der Phil.-Hist. Classe der Kais. Ak. der Wiss.*, Vol. 67), p. 50 (204).
21. C. S. Boswell, *An Irish Precursor of Dante*, p. 174.
22. The metamorphoses of the souls bitten by serpents in the *Inferno* XXIII and XXIV, for instance, are reminiscent of the beast on the icy lake in *Tundal*; and the lake itself may have suggested to Dante his final frozen circle inhabited by Lucifer. See further Boswell, op. cit., pp. 227–9; and Bar, op. cit., p. 129.
23. See, for example, the miniature in the *Très riches Heures du duc de Berry* and the painting by Hieronymus Bosch (reproduced by G. Lote, *La Vie et l'œuvre de François Rabelais* [Paris & Aix-en-Provence, 1938], Plates IVb and V). Verdeyen & Endepols mention another MS, dated 1474, containing twenty fine miniatures (op. cit., I, pp. 116–7). The *Très riches Heures* miniature is also reproduced in Robert Hughes, *Heaven and Hell in Western Art* (London, 1968, p. 183), q.v. for the iconography of Hell in the Middle Ages.
24. For general information on the legend and its origins see especially T. Wright, *St Patrick's Purgatory* (London, 1844); S. Eckleben, *Die älteste Schilderung vom Fegefeuer des heil. Patricius* (Halle, 1885); Ph. de Félice, *L'Autre Monde: mythes et légendes. Le Purgatoire de saint Patrice* (Paris, 1906); Verdeyen & Endepols, op. cit. (study on the Purgatory by Endepols in Vol. I, Part III); Seymour, op. cit., Ch. VII; S. Leslie, *St Patrick's Purgatory. A Record from History and Literature* (London, 1932); K. Warnke, *Das Buch vom Espurgatoire S. Patrice der Marie de France und seine Quelle* (Halle, 1938), pp. iii–vi; Bar, op. cit., pp. 93–100; Patch, op. cit., pp. 114–6 *et passim*; M. de Riquer, *Historia de la literatura catalana*, II (Barcelona, 1964), Ch. XI; Kenney, op. cit., pp. 354–6.

25. See A. Nutt's essay in Meyer & Nutt, op. cit.
26. Translated by L. E. Swift (Dublin, 1809). See Ch. CLXXII, p. 229.
27. Ed. J. F. Dimock. See Vol. V (London, 1867), pp. 82–3. Lucien Foulet was not convinced of Giraldus' ignorance of the *Tractatus* ("Marie de France et la légende du Purgatoire de saint Patrice", *Romanische Forschungen* 22 [1908], pp. 599–627 and especially pp. 616–7). See also F. W. Locke, "A New Date for the Composition of the *Tractatus de Purgatorio Sancti Patricii*", *Speculum* XL (1965), pp. 641–6.
28. Two versions (α and β) are edited by Warnke, op. cit. The original classification of the Latin MSS into two groups was made by H. L. D. Ward, *Catalogue of Romances*, II, pp. 435–92.
29. A possible reference to a pilgrimage to the Purgatory is found earlier, about the year 1152 (Seymour, op. cit., p. 178); but this is rather suspect, and if the place is the same, there is no evidence that the legend as we know it was as yet associated with it.
30. Locke, op. cit., argues from the period of the abbacy of Henry of Warden for a dating of 1208–15.
31. Discussed by C. M. van der Zanden, *Étude sur le Purgatoire de saint Patrice* (Amsterdam, 1927), pp. 71–5.
32. Apparently Stephen, King of England 1135–54: see M. Mörner, *Le Purgatoire de saint Patrice par Berol* (Lund, 1917), pp. xvii and xxviii–xxix.
33. Van der Zanden has commented on the similarity of these figures to Cistercian monks (op. cit., pp. 72–3).
34. In text β the Epilogue is somewhat expanded and occurs after the narratives.
35. Warnke, op. cit., pp. xi–xxiv. See, in addition to the works already mentioned, Becker, *A Contribution* ..., pp. 91–3; Asín Palacios, *Islam and the Divine Comedy*, pp. 190–1 (an attempt to show Moslem sources); van Os, *Religious Visions*, pp. 58–67.
36. For this vision see Boswell, op. cit. Ed. with translation by J. Vendryès, "Aislingthi Adhamnain", *Revue Celtique* XXX (1909), pp. 349–83.
37. Lists are given by G. P. Krapp, *The Legend of St Patrick's Purgatory; its Later Literary History* (Baltimore, 1900), pp. 31 ff.; H. Delehaye, "Le Pèlerinage de Laurent de Pászthó au Purgatoire de s. Patrice", *Analecta Bollandiana* 27 (1908), pp. 35 ff.; Verdeyen & Endepols, op. cit., Vol. I, Part III, Ch. 4; Warnke, op. cit., pp. xxxix–xlii.
38. Op. cit., *passim*. See too Verdeyen & Endepols, op. cit., Vol. I, Part III, Ch. 3; Bar, op. cit., pp. 99–100.
39. See Boswell, op. cit., p. 235; Bar, op. cit., p. 129.

CHAPTER III

THE CHURCH'S WITNESSES:
THE ANGLO-NORMANS

IN the Middle Ages the English, whether of Anglo-Saxon or
Norman French stock, showed particular interest in visions
of the Otherworld. Perhaps this was an early manifestation of
that cast of temperament which still shows itself in a taste for
the supernatural and the good ghost story. So the legends of
Hell that were composed in Latin soon found their way into
one or both vernaculars, the native English tongue[1] or the
socially more respectable Anglo-Norman. It is the versions in
the latter language that will be reviewed in this chapter.

From references in Anglo-Saxon literature of the tenth and
eleventh centuries it appears that the *Vision of St Paul* was
known and appreciated in England at that time, in some of the
redactions as well as the Long Texts. The first version of it to
have come down in French is probably that of Adam de Ros,
dating perhaps from the end of the twelfth century, though the
earliest of the six surviving manuscripts can only be placed
about the middle of the thirteenth.[2] From his humble address
to the "Seignurs . . . a Deu vouez" at the beginning of his
poem (he writes in rough and ready octosyllables) and from his
reference to himself as "God's servant" at the end, one may
deduce that he was a simple monk translating from the Latin
for the benefit of his brethren in the monastery. This is usually
supposed to have been at Ross-on-Wye in Herefordshire,
though a less plausible claim has been staked for Ros near Caen.

He concludes his work by saying that his source has run out
and he will write no more, though he is not tired. He thanks
God and asks for our prayers—the writing has been carried out
in great cold. Poor Adam : we can imagine him in his unheated
scriptorium, which could well have been part of an open cloister,
blowing on his hands to keep them warm enough for the work

of copying onto the parchment his account of the eternal fires
of Hell! He has our sympathy not merely because of this rather
plaintive note, but because his personality does come through
into his stumbling lines. He was no real poet, and the charming
feature of his work is its naïvety: God sends a heavenly angel
called St Michael to a holy man, who is to be led to see the pains
of Hell; the angel goes gladly, for that is his job.

> *Deu prist un angle del ciel*
> *Ke l'en apele Seint Michiel,*
> *A un seint homme l'enveia,*
> *E en après le comanda*
> *Ke deske en enfern l'amenast,*
> *E les grant peines li mostrat.*
> *Li angles i vet volentirs,*
> *Car ce est li suens mestirs.*

(9–16)

The "seint homme" turns out, of course, to be St Paul, who
follows Michael, reciting psalms as he goes. But despite Adam's
extreme poverty of expression, he does succeed in introducing a
lively note into the narrative, especially by his habit of inserting
exclamations of his own, such as: "Ha! sire Deu si fors
turmenz!" (l. 63).

It is possible to speak of these as Adam's own interpolations,
since there is no doubt that the *livre* he mentions as his source
contained the fourth Redaction of the Latin *Vision*. His
episodes appear in precisely the same order as there. He did
substitute his own brief introduction, and also omitted the
torment of the fast-breakers. But this "Tantalus torment",
though one of the primitive features of the legend, tended to
become very corrupt in some of the Latin manuscripts to the
point of its virtual exclusion. So we can say that on the whole
Adam's treatment is a little free (the wheel episode, for instance, caught his imagination and is elaborated for a few lines);
but he did not trust himself to venture far from his model.
Indeed, far from indulging in any literary extravagance, he
reduced the already straightforward Redaction IV to the
simplest of terms.

This is a modest, but deeply pious work written, it would

seem, for a restricted public of no great culture—if it was in fact carried out for the benefit of Adam's brethren in the monastery, it can be taken as a poor reflection on their interest in Latin letters. Yet it did travel beyond his immediate circle, as the surviving manuscripts show; and it inspired at least one miniaturist to illustrate the text with lively, coloured scenes such as Redaction IV is bound to evoke in the minds of those who read it or hear it recited.[3]

Another Anglo-Norman poet produced a version of the *Vision* in very uneven Alexandrine lines by the middle of the thirteenth century at the latest, but more probably in the latter part of the twelfth.[4] The manuscript in which it has come down contains other pious writings by the same man; and in a prologue to his translation of the *Vitae Patrum*, to use his own title, he states that he is writing at the "Temple de la Bruere", Temple Bruer in Lincolnshire, not for clerics, but for the lay folk who have no Latin. Although this poet has for long been known as Henri d'Arci, it has been shown that this is the result of a misunderstanding and that Henri was in fact the influential Templar to whom he was dedicating his writings. I shall therefore follow Professor Legge in referring to him simply as the Templar.[5]

He too has *enromancé* (to use his own phrase) the Latin Redaction IV or, more probably, an earlier, unclassified version of this redaction.[6] His versification is erratic, even by Anglo-Norman standards; and like Adam he seems to have set more store by the content than by the form of his work. He makes no secret of his intention of edifying the "laie gent", and says at the end of another of his poems that he has left out certain sections in which he saw no useful purpose ("en qui je ne vi geres d'utilité").[7] He may have intended to use his *Vision* in church as a rhymed sermon: we know that the Templars served one church, that of Guiting in Gloucestershire, in the early thirteenth century.[8] This would explain his insistence on the merits of regular and sincere churchgoing, as when he speaks of those who suffer in the internal river as the result of their negligence. And he concludes his poem by devoting some thirty lines to the praise of Sunday, starting from the brief injunction in the Latin: "Ideo, qui custodierint ipsum diem sanctum

habebunt partem cum angelis Dei."[9] Christ, says our Templar,
was born and resurrected from the dead on a Sunday, the day
on which He also performed His miracles. The Last Judgment
will be on a Sunday; and because of the holiness of the day we
must commit no sin then or do anything but go to church to
pray and hear the word of Christ from the preacher, except that
we should visit the sick, bury the dead, feed the hungry, clothe
the naked, reform sinners and go to see those who are in prison.
We should also house the poor and strangers, comfort orphans
and widows, and bring peace between those who quarrel.
Those who act thus will go to Heaven when they die.

So, as with Adam de Ros, we can see here something of the
poet's personality coming through his work as he indulges in
slight elaboration and adds a little pious commentary and
exclamation. Rather less naïve than Adam, the Lincolnshire
Templar seems a sincere and god-fearing man, strenuous as we
would expect a Templar to be in his attempts to demonstrate by
example the value of a righteous life.

The third Anglo-Norman poet to treat the *Vision of St Paul*
is also anonymous. Furthermore, he was a plagiarist; for as I
have shown elsewhere, he contented himself for reasons of his
own with re-working the Templar's version into what passes for
octosyllabic couplets.[10] The demands of rhyme and metre
forced him to a certain amount of re-arrangement and padding,
and he was not above making a few careless slips: the Templar
might have been amused, for example, to find one of his own
pious interjections being credited to St Paul himself. But the
plagiarist did seriously depart from his model at three points,
by making clumsy interpolations which show that he knew in
addition a different and rather fuller version of the Fourth
Redaction.

One of the reasons for supposing that the Templar's source
was an early form of this Latin Redaction was that he omitted
the episode of the infernal wheel. Now apart from the fact that
the wheel was one of the most characteristic features of the
Redaction, it was also one of the most popular—we saw how
even Adam de Ros could not refrain from filling out its description a little. The plagiarist, regretting its absence from his
model, contrived to bring it back, but out of its rightful place.

It replaces in fact the Templar's rendering of the punishment of the fast-breakers, and is fused to the description of the place of ice and fire, so that the sinners on the wheel are subjected to extremes of cold and heat. This is just another illustration of how the topography of Hell can be modified by the vagaries of literary transmission.

Then there is a fragmentary interpolation of the episode of the impure bishop,[11] which is inserted into the middle of Christ's harangue to the sinners. It had already appeared, in the form given to it by the Templar, immediately after the intrusive wheel episode. I speak of the "impure bishop" although in this version he is replaced by two pleasure-loving priests, of whose sins we learn, but not their precise torments. The same substitution is found in Adam de Ros ; but since this is the only detail in which the two poems agree against common tradition, we are forced to assume that both used a variant reading of Redaction IV.

The third interpolation appears as a mutilated allusion in one of the two manuscripts to the devils who were torturing the souls of the damned. It occurs at the point where the story breaks off, and is doubtless a reference to the infernal porter and his dog Cerberus, who appear in certain Latin manuscripts. What seems to have happened, then, is that the plagiarist knew a form of Redaction IV other than that used by the Templar, and that he carelessly tricked out his poem with scraps of translations from it. It may be pure coincidence that such a version immediately follows his *Vision* in the Cambridge manuscript.

Little more remains to be said about this rather drab character. His real concern was simply to give the Templar's poem a new, and still very unsatisfactory, form, perhaps with the idea of introducing some order into the metrical chaos of his model. Cleric or layman ? It is impossible to say. He may have shared the general view that a devout exercise of this kind would gain him credit and some remission of purgatorial pains when the grim hour struck ; but if so, we might have expected a less slipshod approach to his task.

An Anglo-Norman version of the *Gospel of Nicodemus* will not detain us long.[12] Probably composed in the second half of the thirteenth century, it gives us no hint of the condition or personality of its author. Even in the prologue he uses the first person plural instead of the singular form, and this is symptomatic of his complete anonymity. His avowed purpose is "to increase the belief of those who are in doubt" (ll. 23–4). As for his source, he merely says that he had seen the story in writing; but the poem's extreme fidelity to the Latin A text leaves small room for doubt on that score. We can see how he tried to keep strictly to the sense of his model, even at the expense of his versification, the familiar octosyllabic couplet. But we know that late Anglo-Norman standards were by no means those of the continental French, so he must not be judged too harshly for this. It is even possible to add a word in his favour: he did avoid an excessive use of *cliché* and padding in his verse.

The depredations of time on libraries and individual manuscripts prevent us from saying how many infernal visions and anecdotes were turned into French on English soil in the course of the Middle Ages. The most productive century in this respect was probably the thirteenth. Gregory's *Dialogues*, for instance, were translated in about 1213 by Angier, sub-deacon and later canon of St Frideswide's at Oxford.[13] Angier used the eight-syllable line, as did the man who translated Gregory's account of the soldier's vision and included it in his *Manuel des Péchés* some half-century later. This work has been attributed on insufficient evidence to Robert Grosseteste, Bishop of Lincoln.[14] An interesting point is that whereas its author recounted the soldier's vision, he passed over that of Stephen. Could it be that the element of divine error in the latter was too much for him to stomach?

I mentioned in an earlier chapter that William of Malmesbury incorporating Hetto's *Vision of Wettin* in his *Miracula Dei genetricis*, deliberately left out the visionary's sight of Hell and the damned. William's work was twice turned into Anglo-Norman, the first time by Adgar in the third quarter of the twelfth century.[15] It is easy to detect a note of regret in Adgar's words as he says that he is following his model in leaving aside the vision of the penance endured by emperors, bishops and abbots:

> *Plusure choses d'icest afaire*
> *trespas, sulunc mun essampleire,*
> *de l'avisiun que cil vit,*
> *dunt mis aucturs un mot ne dit;*
> *d'empereurs, evesques, d'abez,*
> *dunt vit mal e dolur asez.*
> *A mei n'afiert nule rien a dire,*
> *fors ceo, k'afiert a la matire.*

(185–92)

Only his conscientiousness as a translator, it seems, prevented him from embarking on a description of Wettin's sight of the places of retribution.

The Irish legends were on the whole well served by their Anglo-Norman adaptors, and the first translation we must look at is a considerable literary monument in its own right. It is a version of the *Voyage of St Brendan*.[16] There is no evidence that the author of this poem had any interest in Celtic literature as such, and he makes it clear in his prologue that he has undertaken the work at the behest of Adeliza of Louvain, wife of King Henry I of England.[17] This would date the poem after 1121, and perhaps soon after Adeliza's arrival in England in that year. The only direct information we have on the author's identity is when he names himself, cryptically, as "li apostoiles danz Benedeiz" (l. 8). In E. G. R. Waters' view, the only certain conclusion to be drawn is that Benedeit was a cleric (probably a Benedictine) having some contact with the royal court, where Queen Adeliza seems to have been something of a literary patron.[18] Any further identification must be based on assumption; and as there is no evidence that *li apostoiles* indicates any particular rank in the Church hierarchy, we can say no more than that he was writing in the first quarter of the twelfth century and had presumably established some sort of literary reputation to have imposed upon him the task of turning the story of St Brendan into French ("en letre mis e en romanz" l. 11).

Let us see how Benedeit handles those parts of the poem that are relevant to our theme. We notice first that whereas those scenes constituted about one ninth of the *Navigatio*, with Benedeit they occupy 392 lines of a total of 1,840, that is over a fifth of the whole. Moreover, whereas he has abbreviated parts of the original account, notably at the beginning, we shall see that he goes out of his way to elaborate some of the "infernal" passages. So the change in relative length is certainly deliberate.

Three episodes interest us; and the first is the description of the island of forges. In the *Navigatio* we are told of the forges at the beginning of the episode, but only at the end do we learn that the pilgrims have been near Hell. Benedeit, on the other hand, describes the appearance of the island, then reveals through St Brendan that the boat is being drawn towards Hell, and proceeds to a more detailed topographical description of the place. That there is a forge on the island we learn only when the "barbarian" (here a demon, *malfez*) runs into it after sighting the voyagers. No others are mentioned at any time during the episode. The change is slight, but interesting: in the Latin, this was an island of forges first and only incidentally an infernal region; Benedeit conceives it primarily as Hell, and he mentions casually that there was a forge on the island. Throughout he is interested in the infernal characteristics of the place and its inhabitants and is at pains to emphasise this in his descriptions.

The approaching monks see it as a place of smoke and fog, surrounded by great darkness; and from afar they hear sounds of woe. Brendan warns them what the island is, for he knows well that they are close to the pit of Hell. Then follows the more detailed description: there are deep, dark valleys and ditches, from which fly up fiery blades; the sound of the fires is louder than thunder; and flames, sparks and blazing rocks leap up so abundantly as to dim the light of the sun. We hear too that there is a mountain on the island. All this is reminiscent of the topography of Hell as described in various medieval visions and particularly that of Drycthelm, which Benedeit could well have known. He similarly expands the description of the devil, who carries a great hammer, has blazing eyes, and belches fire; and he gives a vivid account of the hurling of the fiery missile. Towards the end of the episode there is a markedly moralising note. The monks see many devils and hear the weeping and wailing of the damned. Benedeit comments that just as the holy man's pious joy is increased by suffering and privation, so is theirs by the sight of the destination of the damned.

The poet's didactic preoccupations show through likewise in the second episode, that of the smoke-capped mountain. The lost companion cries that he is carried off *for his sins* ; and then, as the monks look back, they see Hell wide open, hurling flames, blazing débris, pitch and sulphur up to the clouds.

The passage concerning Judas is the most expanded of the three, occupying 284 lines. The extra material consists mainly of Judas' account of his sins, his bitter repentance, and a lengthy description of the torments he suffers. I cannot agree with Waters that Benedeit has attempted to create sympathy for the traitor,[19] though his miserable condition and his self-reproaches may inspire pity in the modern reader. The poet, as I see it, wished to show just how terrible was Judas' crime and how richly deserved his punishment. As for Brendan's intense grief and his abundant tears (which were not described in the *Navigatio*), surely they are intended rather to reflect the saint's holiness and goodness than to engender sympathy for Judas. We are forcibly reminded of St Paul weeping for the damned in Hell and his intercession on their behalf,[20] and in the *Vision* there is no question of an attempt to arouse sympathy for the sinners.

Benedeit's treatment of the Judas episode, then, seems motivated by this same desire to moralise that we have detected in the earlier passages. But he has introduced further elements. Before the pilgrims' encounter with Judas, St Brendan arms them with the sign of the cross. The traitor's plight on his rock is described more graphically than in the *Navigatio* and not without literary skill. Then come Judas' lamentations and the expression of his despair, whereupon Brendan makes the sign of the cross over his company, and the sea grows calm. He asks the unknown victim why he suffers thus, and in a low, hoarse voice Judas tells who he is and enumerates his crimes. Not all of his account is scriptural. When he tells the holy man that he is at this moment enjoying respite from his punishment,

Brendan enquires about the place and nature of his usual torments, and Judas embarks on a long description of the terrible
pains of Hell. This is all foreign to the *Navigatio*.

Very close by are two Hells, and Judas alone has to suffer the
torments of both. There is an upper and a lower one, separated
by the salt sea. The upper one is burning, the lower stinking
and cold. He spends a day and a night in each alternately.
The idea of an upper and a lower Hell originated with the
Augustinian conception of Purgatory as a kind of upper Hell, a
doctrine elaborated by Gregory the Great, who inferred from
Psalm lxxxv. 13 that there is one Hell below and another, higher
one on earth (*Dialogue* IV, 42).[21] The idea is further evolved in
the *Elucidarium* usually attributed to Honorius Augustodunensis and probably written soon after 1100. Honorius was, then,
a contemporary of Benedeit, had connections with Canterbury,
and spent most of his life in the Irish Benedictine community
at Ratisbon.[22] In the third book he links the doctrine with the
nine pains of Hell as follows :

> Duo sunt inferni : superior et inferior. Superior infima
> pars hujus mundi, quae plena est poenis ; nam hic exundat
> nimius aestus, magnum frigus, fames, sitis, varii dolores
> corporis ut verbera, animi ut timor et verecundia. . . .
> Inferior a utemlocus spiritualis, ubi ignis inexstinguibilis, de
> quo dicitur : "Eruisti animam meam ex inferno inferiori
> (*Psal.*, lxxxv. 13)." Qui sub terra esse dicitur, ut, sicut
> corpora peccantium terra cooperiuntur, ita animae peccan-
> tium sub terra in inferno sepeliuntur . . . (§ 13)

The nine forms of torment in the lower Hell are : terrible fire
that burns without light ; extreme cold ; undying reptiles—
serpents and dragons ; unparalleled stench ; subjection to
flails ; palpable darkness ; the confusion of sinners ; the
horrible sight of demons and dragons ; fiery chains binding
the sinners' limbs. It will be noticed that these torments do not
correspond to those which Benedeit goes on to describe.

On Monday, Judas is in the upper Hell hooked on a wheel that
turns like the wind which blows it about through these regions.
On Tuesday in the lower Hell he is chained and reviled by

demons, then laid on a spiked bed to have lead and rocks heaped upon him. His body is pierced through and through by spits. Back in the upper Hell on Wednesday, he is alternately boiled in pitch and bound to a red-hot stake between two braziers and roasted. On Thursday he is below again in a terribly cold and dark place. Friday sees him flayed, in the upper Hell, by devils who then use a fiery stake to thrust him down into salt and soot, whereupon a new skin forms. This torment is repeated ten times a day; then the devils force him to drink molten lead and copper. On Saturday he is plunged into a deep, black dungeon in the lower Hell, where the stench is so vile that he wants to vomit. But he cannot, because of the copper he has drunk: instead, he swells to the point of bursting. Then, between midday and none on Saturday, he comes to the place where he is now.

Benedeit, with his vivid imagination and originality of expression, is by no means incapable of having invented these gruesome scenes himself. However, in some he seems to be following tradition and perhaps a written source. The appearance of a wheel in Hell is significant as being the earliest mention of this form of torture in French vernacular literature. It is not a fiery wheel, which suggests that Benedeit may not have been thinking of the one in the *Vision of St Paul*. It could be a reminiscence of *Aeneid* VI, though the resemblance would still not be striking, and we have no other evidence of the poet's knowledge of Virgil's text. The idea of the wheel being blown about through Hell by the wind is curious and, in my experience, unique—at least if one disregards the mobile wheel in the later *Vision of Gunthelm*, plainly borrowed from Benedeit.[23]

The pouring of molten metals into a sinner's mouth occurs in the early ninth-century vision of a poor woman quoted by C. Fritzsche;[24] but as, in the *Navigatio*, Judas said that sometimes he burned like liquid lead in a pot, Benedeit may have played with that phrase to produce the form of torture we find here. We are on surer ground in ascribing one or two features to current traditions regarding the nature of Hell: the juxtaposition of great heat and cold, for example, and the abominable stench both occur in the list just quoted from the *Elucidarium*; but they are also found in many other visions, indeed in the majority, including that of St Paul.[25] Only slightly less common are the "culinary" forms of torture (spitting, roasting, and so forth) and the introduction of infernal winds.[26] I have found no other possible sources for the remaining forms of Judas' punishment, unless his flaying is a development of the fifth torment described in the *Elucidarium*. Those inflicted on Tuesday, Friday and Saturday are almost Dantesque in their hideous ingenuity; and they all must have appealed to the medieval public, if we can judge by the way in which miniaturists lavishly decorated three of the manuscripts at this point.[27]

The other differences between Benedeit's treatment of this episode and that of his source have been noted by Waters. They consist mainly of slight abridgments and are not important, though it is surprising to find Benedeit omitting some details of the encounter with the devils at the end of the passage. But on the whole, as we have seen, it was the infernal element in the narrative that most interested him, and in this sense he seems to have reflected the outlook of the society in which he lived. For the Celtic elements in the story he had no particular regard, indeed he is unlikely to have understood them. To be sure, they had been largely submerged in the already much Christianised *Navigatio*; but by insisting on the infernal characteristics of the episodes we have considered, he concealed them even further.[28] There is no sign of the later vogue for the marvels and enchantments typical of Celtic romance. Benedeit's attitude is simply that of the ordinary churchman of his day: a desire to moralise on the mortal dangers of sin and to instruct by example. He himself appears to have been well versed in Church teaching on the subject; but for us his chief appeal lies in a power of illustration and a literary talent above the ordinary for his day.

The *Vision of Tundal*, the second of the great Irish legends, also had at least one Anglo-Norman translator.[29] His poem is only partially conserved, in MS 312 of Trinity College, Dublin. Although this dates from the fourteenth century, its editors consider the work to have been written some hundred years earlier. Composed in very ragged Alexandrines, it breaks off after 364 lines, in the middle of the bridge episode. The anonymous author addresses his audience with a greeting: he will put a Latin story he has found into French for those who have no learning. The source would seem to belong to A. Wagner's second category of Latin manuscripts. Most of the prologue is omitted; but this was commonly done by the writers of the Latin as well as the vernacular texts. Otherwise, what survives of his translation is fairly full, leaving out only inessentials. And it is strongly marked by his personality, being quite animated and showing touches of deliberate originality. We may, for instance, compare his version with the Latin text at the point where Tundal, feeling himself at the point of death, speaks of his axe, which he had brought with him and laid aside when he sat down to eat:

> Uxori socii sic commendavit: Custodi, inquiens, meam securim, nam ego morior.[30]

> > *Orriblement s'escrie, le color luy est mu:*
> > *"Dame del hostel cea ven ! ou es tu?*
> > *Mon acche moi gardez, car tote a morir su;*
> > *Plus ne puis parler; merci, seignur Jhesu !"*

> > (35-8)

(He gives a terrible cry and turns pale: "Mistress of the house, come here! Where are you? Look after my axe for me, for I am about to die; I cannot speak any more; have mercy on me, Lord Jesus.")

The poet elaborates too in his treatment of the beast Acheron. He says that this torment is for the greedy, since they are never satisfied with worldly goods, just as Acheron's thirst is never quenched, even by a river.

The obviously corrupt nature of the text does not flatter its author's skill; and the editors' judgment is a little severe when they suggest that this is a banal production of a workaday rhymester. With due allowance made for the poor condition of the text, the poem can be considered a satisfactory literary achievement by Anglo-Norman standards. The technique is particularly interesting in that the writer treats the different episodes in passages of varying length, each carrying the same

rhyme throughout, after the fashion of the *laisses* of a chanson
de geste. So he had planned his poem with some care and
originality; and this makes us more lenient in assessing his
merits. Alive to the demands of technique, he did not allow it
to mummify the narrative, and for this alone we should be
grateful to him.

It appears from the opening lines and from its epic style that
the poem was intended for oral delivery, perhaps from the
pulpit. There are some indications that the author was a cleric.
He is translating for those who have no Latin, whereas he himself shows considerable competence in the language. He seems
to have known his Scriptures well, and was able to assign one
of Marcus' unacknowledged quotations to its general biblical
context.[31] A smaller point is that he unnecessarily allots the
first torment to *lay* homicides. But whether or not he was a
practising priest, he plainly conceived his work as a pious
lesson to be read or recited to a reasonably cultivated audience.
He enjoyed the task of trying to give the legend the elegance of
form that it merits; and while our assessment of his achievement is hampered by the fact that only part of his poem has
survived, and in a poor copy at that, he does have the distinction
of having composed the only existing verse rendering of the
Vision of Tundal.

Of *St Patrick's Purgatory*, on the other hand, five rhymed
translations have come down from Anglo-Norman territory
alone. Perhaps the earliest is by a certain Marie, traditionally
identified with Marie de France; and it is usually dated soon
after the appearance of the *Tractatus*, that is to say about the
year 1190.[32] Marie twice tells us that she is translating, presumably from a Latin original. Her second reference to her
source occurs at the end of the poem:

> *Jo, Marie, ai mis en memoire*
> *Le Livre de l'Espurgatoire*
> *En Romanz, qu'il seit entendables*
> *A laie gent e convenables.*

(2297–300)

(I, Marie, have committed to writing in the Romance tongue the book of the Purgatory, so that it may be understandable and suitable for lay folk.)

A comparison with the Latin texts shows that up to l. 2056 her translation corresponds quite closely to the reading of the Group α manuscripts, and thereafter is closer to Group β. She has, in fact, worked very faithfully from her model. There is a small amount of amplification, which does not add to the basic meaning of the Latin ; but only twenty-two lines can be called completely original (ll. 1–8, 1019–20, 1053–4, 1119–20, 1667–8 and 2297–302). These comprise the Prologue, Epilogue, and four quite commonplace pious interjections. Each of the latter appears as a complete couplet, suggesting a measure of sincerity rather than padding put in out of necessity. As for the omissions and discrepancies between Marie's text and the *Tractatus* as we know it, these are very small matters and contribute in no way to our knowledge of the authoress or her text.

Despite the attention of scholars, Marie de France remains an enigmatic figure, and is latterly even in danger of becoming a trinity of like-named ladies (the qualification "de France" appears only in her *Fables*), if not of disintegrating entirely.[33] However, for lack of positive evidence to the contrary, I can only repeat the common view that, despite her Continental origin as indicated by her name, she lived and wrote in England, that she was well known to royalty, and that she enjoyed a considerable literary reputation. The most widely accepted chronological order for her three works is *Lais, Fables, Espurgatoire* ; but it may be wondered how she could have come to translate the Purgatory legend from the Latin after stating in her Prologue to the *Lais* :

> ... *Començai a penser*
> *De aukune bone estoire faire*
> *E de latin en romaunz traire;*
> *Mais ne me fust guaires de pris:*
> *Itant s'en sunt altre entremis.* (28–32)

(I began to think of writing some good story, turning it from Latin into Romance ; but this would not have been of much profit to me : so many others have undertaken it.)

We must suppose that either she had failed at that time to find a *bone estoire* in Latin such as would appeal to a noble public, or else when she came to write the *Espurgatoire* she was catering for a different class of public, for whom she considered a translation from the Latin to be better suited. In any case, it is unlikely that the *Tractatus* was in existence at the period when she wrote the *Lais*.

If the *Espurgatoire* had been primarily intended as entertainment for the nobility, Marie would hardly have stated so baldly in her Epilogue that she translated it for the benefit of the *laie gent*. Moreover, there is no dedication to a high personage as in the *Fables* or the *Lais*;[34] so it seems that she intended her account of St Patrick's Purgatory for a wider public, for whom it would have been more *convenables*—fitting, probably because it was instructive. One identification that has been proposed is with Marie, Abbess of Shaftesbury; and D. Knowles has pointed out that the great English nunneries were seats of considerable culture in the twelfth century, and that they probably served as places of education, especially for the daughters of noble families.[35] In these circumstances it would not be surprising to find an abbess translating with a didactic purpose such a work as the *Tractatus*.

Of course, if we are dealing with a single Marie, she was gifted with literary skills and judgment above the average, so she had an eye too for the *bone estoire*; and the clarity and orderliness of the *Tractatus* would have appealed to her. So also would the fact of its hero being a knight; for she was something of an aristocrat at heart, dabbling in the problems of courtly love and delighting in the atmosphere of chivalry.[36] We notice too that in her translation she has underlined the fact that Owein remained a knight on his return from the Holy Land, instead of going into religious orders.[37] It seems fair to conclude that if one quality that drew Marie's attention to the *Tractatus* was its salutary moral tone, another was its value as an adventure story. This would be in keeping with her personality as it emerges from her other works.

The second Anglo-Norman version of the Purgatory legend is by Berol (not the same as the poet of the *Tristan*) and is carried in two manuscripts.[38] One of these was written in

England, probably soon after 1250, and the other is the work of a copyist living in the south-east of France in the fourteenth century. So here is evidence that the poem enjoyed some success in widely separated areas. Consisting of 884 Alexandrine lines grouped into monorhymed quatrains, it may have been composed at the end of the twelfth or beginning of the thirteenth century. As Berol says he is putting the story into Romance (l. 2), we can assume a Latin original, perhaps belonging to the α Group. But he was much more free with his material than Marie, and in particular abbreviated the *Tractatus* considerably. Major portions omitted are the Dedication and Prologue, the story of the old homicide and that of the bantered prior, the description of the procedure to be followed by intending pilgrims, and the testimonies and appended narratives at the end of the work. The two parenthetic homilies of the Latin are also passed over. The effect of this compression is to make the work more compact and entertaining; but we cannot tell how much was due to the particular source used by Berol. We are on surer ground in ascribing to him certain alterations and additions which are not found in any extant Latin text, and which reveal something of the kind of man he was.

The original Prologue is replaced by a short moralisation ending with a reference to *Psalm* lxvi. 12. There follows a quatrain giving a brief geographical description of Ireland, and this is repeated a little further on in rather different words. Just beyond Ireland lie the coagulated sea (*mer betee*) and the magnetic isle, both traditional perils for navigators and probably familiar to Berol through *mappemondes* or similar works. These twin passages are an instance of a stylistic device favoured by him, namely the repetition of lines with slight variation: it is reminiscent of the *expolitio* technique recommended in rhetorical treatises, and may reflect some degree of school training.[39] Berol cannot be accused of having condensed the story out of laziness, when he is prepared to bring in this element of expansion for stylistic reasons. He is fond, too, of amplifying the dialogue: for instance, the words addressed by the demons to Owein, who has just witnessed the activities in the first "plain", virtually repeat the previous description of the torment.

A small point, but one which may illustrate the poet's readiness to depart from his model, is a possible reminiscence of the *Vision of St Paul* at the moment when Owein is delivered from the pit of Hell. Berol says that he moved away a little because of the stench of the place; and this reminds us of Paul's reaction to the opening of the pit in the *Vision*.

On Owein's return from the Holy Land, there is no question of his taking monastic vows: he is merely said to have subsequently led a righteous life. Is this a hint that Berol was not himself a monk? Perhaps; but in any case, the end of the poem leaves us in no doubt as to his deep piety. He insists first on the truth of his account:

> *Ki de ren me mescreit aut vers le pays:*
> *Uncore i est l'entree e serra mes tut dis.*
>
> (Cheltenham MS, 865–6)

(If anybody disbelieve anything I say, let him go to the country: the entrance is still there, and will be for ever.)

These lines contain the same sentiment as that expressed by Caesarius of Heisterbach, probably a contemporary of Berol's, in his *Dialogus miraculorum*: "Qui vero de purgatorio dubitat, Scotiam pergat, Purgatorium s. Patricii intret et de purgatorii poenis amplius non dubitabit."[40] To both men the story was no mere legend; and as we have seen, they were not unduly credulous for their day. So Berol believed in what he wrote, and used the account consciously as a piece of Christian propaganda. In his Epilogue, he points with great insistence the moral that our greatest hope is penitence. Earlier, he had devoted rather more space than did the *Tractatus* to the description of Owein's sins; now he makes it clear that for him the kernel of the story lies in a sinner's redemption through repentance. The moralist once more overshadows the poet, real though the latter's merits are.

Our knowledge of Berol is confined to what we can deduce from this single work. Most probably he was a man of the Church; and training in a monastic or cathedral school might account for a literary touch more deft than that of most of his compatriots. But we may be sure that formal elegance was of

TE 3. Owein in St Patrick's Purgatory. Oxford, Queen's College MS 305. French, late 15th century.

secondary importance to him : he was more keen to instruct
than to impress. Versed in the Scriptures and perhaps in other
apocryphal legends as well as in some of the pseudo-scientific
lore of his day, he has turned his modest learning to an active
purpose, namely to strengthen by the legend's concrete example the faith and Christian observance of the people.

Another version of *St Patrick's Purgatory* written in England,
this time by an anonymous poet, is extant in two manuscripts
that may share a common model.[41] Its editor hazards the early
thirteenth century as the date of composition. Again we are
faced with a translation from the Latin :

> *Une merveile vueil descrivre;*
> *Je su requis, ne l'os dedire;*
> *De latin la dei estrere*
> *E pur lais en romans fere.*
>
> (7–10)

(There is a marvel I wish to describe : I have been asked to,
and dare not say no. I have to take it from Latin and put it
into Romance for lay people.)

The model seems to have been a Group α manuscript. The
suggestion of patronage in the above quotation reminds us of
similar statements in the poems by Marie de France and Berol.
Although we cannot write off these claims as baseless, it is as
well to remember that they are directly inspired by Henry of
Saltrey's mention of the request of the Abbot of Sartis at the
beginning of the *Tractatus*.

The lines I have quoted suggest that this poet too was a
churchman ; and those that precede are full of the terminology
of the preacher :

> *Pur la bone gent conforter*
> *E pur la male amender*
> *Ad Dieu fet meinte merveile,*
> *Sauntz qui ne se meot esteile,*
> *Ne le fueille ne chiet del raim,*
> *Par qui oisel n'ad point de faim.*
>
> (1–6)

VH D

(To give comfort to the good people and reform the wicked, many marvels have been performed by God, without whom no star moves nor does the leaf fall from the branch, and through whom no bird goes hungry.)

And later we catch the liturgical phrase in :

> *Quant ce out dit, en ciel monta,*
> *E si regne in secula.*

(53–4)

(Having said this, he went up to Heaven, where he reigns *in secula.*)

The Epilogue is full of pious exhortation, opening like the Prologue with an exaltation of the divine power and going on to speak of the virtue and necessity of confession. God does not wish a sinner to die, but rather that he repent—we hear again the notes of the professional theologian,[42] even more so than with Berol, who drew a similar lesson. The poet further betrays his veneration of the Virgin, to whom the sinner should pray for help; and other, slighter, indications of his clerical outlook are to be found. Finally, after all his adventures, Owein is said to have entered the monastic life before dying a pious and holy death.

However, despite the tendency to preach at the beginning and end of his poem, the writer does not weary us with his moralisings. Like Berol, he wastes little time once embarked on the narrative; and besides making the same major omissions as his fellow Anglo-Norman, he leaves out such features as the gift of the staff and Gospels to St Patrick and simplifies much of the detail of the *Tractatus*, so that his poem is completed in 859 octosyllables. In general, his treatment is free and lively, but naïve in tone. An unpretentious person, he was not out of contact with things secular. Referring to the story he is about to tell, he says :

> *Ce valt pluz que conter fables,*
> *Eschés juer ou a tables,*
> *Ou sourdent sovent grands tençons*
> *E autres mesprisiouns.*

(13–16)

(This is more worth-while than telling fables or playing at
chess or backgammon, which often gives rise to violent
quarrels and other outrages.)

But perhaps the most interesting passage in the whole poem is
his description of the infernal wheel, or rather wheels, for he is
not content with just one. To the whole episode he devotes no
fewer than fifty lines ; and the striking feature is the way in
which he describes minutely the construction of the wheels,
using the technical terms of the wheelwright's trade. His experience reached out beyond the cloister.

Versatile though he may have been, he was no great scholar
or literary man. His versification is only approximate ; and the
lines are mainly pedestrian with a good deal of padding and
trite phrase. Occasionally, though, he does mint a good or
colourful one. Of the sinners in the third place of torment he
says that they were as full of burning nails as a hedgehog of
spines ; and the bridge was so high, narrow and frail that even
a devil could not have crossed. But on the whole the translation
is simple and artless. Its straightforward manner is that of the
rhymed sermon, and it is doubtful if the author had any higher
pretensions.

The last Anglo-Norman version to have been edited again
dates from the thirteenth century.[43] It survives in one complete
manuscript and one short fragment, the whole poem containing
1,794 lines, that is some five hundred less than Marie's. The
author nowhere gives his name or the nature of his source,
saying simply that he will tell the truth as he found it in writing.
The *escrist* he refers to is likely to have been another α-type
manuscript of the *Tractatus*, but if so he took considerable
liberties with it, as well as omitting the Prologue and final
testimonies. It is only because of these omissions that the poem
is shorter than Marie's ; and it is noticeable that the author has
chosen to pass over only such material as is irrelevant to the
main story. For the rest, the tendency is rather to amplify than
to reduce. Thus at the beginning of the narrative, the description of St Patrick's mission to the pagan Irish is fuller than the
Latin, and more animated. An entirely new conception is
added, when we are told that Christ appeared to the saint *in his*

sleep; and when Patrick awoke in the morning, he knew that his dream had not been an empty one, because he found the staff and Gospels which Christ had given him as he slept before the altar. Then, in place of the first description of the ritual for entering the Purgatory, we find an original passage telling how many people were converted by the miracle. And to prove the truth of it, says the poet, I will tell you of something that happened quite recently. Then he rejoins the Latin account of the knight Owein's resolve.

As well as the major additions, we notice a good deal of elaboration of detail, as for instance the mention of the prior's breaking the wax of the bishop's letter when Owein hands it to him. A small touch, but one which enlivens the telling. And in his description of the torments, our poet tends to make them even more hideous than in the original. So, in the second plain, sinners are set upon by demons, who rend them with their hooks, tearing flesh and nerves apart. And in the third, the nails are so thickly planted in the sinners' bodies that the finest needle in the world could not be inserted without touching one of them. The poet even adds explanations of his own regarding certain of the punishments : those in the fourth plain are for the non-repentant who died in mortal sin ; and the degree of punishment accorded to the sinners in the bath-house, he explains, corresponds to their crime. From these examples it can be seen that what has been added to the story is the minor event, the vividly descriptive detail, the word of simple explanation. The author has not gone out of his way to strengthen the didactic flavour, but has rather cut out passages that he thought tedious, such as the homily which, in the Latin, linked the descriptions of Purgatory and Paradise. He has, it is true, expanded the later reference to the expulsion of Adam from the Earthly Paradise ; but here again he is telling a story (that of the Fall) and not moralising for its own sake. The result is a lively narrative, bare of rhetoric, where the action and visual qualities of the legend are stressed rather at the expense of its spiritual value.

Does it follow that the poem was composed by a layman ? The elaboration of the story of the Fall might point in the other direction, as might the fact that the author, unlike Henry of

Saltrey, makes Owein take the habit on his return from the
Holy Land. And he does begin by saying that he is writing
"en honurance Ihesu Crist". Against this can be set the lack
of any particular sign of piety or of the desire to make religious
propaganda.[44] We are left with the picture of a man who took
pleasure in his work and has passed some of it on to us. There
is no sign of tiring as with so many hack rhymesters when
commissioned to translate a work of any length : if anything,
the section dealing with Paradise is developed more fully than
that describing Hell—an unusual occurrence, and a point in
the poet's favour. We would have liked more information as to
the identity and class of this agreeable person.

One other Anglo-Norman rhymed version of *St Patrick's
Purgatory* remains to be considered. It is anonymous and has
not yet found an editor, though short extracts have been published from the single thirteenth-century manuscript which
contains it.[45] With Marie's poem, it is the most complete of
the vernacular versions, containing in its 1,776 octosyllabic lines
virtually everything offered by the *Tractatus* except the two
interpolated homilies. The appended testimonies are faithfully
translated; and here as at other points the rendering stands
closer to the Latin Text β than to Text α.[49] And the author has
gone even further than Marie in retaining the original Dedication and Epilogue, though in an abbreviated and adapted form.
From the Prologue, the translator omits all mention of Gregory
and Augustine, except obliquely as "li seint". Add to this
omission that of the single tooth of the old prior blessed by the
angels, and we have virtually the sum of his abbreviations :
for conscientiousness we can again compare him with Marie.

His translation betrays a good knowledge of Latin and is for
the most part very close indeed to the *Tractatus*, with a mini-
mum of poetic licence and padding. Here and there we come
across slight elaboration of detail. Thus he adds the notion
that the grotto widens as his hero "Oen" proceeds; he lists
at some length the parts of the body transfixed by burning nails
in the third plain; and when Owein is in the infernal river, we
are told that he was weak from his efforts to evade the demons
and climb out before he finally called on Christ. Certain
passages are slightly rearranged, perhaps in an attempt to im-

prove the sequence of the Latin.[47] But there are no errors of
translation due to apparent ignorance, a point decidedly to the
poet's credit. His verse is straightforward without being naïve,
and entirely lacks the studied rhetorical devices of the schools.
Such rhetoric as we find in the *Tractatus* (I think particularly
of the figures in the description of Owein's entry into the
Purgatory) is reduced to more everyday terms. Moreover, we
noticed that the rather erudite references in the Prologue to the
writings of Gregory and Augustine have been left aside. So
simplicity and directness are the dominant features of the work;
and we might attribute them to a lack of imagination but for the
personal Epilogue to which the poet treats us.

   This is of unusual interest. It follows on from the abbreviated rendering of the original Prologue and occupies 66 lines.
First there is a stern complaint that the world is more corrupt
now than ever before : we must take care not to be caught in our
sin on Judgment Day. And here the poet suddenly emerges
from his anonymity, giving rein to his own feelings in verse
that has some eloquence and is, in places, almost worthy of the
indignation of a Rutebeuf. Plainly he is speaking from the heart
as well as the mind when he compares his own times with those
of the Old Testament (and this, I surmise, was his favourite
reading). He pursues his argument along metaphorical lines
before commending his audience to God and asking our prayers,
so that he may be led out of temptation in Egypt, and come to
Jerusalem and the feet of God. Let us pray together that our
sins be forgiven and nothing remain to be purged away after
death.

   In this conclusion, the poet refers to his work as a *sermun*, to
be delivered in all probability to a lay audience; and to it he
has added his own postscript with a fine emotional flourish.
His declamatory style forcibly suggests that he was himself a
preacher, and probably not under monastic vows. In this connection, we notice that he in no way tones down Henry of
Saltrey's lavish praise of the Cistercians; so if he did wear the
habit, it would most likely be the white. But more probably he
was a secular priest or else a friar. It is fortunate for us that he
chose to write his own epilogue to the legend, for he reveals
himself as a creative writer (perhaps it would be more accurate

to say an impassioned preacher), whereas otherwise his personality would have been lost to us. How often, I wonder, do we misjudge the character of the faithful translator ?

Now the time has come to assess the lessons to be drawn from this examination of the Anglo-Norman contribution to our theme. It has long been recognised that Anglo-Norman literature has markedly pious leanings.[48] Many of its serious texts were used on an equal footing with Latin works in the schools which abounded in England at the period when the language flourished.[49] Consequently it is not surprising to find these numerous treatments of the infernal visit, treatments which in every instance are pious in outlook and serious in intention, sometimes indeed firmly didactic. This confirms and underlines the conclusions of other scholars ; but it is possible to go further and form some opinion on not only the spirit of the works but also the artistic sensibility they reflect. The question of Anglo-Norman versification is so thorny that I can do no more here than repeat that by continental standards their metrical structure leaves much to be desired. If we could be sure of Anglo-Norman criteria, we should no doubt have to modify our criticism, though hardly withdraw it altogether. Leaving aside strictly prosodic considerations, we find that these poems (for none of the texts are in prose) have much to commend them.[50] The stories are for the most part told with a directness and economy which it is refreshing to find at a period when padding was so often the first stand-by of the mediocre poet. Personal interjections and original turns of phrase afford us a glimpse of the man behind the work ; and the net result, though not a broadening of the poetic and spiritual vision as a whole, is to enhance the actuality and liveliness of the original.

This amounts to saying that the Anglo-Norman writers were endowed with real imagination, but imagination which worked within limits and was applied to matters of detail. It is the same quality as is revealed in the excellence of contemporary English craftsmanship in the fields of miniature-painting, embroidery and the goldsmith's art. Here, as in our texts, there is a vigorous originality that testifies to a general creative spirit abroad in twelfth- and thirteenth-century England, a spirit which is further seen in those native English visions included by Vincent de Beauvais in his *Speculum Historiale*.

If the Anglo-Norman authors put something of themselves into their poems, they show at the same time a general lack of affectation. With an Adam de Ros this even becomes naïvety. They are, for instance, not so bound by conventional techniques as to allow their literary care to put a strait-jacket on their material. Perhaps they were less well-schooled than some continental writers; but a more telling reason is surely their ardent and obviously sincere piety, which ensured that for them content was more important than form. We never have the impression that the Anglo-Norman poet is simply paying lip-service to his religion; and it is usual for him to increase rather than diminish the moral content of his source.

It may well be argued that the use of Anglo-Norman as a literary language had lapsed before the descent theme had had time to become sterile and that this accounts for the almost total lack of lifeless treatments in it. There may be some truth in this, but a study of continental texts written during the same period will show a rather different situation there. Another point worthy of consideration is that all of the Anglo-Norman works are in verse. The preponderance of poetry over prose is a general feature of the legend literature written in England. The reasons given by J. Vising, namely that prose did not come into vogue before Anglo-Norman literature was in its decline and that it appealed to a more cultivated class than the metrical legends,[51] go some way towards an explanation. On the other hand, as we shall see, a number of French or Provençal prose versions of all the major pious legends I have reviewed were circulating by the thirteenth century; and it is rash to suppose than none of the Anglo-Norman works were written for a cultivated audience. If the later writers in England did not choose to employ prose it was not merely for lack of opportunity, but because they preferred verse for their narratives. Perhaps they felt prose to be too lifeless a medium; and while it was esteemed in France as giving a more truthful flavour to the legends, it was a less appropriate outlet for the vigorous Anglo-

Norman mentality. The general public appears to have shared the writers' preference.

By their choice of medium, these poets show themselves, then, to be conscious artists ; and on the whole they do seem to have taken some pride and interest in their work, which they carried through zealously, without flagging. But in nearly every case, I have suggested that they wrote for utilitarian ends rather than entertainment. Of course they wished to make the moral dose as palatable as possible, and in doing so were able to satisfy their own circumscribed artistic ambitions. But the impression remains that they believed in their stories as well as in the lessons implicit in them. They were conscious of acting, if only at second hand, as witnesses to the frightful truth of Hell and damnation ; and they speak with the confidence born of an awareness that they are addressing a far from unreceptive public.

NOTES

1. For the visions in English see A. B. van Os, *Religious Visions*.
2. Published from a defective copy of one MS by A. F. Ozanam, *Dante et la philosophie catholique du treizième siècle* (Paris, 1839) ; and from the five MSS known to him by L. E. Kastner, "The Vision of Saint Paul by the Anglo-Norman *trouvère* Adam de Ross", *Zeitschrift für französische Sprache und Literatur* 29 (1906), pp. 274–90 (I quote from this edition). For general discussion of the vernacular versions see P. Meyer, "Notice sur un MS bourguignon . . .", *Romania* VI (1877), of which § VI (pp. 11–16) treats "La Descente de saint Paul en enfer" ; *idem* in "Notice sur le manuscrit fr. 24862 . . .", *Notices et extraits des manuscrits de la Bibliothèque Nationale*, Vol. 35, Part I (1896), pp. 131–68 ; H. L. D. Ward, *Catalogue of Romances* . . . , II, under "Visions of Heaven and Hell", pp. 397 ff. ; Walter Meiden, *La Descente de Saint-Paul en enfer* (unpublished thesis : see *Abstracts of Doctoral Dissertations*, No. 50 [Ohio State U.P., 1946]) ; *idem*, "Versions of the *Descente de Saint-Paul*", *Romance Philogy* VIII (1954), pp. 92–5. On Adam de Ros's version see also K. V. Sinclair, "Anglo-Norman Studies : The Last Twenty Years", *Australian Journal of French Studies* II (1965), p. 140. And for the possibility that Adam belonged to the Cistercian house of Dunbrody in Leinster and was flourishing in the year 1279, see M. Dominica Legge, *Anglo-Norman in the Cloisters* (Edinburgh, 1950), pp. 53–4, 122.
3. The British Museum MS Cott. Vespas. A. VII is so illustrated, and Kastner in his edition gives a description of each miniature. For the illustrations to the version of the *Vision* in the Toulouse MS 815 see Paul Meyer's edition in *Romania* XXIV (1895), where four of them are reproduced between pp. 368 and 369.
4. Ed. L. E. Kastner, "Les Versions françaises inédites de la Descente de

saint Paul en Enfer", *Revue des Langues Romanes* 48 (1905), pp. 385–95 ;
R. C. D. Perman, "Henri d'Arci : the Shorter Works" in *Studies in Medieval French presented to Alfred Ewert* (Oxford, 1961), pp. 279–321 (the text is on pp. 309–16 and is followed by the Latin Redaction IV). See also Sinclair, op. cit., pp. 131–2. The single MS (Paris, B.N., fr. 24862) was examined by Paul Meyer in *Notices et extraits* . . . , 35.I, pp. 131 ff. ; and he concluded that it was written in England in the middle of the thirteenth century. Kastner proposed a rather earlier date for the composition of the poem.

5. M. Dominica Legge, *Anglo-Norman Literature and its Background* (Oxford, 1963), pp. 191–2, 274.

6. D. D. R. Owen, "The *Vision of St Paul* . . .", *Romance Philology* XII (1958), p. 38.

7. *Vie de sainte Thaïs*, l. 154 (ed. Perman, op. cit., p. 285).

8. J. R. H. Moorman, *Church Life in England in the Thirteenth Century* (Cambridge, 1945), p. 51.

9. *Romania* XXIV, p. 375. With the Templar's account of the scriptural events that are supposed to have taken place on Sunday we may compare the conclusion of the Latin Redaction IIId (H. T. Silverstein, *Visio Sancti Pauli*, p. 195). For the sources of this tradition and notes on the observance of Sunday in the Middle Ages see ibid., pp. 80–1.

10. Owen, op. cit., pp. 39–42 ; cf. Perman, op. cit., p. 308. The poem is found in two MSS (Toulouse 815 and Cambridge, Corpus Christi College, 20). For their dates see Paul Meyer in *Notices et extraits* . . . , 35.I, p. 156. He edited the text from the Toulouse MS only, "La Descente de saint Paul en Enfer, poème français composé en Angleterre", *Romania* XXIV (1895), pp. 357–75 ; see also pp. 589–91.

11. A number of Latin manuscripts do not specify the sinner as a bishop (Silverstein, op. cit., p. 114, n. 56).

12. Published in G. Paris & A. Bos, *Trois versions rimées de l'Évangile de Nicodème* (Paris, S.A.T.F., 1885). See also Paul Meyer, "Légendes hagiographiques en français", *Histoire littéraire de la France* 33 (1906), pp. 356–7.

13. The Bibliothèque Nationale in Paris has at least sixteen French manuscripts containing the *Dialogues*. For Angier's version see T. Cloran, *The Dialogues of Gregory the Great, translated into Anglo-Norman French by Angier* (Strasbourg, 1901) ; and Legge, *Anglo-Norman Literature*, pp. 208–9.

14. Ed. F. J. Furnivall (London, 1862), ll. 1925–2060 ; and by A. Jubinal (who was unaware of its source) under the title "De la Peine d'Enfer" in *Nouveau recueil de contes, dits, fabliaux et autres pièces inédites des XIIIᵉ, XIVᵉ et XVᵉ siècles*, II (Paris, 1842), pp. 304–8. See also E. J. Arnould, *Le Manuel des péchés* (Paris, 1940), pp. 125–6 ; Legge, *Anglo-Norman Literature*, p. 214.

15. William's version, with the two Anglo-Norman translations, has been published by A. Mussafia, "Studien zu den mittelalterlichen Marienlegenden, IV", *Sitzungsberichte der Phil.-Hist. Classe der Kais. Ak. der Wiss.* 123 (1891), pp. 34–50.

16. Ed. E. G. R. Waters, *The Anglo-Norman Voyage of St Brendan* (from all MSS) ; H. Suchier, "Brandans Seefahrt", *Romanische Studien* 1 (1875), pp. 553 ff. (diplomatic transcription of London, B.M., MS Cott. Vespas. B.x.[1]) ; Francisque Michel, *Les Voyages merveilleux de saint*

Brendan à la recherche du Paradis Terrestre (Paris, 1878—using the same MS as Suchier); T. Auracher, "Der Brandan der Arsenalhandschrift BLF 283", *Zeitschrift für Romanische Philologie* 2 (1878), pp. 438–57 (diplomatic transcription of the version in Paris, Arsenal, MS 3516, usually considered to be a "modernised" form of Benedeit's poem and dating from the middle of the thirteenth century. It was probably revised by a Picard: see Waters, op. cit., pp. xxi–xxii; and *Histoire littéraire de la France* 33, p. 342). See further Legge, *Anglo-Norman Literature*, pp. 8–18; Sinclair, op. cit., pp. 132–3.

17. A good case can, however, be made from a variant reading that the queen in question was Maud, Henry's first consort (Legge, ibid., pp. 9–10).
18. Philippe de Thaun's *Bestiaire* and a lost *chançun* by a poet named David were also dedicated to her (Waters, op. cit., pp. xxiii–xxiv).
19. Ibid., p. xcv.
20. The Latin account of Brendan's intercession and his obtaining a further respite for Judas was almost certainly inspired by the *Vision of St Paul*, and Benedeit may well have had the *Vision* in mind. It is interesting to find that the possibility of such intercession was emphatically denied by Gregory the Great (*Dialogue* IV, 36). For knowledge of the *Vision* in England before this period see Silverstein, *Visio Sancti Pauli*, pp. 6–9.
21. See Silverstein, ibid., p. 56, and n. 71, pp. 115–6. The concept appears in Redaction V of the *Vision of St Paul* (ibid., p. 196).
22. See Yves Lefèvre, *L'Elucidarium et les Lucidaires* (Paris, 1954), who gives the text of the *Elucidarium* (from which I quote) on pp. 359–477.
23. See above, pp. 17–18.
24. "Die lateinischen Visionen...", *Romanische Forschungen* 2 (1886), p. 278.
25. If we equate the deep, black dungeon described here with the pit of Hell as shown in the *Vision*, a direct reminiscence of the latter seems very likely.
26. Among twelfth-century texts, see especially *St Patrick's Purgatory*. Winds are found torturing sinners in pre-Christian Hebrew literature such as the *Book of Enoch* (translated by R. H. Charles, London, 1917), in the Zoroastrian Otherworld in ancient Persia (C. S. Boswell, *An Irish Precursor of Dante*, p. 71), and in Moslem eschatology (E. Cerulli, *Il "Libro della Scala"* [Vatican, 1949], Ch. LIV, §§ 137–8: God will flay sinners with the mighty wind of Hell before they are burnt in the fire).
27. Waters, op. cit., p. xcv, n. 2.
28. The smoke-capped mountain is an example of this. In the *Voyage of Maelduin* it is an island of laughers and players from which the supernumerary traveller cannot return (Whitley Stokes' translation, § 31). In the *Navigatio* it is a fearsome isle inhabited by demons. Benedeit makes it Hell itself. This is a far cry from the episode as it appeared in the *Voyage of Bran*, where it resembles that in *Maelduin* (K. Meyer & A. Nutt, *The Voyage of Bran*, § 61).
29. The incomplete verse rendering is published by V. H. Friedel & K. Meyer, *La Vision de Tondale (Tnugdal)*, pp. 63–86.
30. A. Wagner, *Visio Tnugdali*, p. 8, ll. 6–7.
31. In l. 170 he refers to "la prophecie Dauid" verses 7–8 of *Psalm* xci (Vulgate xc). This may, of course, have been glossed for him in his model.

32. Ed. T. A. Jenkins, "*L'Espurgatoire seint Patriz*" *of Marie de France* (Philadelphia, 1894: the 2nd edn. appeared in *The Decennial Publications of the University of Chicago*, VII [1903]); K. Warnke, *Das Buch vom Espurgatoire S. Patrice der Marie de France und seine Quelle* (from which I quote). Following F. W. Locke's questioning of the date of the *Tractatus* (see above, p. 50 n. 30), Richard Baum, in *Recherches sur les œuvres attribuées à Marie de France* (Heidelberg, 1968), envisages the possibility of a correspondingly later *terminus a quo* for Marie's poem.

33. Theories as to her identity are reviewed by U. T. Holmes, *A History of Old French Literature from the Origins to 1300* (New York, 1948), pp. 188–9. See too A. Ewert, *Marie de France: Lais* (Oxford, 1944), pp. v–x; and for the most thorough and recent examination of the question, Baum, op. cit.

34. Lines 9–24 of the *Espurgatoire*, which refer to a patron for whom it is being written, are simply taken over by Marie from her Latin original.

35. See D. Knowles, *The Monastic Order in England* (Cambridge, 1941), p. 138. Cf. M. Dominica Legge, *Anglo-Norman in the Cloisters*, p. 49.

36. See S. F. Damon, "Marie de France Psychologist of Courtly Love", *Publications of the Modern Language Association of America* 44 (1929), pp. 968–96.

37. Ll. 1919–32. This anticipates the Latin account by a few paragraphs (Warnke's edn., p. 142).

38. Ed. M. Mörner, *Le Purgatoire de saint Patrice par Berol*. Paul Meyer thought it was composed in western France or England; Mörner, following J. Vising, prefers England.

39. *Expolitio* was taught as a form of *amplificatio* (E. Faral, *Les Arts Poétiques du XIIe et du XIIIe siècle* [Paris, 1923], p. 63). However, it is commonly found e.g. in the epic (see E. R. Curtius, "Zur Literarästhetik des Mittelalters, II", *Zeitschrift für Romanische Philologie* 58 [1938], pp. 216–8).

40. Quoted by Warnke, op. cit., p. xxxvi.

41. Ed. J. Vising, *Le Purgatoire de saint Patrice des MSS Harl. 273, et fonds fr. 2198* (Gothenburg, 1916). The London MS dates from the first half of the fourteenth century and gives the better readings; the Paris MS is from the fifteenth century.

42. Cf. such scriptural passages as *Ezekiel* xxxiii. 11, *Luke* v. 32 and xv. 7, 10. They may be liturgical reminiscences (see St J. Seymour's notes to the *Vision of Tundal* in *Irish Visions of the Other World*, pp. 163–4).

43. C. M. van der Zanden, *Étude sur le Purgatoire de saint Patrice, accompagnée du texte latin d'Utrecht et du texte anglo-normand de Cambridge.*

44. Van der Zanden's suggestion that there are traces of Mariolatry is misleading, since the references to the Virgin are mere *cliché*.

45. London, B.M., Cott. Dom. A.IV (fol. 257^r–267^r). Extracts published by E. Kölbing, "Zwei mittelenglische Bearbeitungen der Sage von St. Patrik's Purgatorium", *Englische Studien* I (1877), pp. 57–121; and by Ward, *Catalogue of Romances . . .*, II, pp. 468–71.

46. E.g., the omission of the sprinkling of holy water before Owein's entry into the Purgatory (fol. 258d: cf. Warnke, op. cit., p. 42); and Owein's former intimacy with the king (fol. 264c: cf. Warnke, p. 138).

47. E.g. with the dimensions of the second plain (fol. 260b); and the first two characteristics of the bridge are transposed (fol. 262b).

48. See, for instance, J. Vising, *Anglo-Norman Language and Literature*

(London, 1923), pp. 36 ff. ; E. Walberg, *Quelques aspects de la littérature anglo-normande* (Paris, 1936), Ch. II ; and M. Dominica Legge's two books, *Anglo-Norman in the Cloisters* and *Anglo-Norman Literature and its Background.*

49. O. H. Prior, "Remarques sur l'anglo-normand", *Romania* XLIX (1923), pp. 186–70.

50. The remarks that follow are only partially true for three of the texts : the anonymous Anglo-Norman version of the *Vision of St Paul* (a *remaniement* of the Templar's poem) ; Marie's *Espurgatoire* (but Marie was of continental origin) ; and the anonymous Anglo-Norman translation of the *Gospel of Nicodemus.*

51. Vising, *Anglo-Norman Language and Literature,* p. 44.

CHAPTER IV

THE CHURCH'S WITNESSES:
THE FRENCH

WITH the Anglo-Norman translators it was possible and, I hope, legitimate to characterise in general terms their attitude towards their material : with the French it will be more difficult to do so. Even so, we shall find them handling much the same body of pious legend in a manner significantly different from that of their insular counterparts. Their treatment of the *Vision of St Paul* provides an immediate example.

The first text to be cited is not a full translation of the *Vision*, but it is none the less interesting for that. *Li ver del juïse* is a monitory poem on the Day of Judgment composed in assonanced Alexandrines, possibly in the Liège region, though this is by no means certain.[1] Despite the fact that the two manuscripts which carry it date from the thirteenth century, its editor believed, and with some support, that it was written early in the twelfth. If this is so, it is by far the earliest French text to show the influence of the *Vision*. For the unknown author, in an attempt to amplify his account and give it added authority, has drawn liberally from that source. Not, however, and here is the interesting point, from the most popular Redaction IV.

At the death of a sinner, we read, devils sit on his chest waiting for the soul to leave the body. They have a scroll whereon the person's sins are inscribed and promise it dire torments in "lo doleros païs" (a term that keeps recurring). The writer goes on to describe the joys awaiting the souls of the pure and godfearing, for

> *Ce reconte sainz Polz, ki les duelz d'enfer vit.*
>
> (l. 228)

In Hell, the saint beheld a man and woman all ablaze, beset by demons, and with their bodies pierced through by ninety and

nine torments. Accosted by Paul, they tell him that their evil
life has brought unceasing punishment upon them : frost and
hail and a fierce wind that pierces them through. There are
seven towers, they say, in Hell, each the repository of ninety-
nine torments ; and they beseech Paul to tell all this to the
living.

Then we learn how the fallen angels have become the
guardians of Hell, again according to St Paul's testimony
(l. 228 is repeated here and elsewhere and forms a kind of refrain). The poet continues his description of the infernal pains
and of the hideous appearance of the guardians of Hell. The
sinners gnaw one another and are tortured by toads, serpents,
and burning chains. In the rushing, cutting river of Hell the
souls are plunged three times every day, and then they are boiled
in cauldrons and roasted on grills. In this grim land sinners
suffer extremes of hunger and thirst, and they long for the sight
of God though they may never see Him. On Judgment Day
murdered infants will seek justice from God ; and their slayers
will be in Hell along with all the false and wicked, languishing
in a deep, gloomy dungeon whither Our Lord descended for
the saving of our souls. It is as deep as the distance from heaven
to earth. The poet then passes to a description of the signs of
the Last Judgment.

Far from trying to conceal his source for the part of his work
I have summarised, he uses the name of St Paul as an insistent
leitmotif. But his freedom of treatment has to some extent
obscured the outlines of that source. Was it the Long Latin
version of the *Vision* or one of the redactions ? There are good
reasons for supposing that it was the former ;[2] and this is of
considerable interest, since no other French vernacular text is
based on the Long version. It might even be taken as support
for the early dating, at a time before the fourth Redaction had
achieved its wide currency.

There is another intriguing aspect of *Li ver del juïse*. In his
free treatment of such material as he had to hand, the poet no
doubt added here and there an extra touch of his own. So
perhaps it is by chance that one or two features have their
nearest parallels, so far as I am aware, in Moslem eschatology.
Thus the architecture of Hell with its seven towers is quite

foreign to the *Vision*. But the Koran shows Hell as having seven
gates; and from the second century of the Hejira, Moslem
tradition divides the Underworld into seven separate regions.[3]
Another similarity is the stress placed on the mighty wind of
Hell;[4] and though it is true that infernal winds are encountered
in many Christian visions, they are seldom given such promi-
nence as here. The fall of the disobedient angels into Hell is
again a commonplace of Christian tradition; but whereas it
is not referred to in the *Vision*, it does occur in the story of
Mahomet's journey to the Otherworld. That the latter itself
owed something to the *Vision* is suggested by its use of motifs
such as the reading by sinners of the scroll of their wicked
deeds,[5] but the other parallels with *Li ver del juïse* cannot be
accounted for in this way. And although it would appear unlikely that the Frenchman borrowed at first hand from Moslem
legend, the possibility should not be dismissed that there was
some indirect influence from a tradition of which certain
aspects at least were familiar to scholars in France by the
twelfth century.[6]

Whatever the truth of the matter, it is plain that this early
poet showed some degree of originality in adapting his source or
sources to the needs of the moment. He had literary talent too:
the verse has something of the vigour and directness of the
chanson de geste, calculated to grip the attention of an audience
—or congregation. For his main purpose is clear: he was providing a work of edification, an exhortation to righteousness.
So it is a fair assumption that he was a monk or priest, especially
as he used a text of the *Vison of St Paul* that would hardly have
existed anywhere but in the library of some religious institution.
A man not lacking in education, and fired with preaching zeal—
it is fitting that he should stand first in the line of those we know
to have put the vision to use in the French vernacular.

Three full continental verse translations of the *Vision* have
survived; and the first, perhaps from the Ile-de-France or
from rather further east,[7] is found in a single manuscript dating
from the middle of the thirteenth century.[8] The anonymous
poet opens with a cry from the heart. He wishes, he says, to
break with the practice of "li autre trouveor", whose only care
is to please their public with lying tales and adventure stories.

But though they abandon the joys of Heaven for those of this life, they are beguiled by the Devil, and God will take His vengeance when He comes to judge them; for then they will be cast into the undying fire.

> Por ce feu que ge tant redout
> Vos di ge, saignor, tout debout
> Que ge vel laissier la folie
> Et amander, se puis, ma vie.
> Ne vel pas de fable paller
> Ne mon tans en folie user;
> Ainz vos dirai, se onques puis,
> Ainsin comme en l'escrit le truis,
> Grant partie de la doulor
> Qu'an anfer souffrent pecheor.

                                                (57–66)

(On acconut of this fire that I dread so much, I tell you straight, sirs, I will forsake folly and improve my life if I may. I will not recite fictitious tales and spend my time on foolishness; but so far as I can I shall relate to you, just as I find it in the written word, a large part of the anguish that sinners suffer in Hell.)

The account of St Paul's vision follows.

This man, then, was a *trouvère*, a professional poet in the ranks of the laity, who decided to abandon the type of literary production that he criticises and turn his talents to the profit of his soul rather than his purse. At the same time, this is not simply a personal exercise in piety, for the *saignor* he addresses in l. 58 were his public—secular or clerical: the form of address would do for either. It may be, of course, that these opening lines are but a literary device appropriate to the burden of his story; for complaints about the moral and literary failings of professional rivals are commonly found at the beginnings of medieval poems and particularly of those that set out to instruct. Yet there seems to be a ring of sincerity here, evidence perhaps of a genuine spiritual experience—though the poet leaves us to guess whether his discovery of the *Vision* had anything to do with it.

Four times he refers to his written source (*escrit*: ll. 64, 136, 180, 484); but he does not say whether it was in Latin or the vernacular. Once more we must look beyond the common Redaction IV, from whose scheme the poem departs in several respects. St Paul is first of all led up to Heaven, which has its foundations upon a river. There is a dark place full of grief and fire, with flames thrown up to the sky. Next Paul sees the fiery trees (the sinners' crimes being specified) and the furnace, where there is a fearsome, multi-headed dragon named Partimor. It swallows up sinners, and from it issue serpents. The fiery wheel does not appear, and the river, which is burning, has no bridge. Sinners are immersed there as in Redaction IV, but for different faults. St Paul then sees a dark ditch of immeasurable depth where unrepentant atheists languish irredeemably with their tongues gnawed by serpents. Elsewhere is a burning river where men and women eat their own tongues and have their bodies preyed on by worms. They are perjurers, traitors, those who spoke evil and were envious and disdainful. In the pit, deep as the distance from Heaven to earth, are black men and women (the adulterers) and naked souls cursing the day they were born. When the pit is opened, Paul sees them clearly. Their groans are as loud as thunder. Then Paul and his guide see the soul of a sinner carried off to Hell by seven devils, who boil it in the deep infernal cauldron. From this point the account is similar to Redaction IV, though a noteworthy omission is the reading of the scrolls of wicked and good deeds. The poem ends, after a reference to Cerberus grieving over the sinners' respite, with an appeal to God to bless those who keep Sunday. There is no mention of the number of torments other than the statement in the prologue that a hundred tongues would not suffice to tell the fifth part. The work is complete in 490 lines.

I have shown in another place that the only way to account for all these elements is to assume that the poet was working from a source, probably Latin, similar in most respects to Redaction III, but incorporating some very early material besides.[9] Indeed, one interesting feature is shared by the Coptic text of the Long version of the *Vision* and can be ultimately traced back to the *Revelation of Peter*. This is

the reason given for the punishment of those who hang by
their hair from the fiery trees : they are the ones who went
against nature by making their hair lighter—the "artificial
blondes" of the day (in the *Revelation of Peter* women who
adorned themselves for adultery were suspended by their
hair above boiling mire). "When lovely woman stoops to
folly . . ." !

In the absence of the model from which he was working, it is
a matter of conjecture how much the Frenchman personally
contributed to the legend. In places he seems to have expanded
the original, as in the episode of the adulterers (ll. 287–306)
and in St Paul's prayer on behalf of the sinners (ll. 427–34).
The latter, along with the prologue and one or two pious exclamations, would appear to confirm his devout intentions. It is
in the prologue that his literary gifts, such as they are, are best
displayed ; but there is nothing out of the ordinary, and we
find the usual tricks of the trade, the usual monotony in the
introduction of each individual torment, the usual restricted
vocabulary. We might, perhaps, have hoped for something
better from a professional poet.

The Alexandrine, or Burgundian, version of the *Vision* is
carried by seven manuscripts[10] and is written in twelve-syllable
lines arranged in monorhymed quatrains. Its alternative title
has arisen from the fact that one (the London) manuscript is
written in a Burgundian dialect, though this does not seem to
be the region of the poem's composition.[11] Although none of
the manuscripts can be dated before the end of the thirteenth
century, the fact that the version was adapted, as we shall see,
by Geoffroi de Paris by the year 1243 allows us to take that date
as the extreme *terminus ad quem* for its creation. The author's
name does not appear, and all we know of him is that he had
passed through the schools ("J'a apris a escole, sou sa por
escriture", l. 5). His opening call : "Beau soignor et vos dames
. . . !" implies a mixed audience, not necessarily noble, but
presumably lay. He addresses them at frequent intervals
throughout the 700-line poem.

This is a very competent, if prolix, piece of work ; but its
interest is not confined to its literary qualities. For despite its
editor's claim that it is based on the fourth Latin redaction, it

contains some unusual features, and these will be highlighted in the following summary.

Under Michael's guidance, Paul was shown each of the three Heavens, but he might not tell what he saw there. Before his death he was also shown the pains of Hell. He saw the fiery trees and the furnace with its seven torments. [At this point the London MS interpolates a wheel episode discussed below.] Then, in Hell proper Paul saw a great wheel of black fire. It was a thousand fathoms across and turned slowly, throwing off sparks of mighty heat. Round its rim were a thousand projections (*cheviles*) as sharp as swords. A devil formed of hell-fire itself and having the appearance of a feathered angel struck sparks from the wheel a thousand times a day, and at each blow it turned a thousand times. A thousand other devils brought the souls of sinners to be impaled on the projections. When they were as black as coal, the devils caused the wheel to strike against a stone (*perron*) with a noise so great that the whole of Hell trembled. The broken sinners fell off and were strewn about as the devils brought more souls to be tortured. The wretches put out fiery tongues and cried for death. They were the proud and pitiless rich. Next the saints came to the infernal river with its razor-sharp bridge, then saw the fate of the infanticides, and after that came to a steep rock. It was a thousand fathoms high and very steep, but rising in steps. On each of the thousand ledges was a different torment: a red, cruel wind at the top, then fire, snow, frost, burning coals, cutting steel, and other pains. Around the base was a deep ditch full of serpents, whose only food came down from above. There too were a thousand devils like feathered angels, but with great claws. They cast down a thousand souls a day from the summit of the rock to the serpents below; and an additional torment for the wretches was that they chewed their own tongues. They were the usurers. Next are described the punishments of the fast-breakers and those who harmed widows and orphans, of the unchaste bishop, and of the unbelievers. After seeing a newly-dead sinner read the record of his sins before being cast into Hell, Paul was taken up into

Paradise where he saw joys that cannot be told. Finally he witnessed the soul of a righteous person being caught up into Heaven after reading the list of his good deeds.[12]

All this adds up to a version considerably more detailed and lurid than that of Redaction IV, more graphic indeed than that of any of the extant Latin texts. No doubt the Frenchman must be allowed his portion of expansion and illustration ; and the frequent moralising addresses to the audience are almost certainly his. Nevertheless, an important divergence from the fourth redaction, namely Paul's sight of the three Heavens before and Paradise after Hell, has its parallel in the Long Latin text, while a striking analogue to the rock torment is to be found in the *Revelation of Peter*. This poet too was plainly following a fairly early Latin text that has as yet escaped classification.[13]

The infernal wheel, perhaps because it was the only mechanical contraption commonly found in Hell, certainly caught the imagination of these medieval poets. The description here shows some macabre ingenuity ; but not content with this, the scribe of the London manuscript introduced a further account of a wheel (ll. 87–136), borrowed, it seems, from a legend in the popular collection *La vie des anciens Pères*.[14] He did not even bother to change its metre from the original octosyllabic rhymed couplets ; and this prompted both Paul Meyer and Kastner, who were unaware of its source, to make some rather ill-judged comments on the versification.

In fact the true author of the Alexandrine version was well skilled in the metrical art, and there is a real professionalism about his treatment of his subject. He was no popular rhymester whose piety outran his competence, but a man who knew how to handle his narrative with its elements of description and dialogue to quite good literary effect. His work bears the stamp more of the *trouvère* than of the devout amateur.

The same can be said for Geoffroi de Paris, who tells us at the end of his *Bible des sept états du monde*[15] that he completed this lengthy poem in the year 1243. Along with biblical material, it contains an assemblage of pious legends that Geoffroi compiled from various sources, adding little of his own apart from the

octosyllabic metre where this was lacking in the original. One
of the legends that he worked in was the *Vision of St Paul* and
in a form which, despite its editor's failure to realise the fact,[16]
is demonstrably a re-arrangement of the Alexandrine version.[17]
His method was to convert the six-syllabled hemistich of his
model into a full octosyllabic line, and this inevitably led to the
use of padding and cliché.

There is little more to be said of his version. He was no poet
in the creative sense, simply an adequate versifier who had
achieved considerable facility in fashioning the octosyllabic line.
Of himself he tells us nothing apart from his name; but although this is the same as that of the chronicler and hagio-
grapher living in the same century, the identity of names cannot be taken as an indication of the identity of the persons involved.[18] Our Geoffroi, it seems, was no more than a hack
writer who was content to suppress his personality in the
interests of his literary retail trade. That he intended his work
to be recited or read aloud to a lay audience is clear from the
opening lines of the prologue, where he calls his hearers to
silence:

> *Gent debonneire, gent courtoise,*
> *Or faites paiz, taisiez la noise;*
> *S'entendez tuit, gent honourée*
> *Qui vers Dieu avez la pensée.*[19]

Unless he was a preacher himself, he was probably some honest
literary journeyman.

The prose versions of the *Vision* present on the whole fewer
points of interest than the verse texts. They were of course
made to be read; but the reading was very often aloud to a
group of people—by the preacher to his flock, perhaps, or by
the court chaplain to his noble audience. So they were not
necessarily produced for private consumption alone and could
have reached quite a wide public. From the thirteenth century
the man who sought to instruct might prefer to write prose
because of the air of greater realism and truth that it imparted to
the narrated facts. The rhetorical flourishes and padding of the
poet, his *mensonges* as his detractors might call them, need have
no place in sober prose. But the very omission of the frills and

additions to the original text meant that the writer would have less chance to intrude his own personality; and this is the case in most of the prose texts we shall consider.

There is a prose rendering of St Paul's vision in an inedited text found in the MS 951 of Trinity College, Dublin,[20] which dates from the thirteenth century and contains other pious legends in French, including prose accounts of the *Voyage of St Brendan* and *St Patrick's Purgatory*. There is no indication whatever of the continental French translator's name, station in life, or purpose. A comparison of his text with Redaction IV shows that he was translating direct from the Latin and not simply transposing into prose one of the vernacular rhymed versions. What few omissions there are may derive from the model: the translation is adequate and capable for its day, and no doubt its author did not intend it to be more.

We can contrast his method with that of the man who put a fragmentary résumé of the *Vision* into an anonymous fifteenth-century compilation of pious legends of Picard or Flemish origin.[21] His concern was to select a few of the infernal torments with which to introduce a homily directed against adulterers. The sight of Paradise and the respite theme are passed over: only the lurid, agonising details interest him. And here is another case of the wheel punishment being elaborated, this time by means of a detail or two culled from a version of *St Patrick's Purgatory*.

The existence of two Provençal versions of the *Vision* provides more evidence, if that were necessary, of the very wide diffusion of the legend in both time and place. The first seems to date from the thirteenth century[22] and is a rather abbreviated and corrupt rendering of a Redaction IV text. There is no clue as to the writer's personality or aims.

The other Provençal version is a fuller and more interesting text. It is found in a manuscript dated 1466, where it follows an account of the visit of a Catalan knight, Ramon de Perelhos, to St Patrick's Purgatory and a version of the *Vision of Tundal*.[23] Once more we appear to have a translation from the Latin, and once more from a model that stands outside the system of classification evolved by Silverstein. A brief outline will show its main characteristics.

St Paul was in prison when he was caught up in the spirit by Michael to see "lo fondament de yffern". He was led across the river Oceanus in whose waters was a terrible dragon. He saw the fiery trees before the gates of Hell, and Michael specified the groups of sinners hanging there. Then they saw the different groups immersed in the river and, in Hell itself, a multicoloured furnace burning in a place of great depth. Souls in a fiery river were eating their own tongues and were gnawed by vermin: they were those who harmed widows and orphans and who practised usury. Black women were being tormented by fire, vermin, and a demon with horns of fire. They were unchaste, slew their children and their husbands, and were witches. Paul saw the seven-sealed "hill" (*pueg*, a mistranslation of Latin *puteus*) and the souls of a sinner and a righteous person receiving their just reward. Paul and Michael and a million angels prayed that the sinners might have respite from their torments on Sundays, and this was granted.

Silverstein rightly pointed to the Latin Redactions I and II as providing most of these features. But other elements, such as the detailing of the crimes of the sinners hanging from the fiery trees, must also bring Redaction III into the reckoning (there are certain parallels with the first of the continental French versions we considered). But the Provençal writer is scarcely likely to have produced an eclectic text from his reading of two or three Latin versions; so we must accept the alternative explanation of a further lost redaction or sub-redaction.

The wide dissemination of Latin manuscripts of the *Vision* is impressive enough, but with the accumulation of the evidence for variant versions and redactions that no longer survive, we are forced to recognise in this legend one of the most universal and influential of medieval traditions, pious or profane. In the last chapter we saw how three Anglo-Normans, writing between the end of the twelfth century and the end of the thirteenth, put the story into earnest if unambitious rhyme such as an unsophisticated audience could understand and appreciate. They used the straightforward Fourth Redaction—perhaps from necessity, but possibly out of preference, for the more elaborate versions were certainly known in England from quite early in the Middle Ages. Now we have seen how the continental poets opted for the "earlier", fuller redactions when they came to make their translations or adaptations. The chances are that they knew the most common Fourth, but that they saw more opportunity to exercise their literary talents on the longer texts. If the author of *Li ver del juïse* was a cleric, and we cannot be sure, the indications are that the other three poets were not; but in all four cases we sense a literary awareness largely absent from the work of the Anglo-Normans.

From the thirteenth century, prose appears as a vehicle for the transmission of the *Vision*; and in the prose texts we miss both the simple didactic zeal of the Anglo-Norman poets and the greater sophistication of their Continental counterparts. Their authors were inspired by neither religious fervour nor literary ambition. For them the legend was simply an edifying story suitable for inclusion in compilations of the kind demanded by a growing reading public. Their accounts tend towards the résumé, and there is a noticeable deterioration in the material itself as well as in the way in which it is handled.

Proof of the *Vision*'s popularity is to be found not merely in the surviving texts that present it in one form or another, or in the evidence that can be assembled for other versions now lost. For one comes across traces of its influence on numerous other medieval works, secular as well as religious, and some of these we shall encounter in the course of this study. It was the form of the *Vision* with its series of sharply defined scenes that was largely responsible for its success. It escapes the tedium of a true sermon in its ignorance of theological subtlety, pointing its morals through images worthy to be illustrated as in the miniatures that accompany the Provençal version of the Toulouse manuscript. Trees, furnace, wheel, bridge and terrible pit— the common folk and their masters would see all this in their mind's eye. And then came the divine intervention in the miracle tradition, the Son of God with diadem on head descending from Heaven to grant the sinners their weekly respite. Here lies the importance of the vernacular texts : they disclosed the infernal topography to the lay folk and helped to plant in their minds the main features of the medieval vision of Hell. More-

over it was above all through the *Vision of St Paul* that the
theme of a mortal being privileged to visit the Christian Underworld and to return with news of what he has seen was popularised in western literature. It is fitting that in his *Inferno*
(Canto ii, 28) Dante should have mentioned his precursor into
the dolorous realm.

I turn now to the non-dramatic French accounts of the Harrowing of Hell. Appropriately enough, the first vernacular text to
contain the infernal journcy theme in any of its forms is the
tenth-century *Passion du Christ* of the Clermont-Ferrand MS
189.[24] While the tradition of Christ's descent has remained
current and been generally accepted from the earliest centuries
of our era down to the present day, its literary presentation has
varied in detail and in degree of elaboration. As an article of
the Creed, its earliest appearance within the Gallican Church
is in the first half of the sixth century, when Caesarius, Bishop
of Arles, incorporated it in one of his sermons.[25] Later in the
same century it was seemingly borrowed by Venantius Fortuna-
tus, Bishop of Poitiers, from the Aquileian Creed; and by the
ninth century, when the Creed was finally accepted into the
Roman Hours office, it had become a recognised article of faith
in the *Textus Receptus*. Once in the official guardianship of the
Church, its basic elements were safe against serious modification.

However, despite the baldness of the article itself (*descendit
ad inferos* or *ad infera*), it was likely to evoke a more elaborate
picture in the minds of its medieval hearers, since they could
well have been familiar with what may be called homiletic treatments of the tradition, even before the *Gospel of Nicodemus*
became widely known.[26] Expanded treatments are found in
France from the fourth century. In one of his hymns, Hilary of
Poitiers described Christ's descent and decorated his account
with elements from pagan mythology—Styx, Phlegethon, the
fierce guardian of Tartarus (Cerberus). There are Classical
reminiscences, too, in fourth-century adaptations by Ambrosius
and Prudentius, in a long poem by Audradus in the Carolingian
period, and even in a late ninth-century sequence from the

abbey of St Martial in Limoges.[27] But by the latter date the *Gospel of Nicodemus* was making its reputation in the west.

The *Passion du Christ* was probably composed in the north-east of the *langue d'oïl*, and meridional features in its language can be ascribed to the southern copyist. It describes in some twenty octosyllabic lines how, before the third day, Christ descended into Hell, overcame Satan, and released from their captivity the first man and all his descendants (*ensfant*, 1. 378), "for never was there mortal man who had not gone to that Hell" (ll. 381–2). He paid not with silver and gold, but with His blood, delivering all from Hell and lodging them in Paradise.

The account is more than a simple paraphrase of the article in the Creed, and there is nothing to suggest that that was its immediate inspiration. From its context, it is true, we see that it uses the same tradition concerning the time when Christ made His descent, namely between His burial and resurrection. This was the general belief in the Middle Ages, though there was a certain amount of confusion, which is reflected in the later vernacular texts.[28] The *Gospel of Nicodemus* does not indicate the moment of the descent, and its influence is nowhere apparent on this episode of the *Passion*. The vanquishing of Satan and the deliverance of Adam and his seed are already commonplaces by this date. Indeed, in one instance there is a contradiction to the testimony of the Latin *Gospel*, Version A. There it is specified that those delivered from Hell were the righteous,[29] but here it is emphasised that all were redeemed. The latter idea runs counter to the accepted dogma in the Middle Ages, evolved after a period of doubt. Among the early Gnostics, Marcion had held the curious view that whereas Cain, the Sodomites and the Egyptians were redeemed, Christ left in Hell the souls of Enoch, Noah, Abraham and Abel. Naturally, this view found little support, and the more usual one was that of Tertullian, who saw Christ delivering only the patriarchs of Israel. On the other hand, the influential Origen, while maintaining the evangelisation of the dead, suggested the complete spoliation of Hell.[30] In the west, Gregory the Great believed that only the righteous were released from their imprisonment; and both Bede and, later, St Thomas Aquinas held the same view, adding that the just souls had awaited Christ's coming in a place where there was no torment.[31]   Further evidence is supplied by the professions of faith made by two Councils : that of Toledo in the seventh century, and the sixth Council of Arles in the ninth.   In both cases it is stated that Christ delivered the *sanctos*.[32]   Perhaps one should not attach too much importance to this statement in the *Passion*, but it may be inferred that the author was not much concerned with doctrinal theology.

Nevertheless there can be little doubt that he was a man of the Church.   This is borne out by certain formal considerations,[33] and by the ring of his terminology throughout the poem and especially in the Latinised *explicit*.   Like other of the earliest French texts, this has all the marks of a work aimed at illustrating aspects of the Christian faith for an unlettered public.   The author's intentions were didactic rather than literary.

A list of all the French texts containing a description of or reference to Christ's descent would be long indeed.   I shall limit myself, therefore, to mentioning a few representative ones and looking rather more closely at those which treat the subject in some detail.   The accounts fall broadly into two groups : those based on the *Gospel of Nicodemus* and those apparently ignorant of it.   The latter category is certainly the larger ; but in it the references to the Harrowing are relatively undeveloped, so it will suffice to give some idea of how diverse these texts are and of their different ways of handling the tradition.

In the realm of purely pious literature there is first of all a straightforward translation of the article of the Creed copied in the thirteenth century into an earlier Latin manuscript :

> *A enfer descendi, si en traist ses amis,*
> *Et au tierc jor resuscita toz vis.*[34]

Or there is the early reference to the divine descent in the First Latin Redaction of the *Vision of St Paul* that found its way into the Provençal version in the Toulouse manuscript.   But many other pious writers liked to show their knowledge of the Creed by describing briefly the events of Christ's life whenever the opportunity presented itself.

Joinville, in his own *Credo*, gave his personal reflections on the descent story, introducing the (unoriginal) comparison between Christ's deliverance of the souls and Samson's extraction of the honey from the lion's carcase.[35] Rutebeuf, in his *Dist de Nostre Dame*, was less expansive, though not entirely orthodox when he represented Christ's soul breaking down the gate of Hell and rescuing His *amis*, while the body remained on the cross.[36] His descent from the cross itself is reminiscent, as we shall see, rather of the so-called *Passion des Jongleurs* than of the Creed; but although the *Passion* was based on the *Gospel of Nicodemus*, this particular feature was not, and there is nothing here to show direct knowledge of the *Gospel*. Then, passing to the middle of the fourteenth century, we find Guillaume de Deguileville mentioning the theme more than once in his *Pèlerinage de l'âme*; and in one passage, describing the signs of the zodiac, he places Christ's descent under Leo, the all-devouring.[37]

It is typical of the Middle Ages that memories of the divine victory should not be confined to pious writings. For instance, they are not uncommonly found in the epic literature of the twelfth century. The hero of a chanson de geste may fall to his knees before a battle to seek God's aid and affirm his own belief. To give a single example, from the *Couronnement de Louis*, Guillaume utters a long prayer before his fight with the pagan Corsolt, recalling the main episodes of the Holy Story. He remembers how Christ rose from the tomb on the third day and proceeded to free His friends from Hell.[38] Here is a third tradition regarding the moment of the descent and which we shall find recurring in the late dramatic *Passion d'Autun*.

A strange mixture of Christian and secular (even pagan) motifs is offered by some of the courtly romances. If the knight often appears to derive his greatest inspiration from a lady, we are reminded from time to time of the religious basis of chivalry, and allusions to pious legend are not infrequent. Chrétien de Troyes' Perceval is given instructions by his mother before he sets out to seek his chivalric destiny, and she mentions the Harrowing in terms consonant with the article of the Creed.[39] The tradition appears again and again in romances of Celtic inspiration, sometimes, as we shall see, in a more elaborate form. It is also to be found in works that show characteristics of both epic and romance. Thus in *Huon d'Auvergne* Eneas describes

Christ's descent to Huon, telling how He entered Hell in glory and released Adam, Seth, Abraham, Isaac, Jeremiah and all the prophets.[40] Elsewhere (ll. 9424–36) Huon sees the very gateway where Christ made His triumphant entry. The gate itself, destroyed by the Redeemer, will only be restored at the Last Judgment. The author of this poem may have had in mind the events as told in the *Gospel of Nicodemus*, but the evidence is too slight to be conclusive. However, I shall now review certain texts where there can be no doubt of the *Gospel*'s contribution.

In vernacular works there is no trace of its influence before the end of the twelfth century, but from that time onwards it made a great impact.[41] First there are those where the tradition was introduced merely as incidental material. This is the case with Robert de Boron's *Roman de l'Estoire dou Graal* (*Joseph d'Arimathie*), composed perhaps about 1200.[42] At the beginning of the poem we are told that Adam and Eve and all the prophets and patriarchs went straight to Hell when they died, and there they confidently awaited Christ's coming. Later His coming is described, and we learn that all the good souls were delivered. In one manuscript, this romance is immediately followed by a fragment of Robert's *Merlin*, and this opens with Christ already in Hell. It goes on to speak of the devils' rage and their discussion of Christ's nature;[43] and this is sufficiently extended to indicate *Nicodemus* itself as the source rather than the *Passion des Jongleurs*.[44] In the fourteenth-century prose romance *Perceforest* the account of Christ's Passion and descent is taken directly from the *Gospel*, though the descent episode itself is curtailed.[45]

It would be surprising if the tradition were not mentioned in that work which takes up so many medieval themes, the *Roman de la Rose*. In fact, Jean de Meung does put into the mouth of Nature a reference to the fear of the "deu d'enfer" when Christ came to break Hell's gates with the wooden staff in order to deliver his friends.[46] Despite the brevity of the passage, it seems likely that Jean had in mind one of the versions of the *Passion des Jongleurs* when he wrote it, for the "baston de fust" he speaks of is surely the cross with which Christ strikes the gates of Hell in some manuscripts of that work.[47]

Turning now to the more important renderings of the

Gospel of Nicodemus into the vernacular, we find that it was translated at least three times in the course of the thirteenth century.[48] The first of these translations was probably that of André de Coutances, who was writing in Normandy at about the beginning of the century. He was followed by an otherwise unknown poet called Chrétien, who hailed perhaps from Champagne or the east of the Ile-de-France; and then a third version was made probably after 1250 by the anonymous Anglo-Norman whom we met in the last chapter.

André de Coutances addresses his poem to a certain "dame de Tribehou" (l. 109), to whom he is in some way related. The first 118 lines form a prologue in which the poet tells us more of himself. In the past he has been fond of "sonez & dances" (l. 2),[49] but now he wishes to treat a more profitable subject pleasing to God. He shows his great reverence for the Virgin and testifies to the importance of her cult among his contemporaries, but says that he cannot rise so high as to sing her praises. Instead he will write in the Romance tongue a story related by Nicodemus. So here we have a man of good birth and who had passed through the schools (he calls himself *mestre* in the first line)[50] hoping to gain favour with both God and a lady of his kin by translating *Nicodemus* into French verse. A cultured poet, he intended his work to appeal to a cultured *milieu*; and his aims were not altogether those of the Christian propagandist, even though he was treating his subject sincerely and without levity.

By the poetic canons of the day, André's poem is well written, with fairly rich rhymes, no excessive padding, and a quite varied vocabulary. It is impossible for us to make close comparisons with the original in the absence of a critical edition of such Latin texts of the *Gospel* as were available at that period; but we can say that while the events narrated agree substantially with the text of the Latin Version A, a good many of the alterations of detail do show the poet emerging from behind his work.[51] There is a good deal of elaboration, particularly in the dialogue, some of which is merely suggested indirectly in the Latin. But tedium is avoided, and this section of the poem strikes a really lively, personal note.

The dialogue between Satan and Enfer is highly animated;

and one of André's most important modifications of the original
is that here Satan is afraid from the beginning, but feigns re-
assurance. Enfer complains to his fellow that he has been
duped by Christ's apparent fear of death, which was no more
than a trick; but he shows by his words that he is not taken in
by Satan's now confident pose. Even the divine voice utters its
summons to open the gates in very human terms:

> & dist la voiz: "Orribles bestes,
> Princes d'enfer qui leenz estes,
> Ovrez voz portes ..."

(ll. 1369–71)

In the Latin the figure of Death is a little obscure, but seems no
more than a pseudonym for Satan. André, however, has
developed more fully the idea of the infernal trinity, and in his
poem Christ first casts Mort into the abyss and then binds
Satan and delivers him to Enfer. Mort is described as the
standard-bearer and constable of Hell. After Christ's action
the legions of Hell call to their leaders to rise up again, complaining that there is no more sorrow in the infernal regions,
and that Clotho, Lachesis and Atropos will now have an un-
welcome rest. And yet we are told that only the good souls are
delivered and taken by Christ to Paradise, a point that is
stressed and repeated (apparently by the copyist) in the last
line of the poem.

After André's version, that of Chrétien makes rather tedious
reading: it is all too clear that this is not the illustrious master
of Troyes, despite the fact that both seem to have lived in the
same part of France and were near-contemporaries. At the
beginning of the poem this man tells us that he is translating
from the Latin "in honour of the Trinity"; and at the end he
repeats this information and adds his name, which he had not
wished to give earlier because he was a sinner. This is all we
know of him. He was no great scholar, and his insistence on the
fact that he used a Latin original may reflect a rather naïve pride
in his ability to do so. He has made a few slips, but on the whole
his translation is faithful—the product, it seems, of a negative
personality. Additions to the original amount to no more than
the usual padding of the second-rank poet; indeed, the ten

PLATE 4. The Harrowing of Hell. Oxford, Bodleian MS Douce f. 4.
English, mid-15th century.

dency is to leave out an occasional detail of the original, but
without serious consequence to the narrative. The treatment of
Part II of the *Gospel* is in 840 octosyllabic lines, compared with
André's 1,214. While reasonably correct, the verse is un-
inspired and shows less command of both technique and
vocabulary than does André's; and while Chrétien's dialogue
sometimes has a little life, the best of it is drab beside that of
his predecessor. It is a work of simple, unpretentious piety,
such as we have come to associate with the Anglo-Normans
rather than the continental writers. And so it is interesting to
note that the sole surviving manuscript was prepared by an
Anglo-Norman copyist.[52]

From the close of the thirteenth century or the beginning of
the fourteenth, a Provençal poem has come down which is of
some significance for the later history of the legend.[53] It is a
translation of the *Gospel of Nicodemus* into octosyllabic verse;
but the descent episode is here based on a Latin B text instead
of the usual A redaction. It contains the following characteristics of Version B : Christ's coming is heralded by the appearance in Hell of the good robber bringing the glad news;
Christ immediately follows, and the defences of Hell cannot
prevail against Him; He casts Satan into the midst of Hell and
chains him by the hands, feet and neck; Adam and Eve and
then John the Baptist[54] praise Christ and thank Him for their
approaching deliverance; Christ thereupon divides the souls
into two groups—some He will take to Paradise, but some must
stay in Hell; the saints beg Him to leave behind in Hell the
sign of the cross as an eternal proof of His power over Satan
and the devils; this He does, then leaves the infernal regions
with His elect, while the others stay in the depths.

Prose versions of the *Gospel* are found in quantity from the
thirteenth century[55] and fall into two distinct categories,
according to whether they are ultimately based on Latin A or
Latin B. The account contained in the fourteenth-century
Paris, B.N., MS fr. 187 may serve as an illustration of the first
type.[56] It is a fairly faithful and colourless translation, prone
only to slight abbreviation, as in the description of the defences
of Hell. Vincent de Beauvais included the Latin text of this
version in his *Speculum Historiale*,[57] and it also occurs in the

VH E

Legenda Aurea (where the form is somewhat abridged, e.g.
Christ does not deliver Satan into the power of Inferus, and the
subsequent squabble of the demons is omitted).[58] Some of the
French translations we have may be based on one or other of
these works.

E. Roy assumed the Provençal rhymed translation to be the
source of the second prose version, though without offering
complete proof.[59] Certainly both offer the characteristics of the
Latin version B; and we have the Provençal poet's assurance
that he was translating from the Latin. Roy believed the poem
to have been translated into French prose in the fourteenth
century, with certain rearrangements, and that the French
version was then retranslated into Provençal prose.[60] His name
for this redaction of the legend is *La Passion selon Gamaliel*,
since Gamaliel and not Nicodemus is the supposed author;
and he lists nine manuscripts and one *incunabulum* in which it
occurs.[61]

Brief though it has been, my survey of the vernacular translations of the *Gospel of Nicodemus* has sufficed to show how
widely the legend was disseminated in the Middle Ages, from
both a chronological and a geographical point of view. Translations are found dating from the very beginning of the thirteenth century on to the end of the period, and originating from
all corners of France as well as the Anglo-Norman domain.
Its appeal would not be limited to a particular class; and with
the reduplication of manuscripts, particularly in prose, it must
have become one of the texts most commonly accessible to the
reading public. Indeed it could not fail to find popularity. It
was an amplification of a biblical and therefore unimpeachable
narrative; but more important still, it treated what to the
Christian are the most significant events of all time: the
Passion, Crucifixion and Resurrection of Christ. The faithful
would show especial interest in the descent episode since this,
though an article of belief, is not described in the canonical
Scriptures. It was on the events recounted by the *Gospel* that
the Christian based his own hope of personal salvation; so
despite recommendations of caution such as the one found in
the *Legenda Aurea*, he found not only entertainment in the
work, but comfort too.

There is, however, evidence that the acquaintance of the laity with the expanded story of the Harrowing of Hell came above all through a rather different version which, although based on *Nicodemus*, is more an adaptation than a translation. It had begun to circulate in France by the beginning of the thirteenth century, or perhaps by the end of the twelfth.[62] The influence of *Nicodemus* is clear, but the events are presented in a very much shorter form. For example, we are not told that Karinus and Leucius witnessed the Harrowing and related it after their own resurrection. Consequently we are not with them in Hell at the beginning of the episode, where Christ's arrival and entry are narrated quite briefly. Nor are there the long dialogues between Enfer and Satan, and Christ's punishment of the latter is not normally described. The account, which is invariably in octosyllabic lines, usually occupies about a hundred of them. The number of manuscripts in which it is found[63] proves the popularity of the work in both France and England (though its continental origin must be presumed); and this in turn explains the considerable variations between the individual texts that lead one to suspect that oral transmission played an important part in the poem's diffusion. This is suggested by its usual title, *La Passion des Jongleurs*. The whole poem, of which the descent episode is only a part, is often found joined to other works of a biblical or hagiographical nature.[64] The descent itself was considered by Becker to have originally had an independent existence,[65] but there is no certain proof of this. Pfuhl sub-divided the extant texts of the poem into three main categories,[66] and the first version, which he published, contains the descent episode in the following terms :

At the moment of Christ's death on the cross, before the Resurrection, His spirit leaves the body and goes straightway to Hell. At the gates, He orders the infernal princes to open, that He may deliver His "friends". They ask who is this King and say that since Adam's sin he and his descendants rightfully belong to them. Christ repeats His command, and the gates open, the chains are broken, and the devils flee. The joyful souls cry their thanks to the Deliverer who has come after they have waited more than a thousand years.[67]

Christ chooses those who were in Hell only through Adam's sin and takes them up into Paradise; but in the fires of torment remain those who did not love Holy Church, peace, justice and the right—all those of evil life, whether lay folk or ecclesiastics.

Pfuhl listed the manuscripts containing a second, "shortened" version of the *Passion des Jongleurs*.[68] The actual descent episode is, however, no shorter than in the first version. The following summary is made from the Paris manuscripts B.N. fr. 24301 and Arsenal 5201.

Christ's spirit leaves the body when He is in the sepulchre. Going at once to Hell, He commands the devils to open the gates. They flee, so He Himself bursts them asunder. He calls to His elect to come forth from Hell. Adam blesses and thanks Christ for His goodness, telling Him of his misery in Hell, where he has had to stay through the fault of Eve. Eve is afraid to approach. Her body is burnt and bleeding. But Christ consoles and pardons her; and, taking Adam with His right hand and Eve with His left, He ascends with them and his *amis* to Heaven. Finally His spirit leaves them and returns to Golgotha.

The third version is found in the so-called *Roman de saint Fanuel*,[69] a work that also dates from the thirteenth century. Becker considered the descent episode to be elaborated from the jongleurs' poem, though it is simply an accretion to the real story of St Fanuel. The Harrowing is described thus:

At midnight after the Crucifixion the guardians of the sepulchre fall asleep, and Christ leaves His tomb to go straight down to Hell. At the gates, He calls upon the demons to open. That day was Hell broken open and despoiled. Christ seized Satan and cast him beneath His feet. Great was the radiance when He entered. Those in Hell see the light, and the Saviour calls them to come forth. From the fire of purgatory[70] Adam hears His voice and blesses Him for His pardon, blaming Eve for his own original downfall. Eve does not dare approach. She is burnt in great anguish of soul and body. But she is pardoned by Christ, who takes Adam with His right hand and Eve with His left and delivers them into Paradise with all the elect. Then He leaves them and returns to Golgotha.

This account presents in common with the so-called "short" version features which are foreign to the redaction published by Pfuhl. Of these the most striking are : Christ leaves the sepulchre to go to Hell ; Adam blames Eve for the original sin ; Christ returns to Golgotha. Close verbal parallels clinch the fact that this is no distant relationship.[71]

We can go further and say that *Saint Fanuel* seems the more primitive : apart from certain preferable readings,[72] it preserves some characteristics of the *Gospel of Nicodemus* that are lost to the other two versions. These are notably the great light which Christ brings into Hell, and the overthrow of Satan. It is possible that the writer who introduced the episode into *Saint Fanuel* knew the *Gospel* and added these touches to an original resembling the short version of the *Passion des Jongleurs* ; but more probably he used an earlier redaction of the jongleurs' poem than has come down in any other form.[73] One further point of interest is that Adam's blaming of Eve, a widespread tradition based on *Genesis* iii. 12, is shared by *Saint Fanuel* and the short version of the *Passion des Jongleurs*, though it is found neither in the first version nor in the *Gospel of Nicodemus* itself.

Before we leave the *Passion des Jongleurs*, some comments may be made on its propagation. Although I have used its widely accepted title, its claim to the patronage of the jongleurs has never in fact been satisfactorily proved. E. Faral made some interesting observations on the subject, illustrated by quotations from the exordia of the *Passion*, of the section dealing with the descent, and of the poems commonly grouped with it (*Roman de saint Fanuel, Evangile de l'Enfance*).[74] He concluded firstly that these poems were intended for public recitation or reading, and no one would quarrel with this. Then he claimed that the performers were professionals, "Car, en dépit de leurs déclarations pieuses et du dessein qu'ils annoncent de moraliser, il ne faut sans doute pas se les représenter comme des évangélisateurs désintéressés : ils exploitent le goût du public pour les narrations dévotes, voila tout. Mais ces professionnels, qui étaient-ils ? Des clercs ? On serait, d'un côté, tenté de le croire. Ils protestent à chaque instant de la véracité de leurs récits, de la sûreté de leur information ; ils répètent qu'ils tiennent leurs histoires de bonne source, qu'ils ont fouillé les livres, les écrits. L'un déclare qu'il a été a 'bonne école' ; l'autre assure qu'il a traduit son poème du latin. Et ces affirmations semblent dénoncer le clerc" (p. 172). But Faral went on to suggest that these claims are simple impostures, pointing to the following lines from *Saint Fanuel* as showing that the poet was not himself a *clerc* :

> *Il n'est nul clerc tant bien letrés*
> *Ne d'escripture doctrinés*
> *Qui sa coulor peüst escrire*
> *Ne sa beauté vous peüst dire.*

(ll. 49–52 ; Faral, p. 169)

(There is no clerk so lettered or so learned in Scripture that he could write down its colour or describe to you its beauty.)

Surely quite the contrary is likely to be true, for the inference is that if no *clerc* can describe the colour then no one can, a compliment by the poet to his own class. Faral's final conclusion was rather non-committal : "Il nous semble au moins acquis que les œuvres précédemment cités appartenaient à des professionnels, clercs ou laïques, peu importe, c'est-à-dire, en fin de compte, si on considère moins les différences de culture que l'identité des modes d'existence, a des jongleurs" (p. 172).

Faral's case seems too subjective to carry conviction. I quote from one of the very passages selected by him :

> *Je ne suis mie enfantomerres,*
> *Ne ne chant pas come jouglerres;*
> *Ains vous depri por cel signor*
> *Qui por nous ot tant de dolor,*
> *Qui souffri mort et passion,*
> *Et qui fut pris comme larron,*

> *Que vous oiez hui en cest jor*
> *La parole nostre signor,*
> *Si me laissiez a vous parler.*
>
> *Signor, ci doivent arester*
> *Les bonnes gens et asseoir;*
> *Mais anemis a tel pooir,*
> *Que vous tornez a gabeor*
> *Les paroles nostre signor.*
> *Se vous volez que je vous die*
> *De Dieu et de Sainte Marie,*
> *Or faites pais, si m'escoutés.*
>
> (*Saint Fanuel* ll. 14–30 ; Faral, p. 169)

(I am no mystifier, nor do I sing like a jongleur ; rather do I pray you for the sake of Our Lord, who for us suffered so much grief, and death and passion, and who was taken like a thief, to harken this day to Our Lord's word and let me address you. Sirs, here should good folk stop and sit ; but the enemy has such power that you mock at the words of Our Lord. If you wish me to speak to you of God and Holy Mary, then hold your peace and listen to me.)

This is an ill-chosen passage to quote in support of the argument that the author was a jongleur. "Imposture", says Faral. Perhaps, but it must be conceded that a literal interpretation of the passage gives the following result : the poet was not a jongleur, but a man of true piety who wanted to instruct his audience with a narrative drawn from the Holy Story. In other words his function, as he states it, was that of the preacher. There is no indication of the place where he was performing, and indeed we would not expect it, since the poem would scarcely be composed for performance on one isolated occasion. But we may notice in passing that the instruction to the people to tarry and be seated could in the Middle Ages have applied to a congregation in church.[75] The line "Que vous oiez hui en cest jor" might be interpreted as a piece of stock padding : on the other hand the meaning "on this day in particular" is possible, referring perhaps to Sunday or a special feast day. So we can say that these lines *could* have been spoken appropriately by a preacher addressing his congregation, in church or elsewhere, on a Sunday or some feast day.[76] The same applies to all the passages quoted by Faral, and in particular we notice the lines from the Paris, Arsenal, MS 5201 :

> Seignor, il fait bon arester
> La ou on ot de Deu parler.

(Faral, p. 170, n. 1)

The tone everywhere is less that of the jongleur who is giving his public their favourite entertainment than that of the preacher trying to gain the people's attention although he realises that other stories are more to their taste.[77]

There is even concrete evidence that the *Passion des Jongleurs* was, in its day, considered as a sermon. In the thirteenth-century Paris, B.N., MS fr. 1822 it immediately follows a poem called *Li sermons de la Crois* and precedes an untitled sermon on the Assumption.[78] And in the Anglo-Norman copy published by F. A. Foster it is headed: "Sermones Mauritii Parisiensis episcopi".[79] While this ascription may be spurious, it is at least apparent that the poem was copied in good faith as a sermon and not merely as a piece of devout entertainment. A study of its literary sources would show its dependence on ecclesiastical writings and traditions such as might have been used by any writer of sermons in the twelfth or thirteenth centuries; but my concern here is with the poem's diffusion rather than with its original composition.

One may wonder why, if the *Passion* did originate in the cloister, it became so widely disseminated during the thirteenth and fourteenth centuries. Its circulation seems to have been so much greater than that of texts like *Li ver del juïse* or even the vernacular versions of the *Vision of St Paul*. Hitherto no one, I think, has looked beyond the jongleurs for a solution, but I would suggest another possibility: the friars. The two chief orders, the Dominicans and the Franciscans, became powerful forces in France from the second decade of the thirteenth century—roughly the time proposed for the original composition of the *Passion des Jongleurs*.[80] The primary aim of both orders was preaching and evangelisation,[81] and it was not long before they were established in England too. Referring to their arrival in this country, J. R. H. Moorman says: "Immediately they began their evangelistic tours which quickly made their mark. In contrast to the rather dreary and monotonous Sunday services which the parish churches offered, these preaching friars provided something which was almost an entertainment."[82] What was the nature of this "entertainment"? Firstly it must be remembered that they used the language suited to their congregation, that is to say the vernacular except when they were addressing a clerical audience; indeed, the friars were specifically enjoined to learn the language of their neighbourhood. Furthermore, it was their custom to bring all manner of lively anecdotes and *exempla* into their sermons, culled mainly from manuals written in Latin. And sometimes, we are told, they would make the sermons more attractive by delivering them in verse.[83]

So there seems to be no reason why the friars should not have used the *Passion des Jongleurs* in their preaching, and if this is so it is surely unreasonable to ascribe its wide diffusion mainly to the jongleurs. The preaching orders, and especially the Franciscans, ministered primarily to the lower classes, and they were particularly fond of chastising in their sermons the great ones of the earth. This spirit is caught in the *Passion*; and although miscreant clerics are among those who feel the lash of the poet's tongue, there is nothing that we cannot imagine being uttered by a stern-principled friar. The Franciscans also paid special attention in their devotions to the life of Christ— His Nativity, Passion and Crucifixion;[84] so altogether the *Passion des Jongleurs* and the poems normally associated with it could not be better suited to their tastes and requirements.

But there is no direct evidence in the poems to show that they were either written or performed by friars. The most we can say is that Robert Grosseteste of Lincoln, a friend and patron of the mendicant orders,[85] may himself have composed a life of Christ in French, presumably including an account of the Passion and Harrowing.[86] I can therefore do no more than suggest an alternative to the jongleurs as propagators of the *Passion*. And if to me the clerical claim seems more soundly based than the secular, it would be rash to suggest that the jongleurs had no hand at all in the matter.

There remains to be considered one more non-dramatic poem

containing a treatment of the Harrowing. This is the *Livre de la Passion*, seemingly a work of the early fourteenth century.[87] It is interesting from two points of view : it shows how an educated man of the fourteenth century felt a need for a new interpretation of the old story; and it represents an intermediate stage between works like the *Passion des Jongleurs* and the later *mystères*.

It recalls the events of Christ's life, and in 49 lines (1806–54) describes His harrowing of Hell. Certain features suggest that the author had the *Gospel of Nicodemus* in mind here, though elsewhere he had made use of the *Passion des Jongleurs*. They are the reference to the time Adam had spent in Hell (l. 1817), and the light that Christ brought into the lower regions (ll. 1843–4). But the conception found here of the Saviour's soul making the descent allied to His divinity (ll. 1810–5) is borrowed from the *Legenda Aurea*.[88]

There follows a description of the four parts of Hell which is coloured by scholastic ideas current at the time : Hell proper is a place of eternal torments, then there is Purgatory, and the two Limbos, one for dead infants and the other for the patriarchs.[89] It was into the latter that Christ's soul descended in order to deliver the souls of the righteous. The connection I have suggested with the *mystères* appears most clearly in an earlier passage which is directly linked with Christ's descent. A devil returns to Hell from the earth with the news of the Redeemer's imminent death. Instead of the message being gratefully received, it provokes a squabble among the apprehensive devils. Its unfortunate bearer is given a beating, and Beelzebub departs to try to prevent the threatened disaster through the agency of Pilate's wife. The scene, which is here described fully in the vernacular for the first time,[90] was to become a common feature of the *mystères*.

A final word may be added concerning the author. Although he says nothing to disclose his identity, Grace Frank is surely right in supposing that he was a *clerc* well versed in the theological traditions and symbolism of his day. His native district may have been to the north of the Ile-de-France, though one cannot be sure of this. Certainly he was a capable poet who wanted to do more than simply re-tell a pious story : along

with his doctrinal preoccupations we must allow him a certain
literary ambition and, indeed, achievement.

I have already spoken of the popularity of the *exemplum* as an
instrument of pious instruction.[91] Some of its virtues, such as
vividness and comparative brevity, were seen in the *Vision of
St Paul*; but though this legend was not canonical, it had a
strong scriptural flavour and so cannot be regarded as a true
exemplum. More typical are the anecdotes from Gregory's
Dialogues which I summarised in the first chapter.

The popularity of the *Dialogues* led to their frequent translation into French in the course of the Middle Ages,[92] and the
earliest such rendering we have dates from the second half of
the twelfth century.[93] It is a prose work written in a Picard
dialect by an unknown author. His choice of prose, while
natural enough in view of the character of the *Dialogues*, does
show that he had no other aim than to make a version of the
work available to those who had no Latin. In fact, the translation is quite faithful and quite colourless, interesting chiefly as
an early example of an unrhymed work of edification intended,
no doubt, to be read to the laity in church or elsewhere.

At least twenty-nine manuscripts contain all or some of the
pious legends known as the *Vies des Pères* or, to distinguish
them from vernacular translations of the true *Vitae Patrum*, as
the *Vie des anciens Pères*.[94] The collection is not in fact a single
work, but an amalgamation of two separate ones, both written
by clerics towards the middle of the thirteenth century. The
first ends with the forty-second legend and is the work of an
Ile-de-France poet; the second was written in a dialect of the
west of Picardy, perhaps by Ernoul de Langy. The combined
work enjoyed great popularity in the thirteenth and fourteenth
centuries.

In many of the *Vies* the infernal powers play a large role, and
visions of demons are common. In one (No. 46) there is the
account of two brothers who were bound together by so great
an affection that when one died and was carried to Hell the other,
though not meriting the punishment, followed him to the places
of torment. Two stories contain a true descent theme, and they

will be summarised as found in the thirteenth-century Paris,
B.N., MS fr. 1546.

No. 21 (fol. 52b-55a): "De cele qui vit sa mere [en]
enfer et son pere en Paradis."

A girl has come to emulate the ways of her devout father
and reject those of her wicked mother. Her mother dies and
is given a splendid funeral; but on the death of her father,
the elements seem to conspire against a burial worthy of his
righteous life. For three days a tempest rages and prevents
any funeral at all; and when on the fourth day it does take
place, it is totally spoiled by the weather, and the body itself
has begun to putrefy. The girl thinks this is a poor reward
for a godly life and so decides to follow her late mother's
wicked example. But God, not wishing to lose her, comes to
her as she lies asleep one night and catches up her spirit from
the body.

She is led in spirit directly to Hell and straightway sees her
naked mother tormented by a flame that passes through her
body and issues from her mouth. Reptiles pierce her cheeks,
rend her face, and emerge from her breasts. The wretch
describes to her daughter how every day she is burnt five
hundred times by the flame and then plunged into icy water.
Much as she regrets her past sins, she cannot die; nor will
she ever have respite, for alms and prayers will avail her
nothing. Then the girl is suddenly led into Paradise, where
she finds her father in bliss. He knows whence she comes,
but shows no pity for his wife. If his daughter fails to lead a
good life, she will find herself in Hell with the heedless rich,
who have to drink molten gold a hundred times a day. Then
she is carried back to her bed. Henceforth she leads a good
life and finally joins her father.

The poet adds that this tale shows the folly of wasting one's
time and neglecting God when in this world; and he uses this
reflection to introduce the description of the infernal wheel
already mentioned in connection with the Alexandrine version
of the *Vision of St Paul*.[95] The wheel burns, cuts and flays its
victims. Moreover it turns in three "gueules" or pits, the first

containing ice and frost, the second boiling metal, and the third noxious filth from which exudes a stinking fog so thick that only the gleam of the fire may be seen. The sinners endure torment according to the degree of their sin. Yet their most bitter punishment is that they can see Paradise and the delight of the blessed.

Some of the tales in the *Vie des anciens Pères* have actually been borrowed from the *Vitae Patrum*; and it is from here that this one has been taken, perhaps indirectly, since it early passed into many collections of sermons and *exempla*.[96] The story seems to be of eastern origin, and analogous situations are to be found in Jewish literature.[97] In the French poem, however, there is a certain amount of amplification, and the wheel is an entirely new feature. The writer has brought his story more into line with the eschatological legends that were so numerous by the middle of the thirteenth century. No direct borrowings can be pointed to: the visit to Hell before Paradise (in the Latin accounts Paradise is seen first) is a common feature in this type of literature, and the torments described here are traditional by this time. The sight of Paradise by those in Hell was widely credited in the Middle Ages. The source of the idea is in *St Luke* xvi. 23, where we are told that the rich man looked up from his place of torment and saw Lazarus in the bosom of Abraham; and this passage is quoted by Gregory in his *Dialogue* IV, 33 in support of the theory that both the damned and the blessed see one another. Our poet may have known the *Dialogues* and even have had IV, 36 in mind when he described the stinking fog that rises from beneath the wheel.[98] But it is likely that most of his elaborations, including perhaps the form of the wheel of torment,[99] sprang from his own imagination and unconscious reminiscences.

So here we can see once again how the pious medieval story-teller delighted in using and elaborating the theme of the infernal journey, and how this was easy for him in view of the store of infernal lore at his disposal, even if he were relatively unlearned. In other words, the description of the pains of Hell had become stereotyped in pious literature by this time and was accepted as a stock way of amplifying a narrative. Regrettably, the poet has not realised that, lacking the vision to develop the infernal scenes along original lines, he would have spent his time more profitably in filling out the cadre of the story which was, it seems, new to vernacular poetry. Is it possible that the public was still demanding the old, hackneyed descriptions of Hell? More probably they had become something of an obsession with the clergy, who were unable to see the didactic advantages of a shift of emphasis and were continuing to plough the by now sterile furrow.

However, in the second of the *Vies* that call for our attention the poet has shown more restraint, and the story has consequently gained in conciseness and pungency.

No. 62 (fol. 125d–127b): "De l'ermite que Jehan l'ange porta en Purgatoire."

For twenty years a hermit lives a life of the utmost asceticism near Antioch and performs many good works. Then he is given the choice by God's angel of spending thirty more years on earth and then going straight to Heaven, or of spending three days in Purgatory before being transferred to eternal joy. His choice is the three days in Purgatory. Accordingly he dies and is transported to that region where, however, one hour seems like a hundred years. Bitterly he complains of his lot, but the angel appeals to St Michael to make the hermit keep the rest of his bargain. He is finally offered once more the opportunity of spending thirty years living on the earth before going to Heaven, and this time he gratefully accepts. So he returns to the body; and after thirty years of privations and mortification of the flesh he obtains his reward.

This legend is of unknown origin,[100] but Klapper has printed the same story as found in a fifteenth-century manuscript.[101] The mention of Antioch suggests that it too originally came from the Middle East. It is rather different in character from the visions and legends we have looked at so far and is not without a touch of humour. The object is not to depict the nature of the torments, but to stress their magnitude and timelessness; and fortunately the French translator has refrained from obscuring the moral with extraneous detail. For it is a simple moral,

neatly told, which is the essence of these *exempla*, intended as
they were to illustrate, and not form, sermons. Their human
interest would have gone far to endear them to a medieval
congregation. Yet while lengthy depictions of the Otherworld
could best be left to the writers of more elaborate vision
literature, these little tales must have helped, in their humble
way, to confirm their hearers in the belief that the horrors of
Hell may sometimes be revealed to ordinary people. Thus they
did help to keep interest alive in the theme of the visit to
Hell.

There is another aspect of the tale "De l'ermite . . ." which I
might mention. It is the making of a bargain by a mortal with a
representative of the Otherworld. Put in these terms, it can be
seen that the theme is linked with that of the infernal pact made,
and later regretted, by a mortal man, who may then be given a
second chance to redeem his fortunes. The Theophilus legend
immediately springs to mind ;[102] and it is significant that its
action takes place in Adana (in Silicia), which is not far from
Antioch whether it be the Syrian or the Turkish town of that
name. Another story of a pact with the devil is attributed to
Amphilochius, bishop of Iconium in the fourth century.[103]
We may deduce that this kind of story relating a bargain with
the supernatural powers was popular in that corner of the Middle
East in the early centuries of the Christian era.

Since we have been looking at one or two stories of eastern
provenance, I may mention another, far more important in
itself, but where our theme makes only a fleeting appearance.
Towards the end of *Barlaam and Josaphat*, Josaphat falls
asleep on Barlaam's tomb and is shown Paradise in a vision.
One French translator, Gui de Cambrai (writing soon after
1214) adds that he afterwards saw the great torments of Hell
prepared for the sinners and many naked souls languishing there
in grief and anguish.[104] Here at least there is no undue digres-
sion to indulge either the poet's moralising propensities or his
taste for the macabre.

Certain of the legends we examined in Chapter I have the
character of more extended, more detailed *exempla*. Two of

them, the *Vision of the Boy William* and the *Vision of Gunthelm*, appear in Vincent de Beauvais' *Speculum historiale*. The formidable task of translating Vincent's work was performed in about 1335 by a hospitaler, Jean de Vignay (or du Vignay).[105] Undertaken on behalf of Jeanne, wife of Philippe VI of Burgundy, this version, which is an assiduous but mediocre production,[106] goes under the title of *Le miroir historial*. It is written in prose.

It may have been the relative sophistication of these legends which discouraged writers in the French vernacular from putting them into verse. They are less straightforward than the *Vision of St Paul* or *St Patrick's Purgatory* : the punishments are rather more complex and less conventional, and the stories do not proceed by such clearly marked stages. Oral transmission and performance would have been correspondingly less easy ; and in any case, by the time they passed to France, prose was becoming more and more appreciated by a growing reading public.[107] So it seems that they never entered the domain of French verse. Apparently composed by clerics in the first instance, they have survived in the work of one cleric and been translated by another for the benefit of a noble and reading public.

Only one of the continental versions of the Brendan legend is in verse ; and using the octosyllabic line like the Anglo-Norman poem, it fails to put it to such good and lively use as did Benedeit. This redaction occurs in the encyclopedic poem *L'image du monde*, which was written in 1245, probably by a certain Gossouin de Metz, though it was long ascribed to Gauthier of the same town.[108] In its original form, however, this didactic work did not include the Brendan story, which was interpolated together with other passages when a second "edition" was prepared in 1247, this time quite possibly by Gauthier de Metz. The legend is introduced by lines telling how the translator found his Latin original at the Benedictine Abbey of Saint Arnoult near Metz and turned it into French so that lay people might understand.[109] This version is contained in many manuscripts throughout Europe. It is a remarkably faithful rendering of the *Navigatio*, though with some tendency to abbreviate rather than expand the descriptive passages, indicative of the author's exclusion of his own personality from the work.

C. Wahlund studied in some detail the prose versions of the legend in French, two of which he published.[110] The first, from the Paris, B.N., MS fr. 1553 and dated 1284, is a faithful Picard translation of the *Navigatio*. Indeed, the translator was more conscientious than competent, and his Latin was apt to let him down from time to time.[111] One must assume that he was a hack worker, operating again in the interests of a lay public.

That the *Voyage of St Brendan* had become a firm favourite with the continental French before the end of the thirteenth century is shown by its belated introduction into the *Image du monde*, but even more clearly by the large number of manuscripts containing the second of Wahlund's prose versions.[112] Much the same remarks as were made about the previous one apply to this, at least in so far as the writer's lack of inspiration and scholarship is concerned. He is distinguished only by a slightly freer treatment and a tendency to condense or eliminate certain details, though some of this may be due to faulty transmission.[113]

A Provençal prose version of the legend may also be mentioned.[114] It is a translation into the Haut-Languedoc dialect of a much abbreviated text of the *Navigatio* and is found in a manuscript of the mid-fifteenth century. The only interest for us lies in the evidence it provides in showing that towards the end of the Middle Ages interest in the Brendan story was not confined to the Frenchmen of the north.

Indeed its history in the French vernacular is a long one. Even before Benedeit composed his poem across the Channel, we have proof that the story was known in France; for there is a reference to it in the works of Ralph Glaber, who died in 1050.[115] I suggested that its appeal for Benedeit lay not so much in the Celtic as in the Christian elements, in so far as it is fair to separate the two. But what are we to make of the reference in the First Branch of the *Roman de Renart* (perhaps late twelfth-century) to a "bon lai breton . . . de saint Brandan"?[116] Should we assume that Renart, playing the part of a jongleur, is using the term *lai breton* loosely and that this is an allusion to Benedeit's poem? Or is it a joking confusion of genres? Or is it possible that someone had composed a work on the subject with an eye more to the mythological than to the Christian content ? This last is but a remote possibility if his starting point was the *Navigatio*.

But to keep to the texts we possess, the legend found its way into didactic compendia in the course of the thirteenth century —the *Image du monde* and Jean Belet's version of the *Legenda Aurea*. As its popularity increased on the Continent, its religious application was not universally observed; for use is made of it in the romance *Baudouin de Sebourc*,[117] and it had actually been satirised much earlier in a short Latin poem.[118] There the writer mocks the legend and the *poeta* who transmits it :

> *O rem miram, risu dignam et plenam stulticie !*
>
> (l. 13)

He says that it is worthy only to be burnt, so full is it of folly. No doubt this was a minority view, for the tale remained at least moderately popular until the end of the Middle Ages.[119] But after Benedeit it lost its vitality ; and in the main the continental renderings are more or less faithful translations of the *Navigatio*.

The success of the *Vision of Tundal* in France was rather more circumscribed. Two prose translations have been published by V. H. Friedel and K. Meyer,[120] and the first is found in the London, B.M., MS Add. 9771. Written originally in the northeast of France, many of its dialectal features have been smoothed out by the fourteenth-century Ile-de-France copyist. This version is reasonably full after omitting all of the Prologue except the date of the vision, such abbreviation as there is being of little consequence to the narrative. The main feature is its anonymity, both literally and figuratively. The author may have been a monk, since he gives in Latin those biblical quotations which he recognises; but his pious peroration, which is fragmentary, is no more than conventional. The *Vision* is followed in the manuscript by another devout work, a sermon on the Seven Deadly Sins.

The second published prose version is more interesting. It, too, was written or at least copied in the fourteenth century, this time by a Frenchman of the south-east. It is found in two manuscripts.[121] There is no direct evidence that it was rendered straight from the Latin, and certainly it is uncommon for prose translators to put as much of themselves into their work as this man has done. But despite the considerable liberties he has taken, there is no reason to suppose that he used anything but one of the common Latin texts.

Although he abbreviates to some extent, and especially towards the end when his energies seem to have flagged a little, at other points he elaborates on the original with apparent relish. In particular he likes to expand his description of the different types of sinners. Thus, the first river is not simply for the proud, but also for hypocrites and Sadducees who banded together against Our Lord and their neighbours (pp. 13–14). The translator expands the list of sexual crimes and their appropriate torments in his treatment of the house of Phristinus and the following episode (pp. 22–3 and 28–9). The Vulcanus torment is for false judges and advocates and for all who oppressed the poor and lowly (pp. 30–1). And King Cormachus' breach of his marriage vow is amply explained (p. 45).

Throughout, this Frenchman embroiders freely on the more lurid details of the Latin, as in the description of the pains suffered in Vulcan's forge; and some of his images are quite telling. The souls there, for instance, are smelted longer than a founder smelts the metal for a bell, and they are hammered as if by a smith who is making little nails (pp. 31–2). He gives his imagination full rein when describing the beast Acheron;[122] and in the account of the monster on the icy lake and the tormented souls there, he even allows himself a flight of lyricism as he enumerates the horrors and the surpassing din: "La dolour, la chalor, la froidor, la puor, l'orror, l'angoisse, la paour, les brais, les cris qu'il getient et qu'il oient des serpens et des ames qui soustenient cel tormant sourmontient touz les tormans deuant" (p. 28). Indeed, one feels that verse would have been his more natural medium, and this is unusual in a medieval prose writer. He exaggerates gaily in his descriptions (as in that of Lucifer, pp. 37–9), and this seems typical of his character.

He is more enthusiastic than accurate, and there are some curious misconceptions in his translation.[123] It is also noteworthy that at first much of the narrative is told by Tundal in the first person, before lapsing into the third for the latter part of the *Vision*.

Despite his down-to-earth treatment of the text and his rather naïve exuberance, there are strong indications that the man was a cleric. His elaboration of the types of sinners comes partly at least from a desire to moralise, and his brief Epilogue contains practical words of advice to the Christian. Moreover, he recognises the scriptural texts and quotes them in Latin, but without attempting to assign them to their context. At one point he even adds a Latin tag of his own.[124] We notice that he does not expect his public to know Latin, however, for he is careful to give the vernacular translation before or after each quotation. So it does seem that he was a simple but imaginative churchman, who wished to turn into French for a public less well schooled than himself an exciting story that had not failed to impress him. He was a man of positive personality, and we are happy to have made his acquaintance.

The *Vision of Tundal* was turned into French prose at least once more in the course of the fourteenth century. For it had been included by Vincent de Beauvais in his *Speculum Historiale* (Book XXVIII, Chs. 88–104), and this, as we saw above, was translated ca. 1335 by Jean de Vignay. Vincent's version is somewhat condensed, but the essential elements remain;[125] and in the fifteenth century it was more than once taken out of the body of the *Speculum* to stand alone as a moral tale, with a tendency towards further reduction.[126]

The remaining prose translations I shall mention are all found in fifteenth-century manuscripts and contribute little in the way of literary merit, although certain features have some interest for us. In two Paris manuscripts[127] we find an adaptation of the legend, omitting the vision of Paradise entirely, and passing over the introductory passages in order to plunge *in medias res*: "Pour avoir cognoissance des paines d'enfer" here follows a vision shown through God's grace to a knight, who afterwards came back to life. First he saw ... And the grisly description of the punishments begins. The author is not interested in the name of his hero (who is referred to simply as "le chevalier" and is not shown undergoing the torments himself), and he passes over the circumstances of the vision. Keeping to the letter of his model is no concern of his, but he does almost always show purpose in his alterations of detail. The opening words are a key to his approach: his aim is to depict the pains of Hell and underline the types of crime for which they are merited. These he elaborates, so that the class of sinners tortured in the burning valley is extended to include such persons as the procurers of abortion and infanticides; and in the house of Phristinus (here unnamed) are the gluttons, the libidinous, drunkards and fast-breakers. When dealing with the punishment of the proud, he is especially severe on the fair sex, calling upon the support of Isaiah in his censure, which occupies a full page. The wretched souls in the valley of forges are lovers of battle and vengeance, along with false judges and advocates and those who fought their neighbours and relations. War is condemned in the ensuing homily. It may be to make the sufferings of the sinners seem more terrible that they and not Lucifer are said to be bound by every member in the pit of Hell. And the writer's purpose is further illustrated by his epilogue:

> Les paines d'enfer sont cent mille foiz plus terribles que on ne sauroit dire ne escripre, dont ung chacun amande sa vie afin que les puisse evader et au reaulme de gloire a grant joye monter, laquelle chouse nous doint acomplir cely qui vit et regne par touz sieclez. Amen.
>
> (Fol. 79^r)

(The pains of Hell are a hundred thousand times more terrible than one could tell or write, wherefore let each amend his life so that he may escape them and go up with great joy into the realms of glory; and may He who lives and reigns throughout all ages grant that we do the same. Amen.)

And to hammer the lesson home, he assures us that if there were a pit as deep as from Heaven to Hell and full of sharp razors, to be cast into this would be the least of the torments. Plainly we are dealing with a churchman moved by the evils of his day to preach the common theme, "Memento mori", and to illustrate it from Tundal's experiences. Believing that his public would more easily be moved to righteousness by fear than by hope, he thought it best to omit the picture of Paradise—a sad commentary on his times. To this end he devoted his moderate talents, producing a work that is drily didactic and lacking the harmony and some of the life of the Latin original. It is a good example of the homiletic use of the *Vision of Tundal*.

Likewise to be found in two Paris manuscripts,[128] the next prose rendering of the legend gives, after a typically abbreviated introductory section, what seems to be quite a faithful translation from a Latin text similar to that printed by Wagner. The *explicit* carries the author's utilitarian and pious intention: it was written "pour l'utilité et le pourfit de nos proismes". And the copyist of the Arsenal manuscript makes it clear that he at least was working for a patron, when he appeals: "Priés pour celli qui l'a fait escrire et qui l'a escrit ossi. Pater Noster, Ave Maria."

The one Provençal version is contained in the Toulouse MS 894[129] and is the only vernacular work from France that states the authorship of the original legend. The writer exhorts people to read or to have read to them "aquest libre, loqual .i. sanct religios, que avia nom Marc, treslatec de grec en lati . . ." It is curious that he should have translated the original "barbarico" by "grec", but there are many other inaccurate readings in the text, which is in itself corrupt. The editor has noted the principal departures from Wagner's Latin text and concludes that they are due to the author's prudery or his desire to simplify: "Il avait sans doute le sentiment que son public ne s'intéressait point aux curiosités de la science ou aux mystères de la théologie."[130] His attitude is that of the simple monk or priest in touch with a lay public, and such additions as he makes to his model are pious and moral in tone. At one point, for instance, he says that it pleased God that Tundal should be converted like St Paul, since he had done or said something which pleased Him and therefore did not merit eternal damnation. And though the opening words of the prologue smack of the conventional, we feel an urgent sincerity behind the appeal to the righteous to be confirmed in their love, obedience and fear of God by reading this book or by having it read.

Two of the author's own additions are reminiscent of features in *St Patrick's Purgatory*. When Tundal is about to suffer the torments of the house of Phristinus, the angel counsels him to rely on God's mercy and invoke His name ; but later, so great was his dismay and confusion when he found himself surrounded by the demons at the pit of Hell that he forgot this injunction and remained in their midst. It will be recalled that the knight Owein protected himself from the ministration of the demons by pronouncing the holy name and that, at the pit of Hell, he almost forgot in his terror to call upon Christ. So it is likely that our author had a taste for Christian visions of the Otherworld and thought they could usefully be turned to the edification of the people. So he translated as best he could— not brilliantly, but with some adroit touches such as enlivening the Latin narrative with occasional dialogue—and, we presume, introduced other changes to suit his purpose and follow the dictates of his conscience. As for his intended public, the prologue seems to point beyond the narrowly clerical world, as does the fact that he appends a translation to his single Latin quotation. But more than this we cannot say.

The Latin manuscripts of the *Vision of Tundal* were widely distributed in the Middle Ages (Wagner listed no fewer than fifty-four in a repertory that is by no means complete).[131] Translations were made into German, Dutch, English, Swedish, Icelandic, Spanish, Italian and Catalan as well as French and Provençal.[132] But in spite of this apparent success, we possess fewer vernacular French manuscripts containing it than we do for the other two important Irish legends or for the *Vision of St Paul*, and of those we have none dated from before the fourteenth century. Scanning Wagner's list of the Latin manuscripts, we at once see a possible reason : only one is in a French library, and was itself copied in the fourteenth century. Even allowing for gaps in the list and for the fact that some French manuscripts may now be in other countries, the evidence is strong that the Latin *Visio* was not widely diffused in the French-speaking domain. On the other hand, we must not forget that in the second half of the thirteenth century Vincent de Beauvais did include it in his popular *Speculum Historiale*; and a Latin metrical version is written in what appears to be a thirteenth-century French hand.[133]

Why, then, is the legend not more strongly represented in the French vernacular? Early texts may, of course, have been lost. But if so, they have gone without trace; and it is unlikely that the picture we have has been seriously distorted by the depredations of time. A more significant factor, I would suggest, is the "literary" quality of Marcus' account, which has a richness of style and detail and a baroque exuberance that would have deterred the workaday rhymester as well as making the work less suitable than its "rivals" for oral presentation as an *exemplum*. It is true that we have the Anglo-Norman verse fragment as well as the early German poem by Alber, but there is no evidence of the story ever being put into French verse on the Continent. With the advent of a wider reading public and the increased popularity of prose, more translations do begin to appear. But still, it seems, the simpler pious legends were more appreciated, and the greater merits of Tundal escaped the public eye.

What, in fact, are the general characteristics of the prose translations? Only two really rise above the level of hack-work: that written by the Frenchman of the south-east and published by Friedel and Meyer, and the brief adaptation intended for homiletic use. Of these the first is unusually personal and even poetical in a modest way, and the second has a stern, "puritanical" vigour. But in each, Marcus' work is reduced rather than increased in stature. The only apparent attempt to attain the breadth of vision and the literary standard of the Latin legend was made by the Anglo-Norman poet; and even this we cannot claim to have been more than a genuine attempt. In a sense, the *Visio Tnugdali* was too "modern" in conception and execution for our medieval writers, and only the technical and spiritual resources of a Dante could have turned it to advantage in the vernacular

In fact, as I mentioned earlier, Dante does seem to have known and used it; and so does the author of *St Patrick's Purgatory*, writing in the same century as Marcus. And in the French vernacular there is an anecdote in the *Livre du Chevalier de la Tour Landry*, written in 1371 or 1372,[134] that appears to owe its form to Tundal's vision. A young and pleasure-seeking married lady is stricken by a sudden malady as she attends mass with her paramour. For three days and nights she lies as if lifeless, wept by her lord and friends. Then she wakes with a great sigh and sends for a priest, to whom she confesses her misdeeds and tells of a vision that has been vouchsafed her. She saw her deceased parents, the pit of Hell open before her, and then the Virgin Mary, who rebuked her for her wicked ways. The priest interprets her vision for her, and henceforth she leads a blameless life.[135]

But generally speaking the *Vision of Tundal*, with its colour, contorted movement and grotesque effects, made perhaps a deeper impression on the medieval artist than the writer;[136] and it may be that these qualities held more appeal for the Anglo-Saxon or German imagination than for the French.

How did the third great Irish legend fare in the vernaculars of France? Of the wide reputation of St Patrick's Purgatory as a place of pilgrimage I have already spoken,[137] so it should not surprise us to find the tale of Owein's adventures told and re-told for French publics from the thirteenth century onwards.

We do not know the author of a version in 1,057 octosyllabic lines composed late in that century in the east of France and extant in a single manuscript.[138] It is not even certain that it was translated direct from the Latin, although this is the assumption made by its editor, who makes detailed comparisons between the French poem and the *Tractatus*. The author's only word on the subject comes in the first line : "Un miracle trovons escrist". And indeed, as we know no vernacular treatment that could have served as the source, and because of the peculiarly uneven quality of the poem, it is probably safe to assume a Latin model. Attempts to classify this hypothetical text have proved inconclusive since the poem, while seemingly based on an α-type manuscript, contains a number of readings closer to the Group β pattern.[139] This is significant only in so far as it draws attention to the inadequacy of Ward's original classification.

When we come to see how the French poet has set about his task, a disappointment is in store. Clearly, he begins with the intention of rendering the legend very fully, omitting only Henry's dedication and prologue; but by the time Owein has entered upon his trials in the Purgatory, his biographer is already tiring. Abbreviating recklessly, he leads the knight through the torments and subsequent joys in little more than 500 lines. Plains one and two are amalgamated and the third omitted entirely, the mountain above the icy river is cut out, as are Owein's second meeting with the fifteen messengers and his visit to the Holy Land. The chapters of the *Tractatus* containing the testimonies and appended narratives find no echo here. There is no question of the story being reduced in length for purposes of artistic effect or in order to increase its tempo for an impatient audience; nor is it likely that the Latin model was abbreviated in this fashion.[140] The truth must surely be that the poet started with good intentions to translate a full Latin text, then wearied of his work and brought it to an end as soon as he decently could. His conscience led him to round it off quite neatly by telling how Owein, on his return, recounted his adventures to the canons at the Purgatory, and how they had them recorded and preached to the Irish, who were thereby converted. Owein himself took the habit and, after a life of service to God and the Virgin, received his reward in Paradise. All this, of course, is foreign to the *Tractatus*. In fact the poet was at no point slavish in his translation. For instance, in his description of the infernal wheel he adds that it is "full of whetted razors" (l. 598). On the other hand, he does not mention the characteristic property that it revolves so fast that only the fire can be seen.

We must conclude that here is a rather slipshod and lazy writer. But on the credit side there is some evidence of an undeveloped talent. He can manage the long sentence with reasonable efficiency, as he shows more particularly at the beginning and end of the poem; and he does not confine his sense groups to a single line or couplet. Sometimes he uses exclamations and even parentheses to good effect.[141] and the general impression is of reasonable fluency. What lacks, in default of fidelity to the original, is rather the sustained pace and Christian zeal of other poets treating the same theme. This makes us wonder if he was an active churchman. Despite a pious epilogue, in which he insists on the verity of his account, and despite his disapproving embroidery of the sins of the old Irishman and other apparent flashes of sincerity, one feels that his heart is not in his work. Certainly he makes his hero become a monk (l. 1020), and elsewhere he elaborates the list of those ecclesiastics whom Owein saw in Paradise (ll. 838–43); but, to counter this, at least one error of translation suggests that his Latin was not of the best.[142] Whoever he was, he does not seem to have been inspired by his text or anxious to inspire others. It is more likely that he was doing a routine job for a none too discriminating master or patron.

Only one other continental French metrical version of *St Patrick's Purgatory* has found its way to us, and this was included in his *Bible des Sept Etats du Monde* by the indefatigable Geoffroi de Paris, whose acquaintance we have already made.[143] From our knowledge of this honest rhymester we would not expect any originality; and when he introduces his poem he makes no attempt to conceal his vernacular source: "Geifroi de Paris la cité / Le vous a del conte rismé" (fol. 154^r). It can be shown that the *conte* to which he refers is the most popular of the French prose versions of the legend;[144] and a revealing comparison can be made between a passage from this version as found in the Paris, B.N., MS n.a.fr. 10128 and the corresponding lines from Geoffroi's poem. I select a passage near the beginning of the legend:

Aprés ce mena nostre Sires seint Patrice en .i. leu desert; et si li moustra une fosse roonde et oscure dedenz; et si li dist que qui enterroit enz verais repentanz et bien creanz par bone entention, qu'il seroit espurgiez en .i. jor et en une nuit de touz les pechiez qu'il auroit fez en sa vie, et verroit les tormenz des mauvés et les joies des bons.

(fol. 163^r)

Aprés ce prist nostre Seigneur
Saint Patrice par grant amor.
En .i. desert leu le mena
Et une fosse li mostra

Roonde et oscure dedenz;
Et dist que qui enterroit enz
Repentanz en confession,
Creanz par bonne entention,
Qu'il seroit purgiez sanz sejor
En une nuit et en .i. jor
De ses pechiez et des mesfez
Qu'en toute sa vie auroit fez.
Des mauvés verroit les tormenz,
Et les joies des bonnes gens.

(fol. 154ᵛ, ll. 61–74)

The manuscript carrying this copy of the prose version dates from about the same time as Geoffroi was writing;[145] and in view of the close similarities between the two texts, even in the matter of orthography, it is tempting to suppose that this could have been the very manuscript from which Geoffroi was working. In any case, the comparison gives an interesting glimpse of the hack versifier plying his trade. And as the resemblance persists throughout the story, the following notes on Geoffroi's deviations from the *Tractatus* can be taken to apply also to the prose version.

The first is the erroneous placing of twelve heavenly messengers in the Purgatory instead of the fifteen found in the Latin texts. The mistake seems to have been made in the original of the prose version, or at least in a very early manuscript, since most of the copies I have studied contain it.[146] It is found in one other treatment of the legend, namely that by Ramon de Perelhos; and I shall later suggest that this too was based on the prose version. Apart from this error, which is significant only in so far as it helps us to trace the literary influence of the prose redaction, the main differences from the *Tractatus* are some omissions and re-arrangements. Thus, the story is taken up after the Latin prologue and account of the old homicide, but information derived from Henry of Saltrey's dedication is inserted after the description of Owein's later life (fol. 169ʳ, ll. 1725–32).[147] Also, the sinful souls in the first plain are tormented by blazing dragons "borrowed" from the description of the second plain.[148] It is, perhaps, noteworthy that the author has

given to the king whom Owein consults on his return the name
of Stephen, taken from an earlier passage in the *Tractatus* ;[149]
and he has also specifically stated that he was Irish (fol. 168ᵛ,
ll. 1654–5). The Latin base text was of the α-Group, and apart
from these discrepancies the translation is full and faithful,
even including the first of the homilies, but ending at the point
where Henry's own epilogue occurred. Geoffroi added his
usual *chevilles* in order to fill out his lines, but did not otherwise
depart from his French model; and he completed this part of
the *Bible* in 1,830 octosyllabic lines. As always, he is an able
and even polished rhymester, but nothing more.

Various other prose versions appeared in the course of the
Middle Ages, but only one is worth more than a cursory glance,
and this will be left for a later chapter. The Dublin, Trinity
College, MS 951,[150] written in France in the thirteenth century,
contains a fairly full account, apparently translated from a β-
type manuscript. The dedication and prologue are given, and
the story is brought to a close before Gilbert's testimony. A
curious feature is that the hero is not named. Nor for that
matter is the translator, who was simply concerned with adding
one more to his collection of pious texts (unless the arrangement
of this manuscript is entirely the work of the copyist).

A third prose redaction is found in the Arras, Bibl. Municipale, MS 587 (879), dating from the fourteenth century.[151] It
appears to have been taken independently from the *Tractatus*,
but the author's proneness to abbreviation makes it difficult to
say to which of the two groups (if either) his source-text
belonged. Much of the introductory matter is left out, and a
halt is called in the middle of Bishop Florentian's testimony;
otherwise, all the important episodes are reproduced.

The portion of the Paris, B.N., MS 15210 that contains the
legend (fol. 60ʳ–77ʳ) seems to have been written in the late
thirteenth or early fourteenth century. The title page to this
section is in a much more modern hand, and the rubric contains
an amusing error :

De l'estat des ames aprés la mort, et de la vision du purgatoire de messʳᵉˢ .st. Patrices, comme ly conte Adam le
Celerier.

The name of Adam derives from a misreading of the two words "a dam" that occur in the *explicit* of the account : "Cil chevaliers recontoit souventes foiz a dam Gilebert le celerier toutes icestes choses . . ." In this text the narrative is so badly mutilated that it scarcely merits classification as a separate version ; and indeed, of the torments in the Purgatory only the demons' bonfire and the bridge are mentioned.

The popularity of our legend in medieval France can be gauged from a review of the prose translations alone, and my list is not intended to be exhaustive.[152] In another form it was included by Jacobus a Voragine in his *Legenda Aurea*,[153] which he compiled about the year 1255, and which was widely known to the end of the Middle Ages and beyond. His is a much abbreviated version with some alterations, including the name of the hero, who now becomes Nicholas and dies thirty days after his return to earth. The *Legenda Aurea* was several times translated into French before the end of our period, notably by Jean Belet ca. 1300,[154] and by Jean de Vignay (the industrious translator of Vincent de Beauvais' *Speculum historiale*) in 1348.[155] The work of the former is in no way a faithful rendering from Jacobus, and the version of *St Patrick's Purgatory* which he inserts is not that of his model, but the most widespread prose version, evidently preferred for its greater detail. Jean de Vignay, on the other hand, confines himself here to a simple translation.

Of much greater interest is a prose adaptation of the legend by the Catalan knight Ramon de Perelhos, of which a Provençal version is extant.[156] But as Ramon tries to hoodwink us by passing off Owein's adventures as his own, I shall say no more of his work until I discuss certain travellers' tales in a later chapter.

Of the seven verse texts of *St Patrick's Purgatory* that I have reviewed, five were of Anglo-Norman origin, all written before the latter part of the thirteenth century. It is natural that a text written in England should find its first public there but there is evidence that it was known on the Continent within fifty years of its composition,[157] and we might have expected a less mundane treatment by the Frenchmen. For the Anglo-Norman poems certainly rise above the French from the point of view of sincere religious feelings, lively narration, and general interest. One of the French works seems the rather casual product of a lazy poet, and the other is that of an un-inspired turner of efficient rhymes. The continental contri-bution to the literary history of the legend lies mainly in the prose translations. They helped to vulgarise the story, if in an unimaginative way, being for the most part examples of the "bread-and-butter" work of the scriptoria. It was left to Ramon de Perelhos to give new life to the story, but in a very different way from the pious Anglo-Normans.

It is perhaps rash to try to characterise in general terms all these continental French treatments of our theme; yet one cannot help feeling that they were created in a climate not quite the same as that north of the Channel, even if similar basic motives were involved. With the Anglo-Normans one sensed that the heart in general ruled the head. But again and again we have noticed a certain professionalism in the continental versions: here a preoccupation with literary form, there the rather uninterested attitude of a man with just another job to perform. The prose writers and compilers of compendia, to whom we found no insular counterparts, brought little zest or imagination to their work. And even with the more competent poets, there is little enough originality to applaud in the handling of the available matter. It is true that those who re-told the *Vision of St Paul* turned for their models to the more extended redactions; but this is about as far as their ambitions took them (though an honourable mention must be made of the man who worked the legend in vivid fashion into *Li ver del tuse*). No poet, it seems, was prepared to grapple in verse with the more extravagantly imaginative *Vision of Tundal*.

By the middle of the thirteenth century, then, the straight-forward, pious account of the infernal visit held, for the French, few new avenues to explore. But the theme was not simply abandoned to the pedlars of worn-out homiletic or literary material: rather it was adapted to other purposes, purposes perhaps more intellectual than those of the devout Anglo-Normans, sometimes frankly irreverent, usually governed at least in part by the wish to entertain. So here too one catches sight of a less involved, professional attitude encroaching on the religious and didactic; and of this a variety of examples will be found later in the book.

NOTES

1. H. von Feilitzen, *Li Ver del Juïse: en fornfransk Predikan* (Uppsala, 1883). For notes on the Oxford manuscript and the versification see Paul Meyer, *Documents manuscrits de l'ancienne littérature de la France conservés dans les bibliothèques de la Grande-Bretagne* (Paris, 1871), pp. 148–50. Feilitzen's edition is reviewed by K. Nyrop in *Romania* XIV (1885), pp. 146–9.

2. I have given my arguments for the use of the Long Latin text elsewhere (*Romance Philology* XII [1958], p. 36). Ground common to it and the *Ver del juïse* is the insistence on the testimony of St Paul himself (also in Redaction VII); the initial description of the fate of souls at the hour of their death (found in the middle of the seventh and at the end of the other redactions); the reference to the slain infants who appeal to God for justice (not in the redactions). The allusion to the Harrowing of Hell, however, is not found in the Long version, but appears in Redaction I; and this suggests that some development may have taken place in the Long text before its use by the Frenchman.

3. Owen, art. cit., p. 36, n. 10.

4. E. Cerulli, *Il "Libro della Scala"*, Ch. LIV, §§ 137–8, and Ch. LX § 150. See Parts II & III for knowledge of Moslem tradition in the West in the Middle Ages.

5. Cf. Cerulli, op. cit., Ch. LXVII, § 165. Both texts probably took this from the *Vision of St Paul*.

6. Cerulli, op. cit., especially Parts II and III.

7. In his unpublished thesis, *La Descente de Saint-Paul en enfer*, W Meiden suggests south-west Lorraine as a possibility.

8. Paris, B.N., fr. 2094. Ed. L. E. Kastner, "Les Versions française inédites de la Descente de saint Paul en Enfer", *Revue des Langue Romanes* 49 (1906), pp. 49–62.

9. Art. cit., pp. 42–4.

10. Ed. Kastner, op. cit., pp. 427–49. An introductory passage of eigh lines is carried in London, B.M., MS Add. 15606 (which is incomplete and in Paris, B.N., MS fr. 24436. As Kastner used a corrupt text, have controlled his readings from other MSS, principally Paris, B.N fr. 24429.

11. Kastner, ibid., p. 428.

12. The London MS omits the sight of Paradise and of the good soul' entry there.

13. See my discussion, art. cit., pp. 45–6. The passage from the *Revelatio of Peter* can be consulted in M. R. James' translation in *The Apocrypha New Testament*, pp. 516–7.

14. Owen, art. cit., pp. 46–7. For details of the interpolated passage, se later pp. 112–13.

15. Paris, B.N., MS fr. 1526, fol. 187^r. For a study of the whole work an

its sources see Paul Meyer, "Notice sur la 'Bible des Sept Etats du Monde' de Geufroi de Paris", *Notices et extraits* . . . , 39.1 (1909), pp. 255–322 ; and J. Bonnard, *Les Traductions de la Bible en vers français au Moyen Âge* (Paris, 1884), pp. 42–54.

16. Kastner, op. cit., pp. 321–51.

17. First noted by T. Batiouchkof (*Romania* XX [1891], p. 25, n. 3). See Owen, art. cit., pp. 47–8.

18. P. Meyer, op. cit., p. 257 ; and Ch.-V. Langlois, "Gefroi des Nés ou de Paris, traducteur et publiciste", *Histoire littéraire de la France* 35 (1921), p. 327, n. 3.

19. Meyer, op. cit., p. 259.

20. Fol. 74^r–79^v. Details of the manuscript are found in Dr Abbot's catalogue (Dublin, 1900), p. 162. I give a transcription of the text in Appendix I.

21. Paris, B.N., MS n.a. fr. 4464, fol. 6^r–7^v. See Owen, art. cit., pp. 48–9.

22. Printed from Paris, B.N., MS fr. 22543 by K. Bartsch, *Denkmäler der provenzalischen Literatur* (Stuttgart, 1856), pp. 310–3 ; and C. Appel, *Provenzalische Chrestomathie* (6th edn., Leipzig, 1930), pp. 177–9. See Owen, art. cit., p. 49.

23. Ed., from Toulouse, Bibliothèque Municipale, MS 894, by A. Jeanroy & A. Vignaux, *Voyage au Purgatoire de St Patrice, Visions de Tindal et de St Paul, textes languedociens du quinzième siècle* (Toulouse, 1903), pp. 123–8. Studies by H. T. Silverstein, "The Source of a Provençal Version of the *Vision of St Paul*", *Speculum* VIII (1933), pp. 353–8 ; Owen, art. cit., pp. 49–50.

24. Ed. G. Paris, "*La Passion du Christ* : texte revu sur le manuscrit de Clermont-Ferrand", *Romania* II (1873), pp. 295–314 ; E. Koschwitz, *Les plus anciens monuments de la langue française : Textes critiques et glossaire* (Leipzig, 1902), pp. 10–37, and in *Textes diplomatiques* (6th edn., Leipzig, 1902), pp. 15–34.

25. F. J. Badcock, *The History of the Creeds* (2nd edn., London, 1938), p. 102 and, for other details of its transmission, pp. 97 ff.

26. The practice of homiletic expansion began in the East. For an early text (by Melito of Sardis in the second century) which represents an intermediate stage between liturgy and homily, see Johannes Quasten, *Patrology*, I (Utrecht, 1950), p. 245 ; cf. J. Kroll, *Gott und Hölle*, pp. 131 ff.

27. See the *Dictionnaire de théologie catholique* (Paris, 1909–50), IV, col. 607.

28. For example, in the version of the *Passion des Jongleurs* published by E. Pfuhl (*Die weitere Fassung der altfranzösischen Dichtung in achtsilbigen Reimpaaren über Christi Höllenfahrt und Auferstehung* [Greifswald, 1909]) Christ makes His descent immediately after His death (ll. 1551–4), as He does in the *Livre de la Passion* (ed. Grace Frank [Paris, 1930], ll. 1806–7). In the *Passion d'Autun* (ed. Grace Frank [Paris, 1934], ll. 1857 ff.), in the Provençal *Passion* (ed. W. P. Shepard, *La Passion provençale du manuscrit Didot* [Paris, 1928], ll. 1621 ff.) and in the *Mystères de Sainte-Geneviève* (ed. A. Jubinal, *Mystères inédits du quinzième siècle* [Paris, 1837], pp. 290 ff. and 332 ff.) He descends after the Resurrection, although the first case is somewhat suspect. For notes on the different traditions see Grace Frank, *La Passion du Palatinus* (Paris, 1922), p. 87.

29. In the Greek text there is no indication as to which souls are delivered ;

VH F

in Latin B Christ casts some into Tartarus and takes others to Paradise (B. H. Cowper, *The Apocryphal Gospels*, p. 386).

30. See J. Monnier, *La Descente aux enfers*, Ch. III.
31. Ibid., pp. 143–4, 159, 169.
32. *Dictionnaire de théologie catholique*, IV, cols. 573–4.
33. The arrangement seems to have connections with Latin hymnody (see P. Zumthor, *Histoire littéraire de la France médiévale* [Paris, 1954], p. 84).
34. Paul Meyer, "Ancienne traduction française en vers du Pater et du Credo", *Bulletin de la Société des anciens textes français*, 6ᵉ année (1880), p. 40.
35. Natalis de Wailly, *Jean, sire de Joinville, Histoire de saint Louis, Credo et Lettre à Louis X* (Paris, 1874), p. 278; Ch.-V. Langlois, *La Vie en France au moyen âge de la fin du XXᵉ au milieu du XIVᵉ siècle*, IV (Paris, 1928), p. 12.
36. E. Faral & J. Bastin, *Œuvres complètes de Rutebeuf*, II (Paris, 1960), p. 238 (ll. 73–83).
37. Ed. J. J. Stürzinger (London, 1895), ll. 10163–286.
38. Ed. E. Langlois (Paris, 1925), ll. 777–82. For other references to the Harrowing in the chansons de geste see Sister M. Gildea, *Expressions of Religious Thought and Feeling in the "Chansons de Geste"* (Washington, 1943), p. 276.
39. Ed. A. Hilka (Halle, 1932) and W. Roach (Genève & Lille, 1956), ll. 583–8.
40. Ed. E. Stengel, *Huon's aus Auvergne Höllenfahrt* (Greifswald, 1908), ll. 10050–4.
41. See R. P. Wülcker, *Das Evangelium Nicodemi in der abendländischen Literatur*, pp. 23 ff.; W. Becker, "Die Sage von der Höllenfahrt Christi in der altfranzösischen Literatur", *Romanische Forschungen* 32 (1913), pp. 923–4.
42. Ed. W. A. Nitze (Paris, 1927). See ll. 11–20 and 593 ff.
43. Printed as an appendix by Nitze, op. cit. (see ll. 1–162). A prose rendering was edited by G. Paris & J. Ulrich, *Merlin, roman en prose du XIIIᵉ siècle* (Paris, 1886).
44. Becker, op. cit., pp. 923–4, suggests a knowledge of both texts and of the Passion sermon. Whether Robert knew the *Gospel* in its Latin form or in a French translation it is impossible to say.
45. Ibid., p. 924.
46. Ed. E. Langlois (5 vols., Paris, 1914–24), ll. 18779–86.
47. See, for example, the passage in Grenoble MS 1137 (Paul Meyer, "Notice . . .", *Romania* XVI [1887], p. 229). This may be the cross which Christ set in the midst of Hell in the Latin Text B (Cowper, *The Apocryphal Gospels*, p. 386); but it could perhaps be a reminiscence of a liturgical ceremony (see later, p. 226).
48. G. Paris & A. Bos, *Trois versions rimées de l'Évangile de Nicodème*. See also Paul Meyer, "Légendes hagiographiques en français", *Histoire littéraire de la France* 33 (1906), pp. 356–7.
49. It may be that he composed a satirical poem, the *Roman des Français*, found in the same manuscript as his *Nicodemus* (Paris & Bos, pp. xvii ff.).
50. The editors (p. xxvi) suggest that he may have studied in Paris. His poem shows some traces of the technique of the schools, e.g. the repetition of a word in the interrogative as in ll. 58–9.

51. It should be mentioned that André has left out the first ten chapters of Part I of the *Gospel*, but we are concerned solely with Part II. The editors made a few relevant comparisons with the Latin Version A (pp. xliii–xliv).
52. Ibid., p. v.
53. Printed by H. Suchier, *Denkmäler provenzalischer Literatur und Sprache*, I (Halle, 1883), pp. 1–73. See also Paul Meyer, "Versions provençales d'Évangiles apocryphes", *Histoire littéraire de la France* 32 (1898), pp. 102–6.
54. Version B as given by Cowper contains no mention of John the Baptist at this point (p. 385).
55. Some are mentioned by Paul Meyer in *Bulletin de la Société des anciens textes français* (1885), pp. 48–9, and in *Romania* XIX (1890), p. 312. See too E. Roy, "Le Mystère de la Passion en France du XIV͏ᵉ au XVI͏ᵉ siècle", *Revue Bourguignonne* 13 & 14 (Dijon & Paris, 1903–4), Part II, p. 324.
56. Other MSS of this type in the B.N. are fr. 409 (fourteenth century) and fr. 966 (fifteenth century).
57. Book V, Ch. 61.
58. Ch. 53. We are warned that the account is subject to caution. Jean de Vignay (see below, p. 116) translated both the *Speculum Historiale* and the *Legenda Aurea* in the fourteenth century.
59. Op. cit., Part II, pp. 324 ff.
60. See also Paul Meyer in *Romania* XXVII (1898), p. 129.
61. For another *incunabulum* see Wülcker, op. cit., p. 28.
62. See Paul Meyer in *Histoire littéraire de la France* 33, p. 355.
63. See H. Theben, *Die altfranzösische Achtsilbnerredaktion der "Passion"* (Greifswald, 1909); Pfuhl, *Die weitere Fassung* . . . (both deal with the MSS in their Introductions); Paul Meyer in *Romania* XVI (1887), pp. 51–2, 228–9, 244–5, and in *Histoire littéraire de la France* 33, pp. 355 ff. F. A. Foster gives further valuable information in *The Northern Passion*, II (London, 1916), pp. 49–58.
64. Cf. Meyer in *Hist. litt. de la France*, loc. cit.
65. Op. cit., pp. 914–5.
66. Op. cit., pp. v–vi. He edits the section of the poem that concerns us. An Anglo-Norman version containing an abbreviated account of the descent (ll. 1473–82) is published by Foster, op. cit., II, pp. 102–25.
67. At this point Geoffroi de Paris, who inserted this version of the descent into his *Bible* (fol. 112͏ᵛ–118͏ᵛ; for details of the *Bible* see above, pp. 89–90), interpolates a passage of 574 lines (published by Pfuhl as an appendix), apparently taken from a non-extant translation of *Nicodemus*. His source is often quite close to Chrétien's version, but presents some minor variations and abbreviations. The interpolation opens with the imprisoned souls learning of Christ's imminent approach and concludes with the raised patriarchs praising God in Paradise. Later in his work, Geoffrey tells the story of Karinus and Leucius as a separate episode (see Paul Meyer in *Notices et extraits* . . . , 39.1 [1909], pp. 303–4).
68. Op. cit., p. vi.
69. Ed. C. Chabaneau (Paris, 1889). The descent episode begins at l. 3324. Jean d'Outremeuse gives a prose rendering of the second half of this poem in his *Myreur des Hystors* (see W. Becker, op. cit., p. 923).
70. This is interesting, since it shows that the *limbus patrum* was unknown

to the writer who, however, found it difficult to believe that Adam had spent his time in Hell.

71. The following parallel passages are taken from the "short" version (S) as found in the Paris, Arsenal, MS 5201 and from Chabaneau's edition of the *Roman de saint Fanuel* (F).

Adam is accusing Eve before Christ:

> "*Mais ce fit Eve ma moillier.*" (S, p. 131)

> "*Ce me fist Eve ma moillier.*" (F, l. 3358)

Eve's grief is described:

> *De sa grant dolor se garmante,*
> *Que tot avoit lo cors sanglant :*
> *En .c. leus va li sans colant.*
> *La lasse famme, l'esgaree,*
> *Est ou feu tote eschevolee.* (S, pp. 131–2)

> *De sa grant dolor se demente,*
> *Semblant fet que molt est dolente.*
> *La lasse fame, la dervée,*
> *Fu el feu toute esquevelée.* (F, ll. 3361–4)

And the final scene :

> *Quant Dex li rois de paradis*
> *Ot d'enfer traiz toz ses amis,*
> *Et il les ot en joie mis*
> *La ou il vot em paradis,*
> *Ses esperit arriers ala*
> *La ou morist en Gorgata.* (S, p. 132)

> *Quant nostre sire Dex li vrais*
> *Ot toz ses amis d'enfer trais,*
> *Et il les ot en joie mis,*
> *La ou il volt en paradis,*
> *Ses deciples pas n'oublia ;*
> *Repairiés est en Gorgata.* (F, ll. 3403–8)

72. E.g. in the first two lines of the last quotations (above, n. 71), where S uses the same rhymes as in the following couplet and the same word, *paradis*. But one should not lay too much stress on such details in view of the long manuscript tradition of all these texts.

73. A fuller study of the filiation of these texts is desirable, but beyond the scope of the present study.

74. *Les Jongleurs en France au moyen âge* (Paris, 1910), pp. 168–72.

75. For medieval church congregations see R. F. Bennett, *The Early Dominicans* (Cambridge, 1937), pp. 96 ff.

76. For the practice of reciting verse sermons, especially during Holy Week and at other festivals, see C. Pinchbeck, "Three Old French Verse Sermons", *Medium Ævum* 23 (1954), p. 1.

77. See in particular the quotation from the *Évangile de l'Enfance* in Faral, op. cit., p. 771.

78. Pinchbeck, op. cit.

79. Op. cit., p. 50.

80. See D. Knowles, *The Religious Orders in England* (Cambridge, 1948), Part II, for a study of the activities of the friars.
81. Ibid., p. 151; and Bennett, op. cit., Chs. V–VII.
82. *Church Life in England in the Thirteenth Century* (Cambridge, 1945), p. 79.
83. G. R. Owst, *Literature and Pulpit in Medieval England* (Cambridge, 1933), p. 227; Moorman, op. cit., p. 80. Cf. also G. Ambroise, *Les Moines du moyen âge* (Paris, 1946), pp. 226–7.
84. A. Fliche, etc., *Histoire de l'Église depuis les origines jusqu'à nos jours*, X (Paris, 1950), p. 393.
85. Knowles, *The Religious Orders . . .*, pp. 180–1.
86. P. Meyer in *Histoire littéraire de la France* 33, p. 356, n. 2.
87. Ed. Grace Frank. It is preserved in five manuscripts. For its date see the Introduction, pp. xvii–xix.
88. Ibid., pp. vii, ix. The latter concept originated with Thomas Aquinas (see J. Hastings, *Encyclopaedia of Religion and Ethics*, IV, p. 655).
89. Bede looked forward to the *Limbus patrum* when he affirmed that Christ had redeemed those faithful who had been awaiting His coming without suffering the torments of Hell (J. Monnier, *La Descente aux enfers*, p. 159). But it was Thomas Aquinas who, in his *Summa Theologica*, first gave the word *limbus* its theological application. Thereafter there was a division between the *Limbus infantium* (or *puerorum*) and the *Limbus patrum*. For a discussion of Aquinas' attitude to the Harrowing and the evacuation of the *Limbus patrum* see Monnier, ibid., pp. 169 ff.
90. Frank, ed., p. v. The scene is treated in ll. 855–92.
91. For information on its history and use see J. T. Welter, *L'Exemplum dans la littérature religieuse et didactique du moyen âge* (Paris, 1927).
92. See above, p. 78 n. 13.
93. Ed. W. Foerster, *Li Dialoge Grégoire lo Pape*, printed with the Latin text. L. Wiese's conclusion (*Die Sprache der Dialoge des Papstes Gregor* [Halle, 1900]) that it was written by 1152 is questioned by Paul Meyer (*Romania* XXIX [1900], p. 319).
94. See E. Schwan, "La Vie des anciens Pères" *Romania* XIII (1884), pp. 233–63, for manuscripts and a discussion of authorship. For the Vitae Patrum, see above, p. 14.
95. Above, pp. 88–9.
96. For the text as contained in the *Vitae Patrum*, Book VI, see J. P. Migne, *Patrologia Latina*, Vol. 73, cols. 995–8. The account given by Honoré d'Autun in his *Speculum Ecclesie*, III, is in *Patrologia Latina*, Vol. 172, cols. 866–7. The tale has been printed by J. Klapper, *Exempla aus Handschriften des Mittelalters* (Heidelberg, 1911), No. 22, and he gives further references.
97. See I. Levy, "La Légende de l'ange et l'hermite dans les écrits juifs", *Revue des Études juives* 8 (1884), pp. 64–73. See especially p. 72.
98. See above, p. 12.
99. Passages in other eschatological texts show interesting analogies with the three "gueules" in which this wheel turns. They seem to correspond to the three rivers seen in conjunction with a fiery wheel by an unnamed visionary, as described in a Priscillianist apocalypse printed by H. T. Silverstein from an eighth- or ninth-century manuscript (*Visio Sancti Pauli*, p. 76): "In medio eius rotam et angelo tartarucho cum uirgis ferreis percutientis rotam et inde uoluitur in gyru et flumine tres."

Cf. too the three pools (of boiling gold, icy lead, and iron) in the *Vision of Thespesios* (above, p. 34). In the *Revelation of Peter* and the *Sibylline Oracles*, wheels of fire revolve in a river (M. R. James, *The Apocryphal New Testament*, pp. 517, 523).

100. See A. Weber, "Zu den Legenden der 'Vie des peres' ", *Zeitschrift für Romanische Philologie* I (1877), pp. 357–65.
101. Op. cit., No. 20.
102. Originally composed in Greek in the sixth century and translated into Latin by Paulus Diaconus in the ninth, it passed into French in the twelfth century and soon became popular in dramatic and non-dramatic form. It contains no actual descent theme, since Theophilus makes his pact at a lonely spot outside the city wall.
103. A. Graf, *The Story of the Devil* (tr. E. N. Stone), pp. 131–4.
104. For various versions see E. Kuhn, "Barlaam und Joasaph", *Abhandlungen der k. bayer. Akademie der Wissenschaften*, I Kl., XX Bd., I Abt. (Munich, 1893); and H. R. Patch, *The Other World*, pp. 102–4. Gui de Cambrai's version is edited by C. Appel (Halle, 1907): see ll. 12891–905.
105. See Paul Meyer, "Les anciens traducteurs français de Végèce et en particulier Jean de Vignai", *Romania* XXV (1896), pp. 405 ff.; Christine Knowles, "Jean de Vignay : un traducteur du XIVᵉ siècle", *Romania* LXXV (1954), pp. 353–77. For his translation of the *Speculum* I have used the copy in Paris, B.N., MS fr. 52. Jean belonged to the Order of Saint Jacques du Haut Pas.
106. There are some defects in Jean's rendering of our legends. For instance, the rubric of the first (assigned to Book XXVIII, Ch. 85) reads : "D'un enfant qui avoit nom Guillaume qui fu crucefiés des Juyfs, par qui la revelation d'enfer fu faite" (B.N., fr. 52, fol. 170ʳ⁻ᵛ). There is a confusion here with William of Norwich, who was martyred by the Jews in 1144 and whom the boy William sees in his vision of Paradise. And in the *Vision of Gunthelm*, Jean omits the novice's wish to take the cross.
107. See H. J. Chaytor, *From Script to Print* (Cambridge, 1945), Ch. V.
108. Ed. A. Jubinal, La Légende latine de s. Brandaines (Paris, 1836), pp. 105–64; A. Hilka, *Drei Erzählungen aus dem didaktischen Epos "L'Image du Monde"* (Halle, 1928), Part I. Jubinal used Paris, B.N., MS fr. 1444, and Hilka Berlin, Staatsbibliothek, MS Hamilton 577. For a discussion of authorship and date see C. Fant, *L'Image du Monde : poème inédit du milieu du XIIIᵉ siècle* (Uppsala, 1886); and O. H. Prior, *L'Image du Monde de Maître Gossouin* (Lausanne, 1913).
109. Hilka, op. cit., ll. 5–12. An almost identical statement occurs in ll. 1767–74.
110. *Die altfranzösische Prosaübersetzung von Brendans Meerfahrt*, pp. 3–101, 103–201.
111. For example, on p. 83 he seems to have had difficulty with *Leviatan*, which he renders as *li dyables*; on p. 85 *faciem Thetidis* has become *le fache de Theodis*, and *refrigerium* ("respite") is translated by *refroidement*.
112. Their dating ranges from the thirteenth to the fifteenth century. Wahlund chooses as a representative text that in Paris, Bibliothèque Mazarine, MS 1716, though it is incomplete at the beginning and the end. Extracts are given from fifteen other MSS, and several more can

be classified in the same group. The usual *incipit* is: "En la vie monseigneur s. Brandan, qui moult est deliteuse ..." An abridged version of the legend is found as an interpolation in the translation of Jacobus a Voragine's *Legenda Aurea* by Jean Belet (ca. 1300); and there the relevant episodes take much the same form as here.

113. Examples of poor translation are *hideus* for *hispidus* (p. 177—on p. 183 it is not translated at all), and *seiche* for *scoriosam* (p. 177). On p. 183 *Leviatan* is rendered by le satan, perhaps through a misreading of an intermediate French text; and on p. 185 the mention of Thetis is omitted. Among the author's abridgments is the description of the smoking mountain.

114. Ed. C. Wahlund, "Eine altprovenzalische Prosaübersetzung von Brendans Meerfahrt", *Festgabe für W. Foerster* (Halle, 1901), pp. 129 ff.; also published separately. Wahlund gives a diplomatic transcription from Paris, B.N., MS fr. 9759 alongside the Latin text as found in Paris, B.N., MS lat. 755.

115. See C. Boser in *Romania* XXII (1893), p. 584.

116. Ed. Mario Roques (Paris, 1948), ll. 2435–8. See Horst Baader's comments in *Die Lais* (Frankfurt am Main, 1966), pp. 35, 233, 235.

117. See later, pp. 190–4.

118. Paul Meyer, "Satire en vers rythmiques sur la légende de saint Brendan", *Romania* XXXI (1902), pp. 376–9. The manuscript dates from the thirteenth century, the poem itself from perhaps the eleventh or early twelfth (J. F. Kenney, *The Sources for the Early History of Ireland: Ecclesiastical*, p. 417).

119. G. G. Coulton (*Five Centuries of Religion* [Cambridge, 1923–50], I, p. 61) quotes evidence from the *Speculum Morale* (late thirteenth-century) that many at that time refused credence to the narrators of visions; and the Brendan legend is very akin to such works.

120. *La Vision de Tondale (Tnugdal)*, pp. 3–62.

121. Paris, B.N., fr. 763, and fr. 12555. The latter seems a copy of the former (Friedel & Meyer, p. 3).

122. The translator calls it Acherouse, "quar elle acoure et deuore les auers ..." (p. 15).

123. See, e.g., Friedel & Meyer, ed., pp. 34–5, and p. 37, ll. 14–15. The translator even ascribed the writing of the *Vision* to St Bernard "quant il escrit la uie saint Malachie, quar elle est iqui escripte" (p. 57: see the editors' explanation, p. 4).

124. "In inferno non est redemptio" (p. 20, l. 18).

125. He himself used an abridgment by Helinand (placed in his *Chronicon* under the year 1149). See H. L. D. Ward, *Catalogue of Romances*, II, p. 424; A. Mussafia, *Sulla Visione di Tundalo*, pp. 7–9.

126. Paris, B.N., MS n.a.fr. 10059 (fol. 175ᵛ–182ʳ) contains a direct translation from Vincent. The *incipit* is: "Cy comance le livre des painnes de purgatoire et d'enfer, ... lequel livre a esté translaté de latin en françois et extrait d'un livre appellé le Miroir des Ystoires." Similarly, the B.N. MS fr. 1556 begins: "Vincent en son Miroiier Historial raconte ..." (here the legend occupies fol. 103ʳ–107ᵛ). This rendering is truncated and much abbreviated.

127. B.N. fr. 12445, fol. 68ʳ–79ʳ (from which I quote), and Arsenal 5366.

128. B.N. n.a.fr. 6524 (fol. 66ʳ–93ᵛ), and Arsenal 3622 (41 folios). The Arsenal MS was written in a north-eastern dialect in the year 1442,

as we learn from a note added by the copyist. That in the B.N., which lacks such information, seems to be a copy of the other in a dialect rather nearer to Francien.

129. Ed. A. Jeanroy & A. Vignaux, *Voyage au Purgatoire de St. Patrice, Visions de Tindal et de St. Paul.* See above, p. 91.

130. Departures from the Latin are indicated at the foot of the text. See, too, Jeanroy's comments on pp. xxvi–xxviii.

131. A. Wagner, *Visio Tnugdali: lateinisch und altdeutsch,* pp. ix–xx. The distribution is: Germany 25, Austria 15, Italy 4, England and Ireland 6, Belgium 2, Paris 1, St Gall 1.

132. See C. Fritzsche, "Die lateinischen Visionen des Mittelalters . . .", *Romanische Forschungen* 3, p. 361; R. Verdeyen & J. Endepols, *Tondalus' Visioen en St. Patricius' Vagevuur,* Vol. I, Part II, Ch. II & III.

133. Wagner, op. cit., p. xxxi.

134. Ed. A. de Montaiglon (Paris, 1854), pp. 73–9. For the dating see p. xiv.

135. I see more parallels with the *Vision of Tundal* than with those of Gregory's *Dialogues* that contain similar themes (see above, pp. 11–12). The lady's character, the period of her trance, the infernal and celestial aspects of her vision, her recovery and conversion are all reminiscent of *Tundal.*

136. See above, p. 49, n. 23.

137. Above, pp. 45–6.

138. Ed. M. Mörner, *Le Purgatoire de saint Patrice du MS de la Bibliothèque Nationale fonds fr. 25545* (Lund, 1920). The date and provenance are discussed on pp. xxvi–xxvii. The *terminus ad quem* is 1317.

139. Summarised in Mörner's edition, p. xv.

140. The parts of the *Tractatus* most commonly omitted in the Latin texts were those not directly treating the Purgatory or the hero (ibid., p. xiv).

141. E.g. ll. 15, 454, 460, 619–20.

142. L. 617 (cf. Mörner, ed., p. xi).

143. See above, pp. 89–90. I quote from the Paris, B.N., MS fr. 1526, where the legend is found on fol. 154 ff.

144. Cf. Paul Meyer in *Notices et extraits . . .,* 39.1 (1909), pp. 309–14. The prose version is edited by P. Tarbé, *Li Purgatoire de saint Patrice* (Rheims, 1842). It is normally recognised without difficulty by its *incipit*: "En cel tens que seinz Patrices li granz preeschoit en Yrlande de la parole de Dieu, nostre Sires conferma son preeschement par glorieus miracles." Some idea of its popularity is given by the fact that the Bibliothèque Nationale in Paris has at least fourteen manuscripts that contain it.

145. See Paul Meyer in *Histoire littéraire de la France* 33, p. 400.

146. I have found two dating from the fifteenth or sixteenth century (Paris, B.N., fr. 25549, and fr. 25553) in which the number of messengers is increased by one. This may be due to analogy with Christ and the twelve disciples rather than to a misreading.

147. I.e. after § 6, p. 144, of Warnke's edition of the *Tractatus.*

148. Geoffroi, fol. 159ᵛ, ll. 678–84; cf. Warnke, op. cit., p. 72.

149. Ibid., p. 36.

150. See above, p. 91. *St Patrick's Purgatory* is found on fol. 86ʳ–111ᵛ.

151. Fol. 137ᵛ–141ʳ. The *incipit* is: "Sains Patris preeschoit en Irlande. Et pour ce que il trouvoit la gent bestial, grant paine metoit de eulz

retraire de lor errour pour la pauour d'infer et pour l'amour des joyes de
paradis."

152. There is, for instance, a further version in two Paris MSS (B.N.,
n.a.fr. 20001 [13th century], and Arsenal 2114, fol. 174ʳ-192ᵛ [15th
century]). The anonymous author ends with some laudatory remarks
on the "moynes gris de l'ordre de saint Benoist".

153. Ed. Th. Graesse (2nd edn., Leipzig, 1850).

154. This translation is found in three manuscripts and some *incunabula*
(see R. Bossuat, *Manuel bibliographique de la littérature française du
moyen âge* [Melun, 1951], No. 4889, p. 464). I have used the Paris,
B.N., MS fr. 183 (fol. 242ᵛ-248ʳ).

155. Published by Pierce Butler, *Legenda Aurea—Légende Dorée—Golden
Legend* (Baltimore, 1899), pp. 122-30. For the date see Bossuat, loc.
cit. ; and on Jean de Vignay see above, p. 116.

156. See later, pp. 219-22.

157. The common prose version must have been written before 1243, when
Geoffroi de Paris translated it ; and the legend was known to Caesarius of
Heisterbach in the first half of the thirteenth century (see above, p. 68).

CHAPTER V

ANTIQUITY AND ISLAM

I F it fell to the Christian witnesses to etch the main contours
of Hell on the minds of medieval men, accounts from beyond
Christendom could serve to impress further upon those who
read or heard them that this was a place of universal punishment
which no sinner could escape. The word of the good pagan,
Virgil, was particularly worthy of esteem; for though the
twelfth century may have earned the label "aetas virgiliana",
the Latin poet's popularity, not only as literary model but also
as prophet and even magician, persisted throughout the Middle
Ages.[1] Of his influence on certain Christian legends I have
already spoken.[2] So it is fitting that we should turn first to him
in this excursus from the main line of our study.

It was in the third quarter of the twelfth century that an unknown poet "translated" the *Aeneid* into French as the *Roman
d'Eneas*.[3] The whole work is rather an adaptation than a
translation, and this is true of the sixth Book, where the hero's
descent into Hades is described.[4] I shall not summarise the
well-known story, but see only how the Old French text
diverges from its model; and for this purpose I take Virgil to
be the model, though it has been suggested that the Frenchman
may have worked from an intermediate Latin prose translation.[5]

The first thing we notice is the comparative brevity of the
episode in *Eneas*, where some 768 octosyllabic lines do duty for
about 900 of Virgil's hexameters. It smacks almost of the
résumé, couched as it is in simple, direct language quite lacking
the richness and polish of its source. Simplification is the key-
note, and it is carried to the point of omitting many of the
proper names that appear in the original and which might have
been unfamiliar to a twelfth-century public. For example, the
name of the Sibyl, Deiphobe, is not mentioned; the Centaurs,
Scyllas, Gorgons and Harpies, Briareus, the Chimaera and the

142

beast of Lerna are lumped together as "mostres orribles / et granz et laiz et molt terribles" (ll. 2421-3); and the meeting with the shade of Palinurus is left out. On the other hand, the poet of the *Eneas* had a fondness for portraits, which he sometimes develops more fully than did Virgil, not always without changing the nature of the person or thing described. For instance, his Sibyl of Cumae less resembles Virgil's divinely inspired priestess than a medieval witch. Charon's appearance is even more grotesque and terrifying than in the original. And most interesting of all is the change that has come over Cerberus (ll. 2563-78): his legs and feet are shaggy, with hooked toes and claws like those of a griffon; his back is sharp and bent, with a hump on the spine, while from narrow shoulders hang massive arms with hands like hooks; on his three sinuous necks are manes of serpents, and three dog-like heads complete the hideous picture. No longer is he a monstrous dog, but rather a dog-like demon with arms and hands instead of legs and paws. Though he certainly has some diabolical characteristics in Classical legend, he is still more of a mythological figure than what we think of as a demon. But in the Frenchman's description we see a stage in the process of degeneration of figures from Classical myth that took place in the Middle Ages. In the case of Cerberus, this process was to continue until he was able to figure on the stage as one of the principal devils in the mystery plays.

The French poet made a number of his own additions, as he did throughout his work. He had demonstrated before his interest in the *merveilleux* and in what passed in his day for general knowledge, so we are not surprised to find an account of the flowers springing from the slaver that fell from Cerberus' jaws.[6] The magic ointment with which the Sibyl anoints Eneas in order to protect him from the stench of Hades is another addition and a feature typical of twelfth-century romance literature (ll. 2393-6). Evidently the poet was puzzled by the function of Aeneas' drawn sword, not realising that steel is a potent protection against malicious spirits;[7] so he states that it provided the light by which the hero was able to see in the Underworld. A further modification of the original is that instead of the Sibyl throwing a drugged cake to Cerberus, she puts him to sleep by casting a spell over him in good medieval fashion.[8]

The possibility that the writer was using a version of the *Aeneid* different from that which we know is perhaps strengthened by one or two changes he has made in the description of Tartarus and its inmates. The crime of Tityos is described (ll. 2737–9), whereas the Latin poem remains silent on the point ; and of greater note is the medieval writer's rejection of Virgil's account of Tantalus' torment (the forbidden banquet) in favour of the more widely known version, found also in Ovid, of the unattainable water and fruit.[9] But it is equally possible that he was using his knowledge of other Classical texts, and particularly of Ovid, to fill out and modify his story. On the other hand, there is one omission that is rather unexpected when we think of the vogue which the particular feature was to have in Christian descriptions of the lower world. I refer to Virgil's mention of the wheels of torment,[10] which remains untranslated in *Eneas*.

One or two reminiscences of Christian eschatological teachings are introduced by the Frenchman. One wonders if the undue emphasis he places on the stench of Hades does not owe something to the *Vision of St Paul* or some similar text. In the same way, his description of the dark fire of Tartarus seems to owe more to the early Christian tradition than to Virgil.[11] This whole passage, where the torments are characterised in general terms and the eternity of the pains is stressed, may be contrasted with the corresponding passage in the *Aeneid*, where it is the crimes rather than the punishments that are described.[12] A moralising touch, too, is added to the lines describing Aeneas' meeting with the shade of Dido.[13] Virgil intended this encounter to represent the purification of and final judgment on their earthly love, for he shows the queen pausing with downcast eyes, then fleeing to join her former husband Sychaeus. But to the Frenchman this was unnatural, since though she was a widow when she met Aeneas, she had still broken her marriage vows to her dead husband. So he shows her holding aloof from him when they meet in the next life ; and as A. Pauphilet points out, this reflects the Church's standpoint that marriage was a bond that even death could not sunder. We also notice that our poet insists less on the presiding influence of the gods than did Virgil, even suppressing the names of Phoebus and Hecate. Perhaps, as Pauphilet suggests, he was conscious of an excess of paganism in the Latin poet, who was trying to illustrate the antiquity of certain Roman religious traditions. This may be so, yet he even exceeds Virgil's paganism in one instance, namely when he indicates in two places that the gods above have no power over the lower realms (ll. 2383-4, 2484-6). But it would be wrong to lay much stress on this, when we have seen his Christian beliefs strongly reflected in his general treatment of the episode.

This continental Frenchman, then, preoccupied as he was with Classical legend, does show through his work as a man of his own age. It has often been noted that his hero is more of a feudal knight than a Roman (or Trojan) figure, but the fact that for him Hades was much the same as the Christian Hell has drawn rather less attention. There can be little doubt that he was a clerk who had passed through the schools, and the theological side of his training seems to have remained strongly impressed on his mind. But for all that, it is clear that he enjoyed his excursion into the Virgilian underworld.

Following Virgil, the author of *Eneas* alluded on two occasions to previous descents into Hades, namely those of Orpheus, Hercules, Theseus, and Pirithoüs (omitting that of Pollux).[14] He might have known more of these from other Classical writers, perhaps even have treated Orpheus' descent[15] in a lost poem, for we know that it formed the theme of at least one twelfth-century work. Gaston Paris, in discussing the medieval French versions of the legend,[16] shows that such a poem existed in the form of a *lai*, but has not survived. From references in certain French texts and from the late thirteenth-century English version, *Sir Orfeo*, it would appear that the lay had more Celtic than Classical features, and that Orpheus' descent had become a visit to a fairy realm. In other words, the myth had lost its infernal characteristics and become assimilated into the popular Matter of Britain.[17]

As far as we can tell, with one exception the story only passed

into French in an authentic form by way of Boethius' *De
Consolatione Philosophiae*, where it is briefly recounted in Book
III, Ch. 12. This influential work was several times translated
into the vernacular, but there is no extant twelfth-century
rendering that contains the Orpheus episode.[18] This does,
however, appear to have been the source of a French rhymed
version of the story which was found in a Geneva manuscript in
fragmentary form and published by E. Ritter.[19] Although
the copy dates from the fifteenth century, the poem's simplicity
of form and language suggest a very much earlier date of composition. Having removed the story from its context in Boethius, the author evidently continued with a description of
the trials of Hercules, including the descent into Hades to
bring back Cerberus:

> *Ausi te vueil je raconter*
> *Coment Hercules pot donter*
> *Cerberus le portier d'enfer*
> *Qui ne dotoit acier ne fer:*
> *Hercules ot un compagnion*
> *Qui Piritous avoit a non,*
> *Qui forment ama d'amor fine*
> *La dame [d'enfer Proserpine] ...*

(ll. 152–9)

(I want to tell you too how Hercules was able to overcome
Hell's porter Cerberus, who feared neither steel nor iron:
Hercules had a companion, Pirithoüs by name, who was
stricken with a noble love for the lady [of Hell, Proserpine].)

So here we have one more fragment of a Classical descent story
in French verse. One cannot suggest the source (it was not
Boethius); but if we can judge from the poet's treatment of
the Orpheus story, he was not one to follow his model slavishly.
For he had elaborated that tale to some extent, seemingly from
his own knowledge of Classical lore (and doubtless bearing in
mind the Christian tradition too). Thus Ixion's wheel, referred to in two lines by Boethius, is here treated in fourteen:
it whirls unceasingly, with its victim attached by feet, hands and
head; but so sweetly did Orpheus play his "instrument" that

it stopped its turning, as if to listen to the melody. The fragment ends in the middle of a similarly amplified account of the
punishment of Tantalus.

Gaston Paris mentions the Orpheus episode included by
Guillaume de Machaut in *Le Confort d'Ami*[20] as being probably
derived from Boethius. But this is doubtful, since Guillaume
mentions the torments of Sisyphus and the Belides, who appear
in Ovid but not in Boethius (or in Virgil). There is, however,
no close similarity with the passage in the *Metamorphoses*; so
perhaps the answer is that Guillaume used none of these
directly, but some other work—maybe a medieval compilation
of Classical legends, since he goes on to speak of Paris and
Helen and of some of the adventures of Hercules. It is interesting to see that Ixion's wheel is said to be surrounded by other,
burning wheels (l. 2525), and that Pluto is also called Lucifer
(l. 2626). Here is a further instance of the influence of the
Christian legends upon the Classical; and Gaston Paris provides another when he mentions a translation of the *De Consolatione* into French by an Italian. This fourteenth-century
writer has made "Olfeus" visit Hell on the suggestion of a
demon, who conducts him thither; and in Hell there was no
devil so roasted that he did not contribute to the laughter with
which the place rang because of the hero's wild exhibition of
joy on finding his wife. The usual pact is made, but Orpheus
loses Eurydice for the second time by turning round, not to
look at her, but because of the terrible noise made by a demon
at his back.[21]

One more presentation of the Orpheus myth must be mentioned. It is included in the long *Ovide moralisé*, of unknown
authorship and compiled late in the thirteenth or early in the
fourteenth century.[22] Here, of course, we have the tale subjected to an allegorical interpretation, but the poet first gives a
straightforward rendering of the account from Ovid in quite
accomplished verse. Then he draws his moral—Orpheus, for
instance, is equated with reason and Eurydice with sensuality;
spiritual and moral properties are attributed to the rivers of
Hades; and allegorical meanings are given to the torments of
Tantalus, Ixion, Theseus and the Belides. And lastly he supplies a religious interpretation of the descent: God was married

to the human soul, but the union was broken through Eve's encounter with the serpent, so that all humanity had to suffer infernal torment.

> *De ce se dolut Diex forment,*
> *Qui l'ame avoit predestinee*
> *Estre s'amie et s'espousee.*
> *Pour la delivrer et requerre*
> *Vault Diex venir dou ciel en terre*
> *Et descendre en la chartre obscure*
> *D'enfer, pour humaine nature*
> *Traire de l'infernal prison*
> *Et pour la metre a guarison.*

(ll. 477–85)[23]

(Greatly did God grieve thereat, for He had destined the soul to be His beloved and His bride. To seek out and deliver it God deigned to come down from Heaven to earth and descend into Hell's dark prison, in order to release human-kind from infernal captivity into salvation.)

Thus we have a typically medieval attempt to bring the Classical legend into line with Christian thought and to suggest in Orpheus a prefiguration of Christ.

As regards, then, the vernacular treatment of the Orpheus story, though nothing has survived that can be attributed to the twelfth century, it did form the subject of a *lai*, albeit probably tricked out in fashionable Celtic costume. From the thirteenth century come translations of the episode in Boethius and per-haps the allegorisation carried out by that pious admirer of the Classics, the author of the *Ovide moralisé*. And in the next century we found a Christianising tendency in Machaut's treatment, as in that of the anonymous Italian who, however, seems primarily to have treated it as an adventure story.

This common propensity to Christianise a Classical story is further illustrated by an episode in the *Roman de Thebes*.[24] Though not a true visit to Hell in that the victim does not return to earth, this incident is treated in a way very reminiscent of the author of the *Roman d'Eneas*. At least it is so treated in one text, that of the Spalding manuscript, which dates from the late fourteenth century, although the *Thebes* itself is likely to have been composed before the *Eneas*.[25] This would therefore appear to be an interpolation, despite the editor's claim that the Spalding manuscript in a number of cases conserves earlier readings than do the others.

The passage in question concerns the death of Amphiaraus. The main text describes briefly (ll. 4832–8) how, amid thunder and earthquake and in fulfilment of his own prediction, the earth opened and swallowed up the hero as it did for Dathan and Abiron. This, with the added biblical allusion, is a terse paraphrase of the account at the end of Book VII of Statius' *Thebaid*. The Spalding manuscript substitutes a longer description inspired, perhaps, by the beginning of the following book of the *Thebaid*, but in its detail more reminiscent of Virgil, and with some admixture of general Christian eschatological lore. There Amphiaraus falls into Hell, the abode of the wretched. He draws his sword, passes the three-headed porter at the gate, and comes to Acheron, a dark, serpent-infested river. Along with his company, who had been engulfed with him, he crosses by a plank ("une planche", l. 4491, reminding us forcibly of the bridge over the infernal river as found in such legends as the *Vision of St Paul*). Next Amphiaraus reaches the river Cochiton with its two ferrymen Acheron and Acharon. It is all ablaze and full of lamenting people. He and his followers pass over and arrive at yet another river, this time full of dragons :

> *Plius est trenchant que nuls rasours,*
> *Plus tost cort qe ne vole ostours.*

(ll. 4521–2)[26]

(It is more cutting than any razor, and flows more swiftly than hawk can fly.)

This is Styx and has no bridge. Tisiphone, with her mane of serpents, bathes there and howls like a wolf. She threatens him with an evil fate for having entered Hell on horseback ; but he passes on, much afraid, and comes at last to King Pluto, who strikes him dead with his trident.

It is hardly surprising that medieval writers should have fallen back on the Christian vision of Hell in their treatment of these Classical descents. It is not merely a question of their having been steeped in that tradition in the schools. The Church saw Hell as one and indivisible and as peopled by sinners from all places and times since the Creation, so there would be no question of one place of torment for the pagan and another for the lapsed member of Christendom. Moreover, as we have found, a number of Classical features had been taken over into the orthodox Christian picture and would have been familiar landmarks to medieval man. And similarly, when he was shown the Moslem otherworld and its denizens, he would have had little difficulty in recognising his whereabouts.

The *Livre de l'Eschiele Mahomet*[27] is a translation into French of a Moslem *hadith* dealing with the Prophet's ascension to Heaven and his sight of the infernal pains. We learn from the proem that it is the work of a certain Bonaventura da Siena, who turned a Castilian version into French and also into Latin in the year 1264.[28] Bonaventura was notary and secretary to King Alfonso X of Castile, and made his translations at the instance of his master. His model was a rendering from the Arabic by a Jew, Abraham alfaquím, and begins: "Ci est li livre qe hom appele en sarrazinois 'halmaereig' que volt tant dire en françois come: monter en alt."

Bonaventura translated the work, he says, for two reasons. The first was to please the king; the second was so that true Christians, hearing all the perverse and incredible things told in the book, should be the more confirmed in their own faith. And he adds that if his French is less well turned than it might be, those expert in the language should forgive him, since it is better that they should have what he has to tell thus than not at all.

With Gabriel as his guide, Mahomet ascends by a marvellous ladder from the Temple in Jerusalem and is shown the various Heavens and the Earthly Paradise. Then Gabriel informs him that God wishes him to see the regions of the damned so that he may instruct his people. (Chs. I-LIII, pp. 40-154)[29]

Mahomet is told of the seven blazing earths below this one, each surrounded by a fiery sea. They are described, one by one. In the first is a mighty, sterile wind with which God will flay the sinners in Hell before burning them. The second contains huge, poisonous scorpions which carry their venom in long, knotted tails. They flay the sinners and then cover them with their venom so that they become as nothing before being remade and suffering their torment over again. Similar venomous beasts inhabit the third and fourth "terres". The fifth is full of sulphurous stones. The angel of Hell hangs the stones about the necks of sinners, and they are set alight after the wretches have been led to Hell. The sixth region houses all the scrolls on which are inscribed the names of the damned and their several crimes. There, too, is a boiling sea of bitter water where those in torment are forced to bathe and drink until they melt away to nothing. Mahomet and his guide come to the seventh region.

This is the Devil's kingdom, where he dwells with his legions. Since his disobedience and fall from Heaven, he has been fettered with iron chains, one hand in front and the other behind, and his feet likewise. He is so huge that he touches our own earth; and the time will come when he will be sent with his minions to commit ravages here. Half of this "terre" is full of darkness, and beyond is the Devil's castle, burning with black fire and surrounded by pits containing poisonous liquids. On one side of the castle is a gate by which one enters Hell itself, and on the other side is a gate with a great wind beyond. (Chs. LIV-LX, pp. 154-66)

Gabriel then gives the Prophet an account of the wonders that will happen on Judgment Day, including the appearance of the bridge Azirat, which will span the mouth of Hell.[30] The Creation is also described. (Chs. LXI-LXX, pp. 168-88)

When Gabriel is questioned about Hell, he takes Mahomet by the hand and leads him to a place whence he can see Hell with its seven terribly hot gates. In front of each is a crowd of devils and sinners, who are brought there daily so that they can see the delights of Paradise and thereby have their pains redoubled. Before each gate are 70,000 fiery mountains, each with 70,000 fiery springs that give rise to 70,000 blazing rivers with 70,000 fiery castles on their banks, each having 70,000 fiery rooms. In every room are 70,000 fiery and hideous women who torment the sinners with their embraces. By each of the rivers are also 70,000 fiery trees with 70,000 different kinds of fruit to each tree; and in each fruit are 70,000 venomous worms. Beneath each tree are 70,000 dragons and the same number of scorpions tormenting the sinners who wish for death 70,000 times a day.[31] Of the gates of Hell, the first is for idolaters; the second for those who abandoned the true faith; the third for those who amassed ill-gotten gains, and for the people called Gog and Magog; the fourth is for gamblers; the fifth for those who forgot to pray and give alms; the sixth is for those who did not believe God's prophets and messengers; and the seventh is for those who gave poor measure. Of the seven parts of Hell, six are for those who did not follow God whole-heartedly. (Chs. LXXI–LXXII, pp. 188–94)

More signs of the Judgment Day are then described, including the weighing of people's good deeds against their bad. In Chs. LXXVI–LXXVIII (pp. 202–10) comes a further description of the Azirat bridge, which has been created as a test for believers and non-believers. It is set across Hell and is more slender than a hair yet sharper than any sword; and for its whole length it bristles with iron spikes and hooks, longer than lances and all of indescribable sharpness. It has seven stages, each twice as long as the previous one. Unbelievers at once fall off that bridge into Hell; other sinners pass a distance according to their merit. At either end are mighty mountains, and flames rise about those who pass over it. The souls can also see the seven gates of Hell. When the sinner falls, he is reduced to nothing by venomous dragons and scorpions and then remade with seventy thick hides, the space between each being filled with poisonous serpents and scorpions that cause him great anguish; and he burns in the flame 70,000 times a day. The angel describes the crossing of the bridge in detail. Then

Mahomet sees the sowers of discord having their tongues
cut out by fiery scissors, adulterers hanging from fiery hooks,
and loose women spitted and dangling from fiery chains. In
the flames are the proud and tyrannical rich. Mahomet, full
of pity and grief, asks to be led away from this place; and
after a further injunction from Gabriel to preach to his people
of what he has seen, he returns to the earth. He tells his
followers of his experiences, which are recorded. (Chs.
LXXIII–LXXXV, pp. 194–224)

The origin of this legend, and of the other Moslem *hadiths*
treating the ascension of Mahomet, bears comparison with that
of the *Vison of St Paul* or of the Harrowing of Hell. For all
three traditions have sprung from brief scriptural texts, a verse
from the Koran in the case of the *hadith*.[32] The Moslem
legends had acquired an elaborate form by the ninth century—
and we may already speak of legends, since by this time different versions of the traditions had emerged. The text I have
summarised seems to owe its general outline to the *Vision of St
Paul*: the holy person is carried away to see both Heaven and
Hell under the guidance of an angel, who gives a commentary
on the various places and things seen. There are also some
similarities of detail, as the reference to the soul's reading of the
record of its good and bad deeds (p. 178), or the visionary's
great pity for the damned. But for the most part the legend is
filled out with material from scriptural, Egyptian, and other
Eastern sources.

It would be interesting to know if this thirteenth-century
translation stands alone in medieval French literature in showing knowledge of Moslem traditions regarding the visit to Hell.
Cerulli has studied the diffusion in the West of the accounts of
the Prophet's visit to the Otherworld and has investigated the
extent to which Moslem eschatology was known to medieval
authors.[33] Certain aspects of it were known to scholars in
France at least by the twelfth century. Thus Peter the Venerable, Abbot of Cluny, visited Spain in 1141 and had some
Molem texts of this nature translated into Latin. In the following century, Jacques de Vitry, Vincent de Beauvais, and the
Englishman Matthew Paris (of St Albans) show among others

some knowledge of Islamic traditions concerning the Otherworld. But none of the evidence is significant for the descent
theme, nor is it drawn from vernacular texts. Cerulli does,
however, examine Dante's debt to Moslem legend, and his
conclusions are far more modest than the claims of Asín.[34] He
believes Dante may have known some of those minor works in
the field that had been translated into a language known to
him.

The manuscript tradition of the *hadith* that I have analysed
throws some small light on the legend's distribution; for the
French translation is preserved in what seems to be an early
fourteenth-century English manuscript, and the Latin text is
found in a manuscript prepared by a Breton copyist, also in the
fourteenth century. A further manuscript containing the Latin
text was copied, probably in southern France, early in the same
century.[35] Thus, soon after 1300 the story of Mahomet's experiences in the Otherworld was known in the south and north
of France as well as in England.

Unfortunately, this fact is of little help in deciding the
question of Moslem influence on the *Vision of Tundal* or on
Li ver del juïse.[36] It may seem hardly likely that a monk would
consciously illustrate his devout Christian work with the ideas
of the infidel. Yet the Middle Ages are full of such paradoxes;
and in the case of the Benedictine Marcus, it is not impossible
that he may have met, in 1148 or 1149, someone returning from
the second Crusade who brought back with him some odds and
ends of pagan lore. As we saw in an earlier chapter, it is likely
that this widely-travelled author of the *Vision of Tundal* met
the spiritual instigator of that Crusade, St Bernard.

Leaving such speculation aside, I have traced no influence of
the French translation of the *hadith* on any other work, and in
that respect it must stand in isolation on this study. It is interesting to read the translator's declaration of intent: to impress upon Christians the errors of Islam and so strengthen
their own faith. Yet the infernal scenes here are not unlike
those of the Christian pious legends: more involved, maybe,
and richer in architectural detail and precision, but similar in
conception and spirit. Like *Tundal* this is a work too complex
to win wide popularity in its day. Indeed, unlike the vernacular

versions of *Tundal*, its form and purpose and the circumstances of its writing stamp it as primarily the work of a scholar.

At the close of this chapter, the point may again bear making that even the evidence gleaned from outside the Christian context played its part in fixing the medieval gaze on the reality and universality of Hell. Details of the Classical Hades were modified a little so that they should conform with the orthodox picture, but with Moslem legend, sharing as it did some of the sources of the Christian tradition and plainly running parallel to it, even this was unnecessary. And so we see the physical aspect of Hell, which over the centuries had been defined largely through the literary accounts of churchmen, being further displayed in literature that stood quite outside the domain of Christian homiletics. In my remaining chapters will be found numerous examples of what might be called the more secular treatment of the subject; but for the moment we will turn to its use in allegory, where it is still possible for devoutness to co-exist with literary art and artifice.

NOTES

1. See D. Comparetti, *Virgilio nel medio evo* (new edn., 2 vols., Florence 1937); J. W. Spargo, *Virgil the Necromancer* (Harvard Studies in Comparative Literature X, Cambridge, Mass., 1934).
2. Above, pp. ix, 6, 35–6.
3. Ed. J. J. Salverda de Grave (2 vols., Paris, 1925).
4. Ibid., Vol. I; ll. 2253–3020 contain the descent episode. Jessie Crosland ("*Eneas* and the *Aeneid*", *Modern Language Review* XXIX [1934], pp. 282–90) suggests that, apart from the change in Dido's attitude, the French version faithfully reflects the original here (see p. 284). A. Pauphilet made some interesting observations in *Le Legs du moyen âge* (Melun, 1950), Ch. III, "L'Antiquité et *Énéas*" (pp. 91–106). He also treats Aeneas' encounter with Dido in Hades in "Eneas et Énée", *Romania* LV (1929), pp. 195–213.
5. Salverda de Grave, op. cit., pp. xxi–xxii. Mrs Crosland (art. cit., pp. 283–4) seeks to prove that there was no intermediary.
6. Ll. 2580–6. The idea is borrowed from Ovid, *Metamorphoses* VII, ll. 406–20 (see E. Faral, *Recherches sur les sources latines des contes et romans courtois du moyen âge* [Paris, 1913], pp. 111–2).
7. Ll. 2431–4. The sword of Odysseus performed a similar function, and the same belief is found in the Scottish Highlands (W. J. Fielding, *Strange Superstitions and Magical Practices* [Philadelphia, 1945], p. 106).
8. Ll. 2598–2602. Cf. Jason putting to sleep the dragon guarding the golden fleece in Ovid, *Metamorphoses* VII, ll. 152–5 (Faral, op. cit., pp. 114–5).

9. Ll. 2747–52. Cf. Ovid, *Metamorphoses* IV, ll. 458–9, and X, l. 41. The Tantalus torment was well known in medieval France. We have seen it occurring in the *Vision of St Paul*, whence it passed into several French texts; and among other works referring to it are Chrétien's *Guillaume d'Angleterre* (ed. M. Wilmotte [Paris, 1927], ll. 903–24), and the treatments of the Orpheus story discussed below.

10. Book VI, ll. 616–7. The wheel torment is normally allotted to Ixion (cf. *Metamorphoses* X, l. 42).

11. E. J. Becker derives it from the *lux atra* of Virgil (*A Contribution to the Comparative Study of the Medieval Visions of Heaven and Hell*, p. 20); but in Hebrew writings the feature is found as early as the beginning of the Christian era (see e.g. A. Lods, *De quelques récits de voyage au pays des morts*, p. 14; M. Dando, *The Conception of Hell, Purgatory and Paradise in Medieval Provençal Literature* [unpublished London Ph.D. Thesis, 1965], Appendix I).

12. *Eneas*, ll. 2753–82; *Aeneid*, ll. 608–27.

13. Ll. 2651–62. See Pauphilet, *Le Legs* . . . , p. 105, and "Eneas et Enée", pp. 211–2.

14. Ll. 2283–4, 2521–30.

15. From the medieval point of view, the most important appearances of the myth in Classical literature are in Ovid, *Metamorphoses* X, ll. 1–77, and Virgil, *Georgicon* IV, ll. 453–527.

16. "Chrétien Legouais et autres traducteurs ou imitateurs d'Ovide", *Histoire littéraire de la France* 29 (1885), pp. 455–525. See especially pp. 500–2 for a discussion of treatments of the Orpheus legend.

17. The French texts mentioned by Paris are the *Roman des Sept Sages*, *Floire et Blancheflor*, and the *Lai de l'Espine* (ibid., p. 500). The lay's source was probably Ovid (ibid., p. 501). For a detailed discussion of its nature and a reference to it in the Prose *Lancelot*, see Horst Baader, *Die Lais*, pp. 201–11.

18. See A. Thomas, "Traductions françaises de la *Consolatio philosophiae* de Boèce", *Histoire littéraire de la France* 37 (1938), pp. 419–70; L. W. Stone, "Old French Translations of the *De Consolatione Philosophiae* of Boethius: some unnoticed manuscripts", *Medium Ævum* VI (1937), pp. 21–30. The episode is not found in Simund de Freine's adaptation (ed. J. F. Matzke in *Les Œuvres de Simund de Freine* [Paris, 1909], pp. 1–60).

19. In "Notice du MS 179bis de la Bibliothèque de Genève", *Bulletin de la Société des anciens textes français*, 3e année (1877), pp. 85 ff.

20. *Œuvres de Guillaume de Machaut*, ed. E. Hoepffner, III (Paris, 1921), pp. 81 ff.

21. G. Paris, op. cit., pp. 501–2.

22. Ed. C. De Boer, IV (Amsterdam, 1936), ll. 1–577.

23. The divisions of the treatment are as follows: straightforward narration, ll. 1–195; moralising and allegorical treatment, ll. 196–443; religious (anagogic) interpretation, ll. 444–577. For early Christian interpretations of the myth along similar lines, see F. Cabrol & H. Leclercq, *Dictionnaire d'archéologie chrétienne*, Vol. XII (Paris, 1936) under *Orphée* (cols. 2735–55).

24. Ed. L. Constans (2 vols., Paris, 1890).

25. Ibid., II, p. ix for details of the manuscript, and pp. 16–17 for a transcription of the passage.

26. The first part of this description is reminiscent of a common property of the testing bridge of Hell: cf. Geoffroi de Paris' version of the *Vision of St Paul* (ed. L. E. Kastner, "Les Versions françaises . . .", *Revue des Langues Romanes* 49, pp. 321–51), ll. 457–8; also its prototype in the Alexandrine version (above, p. 88). The same quality was attributed to the Azirat bridge of Moslem eschatology, as we shall see. For a river flowing "with swords and daggers" see H. R. Patch, *The Other World*, p. 79.

27. Ed. E. Cerulli, *Il "Libro della Scala" e la questione delle fonti arabo-spagnole della Divina Commedia*, Ch. II.

28. The French and Latin texts are printed on opposite pages. The date is given in the explicit (ibid., p. 224).

29. The whole work is divided into 85 chapters, to which I refer along with the page numbers.

30. For notes on the testing bridge of Eastern tradition see Patch, op. cit., pp. 8-10, 82-3.

31. Such enumerations are typical of this text. I omit the less significant ones.

32. See M. Asín Palacios, *Islam and the Divine Comedy*, p. 3.

33. Op. cit., Parts II & III.

34. Op. cit.

35. Cerulli, op. cit., pp. 15–17.

36. See above, pp. 34, 83–4; also Asín, op. cit., pp. 186–90 for some venturesome theories, which A. B. van Os treats with merited caution (*Religious Visions*, pp. 55–7).

CHAPTER VI

ALLEGORY AND SATIRE

THIS is no place to debate the role and nature of allegory in French medieval literature over which, from the thirteenth century, it exerted a powerful, or some might say maleficent, influence.[1] Small wonder, then, that the theme of the infernal journey soon found itself given an allegorical context; and with the placing of the account of Hell within a shell of literary device, a short step is taken away from the brutally direct confrontation of the sinner with his destiny. This does not, of course, preclude a didactic intention on the part of the author, or even a heavily moralising tone; but for the medieval public the pill was a little sugared.

Allegory, it has been said, is most successful when it is representing strife within the emotions or intellect, the *bellum intestinum*. The simplest presentation of this conflict is as an actual battle; and the cardinal virtues and vices formed natural antagonists in this moral strife. That is how Prudentius conceived his *Psychomachia*.[2] A further way of interpreting a prolonged moral conflict within the human mind is to portray life as a journey upon which the traveller may be subject to temptations, but on other occasions may have his courage and integrity fortified. Such was to be Bunyan's method in his *Pilgrim's Progress*.[3] Raoul de Houdenc was the first French writer we know to have thus allegorised a journey through life, for surely this is what his *Songe d'enfer* represents.[4] But he did it without introducing the element of conflict, and in the *Songe* the progress is all too easy and unopposed.

In a dream, Raoul imagines that he is a pilgrim to the city of Hell, and he describes his journey there by a broad and pleasant route. His way leads him through such places as Convoitise and Foi-Mentie, over the river of Gloutonie to

Vile-Taverne; then on to Chastiau-Bordel, through Cruauté and Cope-Gorge, and on past the gibbet of Murtreville until he comes to Desesperance, the Montjoie of Hell. Close by is Mort-Soubite, which is a kind of infernal outpost. So Raoul arrives in Hell itself to find a welcome awaiting him and the banqueting tables laid; for on that very day the King of Hell is holding court. He is personally greeted by Pilate and Beelzebub and sits down with the company to a fine banquet. Upon tablecloths made of the skins of usurers are served many prime dishes: wrestlers with garlic sauce, roast heretics, the tongues of false advocates choicely grilled, and other courses of the same nature, some too revolting to mention. After the meal the King of Hell commands Raoul to read to him from a book of the deeds of wicked minstrels and, well pleased with the performance, pays him royally. Then all the inhabitants set out like knights to seek their prey in the world. So Raoul takes his leave amid warm farewells; and at that moment he wakes.

Raoul de Houdenc seems to have enjoyed a fair reputation in his day, and we shall see that this particular work left its mark on French medieval literature. He was quite a fluent versifier, and his story progresses at a lively pace (it is told in 682 octosyllabic lines). Up to a point, the allegory is well maintained; but it breaks down completely when the pilgrim reaches the goal of his journey, the city of Hell. Apart from the "King of Hell" the principal figures there are Beelzebub and Pilate, both accepted as devils in the Middle Ages. And the feast itself is not described in allegorical terms: it is a simple burlesque, and the details are divulged with repugnant realism. Here Raoul's aim is unambiguous: it is to write a biting satire on the social evils of his day. Every type of miscreant forms an accoutrement to the banquet or else an actual dish—monks and nuns along with robbers and courtesans. So what from another pen could have been an allegorical poem of pious enlightenment has lapsed into rough satire; and clearly it was in this part of his work that Raoul revelled (the final episode in Hell takes no fewer than 300 lines). The result is a sad lack of unity in the poem as a whole on the tonal as well as the structural level. From the

moral point of view, too, one has misgivings. A mortal makes
a not disagreeable journey to Hell, where he is bountifully
welcomed and feasted and sent rejoicing on his way back to
earth. The paradoxical, we might think, verges here on the
flippant.

Whatever the work's technical flaws, we cannot deny to
Raoul the distinction of pioneering the allegorical treatment of
the theme of the infernal journey. He was writing in the early
years of the thirteenth century; but although he composed
other works, there is nowhere any real clue as to his identity.
The common view is that he was a cleric, probably from the
Beauvaisis;[5] and certainly he appears to have received his
literary training in the schools, though the tone of the *Songe* is
secular and unclerical in the extreme. Heretics do come in for
strenuous treatment at his hands (he only devotes less space to
them than to the doxies); and one might point to a pious note
at the end, where he expresses the hope of escaping Hell and
gaining Paradise (ll. 697–82). But this is a pale and conventional
tribute to his religion, insufficient to persuade us that Raoul
was writing from within the Church.

Perhaps the last section of the poem gives an indication as to
his real state. There we are told how he reads aloud to the King
of Hell from a book containing the lives of the "fols menestrels"
(l. 626). He recited, he says, "si bel, si bien, si leonime" as he
could (l. 636), covering the complete list of the crimes and vices
of these men and concluding:

> *Je reting du livre par cuer*
> *Les noms, et les faiz et les diz,*
> *Dont je cuit encore biaus diz*
> *Dire sanz espargnier nului.*   (ll. 648–51)

(From the book I learnt by heart their names, and what they
said and did; and I intend to use this to compose more good
poems, without sparing anybody.)

At first sight, one might think this good evidence that Raoul
was not himself a *menestrel*, but this is not necessarily so. What
is certain is that he was an enemy of the "fols menestrels"—
an enemy, or a rival? He could well be indulging here in one

of the medieval minstrels' favourite pastimes : taunting their rivals. He has remembered their names—why should a monk or priest wish to keep a mental note of the names of minstrels? Raoul says that he will write more verse attacking them. The clergy may have had very mixed feelings towards these people,[6] but they were not in the habit of making direct, personal attacks on them in the vernacular. Furthermore, Raoul seems to be pleading their cause in at least one instance, namely when he refers to the parsimony prevalent in his day. Only in Hell are all and sundry invited to feasts :

> Iceste coustume est faussée
> En France; chascuns clot sa porte:
> Nus n'entre léenz, s'il n'aporte;
> Ce veons nous tout en apert.

(ll. 380–3)[7]

(That custom has lapsed in France ; every one shuts his door : nobody gets in unless he brings something; that is quite plain to see.)

Surely the inference is that here we have a sharp-tongued clerk who has passed through the schools and who, while retaining his religious loyalties, has sought to make his living in the world of secular entertainment. I suggest, then, that he was no priest or monk, nor a jongleur of low degree, but a *menestrel* exploiting the patronage of the wealthy. His treatment of the descent theme is irreverent by our standards, no doubt less so by his own, but certainly not such as would have been dreamed up in the cloister.

Evidence of the esteem in which Raoul was held by at least one of his near-contemporaries is to be found in Huon de Méry's *Tournoiement Antecrist*, written in the year 1234 or soon after.[8] Huon does not disguise his admiration for Raoul, from whom, along with Chrétien de Troyes, he frequently quotes. Much of the material for his poem is taken direct from the *Songe d'Enfer* : Huon is taken to the city of Desesperance, the Montjoie of Hell, to witness the tourney between the heavenly hosts and the powers of darkness. The latter are largely figures from Classical mythology.[9] But this cannot strictly be described as a visit to Hell, since it is clear from the end of the poem that Desesperance is some distance from Hell itself, for the fleeing infernal armies have to take the road described by Raoul to return to their base after the tourney.

About Christmas time in 1340, the Flemish poet Jehan de le Mote finished writing his *Voie d'enfer et de paradis* for Simon de Lille, citizen of Paris and goldsmith to the King of France.[10] In a way, he may be said to continue the tradition of the allegorical journey to Hell begun by Raoul de Houdenc; but there is no indication that he knew the *Songe*, and his approach to the subject is very different, as will be seen from the following summary.

In his sleep one night, Jehan is seized by the desire to travel the road to Hell. Murdre and his pretty wife Desesperance take it upon themselves to be his guides. The journey will take seven days and nights, and on the eighth day he will see Hell within, without, and on all sides. On each of the seven nights of the journey Jehan is lodged with a figure named after one of the Seven Deadly Sins,[11] and they all travel on with him in an ever-growing company. But as Hell is almost reached, the poet senses his folly and tries to escape. At that moment he sees a dark man riding on a black bullock: it is Mors, who immediately strikes him with one of his darts so that he falls lifeless. Jehan's soul is terrified by the appearance of a group of demons and vermin. He is escorted to Hell itself, with its fire-girt wall.

> *Ou mur estoit uns maisonné*
> *Dedens mis et enseëlé:*
> *Seulement chil qui sont parjure*
> *La ardent yver et esté.*

(ll. 1873–6)

(In the wall was set a sealed chamber: there only the perjurers burn, winter and summer.)

There now begins a dispute as to which of his escort is to dispose of the soul, that is to say into which category of sinners he is to be placed. Shall he hang on a gibbet with the gluttons, who dangle above a fire with vermin gnawing their bodies ? Is he to be flung on to a blazing bed, where the slothful are embraced by demons ? Avarice wishes to immure him in a cellar, where sinners have molten gold poured down their throats, or lie on red-hot coins, or are spitted and immersed in boiling water with purses tied round their necks. Ire then leads him to a black, freezing river from which the four chilling winds arise. All his companions try to throw Jehan into this river, where other sinners are immersed; but as he is already flying through the air, his soul is suddenly comforted because of a prayer he had once offered to the Virgin Mary. The devils are dismayed, but Jehan's soul is carried by angels back to his body, which had lain in a ditch since being struck by the dart of Mors.[12]

There follows a vision of Paradise.

Although for the modern reader Raoul de Houdenc's poem may hold more interest than Jehan's, the latter shows greater technical merit. It is written in twelve-line strophes having the rhyme scheme *aab aab bba bba*, a poetic form found from the end of the twelfth century.[13] In some passages, such as the description of the poet's experiences in Hell, the narrative and dialogue are quite lively; but this must be set against much rather characterless verse where Jehan is prone to moralise at length. But the whole story has a much better unity than Raoul's, with the allegorical pattern complete and self-sufficient. There are no deviations from the theme of the journey through life. The poet has indulged in all the seven sins; and so when he encounters Death, Hell appears to have prior claim to his soul. He is saved only because during his life he did not neglect his prayers to Mary. So the construction is clear and logical, and this part of the poem is simply an allegorised miracle of the Virgin. That is not to say that the allegory is maintained on the same level throughout; for, as in Raoul's *Songe*, we find Jehan tending to slip away from the allegorical conceits when he comes to treat what he has seen in Hell itself. But there is no shedding of the cloak of piety, which hangs in sometimes over-ample folds about the whole poem. Jehan makes it clear from the beginning that the book is written first of all in the name of the King of Heaven, then in that of the Virgin and of the saints, and archangels; and on the human level it is composed for the honour and *courtoisie* of a "bourgois douls et reverent", his master Simon de Lille (ll. 25–36). If he was writing primarily for the good of his soul and only secondly for his patron, he was nevertheless at pains to give his story a polished, literary form such as would be acceptable to the discerning Simon and to the noble circles in which both plied their trade.[14]

It is interesting to find that, in order to fill out his description of the dread citadel of Hell, Jehan has had recourse to some of the visionary material that we have already studied. The whole picture is based, whether directly or indirectly it is impossible to say, on the *Vision of St Paul*. Jehan sees the sealed pit of Hell (though here it is shown as a chamber in the wall), the fires of which are reserved for those who did not keep their faith. He sees, too, certain of the damned hanging above a fire, while others are immersed in a foul river. The *lex talionis* principle is very prominent throughout. Other torments belong to the common fund of eschatological material current in his day. So though Jehan may be considered a *trouvère*, the description adopted by his editor, he was well versed in pious legend and may well have had a close connection with the Church. Doubtless he found the moral climate in England to his liking when, as we know, he was enjoying patronage on this side of the Channel.

A third allegorical treatment of the journey to Hell will not detain us long. At present unpublished, it too was written in the fourteenth century and appears to be indebted in no small measure to Jehan's work. My summary is taken from the Paris, B.N., MS fr. 24313,[15] which carries the rubric: "Ch'est li livres de le Voye de Infer" (fol. 1a).

In a dream, the poet decides to undertake the journey to Hell. A damsel appears and offers to conduct him there in eight days: it is Desesperance. She leads him by way of the castles belonging to the Seven Deadly Sins to the gate of Hell, which is a city lying in a hideous valley full of fou smoke. There she says the poet must enter, never to return, since she has promised to lead him there but not back again. However, the poet proclaims his intention to repent and confess his sins, and Desesperance angrily disappears into Hell. The poet sees the horrors of the abyss, with its tortured souls and terrible demons. He sees a black, icy river from which a noisome stench arises. Elsewhere there are serpents and toads that burn and gnaw the hapless sinners. He is dismayed, but a beautiful damsel, Contrition, whose surname is repentance, arrives to comfort him and protect him from the devils. The remainder of the vision is occupied with moral precepts on the value of confession and the necessity of observing the laws of God and of the Church.

There is little that calls for comment. Nothing is known of the author, though his language seems to be that of the northeast. The poem is written in octosyllabic rhyming couplets without notable literary skill, and plainly exploits second-hand material. One noteworthy fact is that the author was not interested in describing the road to Paradise, perhaps finding the infernal path more suitable as an illustration of the need to live righteously and according to the dictates of the Church. The homiletic portion of the work occupies more than a quarter of the whole and is divided into several chapters: "De contrition", "De confesse", "Comment on se doibt confesser des pechiés", "Des .x. comandemens de la loy", "Des œuvres de misericorde", "Des .xii. articles de la foy", "Des comandemens de saincte eglize" and "De satisfation". These surely indicate that the author was himself a churchman.

In the middle of the fourteenth century, the Cistercian monk Guillaume de Deguileville[16] put the allegorical method to cumbrous use in his trilogy: *Le Pèlerinage de la vie humaine*, *Le Pèlerinage de l'âme* and *Le Pèlerinage de Jésus-Christ*. It is the second of these *Pèlerinages* that concerns us. Written between 1355 and 1358, it tells of the soul's visit to the different regions of the Otherworld.

Guillaume falls asleep and dreams that his soul has left his body on the death of the latter. It is escorted by an angel and

VH G

a demon to its judgment in a high, bright region. At the judicial weighing it seems that Guillaume's sins will outweigh his good deeds; but a signed letter of mercy from Christ turns the scales, and it is decreed that the pilgrim soul shall go to Purgatory. Before being taken there he sees sinners deformed according to their crimes. For example, the proud have horns, the eyes of the envious hang out from their heads, murderers have tusks like those of boars, and gluttons have enormous bellies. The soul is conducted to Purgatory by his guardian angel, with a demon trotting hopefully beside him. The purgatorial fire is black, yet transparent, and the pilgrim can see the torments. He himself carries the burden of his sin, but the angel explains that these burdens may be alleviated by the prayers of those on earth; and after what seems an interminable time in the fire, Guillaume does feel his load of sin dwindle away. The angel speaks to him of the infernal pains. (ll. 1–3592)

Suddenly the pilgrim sees Purgatory as a sphere around which is another, misty sphere. It is Abraham's bosom ("le sain Abrahe", l. 3615), whence Christ delivered the patriarchs.[17] These regions, the angel explains, are like a nut, the kernel of which is Hell itself. Around it, like a skin, is the limbo for unbaptised children, with Purgatory around that; and the outermost peel is the *limbus patrum*.[18] After more explanations the soul is led to the earth, where he visits the scenes of his sins and indulges in a long debate with his own body.

Then he is conducted down through the earth, which does not resist his progress, through the *limbus infantium* into Hell. There, surrounded by demons, is Lucifer, seated on a blazing throne and laden with chains. Orgueil, Lucifer's daughter, quarrels with her father and provokes demons to buffet him. They then turn upon her and trample her underfoot while her father sits on her head. The pilgrim sees hypocrites beaten by devils and plunged in fire; and other sinners hang over flames by parts of the body corresponding to their sin. Traitors, armed with knives and their bodies pierced, curse not only their crime but also Christ Himself.

La avoit .i. tournoiement
D'une roe tournant forment.
Du parfont de terre venoit
Par .i. postis et haut sourdoit
Et droitement a une tour
Isnelement faisoit son tour
Si qu'au tour en la tour entroit
Et par en haut bas s'avaloit
En retournant celeement
Au postis et repostement.
Cros de fer estoient fichies
En la roe et fort atachies
Et desciroient deux chetis
Qui estoient a ce postis,
Les quiex aus cols de toutes pars
Estoient chargies de grans sas
Plains d'argent et de monnoie
Que par les sas bien vëoie.

(ll. 4873–90)

(There was the whirling of a swiftly turning wheel. It emerged through a gateway from the depths of the earth and reared aloft; and rapidly it turned just by a tower, so that on its circuit it entered the tower, plunging down from the top to go back through the gate and be hidden and concealed from view. Iron hooks were firmly fixed and attached to the wheel, and they rent two wretches who were by the gate, their backs heavily laden with great sacks full of silver and coinage that I could see clearly through the sacks.)

In the tower is a king, who accuses the two sinners of having betrayed his trust in them. For they had been his servants but had stolen his money by guile, leaving his kingdom defenceless. A devil stirs up the fire beneath them, rails at them, and describes other of Hell's torments.[19]

Next the pilgrim sees the avaricious gnawed by wolves, and the usurers having burning money crammed into their throats; he sees too a furnace where the souls of the impatient and vengeful are burnt like faggots. Afterwards he is shown another wheel, turned by two mighty devils. As it revolves, the sinners upon it (the slothful) strike against a pillar so that their brains are knocked out and their eyes are beaten from their heads. Gluttons have their throats slit and their tongues rent and are grilled over sulphurous coals. Lechers are in a fire where they are gnawed by toads, snakes and other vermin. Then the pilgrim sees a vast ditch burning with stinking fire and full of serpents. In it are sinners being mercilessly beaten by demons while they bewail their lot and the fact that they cannot die. The place, the angel explains, is the "abisme" (l. 5481), the "chaudiere" (l. 5485), the "puis d'enfer" (l. 5486); and there the Jews, pagans, and those who harmed the Church are damned to all eternity. Finally the pilgrim is escorted from Hell by the angel. (ll. 3593–5590)

The above is a mere sketch of the narrative, which is filled out largely by means of moralising speeches put in the mouths of the main characters. There is no escaping the homiletic character of the vision, and Guillaume all too often gives the impression of showing off his theological knowledge. But he was also plainly proud of his technical virtuosity, of which many instances could be quoted. The episode of the traitors on the wheel is a case in point: there is much play on words, and in the explanation of their crime it is hard to see at first whether an image of the wheel moving other wheels (ll. 4895–5038) is intended to be taken in a literal or figurative sense. So far as we can tell, Guillaume did not know Dante, but what he attempted was a vision on a Dantesque scale. Although he did not entirely lack imagination, his step was too ponderous. And the vastness of his vision is unhappily greater than its clarity, with the result that, as in his description of the places of torment, the picture often becomes confused. A rigid scheme such as Dante's might well have helped Guillaume to concentrate his thought. But we must at least give him credit for having attempted a noble synthesis of the medieval vision material, a synthesis for which the time was ripe and which French literature was still awaiting.

The whole trilogy was inspired by the *Roman de la Rose*, which Guillaume held in high regard, and to which he wished to supply the religious counterpart. But he also drew widely on the literature of pious visions ;[20] and in connection with the part of the *Pèlerinage de l'âme* I have just summarised, the *Vision of St Paul* must receive special mention. The suspension of sinners by various parts of the body, the infernal wheels, the stinking pit of Hell are all characteristics of the *Vision* as it appeared in the later redactions. The second description of a wheel of torment is strikingly similar to that given in the Alexandrine version and borrowed by Geoffroi de Paris ;[21] and it was in all probability here that Guillaume found the unusual conception of the wheel striking against a stone as it turned.

The popularity of Guillaume's *Pèlerinages* with later generations has been traced through by E. Faral.[22] Manuscripts abound, many of them richly illustrated. But it was above all in the prose versions that his work became widely known, in England as well as on the Continent. Notably, the *Pèlerinage de l'âme* was thus treated at the request of John, Duke of Bedford, by a certain Jean Gallopes, "le Gallois", between 1420 and 1422. Having already seen something of the English taste for the devotionally orientated macabre, we can readily understand the welcome extended to Guillaume's monumental works in this country. And with the arrival of printed versions from the late fifteenth century, the final public benediction was applied.

None of the texts we have studied so far shows any knowledge of Dante ; and indeed the *Divina Commedia*, though composed soon after 1300, was put to very small use in French literature over the next two hundred years. There were certainly some Italian manuscripts of it in French libraries in the fifteenth century, and it was probably known to a limited circle before then. Christine de Pisan, contrasting it with Jean de Meung's well loved poem, wrote about the year 1400 :

Se mieulx veulx ouir descripre paradis et enfer et plus haultement parler de theologie plus proffitablement, plus poetiquement et de plus grant efficace, lis le livre que on appelle le Dant ... Là orras aultre propos, mieulx fondé plus

soubtilement, ne te desplaise, et où plus tu pourras profiter
que en ton *Romant de la Rose*.[23]

(If you wish to hear Paradise and Hell better described and
theology discussed more loftily and profitably, in a more
poetic and efficacious way, read the book they call Dante ...
There, if you will forgive my saying so, you will hear different
matters treated, that are better and more subtly based, and
whence you may derive more benefit, than in your *Romance
of the Rose*.)

Dante's poem was used by the author of the Franco-Italian
Huon d'Auvergne, which will be considered in the next chapter,
and was familiar to Regnauld le Queux at the end of the
fifteenth century; but otherwise none of the texts reviewed in
this study show the Divine Poet's influence.

No far-reaching conclusions are to be drawn from this
negative evidence, since the diffusion of the *Divina Commedia*
seems to have been very restricted, and the silence of the French
poets may be ascribed rather to lack of knowledge than to lack
of appreciation of the work. Nor is the fact that it may have
been translated into French at the very limit of our period of
great significance for this study. C. Morel published three
French versions,[24] two of which were made in the sixteenth
century. The third, from the Turin, University Library, MS
L.III.17 (a late fifteenth- or early sixteenth-century manuscript),
may have been written a year or two before 1500.[25] The
translation is of the *Inferno* only and remains faithful to the
original[26]—so faithful, in fact, that the unknown author copied
the *terze rime* of his original. Here is a thoroughly conscientious work of literary transposition.

This is the sum of the allegorical treatments of our theme in
French medieval literature; and, as I suggested at the beginning
of the chapter, they betray a somewhat more dispassionate
attitude towards the subject than is found in the exhortatory
productions of homilist and preacher. They are used as
vehicles for interests other than the straightforwardly didactic:
Christian dogmatics, satire on an almost personal level, and of

course the intellectual satisfaction of handling the allegory itself and grappling with literary form. It is interesting, none the less, to find that the "old-fashioned" vision of Hell still exerts its authority and fascination, at the expense, to some degree, of the representation of Paradise and also of the maintenance of allegorical conceit.

NOTES

1. See, *inter alia*, C. S. Lewis, *The Allegory of Love* (Oxford, 1936), especially Ch. II; U. T. Holmes, *A History of Old French Literature*, pp. 301–2; H. R. Jauss, "Form und Auffassung der Allegorie in der Tradition der *Psychomachia*", *Medium Ævum Vivum: Festschrift für Walther Bulst* (Heidelberg, 1960), pp. 179–206; Rosemond Tuve, *Allegorical Imagery. Some Mediaeval Books and their Posterity* (Princeton, 1966).
2. Cf. Lewis, op. cit., pp. 66 ff. For an Old French poem using this theme see the edition by A. Långfors, "Le Tournoiement d'Enfer, poème allégorique et satirique", *Romania* XLIV (1915–7), pp. 511–58.
3. The conception is already found in Seneca (Lewis, op. cit., pp. 68–9).
4. Ed. P. Lebesgue (La Rochelle & Paris, 1908). See Jauss, op. cit., pp. 191 ff.
5. For his life the approximate dates 1170–1230 have been proposed. Lebesgue suggested that he was probably a monk, priest or *clerc* (ibid., p. 14) and favoured the Beauvaisis for his place of origin. For earlier theories see his introductory study. L. Foulet, on the other hand, denied that he was a monk (*Romania* LI [1925], pp. 90–4). Raoul's other works are *Meraugis de Portlesguez*, an Arthurian romance; the *Roman des eles*; and possibly the *Songe de Paradis* printed as his by Lebesgue, op. cit.
6. See E. Faral, *Les Jongleurs en France au moyen âge*, Part I, Chs. II & III.
7. See also Lebesgue, op. cit., p. 20, for similar sentiments occurring in the *Roman des eles*.
8. Ed. G. Wimmer (Marburg, 1888). Huon probably came from the north-west of France (ibid., pp. 10–11). See also Jauss, op. cit., pp. 192 ff.
9. Pluto, Proserpine, Jupiter, Saturn, Apollo, Venus and Cerberus all appear. We noticed that in the *Eneas* Cerberus seemed to be losing his Classical appearance to take on that of the medieval demon. Here he is represented as a three-headed warrior in the infernal horde:
   > Icil fu por mestre tenuz
   > Por ce que .iii. testes avoit.   (ll. 592–3)
10. Ed. Sister M. A. Pety (Washington, 1940). Details of authorship, date and the identity of the patron are given on pp. 2–13.
11. For the appearance of the Seven Deadly Sins in this type of literature see Lewis, op. cit., pp. 70, 86, etc.
12. This section of the poem (4,632 lines in all) comprises ll. 73–2634.
13. Pety (op. cit., pp. 20–1) discusses the versification. I feel her verdict that Jehan's talent "is not enough to give him an honourable position among the *trouvères* of the fourteenth century" (p. 22) to be somewhat harsh.

14. For Simon's interest in literature see ibid., pp. 7–8. Jehan was also patronised by Queen Philippa of England (ibid., pp. 4–5).
15. Other MSS containing the poem are Paris, B.N., fr. 1051, fr. 1534 (incomplete), fr. 1543; and Cambrai 176 (*Cat. gén.*, XVII, 53).
16. Or Digulleville. His name derives from the locality in Normandy, although it is not certain that he was born there, despite evidence in his works of his Norman origin. It is known that he became a monk at Chaalis (near Senlis), and it was there that he wrote his *Pèlerinages*. These have been edited by J. J. Stürzinger (London, 1893–7). Analyses may be found in Ch.-V. Langlois, *La Vie en France au moyen âge*, IV, pp. 244–67; E. Faral, "Guillaume de Digulleville, moine de Chaalis", *Histoire littéraire de la France* 39 (1962), pp. 1–132. See also Tuve, op. cit., Ch. III.
17. The Harrowing is described in scholastic terminology: Christ's soul and His divinity went down to Hell (cf. above, p. 110).
18. The same division, which is perhaps Guillaume's own variant on the more common egg analogy, is given by Regnauld le Queux in his *Baratre infernal* (Paris, B.N., MS fr. 450, fol. 127).
19. A miniature depicting this curious scene is reproduced in Stürzinger's edition (facing p. 162). The idea of the victim watching the punishment of those who wronged him is rare, but not unique. It is found in Christian legend as early as the *Revelation of Peter* (M. R. James, *The Apocryphal N.T.*, p. 509). Faral saw here a topical allusion to contemporary events in France (op. cit., pp. 115–6).
20. See S. L. Galpin, "On the Sources of Guillaume de Deguileville's *Pèlerinage de l'Âme*", *Publications of the Modern Language Association of America* 25.ii (1910), pp. 275–308.
21. See above, pp. 88–90.
22. Op. cit., pp. 128–32. See also Tuve, op. cit., pp. 145–51.
23. Quoted by H. Chamard, *Les Origines de la poésie française de la Renaissance* (Paris, 1920), pp. 219–20.
24. *Les plus anciennes traductions françaises de la Divine Comédie* (Paris, 1897).
25. See E. Stengel, *Philologischer Kommentar zu den französischen Uebertragung von Dantes Inferno in der Hs. L.III.17 der Turiner Universitätsbibliothek* (Paris, 1897).
26. Canto 34 and part of Canto 33 are lacking.

CHAPTER VII

KINGS AND HEROES

I T is a striking fact that almost from the beginnings of French literature we have evidence of pious accounts of the infernal journey being paralleled by profane stories of human beings visiting Hell in their lifetime. Here is an indication not only of the medieval belief in Hell as a genuine, physical location, but also of people's readiness to accept the journey there as a legitimate heroic adventure, devoid of real religious purpose or meaning.

It may well be that by the time the Clermont-Ferrand *Passion du Christ* was written, some time in the tenth century,[1] there was already in circulation a story of which we catch an echo in the *Chanson de Roland*, over a hundred years later. There the following cryptic lines occur :

> *E l'arcevesque lor ocist Siglorel,*
> *L'encanteür ki ja fut en enfer:*
> *Par artimal l'i cundoist Jupiter.*
>
> (Oxford MS, ll. 1390–2)[2]

(And the archbishop slew for them Siglorel, the enchanter who had once been to Hell: Jupiter led him there by the magic arts.)

This, then, is the first reference in French literature to a profane descent. It is a complete episode in three lines : a pagan sorcerer invokes the aid of a powerful demon who takes him to Hell by enchantment and presumably restores him to the earth, where he is one of the Saracens fighting against Charlemagne's rearguard. Unfortunately we know nothing more of the incident, but it may not be without literary and even social significance.

Although no source has come to light, three possibilities

present themselves : either the poet (Turoldus ?) invented the tale, or else he knew of it through written or oral tradition. The first possibility is not strong, since he would hardly have gone to the trouble of inventing such a story to fill but three lines of his poem. Moreover, he had elsewhere made similar references to tales seemingly well known in his day.[3] But if he did invent this passage, we must assume that the conception of the infernal descent was not unfamiliar to him and would not be foreign to the public for whom the *Chanson* was intended. The second possibility would lead to the same assumption, and in this case too the way in which the episode is told suggests that the audience would understand the allusion. And if the poet is referring here to some oral tradition, we must again conclude that the story was well known to his contemporaries. And this is very likely. Belief in the powers of magic and in sorcerers was practically universal throughout the Middle Ages,[4] and pacts between men and demons had been known from ancient times. The Church early condemned the practices of sorcerers and the like in decrees which it continued to issue for many centuries. It is interesting to note that Charlemagne himself had issued capitularies forbidding this kind of activity (sorcery, magic, divinations, enchantments, the practice of "mathematics", etc.),[5] and some of his successors followed his example.

The *Chanson de Roland* was written, then, in an age of great credulity, an age that produced such men as Ralph Glaber who were fascinated by stories like the one these lines appear to summarise. And it is in this light that we must view the episode, realising that the public would be inclined to take it more as fact than romance or, at least, would have no cause to doubt the possibility of a descent of this kind. Only the most enlightened thinkers of the day refused to credit such sorcery; and pagans were more likely than anyone to enlist diabolic aid.

I referred to Jupiter as a powerful demon, although this is not entirely implicit in the text. But as we have already seen on more than one occasion, the gods of Classical Antiquity soon became demons in the Christian Hell, bearing out the natural law by which the gods of one civilisation usually become the devils of the next.[6] So Jupiter would probably be a figure of some standing in the infernal world—higher in rank than the familiar demon who was to come to the aid of the enchanter Corniquant in the *Histoire de Charles Martel*.[7]

With Philippe Mouskés we move forward a century and a half into the realm of pseudo-history. Philippe, a citizen of Tournai, compiled his long rhymed chronicle in about 1243, zealously using all the historical or pseudo-historical material that came his way.[8] He traces events from the fall of Troy to the France of 1242; but for those which occurred before his own day he is totally unreliable, preferring the legendary and highly coloured to the dry bones of fact. Two of the legends that he found and recounted have some interest for us; and the first, the *Vision of St Eucherius*, is briefly told.

It was when St Eucherius ("Eusteres") was in prayer that he was transported by an angel to Hell, where he saw Charles Martel damned in body and soul. The angel advised him that this was Charles's punishment for having misappropriated tithes offered to the Church. In this way he had robbed widows and orphans. After returning to his body, Eucherius told his vision to many of his associates and prayed them to open the tomb of Charles Martel. As they did so, a hideous dragon flew out. But the corpse was entire and not putrefied, though it was black as pitch.[9]

There is little to be said about this legend. It was first related in a letter from the fathers of the Council of Quierzy (858) to Louis, King of Germany.[10] Its chief importance is as evidence that Charles Martel had early acquired a bad reputation in ecclesiastical circles, a reputation that we shall see further exemplified in the romance *Huon d'Auvergne*. The tradition carried by the *Vision of St Eucherius* concerning the reasons for Charles's damnation was widespread in the Middle Ages, but has been ignored in the romance, where the grounds for the king's downfall are quite different.

The second vision of the pains of Hell which Philippe has included in his chronicle is one of more general significance. It is found in several Latin versions and was put by Vincent de Beauvais into his *Speculum historiale* which, as we have seen,

was itself translated in the fourteenth century by Jean de
Vignay. It is the *Vision of Charles le Gros*.[11]

The Emperor Charles has gone to rest one Sunday night
after mass when a terrible voice calls forth his soul from its
body. There appears a guide in radiant white apparel and
holding a ball of shining thread. Charles is told to take the
end of the thread and knot it firmly in his right hand so that
he may be led through Hell.[12] He is taken into deep, fiery
valleys full of burning pits containing pitch, sulphur, lead,
wax and fat, where those who had been bishops under his
father and uncles suffer for their sins. They tell him that in
their time they sowed discord; and if the churchmen and
secular leaders under Charles act similarly, they too will come
here. Black demons with flaming claws fly down to try to
seize the thread in Charles's hand, but they cannot touch it
because of its shining rays. They then try to cast him into the
pits, but the guide duplicates the thread about his shoulders,
and they cannot touch him.

Charles and the angel cross blazing mountains with swamps
and rivers of fiery, molten metal,[13] where many of his father's
chiefs stand immersed to the hair, chin, or navel,[14] complaining that like Charles's relatives they had indulged in slaughter
and rapine for worldly gain. The torments of the powerful
are all the greater because of their position in the world. In
furnaces nearby, Charles sees sinners wallowing in pitch and
sulphur and beset by dragons, scorpions and serpents. These
too he recognises: they had given evil counsel to their own
kings or to Charles himself out of malicious pride and
cupidity. The beasts make for him, but his guide triplicates
the thread about his shoulders, and he is secure.

They descend into a valley that is burning and yet dark on
one side, and on the other beautiful.[15] On the dark side
Charles sees certain kings of his own line suffering torments,
and only the protective thread prevents his being cast among
them by black giants. He then perceives two springs, one
very hot and the other clear and tepid. In the boiling one he
sees his father Louis[16] standing immersed up to his thighs.
Louis assures Charles that he will return to his body, for God

has permitted him to come here to see the torments. Louis himself must spend one day in the boiling water then one in the tepid, the latter granted as the result of the intercession of St Peter and St Remy. Indeed, he may be released from all punishment if Charles and his faithful clergy pray and give alms on his account; already his brother Lothair and his nephew Louis have been released into Paradise. The two boiling barrels that Charles sees to his left are prepared for him unless he mends his ways.

He is then led to the fair side of the valley; and there, in the glory of Paradise, are Lothair and Louis his son. They welcome Charles; and Louis says that his grandson[17] should rule his kingdom. The infant appears; and Charles is instructed to give him the thread in token of his sovereignty over the Empire. This he does, and returns to the body.

Philippe Mouskés' predilection for such historically flavoured visions is shown elsewhere in his work. He describes how Archbishop Turpin was carried off in the spirit to see angels taking the souls of Roland and the dead Christians of Roncevaux into Heaven, whilst Marsile and the pagans are transported by devils to Hell.[18] In another place, the same Turpin is said to have seen a legion of hideous devils riding like horsemen through the air. They announce that they are going to Aix, where they hope to gain possession of the soul of the dying Charlemagne. But on their return they lament that St James of Compostella has flung into the balance so much in the Emperor's favour that his soul has been taken to Paradise.[19]

Unreliable as Philippe is, he asserts the truth of what he tells and affects to despise the tall stories of the chansons de geste. And though a capable poet by the standards of his age, he was not interested in elaborating these legends that he had picked up: rather he tended to condense them. Thus, with the *Vision of Charles le Gros* the circumstances of the vision are omitted; the topography of Hell is less detailed than in the Latin; and Charles's interview with his father is abbreviated. So he does at least affect the attitude of the historian rather than that of the romancer; and the two visions that I have summarised show his particular interest in those accounts which have some political significance. The *Vision of St Eucherius* seems to have been intended originally as a warning to rulers not to encroach upon ecclesiastical rights and privileges ; and the *Vision of Charles le Gros*, of unknown origin and date, appears to have been written as a piece of political propaganda to strengthen the claims of Louis III to the imperial crown.[20] This is not to suggest that Philippe himself had any political axe to grind, but plainly it was that element rather than the pious which interested him. We may contrast his attitude with that of Vincent de Beauvais, who included the legend of Charles le Gros in his *Speculum historiale* (Book XXV, Ch. 50) purely because of its religious implications. So Philippe related his stories tersely and without embroidery. And while this is a commendable attitude for a would-be historian, it precluded the possibility of originality in either the literary or the doctrinal sphere. His approach is entirely secular.

From the brief, factual accounts of the historian we turn now to other texts where the tenuous historical element is disguised and completely subjected to the writer's desire to tell a gripping adventure story. These are what one might call the pseudo-historical romances, successors to and descendants of the heroic chansons de geste. The first we shall study is a prose work produced in the middle of the fifteenth century, but reflecting a much earlier tradition. It is the *Histoire de Charles Martel et de ses successeurs*, still unpublished, and contained in four volumes comprising in all 2,014 folios. They are unique. In the first of these volumes is found a story that may well once have existed as an independent epic poem.[21]

The name of the compiler of this work is unknown, but whoever he was, the only glory he sought was from having rendered into prose a number of rhymed *histoires* dealing with Charles Martel and other figures. It is well known, he says in his prologue, how Pepin and Charlemagne were descended from Charles Martel, but not everybody knows the ancestry of Charles himself and how he came to be king of France. Therefore he will set it out in clear French, faithfully setting the old stories into prose, since this is now preferred to rhyme by the great ones of the land, there being less constraint on the language than with verse. And he adds a note of caution, begging his readers not to withhold their "imagination or understanding" if they find some things hard to believe, since his only concern is to pass on conscientiously what he has found in the said "volume rymé".[22]

The copyist, David Aubert, supplies a few more details. He completed his own work between 1463 and 1465; but the prose adaptation of the verse compilation was made in 1448, as he tells us in a note at the end of the second volume.[23] Some anonymous writer, then, put into prose in 1448 some "anchiennes histoires" that he had found in a "volume rymé". Paul Meyer deduced that the sources for the first part of the work, which contains our descent episode, were most probably two chansons de geste of late vintage.[24] The central figure of the one would be Charles Martel and of the other Girart de Roussillon, whose adventures under Charles are described at length. Of the first, Meyer spoke disparagingly: "Le poème sur Charles Martel paraît avoir été un de ces romans volumineux et compliqués que les pays wallons ont produits en si grand nombre du XIIIe siècle au XVe. Charles Martel y était gratifié d'une généalogie tout à fait fabuleuse, son père étant un certain Eustache de Berry, son aïeul un duc de Berry nommé Gloriant. Il devenait amoureux de Marsebille, fille du roi de France Theodorus, et l'épousait contre la volonté de ce dernier."[25] It would be from this hypothetical poem that the descent story is drawn. It is possible to date it within slightly narrower limits than those proposed by Meyer. If in 1448 the poem was already *anchienne*, then we can assume it to have been composed before 1400; and since I have shown elsewhere[26] that some of its features were probably derived from the *Dialogus miraculorum* by Caesarius of Heisterbach, the *terminus a quo* can be put at a little before 1240, the approximate date of Caesarius' death.

Before any further discussion of the section where our theme is treated, it will be as well to give a brief summary of its contents.

Archefer, the natural son of Charles Martel, is imprisoned by his father for alleged treachery, and is released in order to

go to Hell on an ambassadorial mission. This is the condition
for his pardon. On his way, in Cyprus, he slays the magician
Sorbrin, being at the time in the service of King Grimault of
Sathalie.

Archefer leaves Grimault, having borrowed his magician
Corniquant, whose aid he enlists in his mission to demand
tribute and allegiance from Lucifer. Corniquant offers to go
on his behalf, but the prince insists on making the journey
himself and shows his own prowess in the magic arts as taught
to him by the pagan Sorbrin.

Corniquant invokes a demon who has served him before
and must now carry the two adventurers to Hell and back.
Grudgingly he complies and carries them over land and sea
to the gates of Hell. Lucifer makes a great noise when they
are announced to him, but Archefer puts his demands in the
name of Charles Martel, and the prince of darkness decides
to take counsel. In the meantime Archefer visits the places of
torment where he finds his mother, damned for treason. If
masses are said for her on earth, she will obtain relief from
her punishment.

By this time Lucifer has been persuaded in council that
Charles is an enemy to be reckoned with, so he pledges
allegiance and gives a demon horse and hounds as tribute.
On the horse, Archefer and Corniquant return to Cyprus and
fly from there with Rose, the prince's Saracen love, to Charles's
palace in "Ammarie". Charles is incredulous, but when his
son suggests that he go to Hell himself on the black charger,
he does so, accompanied by Corniquant. He is terrified;
but Lucifer repeats his assurance of homage. And with all
the demons kneeling before him, Charles wishes himself
back to his palace.

There Charles pardons Archefer, who marries Rose, now
turned Christian. Two years later, however, the prince dies.

Some years ago, I considered the relationship between this
story and the romances of *Huon d'Auvergne* and *Huon de
Bordeaux*. My conclusion, from which I have since found no
reason to depart, was that this episode in the *Histoire de Charles
Martel* gives a redacted form of a legend, no doubt forming the

subject of a lost chanson de geste, from which both of the romances are also derived.[27] If this is so, the legend must have existed at least by the end of the twelfth century and possibly much earlier. We have seen something of the bad reputation early given to Charles Martel in ecclesiastical circles, and this may well have been the seed from which sprang the story of how he sent a vassal to Hell and later made the journey himself. I would go further and suggest that in its primitive form our legend showed only the vassal (probably Huon d'Auvergne) making the journey in safety, whereas the king was eternally damned for his injustice. In that case, *Huon d'Auvergne*, which ends in this way, is here closer to the original than is the *Histoire de Charles Martel*.

When we examine the story as we have it in the *Histoire*, we are struck by the extremely secular spirit if the two descents. The motive for Archefer's mission is quite divorced from any Christian conception of the descent theme, since piety has no place in it. He is simply an obedient vassal carrying out his liege lord's command, which entails an ambassadorial mission to Hell with the object of securing the allegiance to Charles Martel of that kingdom's rulers. The whole idea is feudal. Hell is treated as a realm that has stood until now outside Charles's dominion, but which is not strong enough to oppose his demands. Lucifer, in council, decides to become a tributary of Charles and sends him pledges to that effect. Finally Charles himself visits his new vassal state and then returns in safety to his palace. Pious exclamations cannot disguise from us the fact that the story as told here is not very far removed from blasphemy, at least to modern eyes, though the typical medieval audience would doubtless have been more tolerant in its interpretation.

Where the narrative comes closest to the spirit of pious legend, namely where Archefer interviews his mother in Hell, there appears to be a direct debt to such a legend, Caesarius of Heisterbach's story of the landgrave Ludwig.[28] Otherwise, reminiscences are confined to vague and general notions such as the gate of Hell and the torments of heat, cold, stench and reptiles, or to passing allusions to Christ's descent. Clearly the author is no churchman. In one instance, indeed, he shows a surprising ignorance of Church teaching, for it is suggested that Archefer's mother may have her sufferings alleviated, even though she is in Hell and not Purgatory. No, the compiler of the "anchienne histoire rymee" was simply a teller of adventure stories in the epic tradition of the thirteenth and fourteenth centuries, using material which in this case may have originated in ecclesiastical circles and been developed in epic poetry before he came across it. We may suspect that the man who turned the story into prose embellished and modified it more than he admits, but that must remain a suspicion.

This episode in the *Histoire* shows what violence could be done to an originally pious theme—unless I am wrong in suggesting clerical origins, and we are dealing with a late recension of some such secular tale as that alluded to in the *Chanson de Roland*. But by depriving the theme of its predominantly religious associations, the author brings home to us the real epic quality of a true descent story. The hero, like the epic warrior, has to be of stout heart and noble character if he is to survive the journey, which combines the interest of a voyage of discovery with that of a feat of individual valour, one man's courage being measured against the forces of evil. In a way, it is a natural enough extension of the epic theme of a knight venturing into distant lands to pit his strength against the infidel's.

If I am right in my contention that *Huon de Bordeaux* was derived from an earlier form of the *Histoire de Charles Martel*, the epic vigour of the latter has been diffused in the new version. This has had unfortunate consequences for the artistic unity of the story; and one might wonder what brought the author of *Huon* to abandon the descent theme in view of its popularity in his day. For Huon's mission is no longer to Hell, but to the Emir of Babylon (though the king, in sending him, does proffer the opinion that this is a more dire errand than parleying with the devils in Hell).[29] I would suggest that the *Huon*-poet's basic motive was one of burlesque, very much in fashion in the late twelfth and early thirteenth centuries; and if so, the implication is that he regarded his model as a perfectly serious work. In any case, and despite his artistic lapses, it must be admitted that he has brought a good fund of humour into his work, as

well as a fairy-tale element that agreeably bridges the gap between epic and romance.

It would appear that the author of *Huon d'Auvergne* was also
concerned with bringing some of the atmosphere of the romance
into the primitive account of the visit of Charles Martel and his
vassal to the kingdom of darkness. In its extant form, this long
poem dates from the beginning of the fourteenth century and
has survived in three manuscripts, all in a more or less Italian-
ised form of French.[30] It is generally supposed that the existing
redactions were ultimately based on a lost French chanson de
geste; and this, as I have said, I take to be a more primitive
version of the story found in the *Histoire de Charles Martel*,
and which was in existence in the twelfth century. In the following summary I concentrate on the descent episode, to which the
line references apply.[31]

> Huon d'Auvergne is unjustly accused by Duke Sanguin of
> Mongrana of having made love to his betrothed, Sofia, the
> daughter of Charles Martel. Sofia, whom Huon had been
> charged to escort to her future husband, was in fact the guilty
> party; and after Charles has marched against Auvergne
> with his army and Huon has been forced to flee, the true
> circumstances are brought to light. Duke Sanguin apologises
> publicly to Huon, and Charles condemns his daughter, who
> is burnt. (This introductory episode figures in only one
> manuscript.)
> Huon marries the beautiful Ynide, on whom Charles
> Martel soon casts longing eyes. In council he decides to send
> Huon away in order to be more free to indulge his desires.
> The count is to go on an ambassadorial mission to Lucifer in
> Hell, from whom he must demand tribute and allegiance.
> Huon unquestioningly sets out from Auvergne, passes
> through Hungary, where he is unable to find a magician to
> help him in his quest, and then has an interview with the
> Pope in Rome. He is instructed to go on to Jerusalem; and
> prowess in combating the Saracens earns him the honour of
> being crowned king of that city. But he soon sets forth

again; and after many fantastic adventures during which he slays giants and the Sultan of Persia, journeys through weird lands and gets the better of devils, he meets an angel. He is approaching his destination; but first he comes across some pilgrim-hermits, one of whom is his cousin, then travels through the Promised Land and sees the Earthly Paradise, and has more adventures with monsters and demons.

Close by the sea Huon meets the shade of Aeneas, who offers to help him in his quest; and they are joined by the shade of Guillaume d'Orange. All three voyage across the sea in an unpiloted boat that speeds straight to the abyss of Hell. A divinely provided light enables the voyagers to see through the infernal gloom. The water is now full of vermin and fire-breathing dragons. Huon and his companions leave the boat and follow through reeded marshlands a path that leads them to a wall, seemingly of iron and a bow-shot high. Guillaume says they must go through one of its gates, but for the dead who pass there no return is possible. Above the first gate is a painting of a maiden holding a spear: this is Justice. Above another is a dragon crowned like a king: through that one pass the Jewish dead. A third gate shows a lion and is for Moslems. A smaller gateway carries the picture of a fierce, cruel man; but it appears to lack both gate and drawbridge. Aeneas explains that the doors were destroyed by Christ at the harrowing of Hell. They will not be restored until Judgment Day; but so fierce is the glance of the painted man that the damned dare not pass through. Huon is asked by which gate he wishes to enter, and he expresses the desire to see some of his former acquaintances. (ll. 9196–482)

He holds Guillaume by the shoulders, and they rush together through one of the gates. The noise is deafening. First they see those who did neither good nor evil in their lives, and who are now apparently tormented by a rain of metal.[32] In another region are sinners punished according to their works. For example, a robber with both hands amputated roams about in great anguish. Then Huon sees two or three people lying as dead upon biers, with their bodies devoured by vermin and wasps. They are sodomites, and each is tormented by thirty devils. Other sinners, clad in blazing, bloody rags, are the vainglorious who delighted in luxury. At this point Aeneas takes over the leadership from Guillaume. He shows Huon the ruffianly minstrels who, for their trickery, evil-speaking and lechery, are stuck fast in mire and fired upon by mangonels, the stone ammunition representing the treacherous information they carried. Devils lacerate them eternally. Nearby is a soul whom Huon recognises as one of Charles Martel's counsellors. Huon asks why Charles has sent him on this mission, and the tormented soul, Saudin (or Sandin, *P*), replies that it was so that Charles might have Huon's wife. He himself was the thirteenth count to advise Charles to send his vassal on this fearful errand, and already nine of the others have met their death by the sword. Saudin asks, and is granted, Huon's pardon. Huon asks his two guides if this was in fact Charles's reason for sending him hither; and they reply that it was, but whereas Huon will return in safety to the world, Charles himself will come to Hell. (ll. 9483–744)

The travellers come to a river teeming with serpents. It is Acheron. Ten thousand spirits wait to cross in surly Charon's bark; but as they wait a fire-breathing centaur attacks them with his arrows. Some fall into the water to be devoured by the creatures there, while some of those who had reached the boat are knocked off by the combined attacks of the centaur and of Charon. Aeneas rebukes the ferryman for his refusal to carry the travellers, but then he himself is recognised and attacked by the centaur, who is restrained only by the intervention of Guillaume. Aeneas explains to the terrified Huon that this creature was slain at Troy, "si cum te conte Daire" ;[33] and his punishment is simply to pursue the waiting souls. Charon now agrees to take the party aboard. The frightened Huon crosses himself and then complains that he is thirsty. Guillaume demands wine of Charon, who is prompt to supply some that he carries in the boat. It is wine of Auvergne unaffected by cold or heat. Huon exclaims that this is a miracle, but Guillaume points out that the wonders of Doomsday will be greater. They now arrive on the further bank of the river and see punishments too numerous to tell. Once more Guillaume is in the van with Aeneas bringing up the rear. They enter a deep, dark valley full of the wailing souls of sinful clergy of all ranks. (ll. 9745–986)

Huon and his guides now enter the first circle of the great abyss, full of darkness and lamenting souls. It is the limbo of the unbaptised. Huon asks if they will be redeemed on Judgment Day. Aeneas hopes so, for then he too will be saved. Christ has already been to release Adam and the prophets. Next the travellers come to a castle in a plain. It has seven gates. Inside is Ptolemy, the first astrologer, with the other necromancers. For all their wisdom they are unable to find the way out. Beyond the first gate they see the scholars who, wrapped up in their science, were unmindful of God. Past the second gate is Farabi,[34] engrossed in his dialectics, though each word burns like fire and speaks of the wrath to come. The travellers pass the third gate and then the fourth, with the punishments redoubled in each succeeding region. But beyond the fourth wall, the gate of which is more beautiful than the rest, they find a band of tall young people in light-coloured attire, who resemble those foreigners who come to study on the Seine. They are the rival Trojans and Greeks.[35] Huon says he would wish to come here if his soul were damned. One of the spirits wishes to talk with him but is struck on the head by a companion for speaking out of turn. (ll. 9987–10200)

The three travellers pass on and see next a queen running along in great torment. She is Aiglentine, the wife of Gui de Nanteuil who, put to death at her instigation, now pursues her on a fast horse. Now they see the pagan warriors of Aspremont fighting devils whom they take for Christians. Crossing a plain where there is much suffering, they see the Saracen leader Tibaut li Ascler, who had treacherously broken the peace he made with Guillaume. He is pursuing a woman who appears to be Guillaume's wife Guiborc, the former queen of the pagan Tibaut. She runs with loving words towards Guillaume ; but he explains that she is in fact a devil, for the real Guiborc went to Heaven after her death.[36] Further on they see a nobleman on a balcony of a well-defended castle. This is Girart de Fraite, who thinks he is being continually attacked by Saracens, though they are actually demons. This is his punishment for having set himself up in his pride against the mighty Charlemagne.[37] Girart reviles Guillaume, saying he cares not a button for him, since Guillaume has less power in Heaven than he, Girart, in Hell. Continuing their journey, the travellers see a vast crowd of hypocrites in torment for having feigned humility. Huon asks many questions of his guides so that he may give a full account when he returns to the world. (ll. 10201–480)

They reach the fifth gate, which is worked in black and white stone. Here is the abode of the Seven Liberal Arts, founded by Otisiaus (elsewhere named Thesias),[38] who is doomed to a continual chanting of his knowledge. Huon asks if he is punished for his great knowledge alone. No, says Aeneas, only the wicked are damned. He further tells Huon that in this darkness dwell the fallen angels. They pass through the sixth gate to find many people grouped around Pythagoras and singing horribly out of tune. Flames surround them as they remain thus, awaiting the Day of Judgment. Beyond is a stinking lake full of sulphurous fire and swarming with serpents and basilisks. Many souls are already in the lake, and others, chased by demons, throw themselves in. They speak many languages, some that of Auvergne. Huon recognises one as Count Rugere and asks what was his sin. Grudgingly Rugere replies that he was among those who persuaded Charles Martel to send Huon d'Auvergne, the finest man in the world, to Hell so that the king might take his wife. Huon reveals his identity, reaffirms his intention to carry out Charles's bidding, and upbraids the sinner, who flings himself back into the fire to be burnt and gnawed by dragons. Then he sees souls gnawing at one another. Among them are the two traitors who caused Alexander to take poison. Alexander himself chases them with a sharp lance, but can never catch them; then he goes to seek counsel from Aristotle, and so his torment continues day in and day out. (ll. 10481–657)

With his guides, Huon comes to a place of great clamour. There is Judas, and there Ganelon, dragged at the horse's tail. In the depths of Hell Huon sees Cain and the mighty

Pharaoh; but now Lucifer himself approaches. Huon, bidden by Aeneas to have no fear, addresses Lucifer in Christ's name, refusing to salute so base a creature: he is to hold his realm in fief from Charles. Satan says he will take counsel and meanwhile keep Huon hostage in the deepest part of Hell. But Guillaume demands in God's name that Lucifer deliver to Huon what he has asked. Thereupon the Prince of Hell consents to become Charles's liegeman, in token of which he will send the following tribute: a rich litter, a thousand golden singing birds, a priceless crown, and a ring. Lucifer suggests that Huon put the latter on his own finger, but he refuses. The hero's mission is completed, but he is too weak to accomplish the arduous return journey, since he has not eaten for nine days. Guillaume demands food of Satan, and it is supplied. But Huon is suspicious and fears he may offend God by eating. However, Guillaume gives him permission to take the food, for his penance is now completed. He sits, to eat, on a chair which had belonged to him in the world; and this he recognises as a miracle. After his meal he falls asleep. Guillume makes the sign of the cross over him, then puts him in the charge of the demon who had brought the food and tells him to carry Huon safe and sound back to his palace before midnight, without waking him. This is done; and when the count wakes on the morrow he finds himself unharmed in his own city. Guillaume has ascended once more to Paradise. (ll. 10658–827)

Charles is angry at Huon's return and will believe none of his stories. But the devil produces the gifts from Lucifer— including the litter, on which the wretched king is carried off to eternal damnation. A new ruler is chosen: Guillaume Capet. But for Huon there is little rest; and soon afterwards he is slain in combat with the Saracens who are besieging Rome.

How the long, unwieldy descent episode here contrasts with that in the *Histoire de Charles Martel*! Yet a comparison of the whole of the two works can leave us in no doubt that both are derived from a single legend. And clearly too the prose work, with its relatively simple and more coherent development, represents an earlier stage in the legend's life, despite its late date and the fact that it also seems to show some departures from its source.[39] If we had the French poem on which the Italian recensions of *Huon d'Auvergne* seem to be based, the picture would be very much clearer.

It was probably in Italy that the story acquired the Dantesque features which colour so unmistakeably the poem as it has come down to us.[40] A detailed study of all the sources is impossible here, for they are too many and too varied. Dante himself has scarcely woven a more intricate pattern of history and legend than has the unknown author of *Huon d'Auvergne*. It is not difficult to find reminiscences of the French epics (especially *Aspremont* and the Guillaume cycle), of Celtic romance (perhaps represented in the descent episode by the unpiloted boat), of Virgil, of the Alexander legend and other Greek material,[41] and above all of the Divine Poet himself. Indeed, one of the most significant features of this part of the poem is that it represents the earliest known imitation of Dante's *Inferno*, a work which, as we have seen, was largely neglected in medieval France.

The poem's literary value is small because of its very confused and corrupt state in the existing manuscripts. The descent episode lacks the unity of inspiration and logical development of the *Inferno*; and for this reason, although it is far from dull, it bears the stamp of the *remanieur* rather than the true poet. Yet there is no denying its imaginative qualities, which set it apart from many of the texts in the pious tradition. Not that the author's piety is in doubt; but while his sentiment is sincerely Christian, his imagination is largely secular, with curious and rather incongruous results. His devoutness is reflected in such things as Aeneas' longing for redemption, references to Christ's descent and to the terrors of Doomsday, and perhaps more subtly in Saudin's statement that he was the thirteenth of Charles's counsellors to give treacherous advice. It is shown even more strongly in the parts of the poem I have not analysed in detail, particularly in the episodes immediately preceding the descent story. Despite this, Hell is shown as being a relatively innocuous place, at least by comparison with some of the descriptions we have examined. An interesting

feature is that a number of the torments (those of Ptolemy and
the necromancers, the Trojans and the Greeks, the Saracens
and Tibaut, and of Girart de Fraite, Otisiaus, Pythagoras and
his companions) are of an intellectual more than a physical
kind. This is at variance with the usual homiletic approach.
And a distinctly unclerical feature is the lack of any clear
divisions in the infernal regions consistent with the theological
views of the day. There is no mention of Purgatory or of the
Limbus patrum; and the limbo of the unbaptised is not reserved
for children alone.

It is unthinkable, then, that the poet was a cleric. Nor was he
an ordinary jongleur, because in addition to a wide knowledge of
epic and romance he shows considerable familiarity with figures
of Classical history and myth. Moreover, the fate he accords
to the minstrels suggests that he held a poor opinion of them in
general. It seems that he was especially interested in the
scholars of the past, and his relative lenience towards them
reflects a certain sympathy on his part. One wonders if he was
himself a scholar; and the possibility is strengthened by his
reference to the students on the Seine (ll. 10155-8). He may
well have had personal experience of the Paris schools, and
afterwards have been led by his taste for vernacular poetry to
earn a living by his pen. But we cannot penetrate his anonymity further; and our main interest must lie in the comparison
of his treatment of our theme with that found in the *Histoire de
Charles Martel*. Not only may this help to throw new light in a
fascinating corner of literary history, but it shows how it was
felt legitimate to develop and elaborate the theme along purely
literary lines, without special thought of moral instruction. For
Hell had now become one of the stock of "stage properties"
for romance and epic, on a par with the enchanted castle or the
pagan citadel.

In *Baudouin de Sebourc*[42] there are no infernal fictions as elaborate as these last two, but in the course of the long poem there
are two episodes worth examining. I pass over without regret
the rest of the involved story, which was put into Alexandrine
verse about the middle of the fourteenth century in the region

around Valenciennes.[43] It is typical of the later epic, with its mixture of feudal and heroi-comic elements and with its taste for the marvellous, which the two following incidents betray.

Elienor, the Saracen heroine of the poem, needs to explain to her brother, the Saracen king, her temporary disappearance from the palace. She says she was walking in a garden; and as she was about to return to the palace, two black crows descended upon her and carried her straight off to Hell. There she saw her father plunged in a cauldron of molten lead. He sent his greetings to his son the king, along with the message that he must avenge him against the Christian invaders, otherwise his soul would never escape from its torment. Thereupon the crows caught the princess up once more and transported her back to the earth. (III, ll. 362–77)

Later in the poem, Baudouin and his companion Poliban leave Baghdad and set sail on the sea. A tempest drives them far off their course, beyond "la grant mer d'Engletere" (XV, l. 8) and beyond the Irish Sea, until they finally arrive at the Earthly Paradise, which they visit. After a further fifteen days of voyaging they find another pleasant island, where they disembark. Journeying inland, they see a great volume of smoke that blots out earth and sky. Suddenly, from a bush there comes a voice so full of anguish that Baudouin asks if they are in Hell; and Poliban suggests that, having shown them the Earthly Paradise, Christ now wishes them to see Hell. Poliban calls to ask whose the voice is, and the answer is that it belongs to Judas. The travellers are still a thousand leagues from Hell itself; and Judas explains that he is not there only because he has respite from his pains throughout Saturday and Sunday. His Saturday respite is granted him for having once bridged a stream (the stone he used is nearby); and because he once gave money to a poor, sick man, he has further relief on Sunday. He warns the travellers that they are on the road to the house of Cain, where there are three places of darkness. The first is for the still-born children and those who died before baptism; the second is for the pagans and suicides; in the third, where are all the devils, the unconfessed murderers, thieves and usurers suffer their unending punishments. Judas says that for five days in every week he is in the infernal cauldron suffering the dread fires of Hell, where he hopes one day to see Poliban, who delights in the arch-traitor's plight. Having seen and conversed with Judas, the companions return to their ship and set sail. Before long, the wind drives them close to Hell itself. They see demons who, having spotted the ship, bring flaming brands from Hell and cast them towards it. However, an angel comes to protect the voyagers, and the missiles fall harmlessly into the sea,

> ... Mais j'ai oï conter
> En le droite matere de saint Brandon, le ber,
> Que li brandon faisoient l'iauwe en maint lieu flamber.
>
> (XV, ll. 556–8)

(But I have heard it told in the true story of the noble Saint Brandon that the brands made the water blaze in many places.)

Poliban vows that he will take the name of Brandon as a consequence of this adventure with the *brandons*. (XV)

The first episode is scarcely a descent in the true sense of the word, since it is a kind of double fiction, a story invented by one of the fictitious characters. It is curious from another point of view, for Elienor's father is shown to be in a Hell from which he can only be delivered if vengeance is taken upon the *Christians*. It would be interesting to know what was in the author's mind when he wrote this passage. Did he make an unconscious slip as he spoke of the orthodox Hell? Was he wanting to suggest that the king was in a specifically Moslem Hell? Or is it a sly touch of humour and deliberate irreverence? The first possibility is always strong in a medieval work. The strength of the second is increased by the circumstances of the supposed descent, the black birds adding a rather exotic touch.[44] And for the third possibility there are other passages in the poem which might be taken as supporting evidence. Here, for example, are some lines from the first canto:

"... *Tout cil sont non sachant,*
Qui convoitent leur mort et vont en riens hastant:
Car puis c'uns homs est mors, il n'a au sien noiant;
Si le boivent et galent si hoir ou si enfant.
Je tieng a paradis che siecle deduisant:
Quant .i. homs i puet faire son bon et son commant,
Et avoir belle dame et boire des vins tant,
C'on se fache servir en gales et en cant.
Cil qui ont povreté sont en infer manant,
Car je tieng pour infer le regne d'un mescant."

(I, ll. 427–36)

("All those are foolish who look forward to their death and
hurry it on in any way : for once a man is dead, he has nothing to call his own; his heirs or children drink and revel it
away. I think of this merry world as Paradise : when a man
can have his own way here and do as he likes, have a fair
lady and such abundant wine to drink, let him be served in
feasting and song. Those who are in poverty dwell in Hell,
for a pauper's kingdom is Hell to me.")

Admittedly, these words are not spoken by the hero of the poem
(unlike Aucassin's well-known speech in the *chantefable*, which
could conceivably have inspired them),[45] but by the traitor
Gaufroi; and in the fictional anecdote, the doubtful statement
is a whimsy of a Saracen princess. The poet's alibis are sound
in these instances : he cannot justly be charged with irreverence. But there is another case of unorthodoxy—in the second
of the episodes I have summarised. This is in the description
of the "house of Cain", where the pagans are found, not in the
pit of Hell in the company of all the devils, but in what can only
be called a limbo. Whose description is this ? It is given by the
arch-traitor Judas : yet another alibi, but this time more
suspect, since Judas has no reason to lie, suffering as he does
the very torments of the Hell he depicts, and where he hopes
one day to see Poliban languish. For all the evidence, the verdict must be that irreverence on the part of the poet is not
proven. Yet we are entitled to the opinion that this is a mis-
carriage of justice, and the conclusion of Labande does not
detract from our suspicion; for he considered the writer of this

part of the work to be an ex-clerk who preferred good living to the monastic life.[46]

The source of the second episode would be obvious even if it were not mentioned by the poet as being the *Voyage of St Brendan*. He has modified it considerably without improving on the original, which could possibly have been Benedeit's version of the legend. His idea of three infernal regions may have been suggested by the two Hells in Benedeit, but if so his explanation is highly original. The final adventure is a clear imitation of the isle of forges in the *Brendan*. On the face of it, the tone here seems reverent enough despite the unusual description of Hell and the piece of repartee by Judas. But the explanation of the name "Brandon" is ingenious, to say the least; and the inference that this Poliban is none other than St Brendan himself is rather a bold one, suggesting that here at any rate is one saint whom the poet did not hold in great veneration. In this he was following the Latin poet of the preceding century.[47]

There might have been some justification, then, in my leaving *Baudouin de Sebourc* over to be studied in my next chapter, when I shall look at some burlesque versions of our theme. That might also have been the place for a discussion of another descent story if it were extant. As it is we have only an enigmatic reference to it as having figured in a lost epic. In the *Farce novelle a cinq personnages, c'est a sçavoir la mere de ville, le varlet, le garde pot, le garde nape et le garde cul*, which was composed in about 1540, there is an allusion to the valiant Fierabras, who protected "Garguentuas" when he fell down into the nether regions. Abel Lefranc comments: "Cette descente de Gargantua aux Enfers, de même que son trébuchement ne figure dans aucune des rédactions connues [de *Fierabras*]; il faut donc supposer qu'il a dû en exister une qui contenait cet épisode."[48] To this I can add only the comment that this surely was a burlesque of the infernal visit.

The texts reviewed in this chapter show that the writers of secular literature were not above drawing on pious legends if by doing so they could add a further arresting adventure to their tale. The medieval reverence for Christian legend was quite capable of being relaxed in this way, just as the pious writers were not above illustrating their stories by using features from secular or even pagan sources. It would be wrong, however, to think of the treatment of the theme in works like the *Histoire de Charles Martel*, or even less in *Huon d'Auvergne*, as being deliberately irreverent. So real was Hell to medieval eyes that the possibility of its having human visitors did not present the incongruity or profanity which seem to us inherent in the confusion of the physical with the spiritual. Hell could be visited. For medieval people it held varying degrees of terror, but no mysteries. And, in certain cases, it was because of this public familiarity with the nature of Hell that writers of Celtic romance were able to give some of their episodes a distinctly infernal flavour. The hero, or some other person, has to visit a place of great danger (perhaps a relic from a Celtic Otherworld myth); and so, to emphasise the perils of the locality, the author gives it infernal characteristics, yet without pretending that this is the true Hell.[49] Sometimes, as we shall see, their motives were rather mixed. And if irreverence exists for the most part only from the modern standpoint, when the story contains a conscious comic element, there are grounds for suspecting the writer of deliberate levity. This was the case with *Baudouin de Sebourc*; and I shall offer more blatant examples in the next chapter.

Relatively simple secular treatments of the descent theme seem to have existed in epic or epico-romance from the twelfth century at least—and earlier, if we take those three cryptic lines from the *Chanson de Roland* as evidence. Before 1200 it appears that some version of a descent into Hell by one of Charles Martel's vassals was current, and there is no reason to suppose that other similar tales did not exist then. That they have not come down to us may be due to the fact that they would be the type of story more popular with the wandering jongleurs than with the monks in their cloister, because of their lack of any salutary lesson. But although such tales may have existed, the actual descent episodes were probably less fully developed than in the later works. For in the twelfth century, Hell was only just taking shape in the mind of the public, largely through the propagation of the pious accounts. In the following centuries, some stories underwent considerable rehandling and expansion as more illustrative material became available to the *remanieurs*. These conclusions, it is true, are based on very few surviving texts, and we have no means of telling how many others of the same kind have been lost. But it is also noteworthy that those which have come down are continental in origin; and one is tempted to make further deductions concerning a possible difference in attitude to the secular descent story on the two sides of the Channel. First, however, there is more evidence to be assembled.

NOTES

1. See above, p. 94.
2. Ed. J. Bédier (éd. définitive, Paris, 1937). Other versions name the enchanter as Gloriel (Paris and Cambridge MSS) or Gocel (Lyons) and have other minor variant readings.
3. E.g. ll. 207–9, 1562–8, 1773–9, etc.
4. Th. de Cauzons, *La Magie et la sorcellerie en France*, Vols. I & II, *passim*.
5. J. Garinet, *Histoire de la magie en France, depuis le commencement de la monarchie jusqu'à nos jours* (Paris, 1818), pp. 39–40.
6. See J. Seznec, *La Survivance des dieux antiques* (London, 1940), p. 43.
7. See later, pp. 178–80 and Appendix II.
8. Ed. Baron de Reiffenberg, *La Chronique rimée de Philippe Mouskés* (2 vols., Brussels, 1836–8). J. Nothomb suggests 1251 as the *terminus a quo* ("La Date de la Chronique Rimée de Philippe Mousket", *Revue belge de Philologie et d'Histoire* 4 [1925], pp. 77–89). For Philippe's sources see especially F. Hasselmann, *Ueber die Quellen der Chronique Rimée von Philipp Mousket* (Göttingen, 1916).
9. Ll. 1916 ff. (ed. Reiffenberg, I, pp. 79–81).
10. See Dom M. Bouquet, *Recueil des historiens des Gaules et de la France* III (Paris, 1869), pp. 569–60.
11. As Philippe's is not the only vernacular version, I summarise here from the Latin account published by J. P. Migne (*Patrologia Latina*, Vol 179, cols. 1064–8) from William of Malmesbury's *Gesta Regum Anglorum* Book II, Ch. 111, where it is taken verbatim from Hariulf's *Chronica* Book III, Ch. 21. A footnote in Migne points out that some versions wrongly ascribe the vision to Charles le Chauve. Indeed, Philippe Mouskés makes the same mistake. In his chronicle the legend occupies ll. 12571–679 (ed. Reiffenberg, II, pp. 19 ff.) and is somewhat abridged And whereas in the Latin accounts Charles tells his story in the first person, Philippe gives it in the third.
12. This is reminiscent of the ball of thread used by Theseus in the Cretan labyrinth. The analogy is strengthened by the angel's words: "Accip filum glomeris micantis . . . quia per illum duceris in labyrinthaeas in fernorum penas" (col. 1065).

PLATE 5. Archefer receives scroll of magic arts from Sorbrin. Brussels, Bibliothèque Royale de Belgique MS 6. Miniature by Loyset Liédet. 1470.

13. Surely modelled on the Styx, Acheron and infernal marshes of Classical mythology.
14. Cf. the *Vision of St Paul*.
15. In the *Chronique rimée* it is completely hideous.
16. I.e. Louis le Germanique.
17. Louis II of Germany refers to his grandson who became Louis III.
18. Ll. 8288–8325 (ed. Reiffenberg, I, pp. 327–8). Taken from the *Pseudo-Turpin Chronicle*, Ch. 25 (ed. C. Meredith-Jones [Paris, 1936], p. 202).
19. Ll. 11768–819 (ed. Reiffenberg, I, pp. 453–5). Borrowed from the same source (Ch. 32; op. cit., pp. 228–30).
20. Cf. H. R. Patch, *The Other World*, p. 107; A. B. van Os, *Religious Visions*, p. 24.
21. The complete work forms MSS 6, 7, 8 and 9 of the Bibliothèque Royale de Belgique. The episode with which we are concerned is found in MS 6, fol. 285ᵛ–293ᵛ (old foliation) = 289ᵛ–297ᵛ (new foliation). I give a transcription in Appendix II.
22. See Paul Meyer, *Girart de Roussillon* (Paris, 1884), pp. ccii–cciii.
23. MS 7, fol. 435 (see Meyer, ibid., p. clxi).
24. Op. cit.: for information on the *Histoire de Charles Martel* see Ch. VII, § 3, and Appendix II of the Introduction.
25. Op. cit., p. clxiv.
26. "The Principal Source of *Huon de Bordeaux*", *French Studies* VII (1953), pp. 129–39.
27. Ibid. Pierre Ruelle, in his edition of *Huon de Bordeaux* (Brussels & Paris, 1960) does not accept my thesis (pp. 72–3): see my reply to his criticisms in *Cahiers de Civilisation Médiévale* V (1962), pp. 224–5. The question merits further and more detailed study.
28. *Dialogus Miraculorum*, Book I, Ch. 34 (see Owen, art. cit., p. 135).
29. *Huon de Bordeaux*, ed. Ruelle, ll. 2330–3. On one occasion Huon is
    ... *ens l'ille Moÿsant;*
    A trois lieuetes est Infers le puant. (ll. 7085–6)
    This feature is probably borrowed from the *Voyage of St Brendan*.
30. Partially edited by R. Rénier, *La Discesa di Ugo d'Alvernia all'inferno secondo il codice francoitaliano della Nazionale di Torino* (Bologna, 1883); E. Stengel, *Huons aus Auvergne Suche nach dem Hölleneingang* (Greifswald, 1912—ll. 7148–8918), *Huons aus Auvergne Höllenfahrt, nach der Berliner und Paduaner Hs.* (Greifswald, 1908—ll. 9196–10827), and "Karl Martels Entführung in die Hölle und Wilhelm Capets Wahl zu seinem Nachfolger. Stelle aus der Chanson von Huon d'Auvergne nach der Berliner Hs." in *Studi letterari e linguistici dedicati a Pio Rajna* (Milan, 1911), pp. 873–91 (ll. 10828–11534); A. Tobler, "Die Berliner Handschrift des *Huon d'Auvergne*", *Sitzungsberichte der Kön. Preuss. Ak. der Wissenschaften zu Berlin* (29th May 1884), pp. 605–20 (ll. 8919–9195 and other extracts). The MSS are Berlin, Hamilton 337 (=B); Seminario di Padova 32 (=P); Turin, University Library, N.III.19, No. 106 (=T).
31. See Owen, art. cit., p. 129. Line references are from B.
32. The manuscripts are confused at this point.
33. L. 9870. The supposed Phrygian, Dares, is credited with the *Historia de excidio Trojae*.
34. A tenth-century Arab philosopher. Avicenna was his disciple.
35. In P they are geometricians.

VH H

36. In P she is confined to Hell for one unconfessed sin, and Guillaume seeks to help her.
37. One of the several anachronisms in the poem.
38. I have not traced this figure. Marcus Varro is commonly regarded as the true founder of the Liberal Arts (cf. G. Paré, A. Brunet & P. Tremblay, *La Renaissance du XIIe siècle: les écoles et l'enseignement* [Paris & Ottawa, 1933], pp. 97 ff.).
39. See Owen, art. cit. I suggest that the hero's name has been changed; that some features have been borrowed from the story of the Landgrave Ludwig; and that Charles Martel has been allowed to survive, whereas in *Huon d'Auvergne* he is eventually carried to Hell for all time in the infernal litter, a solution that agrees better with medieval tradition.
40. For a discussion of the development of the legend and debts to Dante see A. Graf, "Di un poema inedito di Carlo Martello e di Ugo Conte d'Alvernia", *Giornale de Filologia Romanza* I (1878), pp. 92–110. General features borrowed from the *Inferno* are the architecture of Hell (here somewhat confused), and the constant appearance of legendary and historical figures.
41. There are even striking parallels with the *Odyssey* where, in Book XI, the wraith of Hercules (he himself being among the gods) is in Hades with a strung bow, frightening the souls around him.
42. Ed. L. N. Boca (but published anonymously: Valenciennes, 1841). Boca divided the poem into 25 cantos: my references are to canto and line numbers.
43. E. R. Labande, *Étude sur "Baudouin de Sebourc"* (Paris, 1940), pp. 66–7.
44. Evil spirits in the guise of black birds occur in Christian legend. Peter Damian, for example, recorded in the latter part of the eleventh century how fearful birds rise from a stretch of black water in Apulia on Saturday evenings and return to its depths at dawn on Monday. They are souls enjoying their respite from punishment, and the signal for their return is the cawing of a huge crow (A. Graf, *Miti, Leggende e Superstizione del Medio Evo* [Turin, 1892], I, p. 250). I have already mentioned the demon black birds connected with St Patrick (above, p. 38). And in *Huon d'Auvergne* the hero has to contend with many strange and terrifying birds during his search for the entrance to Hell, being actually transported through the air by two griffins (Stengel, *Huons aus Auvergne Suche . . . , passim*).
45. "En paradis qu'ai je a faire? Je n'i quier entrer, mais que j'aie Nicolete, ma trés douce amie que j'aim tant. C'en paradis ne vont fors tex gens con je vous dirai. Il i vont cil viel prestre et cil viel clop et cil manke, qui totejor et tote nuit cropent devant ces autex et en ces viés cruutes, et cil a ces viés capes eréses et a ces viés tatereles vestues, qui sont nu et decauç et estrumelé qui moeurent de faim et de soi et de froit et de mesaises. Icil vont en paradis; aveuc ciax n'ai jou que faire; mais en infer voil jou aler. Car en infer vont li bel clerc, et li bel cevalier, qui sont mort as tornois et as rices gueres, et li buen sergant, et li franc home. Aveuc ciax voil jou aler. Et s'i vont les beles dames cortoises, que eles ont deus amis ou trois avoc leur barons. Et s'i va li ors et li argens, et li vairs et li gris; et si i vont harpeor et jogleor et li roi del siecle. Avoc ciax voil jou aler, mais que j'aie Nicolete, ma trés douce amie, aveuc mi." (*Aucassin et Nicolete*, ed. F. W. Bourdillon [Manchester, 1930], p. 7.)

Gaufroi's words are certainly less extreme than Aucassin's description of the tedium of Heaven and the rich delights of Hell.

46. Op. cit. For a general discussion of date and authorship see pp. 66 ff. The romance is the work of two different authors; the one with whom we are concerned wrote the first 17,000 lines. Further examples of irreverence in the poem are given by Paulin Paris in his study "Baudouin de Sebourg", *Histoire littéraire de la France*, 25 (1869), pp. 537–93 (see pp. 540, 559, 577–80). He also notes the unsympathetic treatment of monks (pp. 589–90).

47. See above, p. 118.

48. *Œuvres de François Rabelais*, I (Paris, 1912), pp. xxv–xxxvi.

49. Instances may be found in *The Vulgate Version of the Arthurian Romances* ed. H. O. Sommer; e.g. Vol. I (*L'Estoire del Saint Graal* [Washington, 1909]), pp. 220, 248 ff. Another interesting example is in Renaut de Beaujeu's *Le Bel Inconnu* (ed. G. P. Williams [Paris, 1929]), where the reader is left in little doubt as to the infernal nature of the Cité Gaste. This episode (ll. 2778 ff.) includes the appearance of a "demon" horse. But despite images and in some cases symbols taken over from Christian eschatology (further remarkable examples will be given in Ch. VIII), such episodes cannot properly be described as visits to Hell. The closest we come to a true visit is in the fourteenth-century romance *Perceforest*, where the Celtic element is in any case much diluted. There a magician caused an abyss to open so that those watching his performance had the terrifying spectacle of Hell yawning at their feet. They could see the damned being hanged, roasted, boiled, rent apart, or fixed to infernal wheels. (See Jeanne Lods, *Le Roman de Perceforest* [Geneva & Lille, 1951], p. 102 : quoted by J. Frappier, "Châtiments infernaux et peur du diable, d'après quelques textes français du XIIIe et du XIVe siècle", *Cahiers de l'Association Internationale des Études Françaises*, No. 3–4–5 [July 1953], pp. 90–1.)

CHAPTER VIII

PARODY AND BURLESQUE

I T has often been observed, though perhaps not sufficiently
emphasised, that a strong undercurrent of impiety ran
through these centuries so often characterised as the Age of
Faith—partly a reaction, one might think, to the incessant
warnings and threats of the clergy.[1] Lapsed morality, laxity
in leading the Christian life, and criticism and ridicule of
churchmen are not the prerogative of modern times, as a high
proportion of medieval literature confirms. In the romances in
particular a note of pagan indifference to the usual Christian
values is frequently struck. And so in *Guillaume de Dole* we
are shown knights and ladies philandering in a pastoral setting:
they had little thought for their souls; no need there for bells
or churches—the birds were their only chaplains![2] The
Provençal *Flamenca* describes at length how the lovers make their
assignation through words passed stealthily during mass.[3]
Church institutions and liturgical texts are parodied in Latin
and the vernacular, and there are frequent allusions to frivolity
in the observance of Christian rites and ceremonies.[4]

But evidence of open mockery of the mysteries of the Faith
and religious experience is less easy to come by, and what we
have is for the most part the testimony of zealous churchmen.
There is no doubt that some people lacked belief in certain of
the commonly accepted features of Christian doctrine, including Hell and purgatorial punishment, and even God Himself.[5]
And we read of the levity of a jongleur who, being ill received
at a great hall when he proclaimed that he was God's man,
said: "Then I am the devil's man", and was thereupon gladly
taken in by the company.[6] The fact that few surviving texts
contain direct blasphemy or grave irreverence is not to be
wondered at. For it was scarcely prudent to have works of this
kind committed to parchment in an age when there was much

200

devout belief and few did not pay at least lip-service to the
Catholic faith ; and if it was recorded, the preservation of any
irreligious or heretical text through five or six centuries that
have seen revivals as well as regressions in spiritual life would
be a cause for surprise. The few texts we shall look at now do
provide examples of the parodying of essential Christian beliefs,
but in a way least calculated to give offence.

Chrétien de Troyes was a writer of sensibility and tact and was
endowed, too, with a considerable, though quiet, sense of
humour. This, unfortunately, is an aspect of his art that has
been too little studied, or even recognised in the past ; and as a
result, some very wayward interpretations of his romances have,
I believe, been offered. Two of them in particular have suffered
in this way, namely *Lancelot* (*Le Chevalier de la Charrete*) and
the latter part of the *Conte du Graal*, which I take to have been
conceived by Chrétien as a separate Gauvain romance, without
direct connection with the earlier Perceval adventures.[7]
   Our particular concern here is with a section of the *Lancelot*,
which was probably composed within a few years of 1170.[8]
It would take too long to justify now my opinion that the whole
romance was written tongue-in-cheek as a burlesque of the
more extreme cult of courtly love. It may even have been
Chrétien's conscious intention to allow for an appreciation on
two levels, the serious and the comic. But in any case, few
would deny the presence at various points in the poem of
events and situations that hold more than a grain of humour.
And I would claim that the tone was set for the entire work in
the amusingly paradoxical prologue, where Chrétien insists
that he will not flatter his patroness, Marie de Champagne,
but in terms that are most lavish in his praise for her.
   I shall not summarise the well-known story of how Lancelot
rides forth in pursuit of the abducted Guenevere, the mistress
of his heart and object of his every thought. But I do hope to show
that the central part of the romance, which tells of the hero's arrival
in the mysterious land of Gorre and his rescue of the captives
there, is nothing less than a diffuse parody of the traditional
account of Christ's Harrowing of Hell. Let us then see what

evidence there is to back up this rather surprising conclusion.

First there is the visit paid by Lancelot to the strange ceme-
tery, where the finest of the tombs bears an inscription referring to the slab that covers it :

> "*Cil qui levera*
> *Cele lanme seus par son cors*
> *Gitera ces et celes fors*
> *Qui sont an la terre an prison,*
> *Don n'ist ne clers ne gentix hon*
> *Des l'ore qu'il i est antrez;*
> *N'ancors n'en est nus retornez :*
> *Les estranges prisons retienent;*
> *Et cil del païs vont et vienent*
> *Et anz et fors a lor pleisir.*"   (ll. 1900-9)

("He who raises that slab alone and unaided will set free all
the men and women who are captives in the land whence
neither clerk nor noble escapes from the hour he enters ; as
yet none has returned from there : they are held in those
foreign prisons ; and the inhabitants of the country come
and go in and out as they please.")

These words put us in mind of the events following the Crucifixion by their reference to the raising of the stone as well as to
the predicted deliverance of those imprisoned in the land
whence none return.[9]

Lancelot raises the slab and pursues his journey. At this
point, vague reminiscences of the *Gospel of Nicodemus* begin
when an old knight who had been accompanying the hero
chides his son for having wished earlier to fight with him
(ll. 1981-95). We recall the recriminations that flew between
Satan and Inferus in the *Gospel* at the time of Christ's entry
into Hell. And very soon it becomes apparent to us that
Lancelot has actually entered the hostile realm. His arrival is
announced to the inhabitants by a squire, who adds :

> "*Ce dient an cest païs tuit*
> *Que il les deliverra toz*
> *Et metra les noz au desoz.*"   (ll. 2300-2)

("Everyone in this land says that he will deliver them all and subjugate our own people.")

We are reminded of the confidence of the souls in Hell in their imminent deliverance; and their joy is echoed by that of the captives when they learn that this is their saviour:

> *" Seignor, ce est cil*
> *Qui nos gitera toz d'essil*
> *Et de la grant maleürté*
> *Ou nos avons lonc tans esté;*
> *Se li devons grant enor feire*
> *Quant, por nos fors de prison treire,*
> *A tant perilleus leus passez*
> *Et passera ancor assez;*
> *Molt a a feire et molt a fait."*
>
> (ll. 2413–21)

("Good sirs, this is he who will deliver us all from exile and the great misfortune in which we have long languished; and we should do him great honour when, to release us from our imprisonment, he has passed through such perils and has still many more to face; he has much to do, and much he has accomplished.")

Then for a while Chrétien leaves the cadre of the Harrowing to describe Lancelot's passage of the sword bridge. And here, with his mind still running along eschatological lines, he shows familiarity with some such legend as the *Vision of St Paul* or *St Patrick's Purgatory*, with their descriptions of the testing bridge of Hell. Not only does the bridge span a torrent as grim and black "as if it were the devil's river" (l. 3012), but it is razor-sharp[10] and may be crossed only by a true believer:

> *"Mes j'ai tel foi et tel creance*
> *An Deu qu'il me garra par tot."*
>
> (ll. 3084–5)

("But I have such faith and trust in God that He will protect me in all things.")

After his ordeal, Lancelot comes to the castle of King Bademagu: he is bleeding, we notice, from wounds in hands

and feet. From the castle the king and his son Meleagant watch
the hero approach; and they too engage in violent dispute
reminiscent of the quarrel of Satan and Inferus at the coming
of Christ.[11] Like Satan, Bademagu is prepared to receive the
newcomer, though his son shows only hostility. The details of
the two arguments are, of course, quite different: Lancelot's
prime duty remains the rescue of the queen, abducted by
Meleagant. But still phrases recur (as in ll. 3331-4) that keep
before us the equation with Christ's entry into Hell: the courage
of Lancelot's accomplishment is unique, and no such perilous
undertaking had ever been or will ever be achieved.

Now, as if to leave no doubt as to the parallel he is drawing,
Chrétien brings in an explicit allusion to the events of the
Passion. Bademagu says he will heal Lancelot's wounds with
the three Marys' ointment (or better, if such can be found—
ll. 3358-61). The duel with Meleagant is arranged; and all the
prisoners gather as for church on a feast day. The captive
maidens from Arthur's realm had fasted and gone barefoot for
three days[12] to solicit God's help for their saviour (ll. 3514-31).
Their prayers were answered, for the victory went to Lancelot,
who thereby obtained the queen's release. And we are told that
it was the custom of that country that when one person was
delivered, all the others were free to go (ll. 3899-901, cf.
ll. 2112-5). So the captives' joy knows no bounds: they throng
round Lancelot, welcoming him as their predestined deliverer,
each one struggling to touch him. For those who succeeded
there was no greater bliss (ll. 3906-20). In the end, all return
to Arthur's court.

Now though I maintain that this entry of Lancelot into the
land of Gorre and his release of those languishing in captivity
there is an evident parody of the Harrowing of Hell, I do not
suggest that it is in itself a humorous parody. It is true that we
have cause to smile when we reflect that this knight, who is
otherwise abject almost to the point of imbecility in his devotion
to Guenevere, is none the less raised through this parody and
his role of predestined saviour to a state of quasi-divinity. Yet,
considered apart from the underlying burlesque of the romance,
these events have nothing of the comic about them. Here, then,
is a remarkable fact: Chrétien has chosen to parody the most

serious and sublime of the descent stories to serve an overall burlesque effect in this most profane of romances. Rather shocking levity, one might think.

The father of Arthurian romance seems to have had a predilection for otherworldly settings for important adventures, attributable only in part to the Celtic derivation of his sources. One thinks of the Joie de la Cort episode in *Erec et Enide*, the Château de Pesme Aventure in *Yvain*, the Grail Castle, perhaps, in the *Conte du Graal*, and in the same romance Gauvain's adventures in the Château des Merveilles. The lingering existence in this latter place of ancient ladies long since lost to the world demands its equation with some form of otherworld; and, as in *Lancelot*, the context of the hero's visit is a series of adventures turned to burlesque effect.[13]

Soon after Chrétien's death, perhaps, *La Mule sans frein*, a short Gauvain romance, was composed by a poet from Champagne who styled himself Païen de Maisières. This, as I have shown,[14] was a pen-name using a play on the elements of "Chrétien de Troyes"; and in his romance the poet carries further the burlesque tradition as used by the master, notably in the Gauvain adventures of the *Conte du Graal*. In the course of the story, first Kay and then Gauvain ride on the mule of the title in quest of its missing bridle. Their path takes them through a forest full of wild beasts and then into a deep, dark valley.

The valley swarms with reptiles, snakes and scorpions, and other fire-breathing beasts. Even worse is the stench of the place, which is also bitterly cold and scourged by winds. The knights pass through the valley and on a plain find a clear fountain set in a flowery meadow. Further on they come to a black torrent, "li fluns au deable", that seems filled with devils. It is spanned by an iron bridge of no more than a hand's breadth. The sight was too much for Kay; but Gauvain commended himself to God and rode across the bridge, which sagged frighteningly as he went (ll. 167–257, 377–423).

Here again the borrowing from eschatological legend is plain to see, and again it is set in a burlesque context. The valley belongs to the infernal regions, with its typical features of darkness, vermin, bitter cold and wind. The meadow and fountain beyond recall the accounts of the Earthly Paradise normally reached by the traveller after Hell is passed; but with the bridge we are back to the places of torment and the testing bridge over the infernal river.[15] The pleasant region has merely been misplaced.

One other feature of *La Mule sans frein* is worthy of comment, and it occurs when Gauvain has achieved his quest, in the course of which he had slain some ferocious beasts that had kept the inhabitants of a castle cowering in cellars and crypts. They joyfully emerge, and Gauvain is told:

> . . ."*Or dïent en lor langage:*
> *Dieus les a par vos delivrez,*
> *Et de toz biens enluminez*
> *La gent qui en tenebre estoient.*
> *Si grant joie ont de ce qu'il voient*
> *Qu'il ne püent graingnor avoir.*"

(ll. 1030–5)

("Now they say in their own tongue: through you God has delivered them and has given the light of absolute bliss to the people that were in darkness. What they see brings them such great joy that they could not have greater.")

As well as the echo of *Luke* i. 79 (cf. *Isaiah* ix. 2), we catch here once again the phraseology typical of the accounts of Christ's spoliation of Hell.

Our examination of Chrétien's romances and this later poem, apparently by one of his disciples, has disclosed the use of our theme in a parodic vein to fill out a tale of mock-heroic adventure. Most surprising is the particular choice for such treatment of that most august and solemn of all descent accounts, the Harrowing of Hell. The next text to be considered takes this irreverence to even greater lengths.

The fabliau *Saint Pierre et le jongleur* is mentioned by Gröber as a Picard work from the first half of the thirteenth century.[16]

A poor jongleur of Sens loses all his money and possessions through too great a love of wine, wenches and dice. When he dies, a demon who has ranged the countryside for a whole month without finding any prey joyfully seizes the defenceless soul to carry it off to Hell. Meanwhile the demon's fellows have had much better hunting and present to the gratified Lucifer many bishops, abbots, priests, monks, knights, robbers and prizefighters. But Lucifer notices that the last demon has not yet arrived, an opportunity for his minions to vent their spite on this wretched companion of theirs, who is so bad at catching souls. But finally the demon does turn up, bringing with him the naked jongleur, who explains meekly who he is and offers to sing for Lucifer. The Prince of Hell will have nothing of his singing but, out of pity for this ill-clad creature, grants that he may stoke the fire beneath the infernal cauldron. The jongleur swears by St Peter that he is only too glad to get warm, and so he accepts the task eagerly.

One day Lucifer and all the devils go on earth to conquer souls, and the jongleur is given charge of all the damned. If he lets a single one escape, he will have his eyes put out and will be hanged and eaten alive (!). Otherwise, on their return he will be feasted on roast monk with usurer or lecher sauce.[17] Thereupon all the devils depart.

Suddenly there appears the majestic figure of St Peter, who has entered Hell equipped with gaming-board and three dice. Sitting quietly down beside the jongleur, he asks if he would like a game. The jongleur says he has no money; and so St Peter suggests playing for five or six souls. The jongleur is afraid, but he is assured that twenty or so would never be missed. When St Peter holds some newly-minted coins under his nose, he can resist the temptation no longer; so they sit down to play.

St Peter wins steadily; and the poor victim curses him roundly, accusing him of being a cheat and a robber. The jongleur then tries to seize the coins, and when St Peter makes him drop them he grabs the saint's beard and they begin to brawl. But with his shirt badly torn, the poor soul gives in, apologises to St Peter, and proposes a resumption of

the game. It is continued, but always with the same result:
St Peter never fails to beat his opponent by the odd pip.
When the other souls in Hell hear that he is winning, they
cry out to him:

> *" Sire, por Dieu le glorïous,*
> *Nos atendomes tuit a vos."*
> *Et dit seint Pierre: "Je l'otri,*
> *Et ge a vos et vos a mi;*
> *Por vos giter de cest torment*
> *Mis ge au gieu tot mon argent;*
> *S'eüsse mon argent perdu,*
> *Nïent eüssiez atendu.*
> *Se ge puis, ainz la nuiz serie,*
> *Seroiz toz en ma compaignie."*   (ll. 339–48)

("Sir, glory be to God, all our hopes are placed in you."
And St Peter said: "This I pledge, myself to you and you
to me; to cast you forth from this torment I staked all my
money; had I lost my money, your expectations would
have been in vain. If possible, before night falls you will
all be in my company.")

Finally, St Peter wins all the souls from the poor jongleur
and leads them off in great throngs to Heaven.

Lucifer and all the devils return to find no souls either in
the furnace or in the cauldron. He asks where they are, and
the jongleur says that they have been won at dice by an old
cheat. Lucifer is furious and sends for the unfortunate
demon who brought the jongleur to Hell. He has him soundly
thrashed and makes him swear that he will never bring another jongleur or dice-player into his kingdom. As for the
jongleur, Lucifer throws him out of Hell, telling him to go to
God, who loves joy. Never again will he have one of his kind
in Hell.

Ejected from the infernal regions, the jongleur made his
way up to Paradise, where St Peter threw open the door in
welcome. So, adds the poet, let minstrels make merry, for
never will they suffer the pains of Hell. For this they have
him to thank who lost the souls at dice.

This tale, told in 420 octosyllabic lines, shows literary qualities and a wit well above the average for its genre. As I showed some years ago,[18] there are three main strands to the narrative : the character of the jongleur, the *diableries*, and the theme of a divine personage winning possession of all the souls imprisoned in Hell. The first two elements are commonplace enough, so it is to the third that we have to look for what is individual and original in the fabliau. And we realise, of course, that there is only one other account known to the Middle Ages of a divine figure descending into Hell to rescue the captive souls, and that is, once again, the tradition of Christ's descent.

Here, then, we have another case of one of the elaborated descriptions of the Harrowing being put to use in a secular context. But the author of this fabliau showed a temerity far beyond Chrétien's when he used his parody for uproariously comic ends. And that this is a parody can scarcely be doubted when, apart from the main lines of the story and the squabbles among the devils, we find parallels between some of the phraseology here and that used in a variety of pious accounts of the Harrowing. For instance, Christ traditionally spoke of the sacrifice He made on behalf of the rescued souls, but not, as St Peter does here, in terms of money.[19] And the saint's words promising the souls that they would be before nightfall in his company is a direct paraphrase of Christ's promise to the good robber: "Hodie mecum eris in paradiso" (*Luke* xxiii. 43).

Again it is worth commenting that if one takes this as the height of blasphemy, one is not viewing things through medieval eyes. Our poet was no doubt a jongleur himself, and his class had to take many a hard knock at the hands of the Church. So they were not loath, as opportunity arose, to indulge their humour at the expense of its servants, its teachings, or even its texts. The Goliardic *Credo au ribaut* ("The Scoundrel's Creed") was composed in much the same spirit, with the dying clerk bringing the words of the Creed into a monologue even more open to the charge of blasphemy. He believes in dice, not God, and in the tavern more than in Christ. And nobody he has known, he says, *descendit ad infernum* because of a game.[20]

Another of the fabliaux, *Du Vilain qui conquist paradis par plait*,[21] shows irreverence comparable with that in *Saint Pierre et le jongleur*. Its theme too has something in common in that it tells how an unworthy peasant succeeded in talking his way into Heaven. Both show with evident satisfaction the triumph of the unworthy and so set at naught the accustomed warnings of earnest churchmen. Not that I would suggest these two poems to have been composed as a direct attack on the clergy or their religion: their purpose was to amuse. The blasphemy is reckless rather than vicious; and its perpetrators were doing no more than laugh up their sleeves at the unsmiling type of piety that set its face against them. Their public, probably consisting in the main of hard-headed but not humourless townsfolk, would certainly have joined in their mirth.

It is with a sense of anticlimax that we turn to the last of our burlesque texts, for it has little merit or literary interest; and while it shows no greater reverence towards our theme than does *Saint Pierre et le jongleur*, it does not possess the saving grace of wit. It is *Le Salut d'Enfer*,[22] a scurrilous poem of the thirteenth or fourteenth century in which the writer gives greetings on his return from Hell. It begins:

> *Hahai! hahai! je sui venus;*
> *Saluz vous mande Belzebus,*
> *Et Jupiter et Appollin.*

(Ho there! ho there! Here I come, with greetings from Beelzebub, and Jupiter and Apollo.)

The speaker says he has spent the night in the great hall of the demon Tervagan, feasting on heretic with renegade Beguine sauce. And he continues in anti-clerical vein with a description of all the various dishes served at the infernal banquet, apparently in imitation of Raoul de Houdenc's *Songe d'Enfer* or a similar work. The short poem ends with the announcement of a pardon offered by Tervagan, Mahomet, Beelzebub and Lucifer and with the fervent wish that the reader (or listener) may be led off to Hell.

I mention the poem here because it makes no pretence at piety and can be thought of as a burlesquing of our theme.

Certainly the author has worked in a little allegory (the lady Envie is in Hell along with Luxure, who is honoured as queen), but this does not manage to raise the verse much above the level of doggerel : rather it strengthens our suspicion that he took his theme from Raoul, who seems to have been popular with writers of little piety.

This chapter has been devoted to works in which the descent theme was used without didactic purpose, and where there is an ingredient of humour that calls into question the authors' reverence for the pious accounts from which they drew their inspiration. I have used the word parody in connection with Chrétien's *Lancelot* and *La Mule sans frein* although the effect achieved by the use of the eschatological material is not immediately comic. A parody will normally arouse a sense of the ludicrous by inviting a mental comparison of the new work with that from which it was imitated. This is not so in the case of these two romances, where the effect of the pastiche is, if anything, to deepen the serious tone of the episodes where it figures. In this case the humour, as I have suggested, derives not from the imitation itself, but from the context within which it is placed. In both works the hero is elsewhere shown in a variety of humiliating or absurd situations, whereas in the parodic sections he is given a superhuman stature, an aura of near-divinity. What we have, then, is the studied use of incongruity for purposes of comedy. In *Saint Pierre et le jongleur*, on the other hand, the parody is straightforward and designed to provoke less reflective mirth. To this extent, the poet of the fabliau is poking more direct fun at his pious exemplar.

But however we view these texts, they do bear witness to a certain irreverence abroad in France in the late twelfth and thirteenth centuries. I say in France, since nothing similar is, so far as I am aware, to be found in works composed in England. It is of some significance, perhaps, that the fourteenth-century English author of *Sir Gawain and the Green Knight*, in using *La Mule sans frein* as one of his sources, removed all traces of the eschatological background as he made his hero pursue the wintry journey to the Green Knight's court.[23]

NOTES

1. For instance, Ch.–V. Langlois, speaking of the medieval moralists, says: "Et qu'ont-ils vu autour d'eux, que font-ils voir? Les misères qu'on voit encore, jusqu'a celles qu'on croit d'hier: extrême facilité des mœurs, étalage de luxe, soif des plaisirs, impiété 'grandissante'..." (*La Vie en France au moyen âge*, II, p. xxvii). On the other hand, it is true that "Les moralistes noircissent, les fabliaux plaisantent, la littérature romanesque n'apporte que des renseignements sujets a caution" (A. Fliche, etc., *Histoire de l'Église des origines jusqu'à nos jours*, 10, p. 395).
2. Ed. G. Servois (Paris, 1893), ll. 224 ff.
3. Ed. P. Meyer (Paris, 1901).
4. See e.g. Paul Lehmann, *Die Parodie im Mittelalter* (Munich, 1922); or the examples given by Helen Waddell in *Mediaeval Latin Lyrics* (Penguin Books, 1952), and *The Wandering Scholars* (Penguin Books, 1954). And cf. the Feast of Fools (see E. K. Chambers, *The Medieval Stage* [Oxford, 1903], Vol. I, Chs. XIII & XIV; G. G. Coulton, *Five Centuries of Religion*, I, p. 55; Fliche, etc., op. cit., 10, p. 396).
5. See Coulton, op. cit., I, especially pp. 61, 71–3, and Appendix 4, pp. 465–6.
6. Ibid., I, pp. 187–8.
7. See D. D. R. Owen, *The Evolution of the Grail Legend* (Edinburgh & London, 1968), Ch. VII.
8. Ed. Mario Roques as *Le Chevalier de la Charrete* (Paris, 1958). For the following discussion, see also D. D. R. Owen, "Profanity and its Purpose in Chrétien's *Cligés* and *Lancelot*", *Forum for Modern Language Studies* VI (1970), pp. 37–48.
9. Cf. ll. 1934–6.
10. For this property see above, p. 157, n. 26.
11. Ll. 3142 ff. For the dispute, cf. M. R. James, *The Apocryphal N.T.*, pp. 125 ff.
12. This, surely, is a reminiscence of the three days of Easter.
13. See Owen, *The Evolution of the Grail Legend*, pp. 157–63.
14. "Païen de Maisières—A Joke That Went Wrong", *Forum for Modern Language Studies* II (1966), pp. 192–6. See also my "Burlesque Tradition and *Sir Gawain and the Green Knight*", *Forum for Modern Language Studies* IV (1968), pp. 125–45. *La Mule sans frein* was edited by R. T. Hill (Baltimore, 1911) and, as *La Damoisele à la mule*, by B. Orlowski (Paris, 1911). I am preparing a new edition with Professor R. C. Johnston.
15. Cf. especially the visions of St Paul and Tundal and *St Patrick's Purgatory*.
16. Ed. A. de Montaiglon & G. Raynaud, *Recueil général et complet des fabliaux des XIIIᵉ et XIVᵉ siècles* (Paris, 1872–90), V, pp. 65–79 (refs. to earlier edns. on pp. 316–7); R. C. Johnston & D. D. R. Owen, *Fabliaux* (Oxford, 1957), pp. 67–77 (from which I quote); M. Walters-Gehrig, *Trois fabliaux: Saint Pierre et le jongleur, De Haimet de Barat et Travers, Estula* (Beihefte zur *Zeitschrift für Romanische Philologie* 102: Tübingen, 1961). See G. Gröber, *Grundriss der romanischen Philologie*, II.2 (1902), p. 624; cf. E. Faral, *Le Manuscrit 19152 du fonds français de la Bibliothèque Nationale* (Paris, 1934), p. 24.

17. Cf. the feast in Raoul de Houdenc's *Songe d'Enfer* (see above, p. 159).
18. "The Element of Parody in *Saint Pierre et le Jongleur*", *French Studies* IX (1955), pp. 60–3. Much the same arguments were given by Walters-Gehrig in her edition.
19. Might not the lines

> "*Por vos giter de cest torment,*
> *Mis ge au gieu tot mon argent*"

(ll. 341–2)

have been suggested to our irreverent poet by Christ's call to the redeemed souls? Compare, for example, His words in the *Passion d'Autun* (ed. Grace Frank):

> "*Mes amy, or en venés,*
> *Quar en paradis mestier avés.*
> *Bien rayson est que en venés,*
> *Quar je vous ait monlt chier racheter.*"

(ll. 1910–3)

In the *Romanz de saint Fanuel* (ed. C. Chabaneau) the call is:

> "*Issiés d'enfer, boneüré,*
> *De mon sanc vos ai racheté.*"

(ll. 3397–8)

In a version of the *Vision of St Paul* Christ upbraids the sinners in Hell and refers to His sacrifice on their behalf:

> "*Ne ne donnai or ne arjant*
> *Por vos racheter de torment.*"
> (Paris, B.N., MS fr. 2094, ll. 399–400 : ed. L. E. Kastner, *Revue des Langues Romanes* 49, p. 60)

Cf. too the *Passion du Christ*:

> *Argent ne aur non i donet,*
> *Mas que son sang et soa carn;*
> *Deg cel enfern toz nos livdret.*
> (ll. 385–7 : ed. E. Koschwitz, *Les plus anciens monuments . . . Textes critiques*, p. 28)

It is hard to avoid the conclusion that the author of our fabliau had some version of Christ's reported words in his mind as he wrote.

20. Ed. E. Barbazan & D. M. Méon, *Fabliaux et contes*, IV (Paris, 1808), pp. 455–52. See also F. Lecoy, "Le *Chronicon Novaliciense* et les 'légendes épiques' ", *Romania* LXVII (1942–3), pp. 1–52.
21. Ed. Montaiglon & Raynaud, op. cit., III, No. 81; T. B. W. Reid, *Twelve Fabliaux* (Manchester, 1958), pp. 19–22.
22. Ed. A. Jubinal, *Jongleurs et trouvères* (Paris, 1835), pp. 43–5.
23. See Owen, "Burlesque Tradition and *Sir Gawain and the Green Knight*".

CHAPTER IX

TRAVELLERS' TALES

F ROM the world of romance and fabliau, we return now to
reality, or to what certain late medieval writers would have
us accept as reality. Again we are brought face to face with the
common belief that the places of retribution (and, indeed, of
eternal reward) not only had physical existence, but could even
be visited by the stout of heart in some circumstances, provided
the right route were followed. Adventurous travellers were to
be found prepared to undertake the journey; and a few have
left us accounts of their true experiences, though not without
garnishing them with more or less liberal helpings of imaginative detail.

Antoine de la Sale is, to all appearances, a reasonably reliable
witness. He was a Provençal nobleman and squire to Louis III
of Anjou who had, in the course of his travels, heard of the
grotto of the Norcian Sibyl, situated on the summit of the
Monte della Sibilla, not far from Ancona. So in May 1420 he
was tempted to make the journey there and investigate the
strange legends told about other visitors to the grotto. In Book
IV of his *Salade* he has left an account of that journey and of
stories told about the Sibyl in the heart of the mountain.[1]
Although the Paradise of the Queen Sibylla is not strictly a
place of torment, it does present some infernal features, as we
shall see. Furthermore, certain connections with the legend of
St Patrick's Purgatory may justify our interest in it. Antoine's
narrative is sober and factual, and he preserves an attitude of
apparent scepticism towards these tales, which I will briefly
recount.[2]

Five young men of the nearby villge of Montemonaco
once entered a subterranean passage, the mouth of which is
in the grotto, and found that it soon widened so that they

could proceed in comfort. But after about three miles the way was blocked by a rampart of earth from which there issued so strong a wind that they were glad enough to return in safety.

Antoine tells how a certain priest of Montemonaco, Don Anthon Fumato, who was subject to fits of lunacy ("lequel par lunoisons n'estoit mie en son bon sens", p. 82), repeatedly told of his entry into the grotto with two Germans. They had penetrated as far as two metal doors that slam day and night. Then the Germans passed through the doors, having asked the priest to wait for them for the space of a day. Don Athon waited, but they did not appear; and he was forced to return alone. Asked for more details, he said that they had been able to pass the place where the wind was so violent. There was an easy descent for a short way, and then they came to a very long bridge that was less than a foot wide; and below the bridge was a hideous gulf, with the roaring of a river in its depths. But as soon as one puts both feet on the bridge, it is quite broad, and becomes wider still as one goes forward, while the terrible noise of the river diminishes. Beyond the bridge, the cave seems artificially constructed; and at the far end are two artificial dragons with shining eyes that give the impression of life. Thence a narrow passage leads to a smaller cave where are the two metal doors. As the Germans entered, the priest could see nothing beyond; but he heard a sound like people talking.

The people of the district tell yet another story of a German knight and his squire who passed both the metal gates and another which shone like crystal and then came to the abode of the Sibyl. Many men and lovely women dwell there and enjoy pleasures of every kind. But each Friday after midnight the women become serpents and remain in that state until after midnight on Saturday. If the visitors stay longer than three hundred and thirty days in the Paradise, they will never leave. At the last possible moment they do return to the world; but, largely owing to the Pope's delay in granting them a pardon, they finally yield to temptation and return for all time.

Although Antoine's account seems to be given in good faith, albeit "pour rire et passer temps" (p. 63), the stories he relates are not entirely original. In 1391, Andrea da Barberino had included a description of a visit to the Paradise in his *Guerino il Meschino*.[3] It is Guerino himself who makes the journey in search of the Sibyl of Cumae (the influence of Virgil is plain). He too passes the metal gates and comes to the strange realm beyond, where the seductresses become dragons, serpents, scorpions or worms on Saturday and do not regain their original form until Monday morning. He stays in the Paradise for a year. This may well be one of Antoine's sources, either direct or indirect; otherwise we must assume a common source.[4] The whole conception of the situation of the Paradise demands a comparison with that of St Patrick's Purgatory: both are beneath the earth, and access is gained by a passage leading down from a grotto. Andrea da Barberino had put the Irish text to profitable use, but at one point at least Antoine's account shows a direct borrowing from it.[5] The bridge crossed by Don Anthon Fumato and his companions is none other than the Bridge of Dread as it appears in *St Patrick's Purgatory*, growing broader and safer the further the travellers progress. Beyond both bridges is a kind of Paradise, at least in name. However, throughout Antoine's narrative the infernal nature of this place of carnal delight is strongly emphasised: we see the weekly metamorphosis of the Sibyl and her company, and the visitors' fear of mortal sin together with the Pope's reluctance to pardon them. The Sibyl, who has borrowed many of the characteristics of Venus, is a veritable devil. This is just one more case of the divinities, or near-divinities, of one civilisation becoming the demons of the next.

Antoine de la Sale, if we can trust his testimony, visited an entrance to the Otherworld, but remained sceptical about the stories he heard. Should we then credit the moonstruck Don Anthon with these legends? A cleric, he might have put his literary reminiscences to use in tales calculated to impress his more credulous parishioners. Be that as it may, Antoine himself strikes no pose and wishes his narrative to be taken as a simple record of events. The same cannot be said of most of those who have left accounts of their visits to St Patrick's

Purgatory, though doubtless they too wished their stories to be believed.

In the first half of the fourteenth century a Flemish knight, the Sire de Beaujeu, made the journey to the Purgatory, as we learn from the *Chronique des quatre premiers Valois* :[6]

> Monseigneur de Beaugeu par son tres grant hardement fut en l'espurgatoire saint Patrice ou il vit les tourmens infernaux, comme le raconte Heronnet son escuier qui en dit moult de merveilles. Dit Heronnet qu'il vit Burgibus, le portier d'enfer, qui tornoit une roe par cent fois cent mille tours en l'espace d'ung jour et y avoit cent mille ames. Il vit le pont qu'il fault passer aussi trenchant comme ung raseur a l'entree. Il vit le gibet d'enfer. Il vit le puis d'enfer. Il vit le gouffre d'enfer. Aprés vindrent en paradis terrestre.

(My lord de Beaujeu, showing very great courage, entered St Patrick's Purgatory and saw there the infernal torments, as we are told by Heronnet his squire, who relates many marvellous things about it. Heronnet says that he saw Beelzebub, Hell's porter, who turned a wheel a hundred hundred thousand times in the space of one day, and there were a hundred thousand souls upon it. He saw the bridge at the entrance that has to be crossed, sharp as a razor. He saw Hell's gibbet. He saw the pit of Hell. He saw the infernal abyss. Afterwards they came to the Earthly Paradise.)

We are left to guess who was the greater liar, the knight or his squire ; for this description seems to be based on an imperfect recollection of the original legend. Garbled as the account is, it does indicate which of the torments impinged most forcibly on the medieval imagination.

In 1358, Ludovicus de Sur gave, in Latin, an extravagant report of his experiences in the Purgatory, and these were recounted as his own two years later by Louis de France. Of his second-hand adventures we possess copies in Latin and Italian.[7] A Catalan fragment of the same narrative is printed by Miquel y Planas,[8] who was unaware of its source and considered it to be the composition of a fourteenth-century moralist using already popular themes such as the *Vision of Tundal*. The account is wildly romanced, with all kinds of extraneous matter, some taken from *Tundal*, some perhaps from the *Vision of Charles le Gros*.[9] The most startling change is that the demons have become charming temptresses, and the whole journey is as much a test of the knight's chastity as of his Christian faith. Hell even contains a fair "nunnery" inhabited by a company of she-devils. Here is a point of resemblance with the Paradise of the Queen Sibylla, but it is probably fortuitous.

There was also Guillaume de Lille's visit to the Purgatory in 1394–5. His experiences were rather less startling than those of his predecessors. We are told of the event by Froissart in his *Chronicles*.[10] He once asked Guillaume whether, in the course of his journeys in Ireland, he had ever been to the Purgatory. Guillaume replied that, together with an English knight, he had been shut in it from the sunset of one day until the dawn of the next. When they had passed through the door and gone down two or three steps, the heat went to their heads, and they sat down on the stone steps. A great desire to sleep came over them; and they slept all night. On Froissart's asking what he had seen, Guillaume answered that in their sleep they had had strange and marvellous dreams, and he thought that they had seen many more things than they would have done in bed in their own rooms. But he added:

> "Et quant au matin nous feusmes asveilliés, on ouvry l'uys, car ainsi le avions-nous ordonné, et yssimes hors, et ne nou souvint de chose que euissions veu, et tenions et tenons encoires que ce soit toute fantosme."

> ("And when we woke in the morning, the door was opened as we had ordered, and we went out; and we remembered nothing of what we had seen; and we thought, and still maintain, that it was all pure illusion.")

Here at least is a hard-headed account of a night in the Purgatory. But when Ramon de Perelhos went there two or three years later, he was determined to have a better story to tell on his return.

Ramon's account is in fact the most substantial medieval description that we have of a visit to the Purgatory.[11] A well-known Catalan knight and diplomat, he was the son of a man who had been in the service of the King of Aragon and the King of France. He himself had a taste for travelling, and we have proof that on September 6th, 1397, he obtained a safe-conduct from King Richard of England to pass with twenty men and thirty horses through England to Ireland in order to visit the Purgatory.[12] On September 8th he left Avignon for Paris, where he spent four months. With the French king he attended the celebrations held at Rheims in 1398 in honour of Wenceslas of Germany. After his visit to the Purgatory, he returned to Avignon to serve the Aragonese Pope Benedict XIII. The last reference to him we have is in a parliamentary decree by Anselm dated 1405. This much is historical fact; now let us see how Ramon himself describes his adventure.

In 1398, he says, he set out from Avignon for the Purgatory, adding that his father had been chamberlain to King Charles of France. He has had many adventures in Christian and pagan lands but only wishes to tell of his journey to the Purgatory, a journey such as no man had ever made since the death of St Patrick. This brings him to speak of the saint's ministry, of the revelation of the Purgatory, and of the ritual to be followed by those who wish to enter it. Returning to his own experiences, he says that while he was with the Pope (in Avignon), his liege lord, Don Juan, died; so he decided to seek Juan's soul in Purgatory and see what punishments he might be suffering. The Pope tried to dissuade him but finally gave him his bene-diction, and so he set forth. He passed through France and England, staying at both royal courts on the way, and came at last to Dublin. There he was advised to abandon his project on account of the barbarity of the people and the dangers of the Purgatory; but nothing daunted he embarked on the last stage of his journey, accompanied by servants and interpreters. He went to Armagh, where the Archbishop tried to dissuade him from his journey; but he carried on through the barbarous lands of King Yrnel (O'Nial), where the strange customs in-terested him greatly, until he finally came to Processio.[13] There he was joined by the lord of the town with his brother, and they escorted him to the monastery on the island. With the prior they tried to discourage him from entering the Purgatory, but in vain. Ramon followed the prescribed ritual, and a mass was sung. Having made his will, he walked in procession to the gate of the Purgatory, and there he dubbed four knights. Once more the prior warned him of the peril, but Ramon insisted on continuing in order to purge himself of his sins. Then the prior explained what he would find : God's messengers would come to him, instruct him further, and then leave him alone. Ramon entered the grotto with due formalities, followed by "Guilhelm, senhor dc Corsi" (Guillaume de Courcy), one of the entourage of the Queen of England ; but the monks warned them not to speak to one another. Crossing himself, Ramon walked boldly into the Purgatory, and the door was closed on him and his companion. He sat for an hour in the small grotto, sweating in anguish, then fell asleep. There came a clap of thunder, heard in the monastery, and our still drowsy hero felt himself falling. Startled and deafened, he repeated the sacred formula taught him by the prior : "Christe fili Dei vivi, miserere mei." Then the end of the cavern opened, and he walked through, having lost his companion.

From this point we are not surprised to find that Ramon's experiences remind us strongly of those of Owein in the *Tractatus*,[14] but with certain reservations that I shall make later. It may be mentioned here that in the fourth plain he, like Owein, came across some of his acquaintances : King Juan of Aragon, the Friar Minor Frances del Pueg, and his own niece, Aldosa de Queralt, who was still alive when he left his land. All these would be saved, but must first expiate their sins. Aldosa's chief guilt was the use of cosmetics ; Friar Frances had seduced a nun ; of King Juan's sin Ramon refuses to speak. He saw other, closer relatives, all of whom were on the way to salvation.

After his sight of Paradise, Ramon tells us that he found his companion again in the underground hall. They went as far as they could and then sat down, weary and afraid, and fell asleep. There came another clap of thunder, and they found themselves back in the grotto. The door was opened, and they were received back into the outer world with great joy. Ramon then describes briefly his return across Ireland, England and France to Avignon, where he was well received by the Pope. He rounds off his account with a short, pious epilogue, praying God that we may live virtuously and avoid the pains he has described.

No doubt it was on finding that his experiences in the Purgatory did not come up to expectations that Ramon appropriated Owein's adventures as his own, placing them in the framework of his own travels. He wrote, of course, in Catalan, but his original text was unknown to Jeanroy, who referred to Philip O'Sullivan's authority for its existence.[15] This text has since been published by Miquel y Planas; and he, as later M. de Riquer, assumed that Ramon had adapted the Latin *Tractatus* to his own ends. But it can be shown that this is not so. I mentioned above that Ramon placed twelve heavenly messengers in the Purgatory. Now this is a feature of the most common French prose version, whereas in the Latin texts the number is fifteen. Furthermore, Ramon's text, like the French, speaks of fiery dragons in the first plain; and it picks up the familiar story at the same point, namely after the Latin account of the old homicide. And there are other, slighter pieces of evidence which prove conclusively that Ramon found his original inspiration in the popular prose version of the legend.[16] Perhaps he knew the *Tractatus* too; but in any case it is likely that he first came across the story in Paris. For there is a record of an interesting letter sent in 1386 by the Infante of Aragon (later Juan I) to Ramon, who was at that time in the French capital, requesting that he send, in writing and by a trustworthy person, the whole account of that knight who had told of how he had been in St Patrick's Purgatory and what he had seen and done there, for he greatly desired to know.[17] Then in 1394, still a few years before Ramon's visit to Ireland, Juan sent to his daughter the Countess of Foix a book containing a translation of "lo Purgatori de sent Patrici".[18] Here is evidence at the same time of the legend's popularity with a noble public, of one route taken in its penetration into the south, and, one assumes, of Ramon's first acquaintance with it.

The adaptation contains a large amount of fairly faithful translation, and it is chiefly in the framing narrative that we find clues as to Ramon's personality. A teller of tall stories, he plainly expected them to be taken more seriously than the simpler medieval *gab*. Being a natural braggart, he was only too willing to pander to the public taste for tales of unlikely adventure; and he freely admits at the outset that he is telling of his visit to the Purgatory because everyone enjoys hearing of strange and marvellous things. Playing as he did on the gullibility of his friends and contemporaries, he can scarcely be classed among the more pious and reverential purveyors of our theme.

These various records do not lack interest, even if they cannot claim attention as important literature. They are contributed mainly by knights and noblemen, whose blood, perhaps, was still fired with the spirit of chivalric quest and perilous adventure. In the case of the visitors to St Patrick's Purgatory, there may be other reasons for the pilgrimage being made particularly by members of the upper class. Firstly, Owein himself was a knight and so in this respect set a precedent. Secondly, the journey was a long one and lacked the facilities of the great pilgrim routes for travellers of modest means. And having accomplished it, we can understand why a person of rank would be loath to admit that he had been on a wild-goose chase; and this is a plausible reason for the tall stories they retailed on their return, stories which men of deeper piety would have been reluctant to pass off as true experience. So, while we admire the honesty of a Guillaume de Lille, we see in the other tales the reflection of a certain levity on the part of their bearers towards the old pious legends. In other words, their attitude towards them is secular; it is the adventure element in them that appeals, not the pious. Yet we have seen in this chapter remarkable evidence of the influence that the legend of the Irish Purgatory exerted on imaginations throughout the Middle Ages, and a further proof that the theme of the visit to Hell was far more than a literary or didactic device.

NOTES

1. Published by F. Desonay as *Antoine de la Sale: Le Paradis de la reine Sibylle* (Paris, 1930), and in *Antoine de la Sale: Œuvres complètes*, I *La Salade* (Liège & Paris, 1935), pp. 63–130. For a summary and discussion of sources see H. R. Patch, *The Other World*, pp. 265–70.

Desonay discusses the relevant sections of the account in *Antoine de la Sale, aventureux et pédagogue* (Liège & Paris, 1940), Ch. II.

2. I summarise from Desonay's edition in *Œuvres complètes*, I, to which the pages references relate.

3. G. Paris (*Légendes du moyen âge* [Paris, 1903]), pp. 67–109) gives a summary of the story as found in the *Salade* and in *Guerino*, and also tells of his own journey there and that of Pio Rajna. Patch gives a brief summary of and comments on *Guerino* (op. cit., pp. 263–5).

4. Patch prefers the latter solution (ibid., pp. 268–9).

5. Cf. Patch, ibid., p. 267, n. 114. We have elsewhere Antoine's own testimony that he knew the legend: "... En Ybernie, la appert un puis du purgatoire" (*Œuvres complètes*, I, p. 140).

6. Ed. S. Luce (Paris, 1862). See p. 22.

7. The Latin account is published by M. Voigt, *Beiträge zur Geschichte der Visionenliteratur im Mittelalter. I: Visio Lazari* (Leipzig, 1924), pp. 226–45.

8. *Llegendas de l'altra vida* (Barcelona, 1914), § 7.

9. There is a beast much resembling *Tundal*'s Acheron. Similarities with *Charles le Gros* are dragons that emerge from a furnace to attack the traveller, and a venerable man or angel who offers him the end of a kerchief, by which he is led through part of Hell.

10. *Œuvres complètes*, ed. Kervyn de Lettenhove, XV (Brussels, 1871), pp. 145–6.

11. I have used the Provençal translation of Ramon's Catalan text, ed. A. Jeanroy & A. Vignaux, *Voyage au Purgatoire de St Patrice...*, pp. 1–54 (see pp. xiii–xviii for details of Ramon's life). This translation is found in Toulouse, Bibl. Mun., MS 894 and is dated 1466. M. de Riquer gives a full account of Ramon's life and journey in *Historia de la literatura catalana*, II, Ch. XI.

12. T. Rymer, *Foedera, pactiones, etc.*, VIII (London, 1727), p. 14 (quoted by Jeanroy, op. cit., p. xvi).

13. For the identification of the Irish place names in Ramon's account see C. Brunel, "Sur la version provençale du voyage de Raimon de Perillos au Purgatoire de Saint Patrice" in *Estudios dedicados a Menéndez Pidal*, VI (Madrid, 1956), pp. 3–21.

14. See above, pp. 38 ff.

15. Op. cit., pp. xviii–xix. O'Sullivan summarised the account in his *Historiæ catholicæ Iberniæ compendium* (1621).

16. For instance, The *Tractatus* gives the temperature of the wind in the third plain, whereas Ramon and the prose version do not; and in the *Tractatus* the fiery pit is to the south of the icy river, but in the other two texts it is to the east.

17. He was to send "en escrits, per persona certa, tota la relacio per aquell cavaller qui deits que es entrat en lo Purgatori de sent Patrici, feta de ço que ha vist e li es esdevengut en lo dit Purgatori, car fort ho desijam saber." See Miquel y Planas, op. cit., pp. 295–6; M. de Riquer, op. cit., p. 310.

18. "Un llibret en lo qual havem fet trelladar lo Purgatori de sent Patrici" (Miquel y Planas, loc. cit.; Jeanroy & Vignaux, op. cit., p. xxi; M. de Riquer, op. cit., p. 313).

CHAPTER X

HELL ON THE STAGE

To present Hell on the stage in a serious and convincing way was, one might think, a daunting task. Our study has shown that, apart from a certain amount of levity in a handful of texts, the infernal regions were depicted in medieval literature as a place of unimaginable horror; and an actual representation with flesh and blood actors and more or less primitive scenery could not hope to be as spine-chilling as the monitory picture held up by the Church. Medieval painting and sculpture, while suffering the same handicap to some degree, could and did depict gruesome horrors unpresentable on the stage. People in the Middle Ages were quick to grasp the reality behind symbols; but the stage representation of Hell cannot be taken as a symbol in this sense, and even the forbidding *gueule d'enfer* was the result of attempted realism rather than symbolism.[1] Whereas most biblical scenes could be played on the human level and be made more poignant and immediate by dramatisation, the showing of hellfire and its guardians posed quite different problems. The danger was that such displays might weaken rather than confirm the awe and terror inspired by the Church's teachings on the subject.[2]

In fact, the medieval dramatic writers did not shirk the task; and so from the earliest period of the vernacular drama Hell appeared as a recognised *mansion* on the actors' left, in opposition to Paradise on their right. Even the bilingual *Sponsus*, which may have been written late in the eleventh century, shows as its only piece of true action the casting of the foolish virgins into Hell.[3] But the *Mystère d'Adam*, probably from about the middle of the twelfth century, already gives elaborate directions for the staging of the infernal scenes.[4] The play as we have it is incomplete, and it is just possible that the original version contained Christ's spoliation of Hell as its climax. This is almost certainly true of another fragment, the Anglo-Norman *Seinte Resureccion*, which was written some years later,[5] and which includes the following stage directions in its prologue :

> *E une gaole mise i soit,*
> *Les prisuns mettre en destroit;*
> *De l'une part i soit enfer mis,*
> *Leinz serrunt les enemis*
> *Ensemble od les anciens*
> *Ke la serrunt mis en liens.*
> *Le cel ne devez ublier,*
> *U les angles deivent habiter.*[6]

(Let a gaol be placed there for putting the prisoners in durance ; and let Hell be situated to one side, with the devils in it along with the patriarchs, who will be in chains there. You must not forget Heaven, which the angels must occupy.)

We see from the action of the *Sponsus* that the dramatic representation of Hell was not merely the result of the secular staging of religious stories. The text is preserved in a manuscript from the monastery of St Martial at Limoges, and whether or not it was played within the church, it is certainly intimately connected with the cult.[7] So it seems to have been the clergy themselves who first had the idea of representing Hell in this way, albeit they had an eye to giving a wider popular appeal to the holy stories. K. Young has traced the progressive drama-tisation of the Harrowing within the liturgy ;[8] and though none of the texts he cites is earlier than the fourteenth century, it is likely that Hell was used as a locus much earlier. J. Kroll thought that an antiphon dealing with the Harrowing was probably used in the Easter service before the tenth century ;[9] and already by the early thirteenth century Christ's descent was dramatically portrayed in the Easter play of Klosterneuburg.[10] It is important to note that the "staging" of such plays was largely symbolical. Thus, in the fourteenth-century dramatisa-tion from the convent of Barking the representation of the *Descensus* occurred at the chapel of St Mary Magdalen. "Behind the closed doors of this room are imprisoned all the members of the convent, representing the souls of the patriarchs confined in

Hell and awaiting the coming of Christ. After the priest outside has uttered *Tollite portas* three times, the door of the chapel is flung open, and all the imprisoned spirits, carrying palms of victory, are allowed to depart in procession towards the sepulchre during the singing of several antiphons, the last of which is *Cum rex gloriae*."[11] There may have been a little more realism in the Klosterneuburg play,[12] but there is no indication of any elaborate scenery or staging. The fact is not surprising when we consider the obvious limitations of a performance in a church; but there is another important factor, namely the evident preference in ecclesiastical circles for a symbolic rather than a realistic portrayal. An early instance of this is the ceremony for consecrating a new church. Prior to the ceremony, the building is regarded as the abode of Satan. Three times the bishop raps thrice on the closed doors, calling: "Tollite portas, principes, vestras, et elevamini, portae aeternales, et introibit rex gloriae", and each time receiving the response from within: "Quis est iste rex gloriae?" On the third summoning, the bishop declares himself with the words: "Dominus virtutum, ipse est rex gloriae",[13] and the doors are flung open.[14] This is a direct reflection of the Harrowing. So while the Church exploited the use of symbolism in this way, it was not inclined to over-indulge in realistic touches that would tend to be less in keeping with the dignity and mystery of Christian worship. This may well explain why anything other than liturgical dramatisation was liable to evoke protests from devout churchmen such as William of Wadington, who wrote ca. 1300 in his *Manuel des pechiez*:

> *Fere poent representement—*
> *Mes qe ceo seit chastement*
> *En office de seint eglise*
> *Quant hom fet la Deu seruise—*
> *Cum Ihesu Crist la fiz Dée*
> *En sepulcre esteit posé,*
> *E la resurrectiun,*
> *Pur plus auer deuociun.*
> *Mes, fere foles assemblez*
> *En les rues des citez,*

Ou en cymiters aprés mangers,
Quant venent les fols volunters—
Tut dient qe il le funt pur bien—
Crere ne les deuez pur rien
Qe fet seit pur le honur de Dée,
Einz del deable, pur verité.

(ll. 4299–314)[15]

(They may perform a representation—as long as it be done tactfully in a church office, when service is being paid to God —of how Jesus Christ the Son of God was placed in the sepulchre, and His resurrection, so that devotion may be increased. But to hold foolish assemblies in city streets, or after meals in cemeteries, when fools gladly come along— they all say that they do it with good intentions—you should never on any account believe that they do this in God's honour : rather it is in the devil's, if truth be told.)

But now it is time to turn to the appearance of our theme in the French vernacular drama. And as space prevents an exhaustive study, I shall look at the most significant of the surviving texts and lay special emphasis on the elements of realism they contain.

William of Wadington's attack was primarily on what he called *miracles* (ll. 4294, 4318); and although he seems to have given the term a wider application than we do today, we may bear his words in mind as we look at a continental French miracle-play that revolves round a form of the descent theme. It is the *Miracle de un prevost que Nostre Dame delivra*, contained in the famous Cangé manuscript and perhaps over half a century later than William's testimony.[16]

The provost Estienne is shown to be wicked and rapacious, but a redeeming quality is his unswerving loyalty to St Prist. We are shown that his particular crime has been to try to acquire property belonging rightfully to the churches of St Agnes and St Lorens. We learn of the death in Italy of his brother, an archdeacon.

God commands Gabriel to go to Satan and tell him to take
Estienne to Purgatory "en corps et en ame" for his sins:

> *"Et la le bate et le pugnisse*
> *Et le face a peine partir*
> *Sanz l'ame hors du corps partir;*
> *Car je li deffens a li nuire,*
> *Voire, afin que par lui ne muire."*

(ll. 392–6)

("And there let him beat and punish him so that he
scarcely gets away without his body leaving his soul; for
I forbid him in fact to do any harm to him, lest he die at
his hands.")

In Heaven St Agnes and St Lorens, clearly much upset by the
provost's actions, show little sympathy towards him.

The scene changes to Purgatory, where two demons are in
conversation. One has just brought the archdeacon to be
purged of his sins, and the other has been commissioned to
fetch Estienne himself. Then we see the two brothers meet
in Purgatory. The archdeacon admits that his sin too was
avarice, but he knows that he will eventually go to Paradise.
The devils plan to show Estienne all the different forms of
torture at their disposal, and he regrets his lot in this place
where there is bitter death without the chance of dying. What
good, he wonders, was all his devotion to St Prist?

In Paradise his patron saint is actually pleading on his
behalf with St Agnes and St Lorens and eventually obtains
their pardon for him. St Prist then carries his plea for pity
to the Virgin herself, and at her behest God bids her go with
the saints to the place on earth where Estienne was seized by
the devils. She may go no further, but St Prist may then
proceed to Purgatory and bring the provost before the Virgin.
Thereafter he shall be allowed thirty days of life, during
which time he must show true penitence.[17]

To the devils' dismay, St Prist, accompanied by St Agnes
and St Lorens, comes to Purgatory and delivers Estienne
from his torments. He is brought before the Virgin, who
specifies his penitence. He must go to the Pope and tell him

PLATE 6. Scenes of Hell (including the weighing of souls, the Harrowing of Hell, the infernal cauldron, the

of the pains he has suffered. He must also tell him to say a
mass for the archdeacon on the following morning, and then
Estienne's brother will be translated into Paradise. Should
the Pope be unbelieving, he must be brought to see the
Virgin.

So Estienne returns to earth and interviews the Pope, who
suspects his visitor of being a devil. But finally he is conducted
to see the Virgin and God Himself, and the play ends with
general rejoicing and songs of praise.

Despite the absence of stage directions, the miracle was
clearly written for dramatic presentation by means of *décor
simultané*; and this was the end to which it was adapted from
the collection of non-dramatic *miracles* compiled by Gautier de
Coincy about 1225.[18] To make the representation possible,
Estienne is shown to have been carried off to Purgatory *en corps
et en âme*, so that the audience saw a flesh-and-blood descent
enacted before them. But since the play is relatively simple and
nothing elaborate is called for by way of scenery or large casts
(for instance, only two devils and possibly Satan appear), it
could have been presented with perfect dignity and reverence,
more being left to the imagination than performed. But the
author's intentions seem to have been rather different, at least
as regards the infernal scenes. The demons' speeches are extremely lively and even punning in places.[19] And it is more than
likely that words were translated into action:

> PREMIER DYABLE
> *Alons, Vehemot, sanz attendre,*
> *Si le hapons en un sursaut.*
> *Sa, prevost, en enfer le chaut*
> *Vous porterons.*
>
> SECOND DYABLE
> *Non pas, mais nous l'i trainnerons.*
> *En sanglante heure nous fault il*
> *Porter sur noz colz tel ostil.*
> *Tien la, lie le conme un fol*
> *Et par les mains et par le col.*

(ll. 454-62)

(*First devil*: Come on Behemoth, look sharp; let's pounce on him and grab him. Here, provost, we're going to carry you off to warm you up in Hell. *Second devil*: Not likely— we'll drag him there. That'll be the day when we have to carry baggage such as this on our backs. Hold on, and truss him up like a madman by his hands and neck.)

The arrival of the devils on the scene would in no way add to the dignity or moral tone of the story, and this was true of the other miracles in which they appeared.[20] As for the scenery used, the use of the word *enfer* in the above quotation suggests that no fine distinction was drawn between Hell and Purgatory; and no doubt the same set (perhaps the *gueule*) would do service for either in the *puis* where the miracles were presented. Either within or just outside this *mansion* some 250 of the play's 1,339 lines would be played, so there was good scope for knockabout action and even farce. I cannot see the audience's dread of Hell being augmented by such scenes. It has been said of the miracles that "rien ne paraît plus naturel dans ces drames que le surnaturel".[21] That this is so reflects some debasement of the fervent Christian spirit that had pervaded the early epics and saints' lives. While one cannot yet say that familiarity has bred contempt in this sphere, it has led to an intimacy which naturally caused some disquiet in staid and pious circles.

It is the mystery plays with their dramatisation of the Harrowing of Hell that provide most of the material for this chapter. In them Christ's descent is found in its most elaborate form, and in the form that had the greatest impact on the lay public, at least after the thirteenth century. The *Gospel of Nicodemus* had already brought the theme into art,[21] but with its representation on the stage the faithful were able to see the paintings and sculpture brought to life in the most vivid fashion. We do not know who were the first to have the privilege, though we have seen that the action was almost certainly known to the vernacular drama of the late twelfth century. Yet for at least another century we have no further evidence of its use on the stage.

Then, at about the end of the thirteenth century or beginning
of the fourteenth, it was incorporated in a mystery play based on
the *Passion des Jongleurs*.[23] This is not extant, but it must be
postulated as the common ultimate source of three later texts,
namely the *Passion du Palatinus* (which I will designate *P*
in the following discussion), the *Passion d'Autun* (=*A*), and
a fragment found at Sion in the Simplon district and published
by Joseph Bédier (=*S*).[24] Although *P* seems to antedate *A*
in its present form, the section dealing with the Harrowing has
little in common with either the *Passion des Jongleurs* or *S* or *A*,
all of which show close similarities with one another. We may
therefore assume that the episode in *P* has been substituted for
an original to which *S* and *A* both approximate, *A* being a
slightly elaborated re-working of the source, but having the
merit of completeness. So while *P* contains the first dramatic
treatment of the Harrowing in the French vernacular, the
episode in *A* represents the earlier tradition.

There has been some discussion as to the exact nature of *A*;
but its editor concludes that, originally a dramatic composition,
it has had a number of narrative lines added to permit it to be
read aloud. Two such interpolations occur in the descent
episode, but they appear simply to replace original stage
directions.[25] The following is the substance of the episode:

An angel calls upon Christ to rise from the tomb, as three
days have passed since the Crucifixion. Christ promises to
rise at once and go to Hell, whose gates He will shatter so that
He may deliver His friends. At the defences of Hell He tells
the devils of His purpose. They refuse to open at His command, and ask who is this King of Glory. Again Christ bids
them open, and at once the gates burst asunder. He enters
and tells Adam and his seed that they are to be delivered.
Adam says that they have been imprisoned for 4,404 years;
and he blames Eve for his original downfall. Christ thereupon calls to all the souls to come forth into Paradise.

Unfortunately we have to take into account re-arrangements
both by the *remanieur* of the original play (or so it seems) and
by the editor. The former apparently transposed the Harrowing from immediately after Christ's death on the cross, as it

appears in the *Passion des Jongleurs* and in *P*, to the time when He lay in the sepulchre.[26] But to the editor is due the arrangement of the text whereby Christ is called from the tomb before His descent. For she has interpolated between the boasts of the soldiers guarding the tomb and the scene of the Harrowing a passage originally at the end of the Biard account, though it was clearly out of place there.[27] In it, an angel calls upon Christ to rise and comfort His friends; and He replies that He will at once go down into Hell, burst the gates asunder, and lead his friends out (ll. 1866-9). Now Mrs Frank was acting logically in placing these words before the descent, for that is the only place where, as they stand, they have meaning. But it is interesting to compare and contrast them with the equivalent passage in *P*, where in much the same words Christ is summoned from the tomb by an angel and replies that He will rise, having been down into Hell, which He burst asunder, and led forth the righteous (ll. 1720-3). Mrs Frank believes that the whole passage in *P* retains a trace of the tradition of the descent following the Resurrection, since the angel tells Christ to show Himself to his people and comfort them (ll. 1718-9). But surely that reference is to those to whom He was to appear on earth, and not to the patriarchs in Hell. This could have been the original confusion that led to the alteration and misplacement of Christ's speech in *A* or its prototype.[28] The matter would not be important but for the fact that the editorial rearrangment substitutes the descent of the resurrected Christ for His descent from the sepulchre, a conception which the *remanieur* may have preferred as representing the tradition of the Creed.[29] On the other hand, it must be admitted that a good argument can be made out for Mrs Frank's arrangement since, if the Resurrection originally took place after the descent, we should expect to find the call from the tomb immediately before the guardians' dismay in the Sion fragment (between lines 25 and 26). I can only suggest that the confusion had occurred before the writing of the Sion text.

The action of the lost *mystère* appears to have been quite simple: Christ's appearance before the gates of Hell, which He probably struck with His fist or the cross; some show of resistance by the devils; the bursting asunder of the gates;

and the deliverance of the patriarchs by Christ, who may have
remained on the threshold of the *mansion* representing Hell.
There is no indication of any elaborate *diablerie* such as might
have detracted from the dignity of the performance.

The episode in *P* is, as I have said, quite different from that of
A, and must be assumed to have been substituted for the original by one of the *remanieurs* of *P*.[30] In place of the 44 lines of
A we now have no fewer than 216 (ll. 1235–1450).
    The action takes place while Christ is still on the cross, and
it opens with a *diablerie* of the type that was later to become the
stock-in-trade of every writer of *mystères* :

> Satan and Enfer[31] quarrel about the advantages or dangers
> to them of the Crucifixion, brought about by Satan. He is
> confident that Christ no longer represents a danger to the
> infernal powers. Enfer, however, is much afraid that they
> will be unable to withstand their enemy when He comes ;
> and suddenly he sees Christ approaching with a cross in His
> hand. He flees with the other devils and leaves Satan to face
> Christ alone. When Jesus demands that the gates be opened,
> Satan defies Him. (The dialogue here is colloquial and lively
> in the extreme.) The souls perceive Christ's coming and
> welcome Him. He tells them to come forth and He will lead
> them to Paradise. The souls thank Him, for now deliverance
> has come after more than a thousand years ("mil anz et
> plus", l. 1447).

The last few lines, including the term of the souls' captivity,
correspond with the *Passion des Jongleurs* as published by
'fuhl,[32] as does the conception of Christ's spirit making the
descent while His body was still on the cross. But for the rest,
the episode is a free paraphrase of parts of the *Gospel of Nicodemus*. This is an historic moment in the development of the
mystères, since here for the first time we have a writer who
appreciated the dramatic potentialities of the dialogue between
the devils as found in *Nicodemus*, and who adapted it to the needs
of his *genre*. And though there seem only to have been four
devils on the stage, all the spirit and hurly-burly of the later

mystery plays is incipient in the scene. The atmosphere i
virtually one of burlesque; and the sharp and ribald insult
flung from devil to devil are only equalled by those applied t
the Redeemer.

The Provençal mystery found in the Didot manuscript[33] ma
not have been written earlier than 1345, the date found on par
of the manuscript. But as regards the development of ou
theme, we are here taking a backward step: the story i
presented in a simple form, with little attempt at dramatic effect
and unless the copy is corrupt, the composition of the scene i
illogical.

> Christ rises from the tomb and takes the good robber t
> Paradise.[34] In Hell, Adam is aware of Christ's coming. Ther
> after a dialogue between Jesus and the devils, who are re
> fusing Him entrance, we are told that He came to the gates o
> Hell and entered. He tells His friends to come forth int
> Paradise, and they joyfully praise God. But then we ar
> apparently taken back before the gates of Hell, and a furthe
> dialogue between Christ and Baraban, a demon, ensue:
> Suddenly God himself appears and bids His Son ente
> Christ does so, calling again to Adam and the other prisone
> to come forth. He finally ascends with them to Paradise.

The source of the episode is unknown, and the editor ha
found no proof of knowledge either of the jongleurs' poem or o
Nicodemus. Perhaps the writer was merely reconstructing tl
scene from memory, for the form in which it is cast is far fro
satisfactory. Were it arranged logically, it would be simple i
the extreme, lacking the fire of the *Passion du Palatinus*, an
with no violent action suggested in the rubrics ;[35] but at least
would possess a certain naïve dignity almost entirely sacrifice
in the later treatments.

With the *Mystères de Sainte-Geneviève*[36] we find ourselves at tl
beginning of the fifteenth century, though they may have bee
written originally in the middle of the fourteenth. The desce

into Hell is found in two independent works, which we may class together here as they are found in the same manuscript[37] and apparently formed part of the repertoire of a *confrérie*. They are the *Passion* and the *Résurrection*.

The scene in the *Passion* is a paraphrase of part of *Nicodemus*.

The devils, Satan and Beelzebub (= Enfer) discuss Christ's coming and decide that He must not be allowed to enter Hell. Christ arrives demanding admission, and Satan orders his companion to bar the gates. The prophets briefly recall their prophecies. Then Christ repeats His demand, and Beelzebub asks who this King of Glory is. After the reply by Habakkuk, Satan declares that the gates are already broken, and then addresses flattering words to Jesus, promising Him never to act against Him again. To the bickering of the devils, Christ says that He will cast Satan, chained, into the infernal prison for ever : Beelzebub is to be his guard. Thereupon the grateful Adam and Eve and their companions are delivered into Paradise.

Again we miss the verve displayed in the *Passion du Palatinus*, but some action is implied when not actually called for in the rubrics ; and Satan's words of flattery faintly echo the technique of the master-devil in the *Mystère d'Adam*. The appeal of this scene is certainly broader than that in the *Passion d'Autun* ; but there are indications that what we have is a redaction of a considerably earlier play,[38] and this would account for the still relatively simple form.

The *Résurrection* reflects an entirely different tradition.

Adam is in Hell, calling for succour in scholastic yet lyrical tones :

> *Doulz Diex, qui a ta formeüre*
> *Me feis par ymaginee faiture,*
> *Et ame et vie me donnas . . .*
> *Vrais Diex, veulles nous secourir !*
> *Nous ne faisons que langourir.*   (p. 332)

(Sweet God, who created me in thy form and image and gave me life and soul . . . True God, deign to succour us ! We do nought but languish here.)

In his entreaties he is joined by Eve, John the Baptist and Noel (Noah). Then "Belgibus, premier deable" expresses to his companion "Belias" the fear that the souls may be redeemed as they have prophesied. Belias says that he would take this ill, if God should fill his Paradise where once they themselves were. And this introduces a description of the devils' fall from grace under Lucifer, their leader. The anxious guardians of Hell decide to put their prisoners to blaze in the great infernal fire with Lucifer. Then God the Son, rising from the tomb, proclaims His intention to accomplish His descent. He will deliver the souls of the patriarchs and the prophets from the Limbo where he knows them to be. The devils are afraid and angry; but Christ, showing the wounds with which He has purchased the souls' deliverance, calls upon them to join Him in Paradise. With the devils' forlorn complaints that no prisoners are left to them through God's breach of faith, the episode comes to an end.

The gulf dividing this presentation of the Harrowing from that found in the *Passion* is manifest. What little dramatic action there was latent in that text has been consciously rejected by this author, save for the necessary appearance of the Redeemer and his leading the souls from Hell. Even the devils here moralise, and the whole scene is full of the terminology of scholastic theology,[39] forcing a comparison with the *Livre de la Passion*, which we studied in an earlier chapter.[40] Disregarding the popular taste, our author, who could well have been a churchman, has realised the serious nature of his subject and treated it with uncommon restraint and lyrical dignity. However, since all the plays in the Ste-Geneviève manuscript appear to have formed a single repertoire, we cannot consider any of them singly without reference to the whole. And though the amount of realism and comic effect in the *Passion* and the *Résurrection* is a good deal less than in the Palatine *Passion*, the rest of the collection makes up for this in full measure. For the other plays show a strange mixture of the pious and the grotesque, which is well prominent in the *diableries*. That these two *mystères* are earlier in origin than the saint plays in the same manuscript[41] suggests that, while they were still considered fit for use at the beginning of the fifteenth century, the public taste had become somewhat more debased since the date of their composition. They were probably retained mainly for the benefit of the clerical section of the audience, whilst the lesser plays were provided as a sop to the layfolk.[42]

So far, the plays we have looked at are no more than precursors of the great fifteenth-century *mystères*, although as far as the descent episode is concerned they collectively show all the chief features of the latter in embryo, except for the vast and exaggerated scale. With the *Passion d'Arras*, probably by Eustache Mercadé who died in 1440, we achieve the final step.[43] The whole work, which was performed over four days, totals 24,945 lines: of these 1,300 are devoted to Christ's descent, which is described in three separate scenes (ll. 17557–729, 18059–231, and 20300–21253). Two of these form a kind of prologue to the Harrowing:

> After St Michael's announcement of Christ's forthcoming descent, Cerberus describes the events of the Crucifixion—to the dismay of the devils, who sense impending disaster. Later, Lucifer scolds Satan for his part in the preparation of the coming catastrophe, but he is pacified in the end and in a lively speech orders the devils to undertake the barricading of Hell. Culverins and cannons are included in the defences! But even these cannot prevail against the Son of God, whose victorious entry into Hell is heralded by the archangel Gabriel.

The *Passion d'Arras*, if it was in fact the first French mystery to give such a broad development to the descent theme, set the pattern for those which followed. Its sources have been studied by W. Becker. The *Gospel of Nicodemus* furnished the ground plan, but upon this have been erected elements from the liturgy and much of the infernal lore current by this time in medieval France. Here for example, are the names of some of the devils in the play: Cerbere, Astaroth, Agrapart, Leviatan, Burgibus, Urbant, Tantalus, Bufar, Nazar, Fernagus, Errouillart, Rifflart, Dentart, Fouant, Zaroës, Frongnart, and "Gombaut le maistre des diablesses". Classical, biblical, epic and popular names are mingled with others that may well be Mercadé's own inventions. In all, the *diableries* take up almost half of the lines devoted to the whole episode, and throughout the play there are frequent scenes in Hell.[44]

It would be an unrewarding task to analyse the relevant scenes in all the fifteenth-century *mystères*.[45] Instead, I shall give a summary of those scenes which bear on the descent episode in Arnoul Gréban's great *Mystère de la Passion*,[46] a representative work that holds a central position among the French mystery plays, and of which it has been said: "Cette œuvre absorbe en elle les essais antérieurs."[47] Composed by 1452, it owes a great debt to the *Passion d'Arras*, just as it was itself to contribute much to the *Passion* of Jean Michel.

We first make the acquaintance of the principal devils in the Prologue, when we are present at the fall of the rebellious angels Lucifer, Sathan, Belzebuth, Astaroth and their tribe. The first soul received by the newly-created devils is that of Abel who, being a just person, is put into the Limbo. There he is soon joined by Adam and Eve. On the first day of the play, Lucifer calls a council to discuss the prophecies of a divine descent into Hell. His summons to the devils might almost serve as a *mise en scène* for the infernal regions:

> *Saultez hors des abismes noirs,*
> *Des obscurs infernaulx manoirs,*
> *Tous puans de feu et de souffre,*
> *Deables, sailliez de vostre gouffre*
> *Et des horribles regions:*
> *Par milliers et par legions*
> *Venez entendre mon procés.*
> *Laissiez les chaisnes et crochés,*
> *Gibés et larronceaux pendans,*
> *Fourneaux fournis, serpens mordans,*
> *Dragons plus ardans que tempeste;*
> *Ne vous bruslez plus groing ne teste*

A faire ces metaulx couller :
Faictes moy bondir et crouller
Tout le hideux infernal porce,
De haste de venir a force
Oyr ma proposicion. (ll. 3705–21)

(Leap forth from the black abysses of the dark haunts of
Hell all stinking with fire and sulphur, devils ; spring up
from your gulf and the regions of horror : in your thou-
sands and legions come and hear what I have to discuss.
Leave the chains and hooks, the gibbets and the dangling
rogues, the well stoked furnaces and biting serpents, and
fiery dragons keener than tempest : don't burn your heads
and snouts any longer in making those metals run : see to
it that all the hideous infernal herd comes bounding and
quivering in their haste to throng together and hear the
news I have for you.)

Later, Satan brings the tidings of Christ's birth, for he is the
devil chiefly concerned with earthly affairs. He is soundly
drubbed and tortured for his pains. Similarly, on the second
day, when he returns with Berich from an unsuccessful
attempt to corrupt Christ, they are both tortured by the other
devils with the consent of Lucifer. Again he tries, with like
result ; and a devil cast out of a Canaanite girl by Christ is
condemned by Lucifer to roast on the infernal braziers. Still
on the second day, all the devils are plunged into gloom by
the news of the deliverance of Lazarus from the Limbo.
Then the hapless Satan returns after another fruitless expedi-
tion to the earth and is once more punished with gusto by his
comrades. They plan to use Judas to betray Christ ; and on
the third day, with his treachery accomplished, Judas is received into eternal torment.

In the Limbo Adam and Eve long for deliverance ; and
God sends St Michael down from Heaven to announce their
imminent salvation. The souls in the Limbo give expression
to their joy, and Lucifer asks the reason. He is alarmed, but
the other devils are confident, and Cerberus promises to keep
the gate of Hell closed. Meanwhile, Satan proudly announces
Christ's impending death ; but now Lucifer asserts that if it

comes about it will mean their undoing; so he sends Pilate's wife to try to prevent the disaster. In Hell there is growing alarm, and Lucifer orders the defences to be made ready, with great armies at hand to defend the barred and bolted gates. Satan returns to announce Christ's approach:

> *Veez cy l'ame Jhesus qui vient*
> *Pour nous despouiller cent contre ung.*
>
> (ll. 26228-9)

(Here's the soul of Jesus coming to despoil us, a hundred to one on it.)

The divine rescuer appears at the gates. He calls in Latin for them to be opened that the King of Glory may come in. The souls in the Limbo ask who this King of Glory is. Then comes the stage direction: "Icy doivent cheoir les portes quand Jhesus frappera sa croix encontre" (here the gates must fall when Jesus strikes them with His cross). Christ says that victory is His, though He has paid a heavy price. He has come to deliver the good prisoners and to make the infernal powers subservient to the cross. He takes Adam by the hand; and then, after a few words from each of the prophets and from Eve, "icy les emmaine Jhesus hors d'enfer et les met en quelque lieu determiné, et tandis font grant tempeste les diables en enfer" (here Jesus leads them forth from Hell and puts them in some specified place, and meanwhile the devils make a great uproar in Hell).[48] The devils are enraged, and Lucifer orders Christ's pursuit. There is great grief in Hell, for although many damned are left, the "flower of the devils' inheritance" has been carried off. Even Lucifer calls for death:

> *Mort, Mort, ou es tu enserree?*
> *Gette l'œil au dueil ou je suis:*
> *Ma fille de moy engendree,*
> *Partout te quiers, et tu me fuys!* (ll. 26375-8)

(Death, Death, where are you locked away? Cast your eye on the grief I am in: daughter of my own flesh, I seek you everywhere, and you flee me!)

But finally he decides to make the best of the situation and
sends for the souls of the two robbers. Michael takes that of
the good one to Heaven, but the soul of the bad one he does
send down to Lucifer in Hell.[49]

A good deal is known of the life of Arnoul Gréban, poet and
musician.[50] It was when he was organist and choirmaster at
Notre Dame in Paris that he composed his vast *Passion*. Of his
sincerity and pious devotion there can be no doubt,[51] indeed
they shine constantly through his work. But this was not
enough for a Parisian audience of the mid-fifteenth century;
and Arnoul has not shirked from accepting and developing the
tradition of the *diableries*. The vivid and macabre quality of the
devil scenes may appear even from the above summary and
without reference to the *mise en scène*. This must have been
highly developed, with separate *mansions* for the Limbo and
Hell;[52] and the scale of the effects may be gauged from those
demanded of the *régisseur* at the moment of Christ's death:
"Icy encline Jhesus le chef et rend l'esperit; et doit trambler la
terre, les pierres se fendre, plusieurs morts ressusciter. le
voile du temple doit partir et rompre en deux" (here Jesus bows
His head and gives up the ghost; and the earth should quake,
the stones split open, a number of dead be resurrected, and the
veil of the temple should part and be rent in two).[53] Such
effects were engineered to appeal to the public; and one cannot
escape the conclusion that it was the spectacle which drew the
crowd. Real though the literary value of Gréban's *Passion* is,
only the discriminating few would come to its performance for
the sake of the poetry or the religious stimulus it sought to
provide; and even they cannot but have been impressed by the
lavish display of scenic effects. One of the great qualities of the
early medieval imagination had been the ability to appreciate
and interpret the symbol. Now we find its place in drama
usurped by a gaudy realism; and the loss in spiritual value is
immense.

On the French stage, then, the *diableries* increased in length and
number as the Middle Ages drew to their close; and with the

insistent striving for realism, the borderline between the hideous and the comic was frequently overstepped.[54] The devils, from being few and relatively anonymous, became legion, and most of them were named. Already in the *Gospel of Nicodemus* Satan and Inferus were invested with some rudimentary psychology, representing in a way the Roland and Oliver of the infernal realm. This elementary psychological treatment is pursued in the later *mystères*. And now Death (Mort) has become a devil in his own right from being originally the allegorical pseudonym of Satan; from Classical mythology the three Parcae are introduced[55] in the company of such figures as Cerberus and Tantalus; Hebrew tradition provides more names—Beelzebub, Astaroth, Belial, Belphegor, Lucifer, Leviathan, for instance; pagans like Agrapart and Fernagus are enrolled from the epic; and finally there are native French creations, popular or allegorical, such as Barbarin, Mauferas, Engignart, Desesperance. An interesting list, consisting largely of Classical names, is given by Jean Michel in his own *Passion*.[56] So in this way the "domestic" scene and atmosphere in Hell was elaborated, and a series of *diableries* came to be demanded by the public by way of introduction to Christ's descent. Any moral value these may have had was submerged by their appeal to the craving for sensation and broad laughter. Thus, when the supreme moment came, its poignancy was reduced by the comic associations built up in the minds of the spectators by the earlier scenes.

Of course, we must beware of isolating these episodes from their context, in which a certain amount of light relief was no doubt necessary. The *mystères* were still devout works. But the secular and comic elements embedded in them throughout their entire length did, as time passed, grow in their relative importance.[57] So the trend in the scenes connected with the Harrowing can legitimately be taken as symptomatic of the whole.

From the Church's point of view the change was to be regretted, although the ecclesiastical authorities were not yet provoked to a general opposition to the mystery and miracle plays. Indeed, their opposition seems to have taken a surprisingly long time to become manifest.[58] For even though, as far as we know, there were no purely comic versions of the infernal visit being acted, the burlesque element in the *diableries* must have influenced the public view of Hell in a sense contrary to the Church's eschatological teachings. Instead of folk leaving such spectacles with their faith confirmed and their terror of Hell increased,[59] they were more likely to laugh at the antics of the demons and discuss among themselves which was the best clown. This was poor theological training. And although performances were not so very frequent,[60] they could have been a contributing factor as well as a by-product of an increasingly light-hearted and irreverent attitude to religion in the later centuries of the Middle Ages. Was it, one might wonder, a sheer accounting necessity to enter on an expense sheet for a *mystère* played at the end of our period such an item as : "A Dieu le Pere . . . donné un pot de vin de cinq sols" (To God the Father one pot of wine at five sous)![61] While it is common to consider the mysteries as one of the great triumphs of medieval Christianity, the staging of Christ's descent together with its attendant *diableries* was, theologically, something of a blunder.[62]

From the doctrinal point of view, a simple and largely symbolical representation would have been safer. Alternatively, the events could have been narrated in the course of the dialogue through the mouths of Karinus and Leucius or some other suitable person, even Christ Himself. In this way much of the danger, but also most of the popular appeal, would be avoided. The technique was, however, used to deal with another "descent" episode in several of the *mystères*. I refer to the so-called *Vison of Lazarus*.

This is not a true vision, but an account of the places of torment given by the resurrected Lazarus. It became in the fifteenth century a recognised episode in the account of Christ's Passion.[63] In the *Gospel of Nicodemus* Inferus refers to Christ's raising of Lazarus ; but as yet there is no exploitation of the latter's experiences during his period of death. We have to wait several hundred years (the date is uncertain) for a reference to his subsequent description of the pains of Hell. This occurs in a pseudo-Augustinian homily, where it is supposed that Lazarus is dining in the house of Simon. In answer to the guests' questions, he gave a detailed and ordered ("per ordinem") account of the gloomy places of punishment.[64] This, it seems, was the starting point of the legend. Then about 1170 it reappears in almost identical form in Petrus Comestor's *Historia scholastica*,[65] though there the words "per ordinem" are omitted. This phrase has some significance, since it infers some sort of fixed disposition of the places of torment; and perhaps it is for this reason that in later accounts it is usual to number the torments or to give an indication of the architecture and topography of Hell.

Of the development of the legend in medieval literature much has still to be learned. Voigt noted a reference to it in the late thirteenth-century *Liber de abundantia exemplorum* along with another to the *Gospel of Nicodemus*, whilst an anonymous *Passio Lazari*, seemingly of the early fourteenth century, makes full use of the *Vision of St Paul* and cannot be said to belong to the same tradition as the French texts.[66] The latter all relate how Lazarus, dining at the house of Simon, tells the assembled company not so much of his own experiences in Hell as of the type of place it is. The account is given quite briefly and has little literary interest, so it will suffice to mention the chief works in which it occurs.

In 1398, Isabel of Bavaria ordered the translation of a *Passion* from Latin into French.[67] This was a non-dramatic prose work containing Lazarus' account of Hell, where there are nine torments.

In the *Passion de Sainte-Geneviève*[68] nine similar torments are described. Here they take the following order: fire for the covetous; fire and ice for the malicious; all manner of vermin, dragons and toads for the envious; darkness for the lustful; the disobedient are beaten by a thousand demons; there is more darkness for other evildoers; the unconfessed recount their sins to one another and indulge in mutual slander; devils and dragons punish those who did not go to church; the very wicked suffer all the torments.[69]

Lazarus' story in the *Passion de Semur*[70] only occupies twenty-six lines. Here we are merely told of the two parts of Hell, one for the good souls (that is the *Limbus patrum*) and one for the wicked. The former are simply in darkness, but the evildoers are in the eternal fire, tormented by reptiles, stretched out upon the earth, and immersed in boiling lead. They suffer proportionately to the degree of their sin.[71]

Gréban's *Passion* contains a version of the legend which shows obvious debts to scholastic theology.[72] The infernal regions comprise four "storeys" arranged one above the other. The highest is the *Limbus patrum*, then comes Purgatory, the Limbo for unbaptised children, and finally the abyss of Hell. Such is the account given by Lazarus on the second day of Gréban's mystery, and in this form it was taken over by Jean Michel at the end of the century.

The other texts I shall mention show a seven-fold division of Hell. Voigt has found such a division linked with a mention of Lazarus' story in George of Krisszafán's description of his visit to St Patrick's Purgatory in 1353.[73] Perhaps the first occurrence in French is in the fifteenth-century prose *Résurrection de Lazare* found in the Paris, B.N., MS fr. 923.[74] It recurs in Regnauld le Queux's *Baratre infernal* of 1480, in the printed *Traité des peines d'enfer et de purgatoire* of 1492, and in the *Compost et Kalendrier des Bergers* of which we have a printed copy dated 1493[75] and many later editions. In addition, Voigt sees the seven torments present (though in a rather confused form) in the Provençal *Suscitatio del Laze*.[76]

It is generally accepted that the notion of seven places of torment is dependent on the medieval conception of the Seven Deadly Sins, and as far as the *Vision of Lazarus* is concerned the proof seems to lie within the texts themselves. The usual medieval order of the sins was : Superbia, Avaricia, Luxuria, Invidia, Gula, Ira, Accidia. In our texts the order varies, but the sins are the same. This is how they appear in the *Compost et Kalendrier des Bergers:*

There are huge mill-wheels turning rapidly, and the proud are attached to them by fiery hooks.[77] The envious are immersed to the navel in a river of ice and are lashed by a biting wind.[78] In a cave, the wrathful are hacked by swords and knives.[79] The slothful are shut in a room full of serpents.

The avaricious are plunged to the neck in cauldrons of boiling oil and metals.[80] In a valley there is a foul river and a table heaped with filth set upon its bank. Here the gluttonous are fed with reptiles and the water of the river.[81] The lustful are sunk in pits full of fire and sulphur.

It will be appreciated that this is a hotch-potch of general infernal lore gleaned perhaps from a number of different legends, but probably with reference only to the author's memory. The sole original feature in the *Vision of Lazarus* in general is that the various pains have been matched, somewhat haphazardly, to the scheme of the Seven Deadly Sins. This arrangement, though useful for inclusion in pious compendia or almanachs, does show how barren the orthodox pious treatments of our theme had become in France by the late Middle Ages. Its contribution to the *mystères* where it appears is negligible. Maybe it helped a little to stir the public's imagination as they learned what lay behind that yawning façade to the right of the stage. But the *Vision* was not dramatic in its origin, nor did it contain the seeds of drama as did the Harrowing. All we can say in its favour is that it was theologically "safe", if apocryphal, in a way in which the dramatisation of Christ's descent was not. But it brought nothing of real value either to the *mystères* or to the common fund of eschatological legends.

Leaving aside questions of theological propriety, we may now consider the aesthetic value of the descent theme in the medieval drama. In the miracle play it merely provides another plot with a lurid setting. As for the *mystères*, only the representation of the Harrowing made any real contribution, but it was an extremely important one. Together with the Crucifixion, with which it is so closely associated, it supplies the emotional climax of the action. From the hour of apparent defeat represented by the cross is snatched the supreme victory over death itself and over the powers of sin and darkness. The tension built up by the Crucifixion scene with its relatively simple *décor* is snapped and dispersed by Christ's triumph over the grave and by the more elaborate setting of the descent scene. The audience suddenly relaxes to laugh at the antics of the rulers of Hell as they are dispossessed of their inheritance by their victorious enemy. It sees with delight the defences of Hell broken down, Satan cast into the pit of the abyss, the patriarchs delivered from the Limbo, and the souls of the eternally damned still plagued by the fires of Hell or revolving on the infernal wheel. From an aesthetic point of view, then, the presentation of the Harrowing is successful—so much so that one feels the plays might have ended here. And seen in this light, even the comic element of the *diableries* has its function. But to return to my former position, it was wholly unfitting that one of the greatest of Christian mysteries should have been trammelled with comic associations and have provided an outlet for emotions pent up during the representation of the supreme Christian act.

NOTES

1. For the appearance of the *gueule* and its derivation from biblical texts see G. Cohen, *Histoire de la mise en scène dans le théâtre religieux du moyen âge* (Paris, 1926), pp. 97–8 *inter alia*, and Plates I & V.
2. For a discussion of this question, see A. Kolve, *The Play Called Corpus Christi* (London, 1966). The Wycliffite preacher cited by Kolve (e.g. p. 21) certainly believed that the stage representation of Hell would lead to its reality being taken lightly.
3. "Modo accipiant eas Demones, et precipitentur in infernum." There is unfortunately no indication of the *décor*. For this work see K. Young, *The Drama of the Medieval Church* (Oxford, 1933), II, pp. 361–9 (the text is on pp. 362–4); Cohen, op. cit., p. 54, and *Le Théâtre en France au moyen-âge* (Paris, new edn., 1948), pp. 14–15; Grace Frank, *The Medieval French Drama* (Oxford, 1954), pp. 58–64. Ed. L.-P. Thomas, *Le "Sponsus"* (Paris, 1951).
4. Ed. P. Studer (Manchester, 1918); P. Aebischer (Geneva & Paris, 1963). For the dating see Frank, op. cit., p. 76; Aebischer, op. cit., p. 19. There is provision for chains, clouds of smoke, and a great din augmented by bangings on cauldrons and kettles (ed. Studer, p. 29).
5. Ed. J. G. Wright as *La Résurrection du Sauveur, fragment d'un jeu* (Paris, 1931), and by T. A. Jenkins, etc. (Oxford, 1943). See also Cohen, *Le Théâtre . . .*, pp. 18–19; Frank, op. cit., pp. 86–92. The usual dating is late twelfth century.
6. Canterbury MS (London, B.M., Add. 45103), ll. 23–30. This is a more redacted version than that in the other MS (Paris, B.N., fr. 902), where the equivalent passage reads:
   Vne jaiole i deit aver
   Pur les prisons enprisoner;

> *Enfer seit mis de cele part*
> *Es mansions del altre part*
> *E puis le ciel . . .*

(I quote from Jenkins' edition.)

7. Young is uncertain. Though usually known as a liturgical play, the *Sponsus* is not derived from the liturgy, nor is there evidence that it was attached to it (Young, op. cit., II, p. 168).

8. Ibid., I, Ch. V.

9. *Gott und Hölle*, pp. 154–6.

10. Ibid., p. 163; Young, op. cit., I, pp. 421–32 (with text). W. Becker had earlier quoted the Fleury *Visitatio Sepulchri* as containing the first direct mention of the descent in liturgical drama ("Die Sage von der Höllenfahrt Christi in der altfranzösischen Literatur", *Romanische Forschungen* 32 [1913], p. 925). This is found in the Orléans MS 201 (178). The three Marys are at the tomb:

Item prima dicat:	*Resurrexit hodie rex angelorum.*
Secunda:	*Ducitur de tenebris turba piorum.*
Tercia:	*Reseratur aditus regni celorum !*

(Young, op. cit., I, p. 396)

11. Ibid., I, p. 167.

12. Suggested especially by the direction: ". . . Ihesus magno impetu tandem confringit portas Inferni" (ibid., I, p. 428).

13. These calls and responses are taken from *Psalm* xxiv (Vulgate xxiii). 7–10.

14. Young, op. cit., I, pp. 102–4. This ceremonial was used in Metz in the ninth century. See also E. K. Chambers, *The Medieval Stage*, II, p. 4; Cohen *Histoire de la mise en scène . . .* , p. 21; Kroll, op. cit., pp. 156–7.

15. Quoted by Young, op. cit., II, p. 417. For the general attitude of the Church see Chambers, op. cit., II, pp. 97–103; M. Henshaw, "The Attitude of the Church Towards the Stage to the End of the Middle Ages", *Medievalia et Humanistica* 7 (1952), pp. 3–17.

16. Ed. G. Paris & U. Robert, *Miracles de Nostre Dame*, II (Paris, 1877), pp. 227–80. *Résumés* are given by L. Petit de Julleville, *Les Mystères* (Paris, 1880), pp. 258–9, and by A. Jeanroy in *Histoire littéraire de la France* 39 (1959), pp. 49–51. On the *Miracles* see Frank, op. cit., Ch. XII; R. Glutz, *Miracles de Notre Dame par personnages* (Berlin, 1954).

17. The theme of the death of the visitor soon after his return to earth is quite common in medieval vision literature and is parallelled in Celtic mythology (cf. Marie de France's *Lanval*, and see L. Spence, *The Magic Arts in Celtic Britain* [London, 1945], p. 80). In the present case a close analogy can be drawn with the legend "De l'ermite . . ." in the *Vie des anciens Pères* (see above, p. 114): in each case the principal figure is sent back to earth from Purgatory as a concession and for a specified length of time, in one case thirty years and in the other thirty days.

18. See the Abbé Poquet's edition (Paris, 1857), cols. 593–604. For a note on the source see Petit de Julleville, op. cit., II, pp. 259–60. The story also figures in the *Legenda Aurea*, where it is incorporated in the life of St Laurence (the St Lorens of our play).

19. E.g. a devil's:

> *Laisse m'en pais; dyable y ait part.*
> *Je cuiday prendre tout ouan*

> *L'arcediacre de Milan*
> *A ce qu'il fust nostre sanz fin,*
> *Mais il a esté si affin*
> *De Dieu a sa fin, et de fait*
> *A fait tant que riens n'y ay fait*
> *Fors que tant, c'est bien chose voire,*
> *Que je l'ay mis en purgatoire.*
>
> (ll. 432–40)

20. In the *Miracle de Théophile*, for example, occurs the Virgin's famous but unbecoming threat to Satan : "Et je te foulerai la pance" (ed. Grace Frank [Paris, 1949], l. 585).

21. Petit de Julleville, quoted by Grace Frank, *The Medieval French Drama*, p. 121. Of this particular play Petit de Julleville remarked : "Dans aucun autre miracle on ne voit le monde terrestre et le monde surnaturel se mêler l'un a l'autre aussi aisément, aussi familièrement" (op. cit., p. 259).

22. See J. Monnier, *La Descente aux enfers*, Ch. X.

23. See Grace Frank, *La Passion d'Autun*, p. 29.

24. *La Passion du Palatinus*, ed. Grace Frank, who dates it, as it stands, from the early fourteenth century (p. x). *La Passion d'Autun*, ed. Frank : this title covers two independent texts, both found in fifteenth-century manuscripts ; but one is incomplete, and it is only the other, known after its copyist as the *Passion de Biard*, which contains the descent scene. The Sion fragment, ed. J. Bédier, "Fragment d'un ancien mystère", *Romania* XXIV (1895), pp. 86–94 ; reprinted by Frank, *La Passion d'Autun*, pp. 160–2, 164–5. The manuscript dates from the late thirteenth or early fourteenth century (Bédier, op. cit., pp. 86–7) ; and it carries only two fragments totalling 87 lines, of which the first 25 give the end of the descent episode. The whole question of the filiation of these texts is discussed in Mrs Frank's Introduction to the *Passion d'Autun*. See also A. Jeanroy, "Le Théatre religieux en langue française jusqu'à la fin du XIVe siècle", *Histoire littéraire de la France* 39 (1959), pp. 4–5, 11–22.

25. Ll. 1878–9, 1908–9. Thus the second reads :

> *Adonc respondit JHESUCRIST*
> *A tout le peuple qu'estoit iqui . . . ,*

in place of the "Or parle Jhesus" of *S* (between l. 23 and l. 24). Cf. Frank, *La Passion d'Autun*, pp. 10–19.

26. P. M. Maas (*Étude sur les sources de la Passion du Palatinus* [Tiel, 1942], pp. 131–2) suggests that scenic considerations may have resolved the author of *A* to make the Resurrection precede the descent, thus avoiding two apparent resurrections from the tomb. Both traditions existed in the Middle Ages ; and while the Creed places the descent first, we have already noticed the other tradition's occurrence in the *Couronnement de Louis* (above, p. 97), where, of course, there is no question of dramatic technique being involved.

27. See *La Passion d'Autun*, pp. 25, 137, 160.

28. That *P* is closer to the original at this point is suggested by its better rhymes.

29. See above, p. 95.

30. Cf. Frank, *La Passion du Palatinus*, p. 86.

31. The personages, unnamed in the manuscript, have been given their

traditional names by the editor (ibid., pp. iv and 86), who concludes tha
this is a copy of a true play modified for reading.

32. See above, pp. 103 ff.
33. Paris, B.N., n.a.fr. 4232. Ed. W. P. Shepard, *La Passion provençale d*
manuscrit Didot. See also E. Roy, "Le Mystère de la Passion en France
du XIVᵉ au XVIᵉ siècle", *Revue Bourguignonne* 13 & 14, Part II, pp. 319-
28.
34. Ll. 1621–32. The descent episode proper occupies ll. 1706–1811.
35. The devils even address Christ as "bos hom" (l. 1724), and He call
them "amic" (l. 1784).
36. Ed. A. Jubinal, *Mystères inédits du quinzième siècle*, II. See also W
Becker, op. cit., pp. 936–41 ; Frank, *The Medieval French Drama*, pp
136–53.
37. Bibliothèque Ste-Geneviève, MS 1131. See Jubinal, op. cit., II
pp. 290–7, 332–46.
38. Frank, *The Medieval French Drama*, p. 148.
39. Cf. Christ's words :
> Sanz ce que de riens soie repris,
> Acompliray ce que j'ay empris
> Quant mon pere glorefié
> Aprés mort m'a vivifié
> Le corps ou mon vray esperit
> Conjointement le resprit
> Par la vivification
> De la glorification
> Divine qui finer ne puet,
> Droit en enfer aler m'estuet.
>
> (p. 338

See Becker's analysis (op. cit., pp. 939–41) and his further suggestion
the influence of the *Gospel of Nicodemus* and the Easter procession.
40. See above, pp. 110 ff.
41. Frank, *The Medieval French Drama*, p. 147.
42. It is clear from internal evidence that the Ste-Geneviève plays we
written for an audience of *lais* and *clercs* (ibid., pp. 136, 153).
43. Ed. J. M. Richard, *Le Mystère de la Passion. Texte du MS 697 de*
Bibliothèque d'Arras (Paris, 1893). See too W. Becker, op. cit., pp. 948
52 ; Frank, *The Medieval French Drama*, pp. 179–80. The *Passion*
Semur (ed. Roy. op. cit., pp. 73* ff.) may be an earlier play, but th
manuscript in which it is found is dated 1488. This work owes much
the *Passion de Ste-Geneviève*, though the descent episode is independen
It occurs on the second of the two days (ll. 8584–742), but *diableri*
occur on both days. There are fourteen named devils in the cast.
44. Studied by O. Geister, *Die Teufelszenen in der Passion von Arras u*
der Vengeance Jhesucrist: ein Beitrag zur Verfasserfrage (Greifswal
1914).
45. Other important *mystères* containing the Harrowing are : the *Passion*
Semur (see above, n. 43); the Provençal *Mystères rouergats* (e
A. Jeanroy & H. Teulié, *Mystères provençaux du quinzième siè*
[Toulouse, 1893] : they are disconnected episodes probably intend
for incorporation into a complete *mystère*. Christ's descent owes mu
to the Didot *Passion*); the *Passion* of Jean Michel (a summary wi
extracts is given by the Parfaict brothers, *Histoire du théâtre françois,*

[Paris, 1734]. Written about 1500, it is an amplification of Gréban's work); the *Résurrection* sometimes wrongly attributed to Jean Michel (see Parfaict brothers, op. cit., II. Some features, e.g. the descent of the good thief with Christ, are taken from the *Passion selon Gamaliel* [see above, p. 102]. It was produced in Paris in 1507).

46. Ed. G. Paris & G. Raynaud (Paris, 1878). For a discussion and further bibliography see W. Becker, op. cit., pp. 953–7; *The Medieval French Drama*, pp. 181–7.

47. Monnier, op. cit., p. 217.

48. The actual descent occupies ll. 26228–336.

49. Further *diableries* occur on the fourth and last day (see ll. 28868 ff., 31925ff., 33331 ff.).

50. See especially P. Champion, *Histoire poétique du XVᵉ siècle* (Paris, 1923), II, pp. 133–88. Grace Frank records the essential facts (*The Medieval French Drama*, pp. 182–3).

51. For his own testimony see Cohen, *Histoire de la mise en scène* ..., pp. xli–xlii (quoting from the final Prologue of the *Passion*, ed. Paris & Raynaud, p. 451); and Frank, *The Medieval French Drama*, p. 184.

52. It could hardly have been more elaborate than in the *Résurrection* attributed to Jean Michel. For the detailed instructions regarding the staging of Hell and the Limbo in this play, see Parfaict brothers, op. cit., II, p. 477; and Cohen, *Histoire de la mise en scène*, pp. 94–5.

53. Ed. Paris & Raynaud, p. 399; quoted by Cohen, ibid., p. 163.

54. For a rapid survey of the whole question see R. Lebègue, "Le Diable dans l'ancien théâtre religieux", *Cahiers de l'Association Internationale des Études Françaises*, No. 3–4–5 (July 1953), pp. 97–105. The Devil as a comic figure on the medieval stage is studied by H. Wieck, *Die Teufel auf der mittelalterlichen Mysterienbühne Frankreichs* (Leipzig, 1887), Ch. IV. For the extravagant lengths to which realism was taken, even at the expense of personal danger to actors and public alike, see Cohen, *Histoire de la mise en scène* ..., Livre III, *passim*, and especially Chs. II & IV.

55. André de Coutances already knew them as devils (see above, p. 100, for his version of *Nicodemus*).

56. Parfaict brothers, op. cit., I, pp. 381–3. For a rather haphazard attempt at classification see Wieck, op. cit., pp. 7 ff.

57. See Chambers, op. cit., pp. 90–1; Cohen, *Histoire de la mise en scène* ..., pp. 261 ff.

58. See Chambers, op. cit., pp. 101–3. There is little sign of any active opposition before the events leading to the Paris Parlement's decree of 1548 forbidding the Confrérie de la Passion to represent mystery plays based on the Scriptures. Even here the Church's hand is not apparent, although the decree was motivated by religious scruples (see Petit de Julleville, op. cit., I, pp. 423–30).

59. The account given by L'Hospital of the audience at a sixteenth-century *mystère* perspiring with terror is clearly ironical (Lebègue, op. cit., pp. 103–4). For a discussion by Lebègue of the popularity of the *diableries* in the sixteenth century and later see *Mélanges d'histoire du théâtre du moyen-âge et de la Renaissance offerts à Gustave Cohen* (Paris, 1950), pp. 222–6.

60. They took place at festival times and seem at first mainly to have been annual events (see A. Thomas, "Le Théâtre a Paris et aux environs à la

fin du quatorzième siècle", *Romania* XXI [1892], pp. 606–11; and Frank, *The Medieval French Drama*, p. 166).

61. Cohen, *Le Théâtre en France au moyen-âge*, p. 62, quoting from the *Livre de conduite* for the Mons *Passion* of 1601.

62. For a discussion of the humorous elements in religious drama, see Kolve, op. cit., especially Chs. VI–VII.

63. See M. Voigt, *Beiträge zur Geschichte der Visionenliteratur im Mittelalter. I: Visio Lazari*. The raising of Lazarus figures in the liturgical drama from the twelfth century (Young, op. cit., I, p. 524, and II, pp. 199–219), but as yet there is no description of Lazarus' experiences in the lower world.

64. "Convivis interrogantibus tristia loca poenarum sedesque alta nocte semper obscuras, Lazarus indicat diligenti narratione, per ordinem; diu quae siti longisque temporibus ignorati invenerunt tandem inferi proditorem." The homily is printed in J. P. Migne, *Patrologia Latina*, Vol. 39, col. 1929, no. xcvi (see Voigt, op. cit., pp. 14–15). For the context of Lazarus' "vision" see *John* xii. 2.

65. Migne, *Patrologia Latina*, Vol. 198, col. 1597, Ch. cxvi (see Voigt, op. cit., p. 15).

66. Voigt, op. cit., pp. 8–13, 16.

67. See Roy, op. cit., pp. 590, 252–3, 478.

68. Ed. Jubinal, op. cit., II, pp. 171–4.

69. The source of the ninefold Hells is to be found in the *Elucidarium* attributed to Honorius Augustodunensis (see above, p. 60) or at least in the tradition which Honorius reflects.

70. Roy, op. cit., p. 107.

71. The torments show a perhaps fortuitous similarity with some of those described in *St Patrick's Purgatory*.

72. Ed. Paris & Raynaud, ll. 15784–862. See Roy, op. cit., p. 220.

73. Voigt, op. cit., pp. 4–6.

74. Fol. 116ʳ ff. See Roy, op. cit., pp. 306–7.

75. Facsimile edition by P. Champion (Paris, 1926). Lazarus' account occurs in Part II.

76. Ed. Jeanroy & Teulié, op. cit., pp. 86–8. See Voigt, op. cit., p. 24.

77. Cf. the wheel in the Alexandrine version of the *Vision of St Paul* (above, p. 88), where a kind of mill-wheel has been represented.

78. Cf. the *Vision of Alberic* (*Bibliotheca Casinensis*, Vol. V, Part I [Monte Cassino, 1894], pp. 191–206), where sinners are immersed in an ice-filled valley to different degrees according to their sin (see H. R. Patch, *The Other World*, p. 111). The Alexandrine version of the *Vision of St Paul* contains a similar torment for fast-breakers (above, p. 88).

79. Cf. the House of Phristinus in the *Vision of Tundal* (above, p. 30).

80. Cf. the bath-house in *St Patrick's Purgatory* (above, pp. 42–3).

81. This is apparently an adaptation of the Tantalus torment (cf. the punishment for fast-breakers in the *Visio Pauli* [above, p. 4]).

CHAPTER XI

HISTORIAN OF HELL

THERE could be no more appropriate work with which to conclude this study than Regnauld le Queux's *Baratre infernal*, which has come down to us in the Paris, B.N., MS fr. 450.[1] Regnauld le Queux of Douai, preceptor to the Comte de Périgueux and a writer and poet of mediocre talent, compiled this volume of infernal lore in the year 1480.[2] It seems that he found more favour with his contemporaries than with posterity, and he is mentioned by the Grand Rhétoriqueur Jean Bouchet in his *Temple de Bonne Renommée* (1516) among those who have graced French literature with their writings. In one place, Bouchet refers to Regnauld's *Mansion céleste*, a work now lost but which was presumably written as a counterpart to the *Baratre infernal*.[3] As I mentioned earlier, Regnauld knew Dante, to whom he specifically refers,[4] and it may have been the Tuscan poet who gave him the idea of undertaking this massive work. But he was certainly no Dante, and Paulin Paris piously exclaims : "Dieu, dans sa miséricorde, ne tire jamais de la foule innombrable des poëtes inconnus maître Regnaud le Queux, auteur de la *Maison céleste*, du *Baratre infernal* et du *Miroir de Court !*"[5]

Regnauld's aims were really of a three-fold nature : scholarly, pious, and literary; and it is hard to say where he himself would have laid the emphasis. But before justifying this statement, I shall review the contents of the *Baratre*. The manuscript comprises 238 folios of prose intermingled with dull, mechanical verse. Throughout, Regnauld quotes liberally from Christian and pagan writers, both in the text itself and in numerous glosses. The whole work falls into two main parts preceded by a long, amorphous Prologue and rounded off by a brief conclusion. The first "livre" is devoted to non-Christian testimonies on the nature of Hell and its inhabitants and is built round a free account of the sixth book of the *Aeneid*. From the rubrics it can be seen that Regnauld indulges in long digressions and explanations and also in some "tidying up" of the Virgilian Hades, which he makes conform to a more Dantesque architectural plan. The second book has a clear internal sub-division. First, Hell and its inmates are described according to the testimony of the Scriptures and various Christian writers (still with copious references to Classical myth and tradition); and secondly, Regnauld proves the very real existence of the places of torment by describing sundry visions and descents experienced by human beings. It is this latter section that particularly concerns us here, and a brief analysis of its contents will illustrate the richness of the material of this kind that was at the disposal of the late medieval writer. I have already discussed in earlier chapters the more important of the accounts, so I shall not now do more than show how Regnauld has introduced them into the *Baratre*. But let me first draw the reader's attention to the formidable list of authorities and sources drawn up by our infernal historian on folios 29^r–30^r of his work. First he names the "anciens poëtes morelz, satyriques, elegyaques, genealogiques, theologues, hystoriques, philosphes et mithologiques" that he has used. Sixty-two are listed. There follow the names of fifty Christian writers and ten biblical and apocryphal books. No doubt Regnauld gleaned many of the references from medieval compendia to which he had access, but we should not under-rate the painstaking scholarship to which the *Baratre* is a monument.

On folio 188^r Regnauld embarks on his description of "exemples, visions et revelations des paines terribles d'enfer"; for, as he reminds us, examples move us more than words—the theory behind so much vision literature. The first anecdote is the *Vision of a Cistercian Novice*,[6] somewhat abbreviated from the version given by Vincent de Beauvais in his *Speculum historiale*. There follows the *Vision of Tundal*,[7] again borrowed from Vincent, with some omissions and minor alterations, and breaking off after the sight of Lucifer. Perhaps Regnauld had reserved the vision of Paradise for his work on that subject. The next story, of the Archbishop Eudo of Magdeburg,[8] occupies folios 204^v–213^v. Probably composed in the thirteenth century, it was based on earlier German legends and deals with a wicked prelate who dies in sin. Immediately afterwards his soul is seen in the possession of devils by a chaplain of the same city. The next two *exempla* similarly describe how demons seize the souls of two sinful men. The first is taken from Gregory's tenth book of *Dialogues*, and the second is glossed "Guillermus, libro de apibus"; but neither are true illustrations of the descent theme. Two folios are then devoted to a literal prose translation of the *Vision of Charles le Gros* (but ascribed here to Charles le Chauve);[9] and Regnauld goes on to tell of Charlemagne's vision of his counsellors in the infernal baths ("es baings d'enfer", 219^v), where they suffer eternal torment for their treachery. Charles is said to have witnessed their lot as he lay on his deathbed.[10]

Once more Regnauld turns to Vincent de Beauvais, this time for the *Vision of the Boy William*.[11] It is rendered faithfully except for the omission of the vision of Paradise. There follows Lazarus' account of his brief sojourn in Hell, where, as I mentioned in the last chapter, the usual seven regions are found, and the sinners are classified accordingly.[12] After two brief anecdotes concerning the wicked Count of Nevers and his damnation come two further accounts from Gregory of the appearance of demons that are put to flight by prayer; and then Regnauld turns to Bede's *Historia Ecclesiastica* for two more *exempla*. The first concerns the damnation of the king's standard-bearer, who was too proud to confess his sins and was consequently damned.[13] The second tells how a sick blacksmith saw in a vision the gulf of Hell opened and Satan in the depths surrounded by his minions Pilate, Judas, and Caiaphas. Since it was too late for the smith to repent his misdeeds, he too was damned.[14] Two further examples of sinners miserably damned are quoted. The first was Lothair's majordomo Ebroyn, who was responsible for St Leger's death; and the other, Ruffino, was the nephew of Cyril, Patriarch of Jerusalem, who saw him in a vision perpetually tormented for having taken too much delight in games. We are familiar with the punishment of Judas as related in the *Navigatio sancti Brendani*;[15] and this, taken from its context, forms the next of Regnauld's illustrations.

Our compiler calls the account which follows "un autre exemple final", but his enthusiasm does not yet allow him to lay aside his pen. The story is told in few words, but it perhaps first aroused in Regnauld that curiosity which led him to produce his *Baratre*, for he says of it:

> *Comme estudiant cela vy*
> *En mon tendre, jeune et bas age.*

(fol. 231ʳ)

(I saw that as a student in the early days of my tender youth.)

A zealous monk, sunk in contemplation outside his hermitage, was led into the depths of Hell, where he saw in a hideous passage a woman, hung by her feet and suitably punished for her immoderation in life.

Regnauld then proceeds to speak of the damnation of a certain Bishop of Paris and of the happier fate of the Doyen of Langres. The latter, in Paradise, explained to a visionary that of thirty thousand people who died when he did, only he and one other were taken to the blessed regions; three were sent to Purgatory, but the remainder were consigned to Hell for all time.[16] This leads Regnauld to relate the story of the girl who saw her father in Paradise and her mother in infernal torment. The tale is as analysed earlier,[17] except that there is no mention of the wheel, and Heaven is not described. The source is given as "Prosper: ad Radulphum".[18] Then, before his brief Conclusion, our compiler quotes from St Marcel an example of a serpent seen issuing from the tomb of an unchaste woman. His final words are directed against those who do not believe in the reality of Hell's deceptions (as reflected in his title), and they express the pious and monitory intentions that underlie the whole work. One can hardly doubt that he believed himself in the truth of the pious stories he recounted; and it was in all sincerity that he reproved those who do not credit the "above-mentioned visions, revelations and examples".[19]

There is no doubting, then, the genuineness of Regnauld's religious beliefs. We see it in his choice of subject and of illustrative texts, in the frequency of his quotations from the Scriptures, and in the moralising asides with which he favours us from time to time and particularly at the end of the work. Its second part reminds us, indeed, of such pious compendia as that of Vincent de Beauvais; but Regnauld has included much more pagan lore than his predecessors, and his list of such sources is impressive. He quotes Ancient writings with obvious satisfaction and even with a good deal of confidence:

> *Partout a sens, qui sens y veult querir.*
>
> (fol. 30ᵛ)

(There is good sense everywhere, if we are prepared to look for it.)

And if he hesitates a moment before Virgil,

> *Que je ne prengs pour texte d'evangile*
>
> (fol. 44ʳ)

(whom I do not take as gospel truth),

he quickly adds that, for his taste, this poet speaks better on the subject of Hell than any other. The extent to which he has used these writers is apparent from the list of rubrics; and throughout the *Baratre* one is struck by the richness of the material, Christian and pagan, from which he has drawn. Though much of this would certainly be borrowed from other encyclopaedic works, the apparent facility with which it is brought into the *Baratre* suggests that Regnauld's own scholarship was not inconsiderable. This is less favourably reflected in his style, which is ponderous at the best and contorted at the worst. His verse shows the influence of the Grand Rhétoriqueur school, and we have seen it praised by Jean Bouchet, one of their number; but Regnauld did manage to avoid their worst excesses in the matter of rhyme and general intelligibility. It is interesting to note that the names of Charles de Gaucourt and Jean Meschineau figure in the Dedication of the *Baratre*.[20] The first was chamberlain to the king and, in 1472, Governor of Paris, as well as being apparently something of a Maecenas to the new school of poetry. Meschineau (Meschinot) was himself a Rhétoriqueur; and his poetry, full as it is of metrical jugglery, achieved some success in his day.[21] In these circles writing was a serious and laborious occupation; so from his affiliations as well as from the *Baratre* itself, we can see that Regnauld was a conscious literary artist.

A fitting description of the *Baratre* might be: a work of pious scholarship with literary pretensions. We must not look for originality, either in content or in expression, or we shall be sadly disappointed. But much of the documentation carried out by Regnauld remains valid and interesting for the modern observer. Although the style is mechanical and uninspired, Paulin Paris was perhaps too uncompromising in his condemnation. For if one accepts the subject as a readable one, then the *Baratre* is readable, if only for the variety of information and anecdote it presents. In essence it is medieval; but in turning its pages one is conscious that the author stands on the threshold of the Renaissance. He has elevated the Ancients to a position of almost equal dignity with the Christian apologists; and he has some acquaintance with Italian letters—Dante and Boccaccio in particular. His taste for the grotesque, however, which is so marked a feature of medieval art and literature, shows him as yet untouched by the Renaissance cult of beauty. But to the old traditions he had little to add; and his work is in many respects a monument upon their grave.

NOTES

1. As yet unpublished. I give its list of contents in Appendix III.
2. It is dated in the course of a verse passage on fol. 28^r.
3. See Paulin Paris' notes on the work in *Les MSS françois de la Bibliothèque du Roy*, IV (Paris, 1841), pp. 171–9.
4. "Dantes le poëte tusque" is quoted as an authority on the source of Acheron (fol. 33^{r-v}).
5. Op. cit., pp. 178–9.
6. I.e. the *Vision of Gunthelm* (see above, pp. 16–17).
7. See above, pp. 27 ff.
8. For information on this legend see A. E. Schönbach, "Nachträge zur Legende vom Erzbischof Udo von Magdeburg", *Sitzungsberichte der Ak. der Wiss. in Wien (Ph.-hist. Kl.)* 145 (1903), Abh. VI, pp. 78–91.
9. See above, pp. 176 ff.
10. The gloss is "Turpinus Karoli Magni cronographus", but this legend does not appear in the *Pseudo-Turpin Chronicle*.
11. See above, pp. 15–16.
12. The classification is according to the Seven Deadly Sins. The order here is: the proud, the lustful, the avaricious, the wrathful, the envious, the gluttonous, and the slothful.
13. Based on *Historia Ecclesiastica*, V, xiii (ed. J. E. King, II, pp. 268–75).

14. Based on *Historia Ecclesiastica*, V, xiv (ed. King, II, pp. 276–9). In the original the sinner is a carpenter.
15. See above, pp. 23–4.
16. See G. G. Coulton on "The chances of hell" in *Five Centuries of Religion*, I, pp. 445–9, and especially pp. 466–7 for this anecdote (quoted from Herolt) and other similar ones. See, too, R. F. Bennett, *The Early Dominicans*, p. 125.
17. Above, p. 112.
18. Prosper of Aquitaine, a disciple of St Augustine, lived at the beginning of the fifth century. I have been unable to trace this story in his writings.
19. For the tenor of Regnauld's closing remarks see the rubrics for fols. 235–6 in Appendix III below.
20. See the rubric to fol. 26.
21. H. Guy, *Histoire de la poésie française au XVIᵉ siècle*, Vol. I : *L'École des Rhétoriqueurs* (Paris, 1910), pp. 17, 19–21.

CONCLUSION

THIS study of the theme of the infernal journey has led us into the highways and byways of medieval French literature ; and we have seen how it was approached by writers of varied callings and social environments, living in different centuries and supplying diverse needs. But for all the disparity of treatment, the theme's real significance does not change : it exemplifies the triumph of humanity over the realm of death, mankind's victory in the ultimate struggle, hopeless though it may seem. And here lie its greatness as a theme and its universality as a symbol. Yet, as we have seen, the men who treated it in our texts never managed to realise its full symbolic potential. After the simple and dignified *Passion du Christ*, the later accounts of visits to the lower regions came to rely on the accumulation of realistic detail at the expense, all too often, of spiritual values. The usual preference of the infernal to the celestial journey only strengthens the impression that, rather than relating the theme through symbolic treatment to mystical experience, its exponents tended to use it as a more of less devout adventure story—and Hell was recognised as a much more adventurous place than Heaven !

The belief in it as a real place was, from the twelfth century, reinforced and coloured by exhaustive descriptions of the locality, its inmates, and its tortures. Just as the earth once took shape and acquired its features after being a vague, fiery mass, so the geography of Hell emerged throughout the Middle Ages from the amorphous "feu pardurable" until it could be seen by the mind's eye in vivid and minute detail. The difficulty then for the writers (had they faced up to it) was to divest their imaginations of the scene and thereby achieve a more sublime treatment of the descent theme. And if it is unreasonable to suppose that they could have done this altogether, they might still have attempted to fuse the realistic and symbolic elements into an organic whole. This was the achievement of Dante ;

but there was no Frenchman equal to the task. A notable, though heavy-handed, attempt was made by Guillaume de Deguileville; and the other allegorists went some way on the road. However, medieval allegory, a less pure and more contrived form of symbolism, fell short of the requirements and tended to break down in the hands of its manipulators. The realistic technique already had too firm a hold, and a regeneration of the theme's spiritual content was hardly achieved.

One factor may be mentioned as of some importance in determining the realistic orientation of the theme, and for this the responsibility lay within the Church itself. The upsurge of religious zeal in the twelfth century was marked by a spate of pious literature, much of it aimed at bringing home Christian eschatological teaching to the laity. But by this time, the jongleurs were doing a busy trade in the secular line, tales of feudal strife and exotic adventure, all decked out to catch the public eye. If the clergy were to compete for the people's attention, they too had to provide their literature with a colour and popular appeal that their more tedious sermonisings on Hell and damnation lacked.[1] So they tried to supply evidence of the sinner's ultimate fate in a palatable, "epic" form, well backed up by circumstantial detail. We have seen the result in the homiletic treatments of our theme.

As time went on, the works embodying it accumulated, but were prone to become stereotyped and arid. Visions of Hell were no longer created, but compiled, with the consequent degeneration of the theme in pious literature. The vernacular fortunes of the *Vision of St Paul* show something of this. The fourth Redaction is already a pious adventure tale, but it is relatively straightforward and concise when handled by poets like Adam de Ros and the Templar. They merely enliven it here and there with personal reflections and the occasional telling phrase. With the Alexandrine version we find literary elaboration on a wider scale; and though the model in this case was not Redaction IV as we know it, it is clear that much of the expansion is attributable to the French author. Of the French prose versions, that in the Dublin manuscript is a straightforward, uninspired translation from the Latin; and the writer of the fragmentary Picard text has borrowed some of the episodes to form a sensational preface for his homily. In neither case is any interest shown in the theme as such. And the pillaging of the *Vision* for its infernal material had been going on ever since the writing of *Li ver del juïse*. Details of it appear in a garbled form in Jehan de le Mote's vision of Hell and in that of Guillaume de Deguileville, who elaborates especially on the wheel of torment. It was seemingly through the *Vision of St Paul* that the wheel became a standard fixture in the medieval Hell, so much so that it appeared on the stage as part of the infernal *décor*.[2] Thus, in the vernacular, the *Vision* was not only elaborated, but also ransacked for material such as had been used to fill out numerous other medieval legends.[3]

As each new treatment of the theme appeared, the collection of infernal lore was increased, so that it became a well from which any one might draw. It is rather ironical now to find the professional poets borrowing from the pious, either to add implausible episodes to their romances (*Huon d'Auvergne*, *Baudouin de Sebourc*), or to give a particular tone to an adventure (*Lancelot*, *La Mule sans frein*), or even recasting a whole story in a profane form (*Saint Pierre et le Jongleur*). One notices, incidentally, that the secular treatments contain rather more action than the pious; and in particular the hero or central figure has more of the spotlight and is less passive than, say, St Paul, or Owein, or Tundal. But, to return to my earlier point the infernal material has become the stock-in-trade of any writer of adventure stories, whether instructive or purely entertaining; and to the public it has become familiar in both contexts.

So far I have been speaking of the theme and the texts in which it appears in general terms; but our survey has shown that a broad generalisation is not necessarily valid for the whole field of study. More particularly I have suggested a need to differentiate between the continental and the Anglo-Norman usage and attitude. What above all characterises the Anglo-Normans in their handling of the theme is an integrity and whole-heartedness that shine through their works. The French contribution stands, for the most part, in sharp contrast. But before I attempt to analyse it, I shall suggest how well placed France was for the reception and therefore the use of eschatological material.

The richest fund of all was provided by the Scriptures. First there was the conception of Hell itself, a place of retribution full of fire and brimstone, with the fallen angels as demons and the Old Serpent himself chained in the depths of the bottomless pit. The Middle Ages made use too of some less obviously infernal features, as when they equated the jaws of Leviathan with the *gueule d'enfer* and represented it thus in sculpture and painting as well as on the stage. And it was from brief passages of the Scriptures, as we have seen, that certain descent traditions originated—those of Christ and Lazarus, together with St Paul's vision of the pains of Hell. So, naturally enough, the pious writers turned often to holy writ both for themes and for illustrative material, of which they found a rich store in Old and New Testament alike, especially in those books of an apocalyptic nature such as *Daniel* and *Revelation*.

One could go further back and trace the influence of earlier systems such as Mazdaism or Orphism or Jewish beliefs that find their way through to our texts ; but the horizons opened by a quest for ultimate sources would be far too wide. Two of our major pious texts, the *Vision of St Paul* and the *Gospel of Nicodemus*, must however be mentioned as having been composed in the eastern Mediterranean region ; and though both have their roots in the New Testament, the former at least seems indebted to earlier, non-biblical writings, and in particular to the *Revelation of Peter*. And while we are in the Middle East, we must not forget that feature of the ancient Persian religion, the Chinvat bridge, which bypassed the Scriptures to enter by way of Gregory's *Dialogues* into medieval eschatology. Nor should we overlook such legends of undoubted eastern origin as passed into the *Vie des anciens Pères*. All this pious material entered France by way of the writings of the early Church, to pass through the medium of Latin into the vernacular texts.

Second only to the contribution from the Middle East, and in some cases mingling with it at an early date, is that afforded by Classical mythology and literature. Few of the texts we have studied show no trace of Classical influence, even if it is no more than the appearance of a single name, like the Jupiter of the embryonic descent story in the *Chanson de Roland*. The actual geography of Hell owed much to Greek and Latin conceptions. For example, the infernal rivers Styx, Cocytus, Acheron and Phlegethon are often mentioned, and the infernal marshes appear in more than one pious legend. Some of the forms of torment are equally dependent on Classical sources, and none more plainly than the unattainable food and drink of the Tantalus legend, or the fearful tortures that Tundal saw inflicted in Vulcan's forge. The origin of the infernal wheel is less easy to establish; but Ixion's well-known punishment must at least have popularised it to the point where it was adopted into the redactions of the *Vison of St Paul.*

If we look at the names of the denizens of Hell quoted in medieval texts, we find a formidable array of Classical names drawn from both mythology and history. Of the historical characters, Nero in particular enjoyed the reputation of being one of the major devils. It is still more interesting to find Virgil, Horace and Juvenal mentioned as demons by a tenth-century grammarian of Ravenna.[4] The old gods, too, are now numbered among the lords of the Underworld and minions of Satan. Also in the tenth century, Pope John XII, we are told, invoked the aid "of Jove, of Venus, and of the other demons".[5] Jupiter, Juno, Pluto, the Parcae and Tisiphone all appeared frequently in French texts, the *mystères* being an especially happy hunting ground for such names. And Cerberus, whom we find already in early redactions of the *Vision of St Paul,* never lost his "popularity" as a demon throughout the Middle Ages, which saw him assigned the role of guardian, herald, and porter of Hell, strangely humanising him in the process. But apart from the devils' names, their very appearance and that of the archdemon himself was influenced by the gods of the Ancient world. For from Pan and the satyrs were inherited the shaggy bodies and cloven hooves so typical of the medieval portrayal of the tribe of Hell.

Of the Classical writers none were more widely known and loved than Virgil and Ovid. From them certain descent stories were borrowed in their entirety by the vernacular writers; but far more often the debt was confined to a few chosen features. If it was probably through Ovid's *Metamorphoses* that such details as Tantalus' torment became well known, the borrowings from Virgil are even more significant. Leaving aside the question of Ixion's wheel, it is very likely that the Middle Ages knew of the infernal rivers and marshes and of the role of Cerberus chiefly from the account of Aeneas' descent into Hades. The conception of Hell as a kind of citadel is not uncommon in the medieval texts, and this may owe something to the city of Rhadamanthus; and the depth of the place of torture next to the pit of Hell in the *Vision of St Paul* was probably borrowed from Virgil's description of Tartarus.[6] The same vision may have used the elm tree at the entrance to the Latin poet's Hades, converting it into the burning trees shown to St Paul. But whether or not this is so, it is undeniable that Classical themes and features were pillaged by the Christian writers to fill out their descriptions of Hell; and the more secular the texts, the greater was the enthusiasm for such borrowing.

A third noteworthy fund of myth-making material drawn upon by some of our authors was Celtic tradition and mythology. In this case the borrowings are of a more general nature. For the *Voyage of St Brendan* and *St Patrick's Purgatory* the original writers used legends current in their day with the aim of presenting their heroes' experiences as real adventures, rather than using the more common vision cadre. We have seen something of the debt of these two legends to native Irish traditions. The *Vision of Tundal*, on the other hand, though set in Ireland and written by a Munster man, seems to owe little to Celtic folklore. But whatever their sources, one must pay tribute to the lively and colourful imagination of both Marcus and the anonymous originator of the Brendan legend. These are the only two of our texts that can confidently be ascribed to Irish writers, and of all the medieval treatments of our theme only Dante's shows more variety and breadth of vision. Thus, the Celtic contribution lies not only in the content of the tales, but also in the manner of the telling. Of their popularity with later medieval writers I have given ample evidence.

If Ireland produced some important pious legends, England could outdo her neighbour in quantity if not in quality. From the time of Bede onwards a large number of visions were recorded, and at least three found their way into French. The English writers showed great inventiveness in amplifying the pains of Hell, thereby increasing the stock of such material available in medieval France. The same may be said of certain German visions,[7] some of which were probably known west of the Rhine although, with the exception of the truncated *Vision of Wettin*, they seem to have left no trace in the vernacular. Turning to Italy, the twelfth-century *Vision of Alberic* may not have passed into France, but Dante was known, if not widely, before the end of the Middle Ages. Lastly, we have seen how Moslem traditions were familiar, at least to a few scholars, by the thirteenth century; and even if French writers made no use of this material (the final translator of the *hadith* was an Italian), they could at least thank Islam for providing one or two demons, including the Prophet himself, to swell the numbers in the Christian Hell.

France, then, was extremely favourably placed for the accumulation of myths, legends and traditions that came in from three points of the compass. French writers more than any others had the opportunity to make a synthesis of the whole or part of this rich store in the creation of new visions. Regnauld le Queux's compendium of infernal lore illustrates most strikingly the abundance and variety of available material; but his capacities were simply those of a compiler, not of a creative artist. It is true that his work was put together in the fifteenth century, but much of its content had been available from a far earlier date. To what use, then, did French writers put their resources? And firstly, what new, native compositions were achieved?

The answer is disappointing. In the realm of purely pious literature the achievement is virtually nil. There is some lively re-handling of earlier material in *Li ver del juïse*, and possibly the development of the artistically barren *Vision of Lazarus*. That is not a great production for an age that raised the Gothic cathedrals and nurtured such Christian leaders as St Bernard and St Thomas Aquinas. At a lower level of piety, the two visions reported by Philippe Mouskés, though originally written in Latin, can claim to have their roots in French soil. The first is without literary merit; and while that of Charles le Gros is rather more developed, it cannot be rated as a very valuable addition to vision literature. Both savour of political propaganda, doubtless a reason for their transmission by Philippe. Then there are the allegorical visions, whose very form implies some artistic design. Raoul de Houdenc's, which set the fashion, deteriorates into a broadly comical situation, so that its main virtue is as a piece of satire. Jehan de le Mote and the anonymous poet, while maintaining a more serious tone, have not created great literature : suffice it to say that the former shows far more adroitness than the latter. Guillaume de Deguileville, keeping a good deal of allegory, attempted a vision in the grand manner ; but the parts of his work dealing with the soul's visit to Hell are disappointing. There he shows little originality, but a good deal of confusion, which makes for rather tedious reading. On the stage, the French contribution is spectacular—the accumulation of the *diableries*, enlivened by Gallic vigour and even wit, and all the extravagant display that attended the Harrowing in the later *mystères*. But this was empty spectacle, unworthy of the end to which it was put. The miracle play we looked at was simply a dramatisation of an earlier story ; but in any case, the descent theme was little developed.

The profane treatments show rather more merit. We should like to know more of that hinted at in the *Chanson de Roland* ; but we cannot assume that it constituted a major work, since we find no other reference to Siglorel's descent. In the *Histoire de Charles Martel* we have a good, brisk handling of the theme ; however, this is purely an adventure story and contains surprisingly little of the otherworld material at the author's disposal (unless we suppose that the original poem was written before the material became widespread in France). If *Huon d'Auvergne* goes to the other extreme in its prolixity, we owe the author small gratitude for having filled out his ground-plan with borrowings from Dante and elsewhere. The descriptions of visits to Hell in *Baudouin de Sebourc* form a small proportion of the whole poem ; and even so, the more expanded one has been taken with little modification from the *Voyage of St Brendan*. Of the descent episode in the lost version of *Fierabras* we know nothing, though it is fairly safe to assume that it too was episodic. Our fabliau, *Saint Pierre et le Jongleur*, is lively and well written, but no more than a very free parody. So thin is it in descriptive detail that it could be put on the stage with little alteration. As for the *Salut d'enfer*, it would be over-generous to credit it with any kind of merit. So when we look back over this native French output in the eschatological field, we are not greatly impressed. There are the slight visions with a political bias, the allegorical poems, a couple of acceptable adventure stories, and one good parody. Might one not have been entitled to expect something more from the creators of the chansons de geste, Arthurian romances, graceful lyrics, the *Roman de la Rose*, and drama on the scale of the mystery plays ? We cannot demand another Dante ; but would it be outrageous to expect new pious creations fit to be classed with the original *Vision of St Paul* or the *Gospel of Nicodemus*, the *Vision of Tundal* or *St Patrick's Purgatory*, with the *Vision of Alberic* or with those attributed to the boy William and the Cistercian novice ? It may be that the satirical use of the theme, known in Ancient times to such as Aristophanes, was rediscovered by Raoul de Houdenc. This was the aspect that was later to appeal to Rabelais when he was writing his *Pantagruel*.[8] And in the seventeenth century, an anonymous and so far un-published work entitled *L'Enfer: satyre* used the theme for contemporary satire.[9] What good use could have been made of it by some witty and sharp-tongued mediaeval poet ! But again we can speak only of missed opportunities.

It is when we turn from the original French creations to examine the vernacular treatments of already existing works that a comparison with the Anglo-Norman texts becomes valid, at least for those French legends that are in verse, date from the period when Anglo-Norman was flourishing, and do have true counterparts in that literature. This limits the field of com-parison to versions of the *Vision of St Paul*, *St Patrick's Purgatory*, the *Voyage of St Brendan*, and the Harrowing of Hell—some seven texts in all. Of these, two (the *Vision de saint Paul* of the B.N. MS fr. 2094 and André de Coutances' trans-lation of *Nicodemus*) share with most of the Anglo-Norman works the characteristic that their authors' personalities do emerge, and in a genuinely pious light.[10] Personalities are suppressed, on the other hand, in translations of *Nicodemus* by Chrétien and the Provençal poet, and in those legends that were simply written as part of pious compilations : the version of the Brendan legend in the *Image du Monde*, and Geoffroi de Paris' adaptations of current vernacular works. All these are pious enough, and they are technically sound. But the impression is left that they are the products of hack poets lacking in the zeal of the Anglo-Normans. The author of the anonymous east French version of *St Patrick's Purgatory* even scamped his work, maybe out of sheer boredom. The last text comparable with those from north of the Channel is the Alexandrine version of the *Vision of St Paul*. Here we find pious inspiration and imaginative quality; but this time there is a conscious artistry such as gives a literary flavour foreign to most of the Anglo-Norman poems, and the author's interest seems to be at least as much in form as in content. What I said earlier of the Anglo-Normans' characteristic contribution may find some support in these remarks.

The remaining French versions of earlier works or legends may be dealt with briefly. A large number are in prose, either standing independently or included in compendia. These are mainly anonymous in both senses of the term,[11] witnesses to the "commercial" propagation of literary material by the medieval scriptoria. But some, such as the translation of the *hadith* and the accounts by Antoine de la Sale and Ramon de Perelhos, are of real interest and illustrate unusual aspects of our theme. Then there are a few poems rehandling borrowed material : the descent stories in adapted Classical legends show Christian concepts breaking through the pagan setting ; the two legends from the *Vie des anciens Pères* are examples of the pious, homiletic treatment ; the Clermont-Ferrand *Passion*, the *Passion des Jongleurs*, and the *Livre de la Passion* contain fairly brief descriptions of the Harrowing and show successive stages in the development towards dramatisation ; and the late translation of Dante's *Inferno* is of interest only as a literary *tour de force*.

Looking over the French use of the theme as a whole, we find that the straightforward pious renderings are in the minority, unless we include all those monotonous prose translations that add nothing to their original, and more often than not lead to its progressive corruption. There are usually other preoccupations to be discerned. This man experiments with allegory; another is a medieval "orientalist", and a third a fifteenth-century student of eschatology; there is a political historian, as well as a number of travellers and adventurers. We have translations and adaptations of Classical legends, a studied transposition of Dante's masterpiece, treatments of the theme by writers of epic or romance (not forgetting its use within a burlesque context by Chrétien de Troyes and his imitator), a good-humoured parody, and a scurrilous satire. We also saw something of the theme's fortunes in the world of theatre. So to a considerable extent its direct pious or homiletic appeal was distorted by more secular considerations, with the desire to entertain rather than instruct looming ever larger. On the one hand there is an attempt to attract the more sophisticated section of the public, on the other the wish to cater for the sensation-seeking and frivolous element.

Light-hearted and irreverent treatments written in various parts of France have come down. They reflect not merely the decline in the theme's spiritual value but also the existence of a somewhat sceptical attitude, or at least *insouciance*, towards the wrath to come. This frame of mind would seem to have become more prevalent as the Middle Ages progressed, but irreverence can be traced in vernacular texts as far back as the *Pèlerinage de Charlemagne*, and the equation "early equals pious" is only broadly true. Perhaps there is a link here with the growth of the towns and the *esprit gaulois*, though the tendency towards scepticism may be traced even in the schoolmen's discussions on the reality of the pains of Hell.

In the past, we have been told too often that medieval man was permanently terrified at the thought of Hell and future retribution. To quote a single instance, E. J. Becker spoke, at the end of the last century, of "the epidemics of terror which pervaded the Middle Ages. ... All the while the clergy was becoming ever more and more powerful, and the people ever more and more panic-stricken at the thought of what even the least sinful of them would have to undergo before obtaining everlasting bliss. And the more panic-stricken the people became, the greater swelled the power of the clergy, till at last the terror of the one became a nervous disease afflicting nations at a time, and the power of the other greater than the world had ever known. It was in such an unhealthy atmosphere that visions flourished in all their power. They are the outgrowth of a fundamentally morbid psychological condition."[12] Few nowadays would take such an extreme view; yet full account has still to be taken of the evidence pointing the other way. How restricted was the public able, for instance, to accept the burlesque treatments of our theme, and presumably to laugh at them? If it be argued that such texts are few, we may reply that works of this kind had the poorest chance of survival, that doubtless a fair proportion of the output has been lost, and that equally certainly some are still waiting to be discovered, or read in the spirit in which they were written.

We should beware of making a too facile generalisation from the words Villon puts into the mouth of his mother (or indeed of applying them to Villon himself):

> "Au moustier voy dont suis paroissienne
> Paradis paint, ou sont harpes et lus,
> Et ung enfer ou dampnez sont boullus:
> L'ung me fait paour, l'autre joye et liesse."[13]

("In the church in my parish I see a painting of Paradise, where there are harps and lutes, and a Hell where the damned are boiled: one frightens me, the other makes me happy and joyful.")

Perhaps such terror of Hell was more prominent in Villon's day, with the general moral and physical depression produced by the ravages of the Hundred Years' War. But generally over the whole period there is no evidence that it dominated the continental French outlook: to judge from many of our texts, the opposite is more likely to be true. Once more, however, reservations must be made regarding the position in England, where all our indications suggest that a more serious view was held of these questions.

I am inclined to turn Becker's argument by suggesting that in France people were early becoming hardened to the thunderings of the clergy on the subject of hellfire and damnation. Perhaps it was when less reaction was prompted by the threats that the priesthood heightened its descriptions of the terrors of Hell, and this move led in turn to increasing indifference on the part of a considerable section of the population. A pathological state of terror at the prospect of hellfire may have been the reaction of a small number of clergy whose way of life, as Becker pointed out, was conducive to nervous disorders. But the ordinary folk could not live in such a state of tension; and to some extent the rather light-hearted treatment of religious themes may have provided a safety-valve.[14] To see a mortal brave the perils of Hell and emerge unscathed would give them a feeling of satisfaction, for in their hearts they all thought of Satan and his crew as real, physical adversaries. The happy ending of these accounts, whether pious or profane, would bring a measure of assurance and an increased faith in humanity. The fear they inspired should no more be over-stressed than overlooked; but I would suggest that the serious Anglo-Norman mentality was more prone to it than was that of the less grave Frenchman, who could more easily shrug it off with a smile.

And here this study ends. I cannot claim that its theme is attractive; but it is one that has a bearing on a great deal of medieval literature as well as on that less definable entity, the spirit of the age. Perhaps by looking at it in its various aspects we can discover something about that still more elusive thing, the French national character—or even, it may be, about the psychology of man himself.

NOTES

1. That churchmen were fully aware of the attractions offered by the secular entertainers some of their exordia testify (cf. above, pp. 70–1, 84–5, 99). E. Faral (*Les Jongleurs en France au moyen âge*, p. 171) quotes the following appeal to his audience by the author of the *Évangile de l'Enfance*:

    > S'avés oï assés souvent
    > Les romans de diverse gent
    > Et des mençongez de cest monde
    > Et de la grant Table roonde
    > Que li rois Artus maintenoit,
    > Ou point de verité n'avoit,
    > Qui vous venoient a talent;
    > Cestui oés devotement,
    > Que tout est fet de Jhesu Crist . . .

2. In the sixteenth century, the wheel is shown in the well-known miniature depicting the setting for the *Passion* played at Valenciennes in 1547 (see G. Cohen, *Histoire de la mise en scène dans le théâtre religieux du moyen âge*, Plate I, and *Le Théâtre en France au moyen-âge*, Plate VII).

3. The *Vision of Tundal*, *St Patrick's Purgatory*, and the visions of the boy William, Charles le Gros, and Lazarus to mention only a few.

4. A. Graf, *The Story of the Devil*, p. 34.

5. Ibid., p. 18.

6. It is as deep as the distance from earth to Heaven: cf. the *Aeneid* VI, ll. 578–9.

7. See C. Fritzsche, "Die lateinischen Visionen des Mittelalters bis zur Mitte des 12. Jahrhunderts", *Romanische Forschungen* 2, pp. 247–79, and 3, pp. 337–69.

8. For Epistémon's descent into Hell see Ch. XXX.

9. Preserved in the Paris, Arsenal, MS 4109. The *incipit* runs:

> Je chevauchois proche de Monmartre dessus une jeune jument forte en bouche et ombrageuse, laquelle m'emportant à son plaisir d'un lieu en autre, en fin me précipita dans une profonde quarrière de plastre qui donne jusques au grand chemin d'Enfer.

Explicit:

> La nuit venoit: tout le monde estoit en desbauche en Enfer, qui me feit me retirer incontinent au Collège des Jésuittes, d'où je partis le matin avec le Diable poste, et m'en retournay à Paris.

10. It is interesting to note that both Norman writers who figure in this study (André de Coutances and Guillaume de Deguileville) were men of deep piety. In this they have affinities with their insular cousins.

11. The second prose version of the *Vision of Tundal* is a notable exception.

12. *A Contribution to the Comparative Study of the Medieval Visions of Heaven and Hell*, p. 3.

13. François Villon, *Le Testament*, ll. 895–8 (*Œuvres*, ed. A. Longnon & L. Foulet [Paris, 1932]).

14. Cf. J. Frappier's remarks in "Châtiments infernaux et peur du diable, d'après quelques textes français du XIIIᵉ et du XIVᵉ siècle", *Cahiers de l'Association Internationale des Études Françaises*, No. 3-4-5, pp. 91–6.

LA VISION DE SAINT PAUL

(Dublin, Trinity College, MS 951, Cl. I.5.19, fols. 74^r–79^v)

(74^r) Ici orrés vous comment sains Pos et sains Michieux li archangeles alerent pour veoir en enfer les grans tormens dont les ames sont tormentees as pecheours qui la sont, et comment il ourent remede par lour proieres.

Al jours del dieme. . . .¹ ce est uns jou. . en quoi li angel. . . esjoissent . . . . greignours que nus autres jours. L'on doit demander qui proia premierement que les armes eussent repos en enfer. Ce fu saint Pous li apostre et saint Michieux li archangeles quant il alerent en enfer pour ce que Dieux vout que saint Pous veïst les paines d'enfer; et il envoia saint Michiel avecques lui pour monstrer li les paines d'enfer. Sains Pous vit devant les portes d'enfer arbres de fu, et peecheours qui (74^v) estoient tormentés et penduz : li uns pendoient pas les piés, li autre par les mains, li autre par lez cheveux, li autre par les cous, li autre par les langues, li autre par les bras. Aprés il vit une fournaise de fu ardans qu . . . . .it flamme par .vii. lieus de d. .erses colours. Illuecques estoient plusorz paines et tormens. En cele fournaise s . . . . . . .ises les armes des peecheours qui ne voudrent faire penitance en cest monde. Li un pleurent, li autre uslent, li autre gemissent, li autre desirent la mort; si ne muerent point, quar les armes ne morront ja. L'on doit molt douter enfer, ou il a pardurable dolour, ou il a tousjours gemissement de cuer et tristece sans leeche et habundance de larmes pour les dolerous tormenz. Il i a une roe de fu ou il a mil cercles; et li angele d'enfer la fiert mil fois le jour, et a chascun coup il bruille mil armes. Aprés ce, saint Pous (75^r) vit un flueve molt orrible, ou il avoit molt de bestes autresi comme li poisson qui sont en mi de la mer, qui devorent les armez des peecheours sanz nule misericorde autresi comme li leu qui manjue le berbis. Illuecques vit saint Pous plusours armes plongiés : li un estoient plongié jusques au genous, li autre jusques au nombrill, li autre jusques as levres, li autre jusquez a sourcieux ; et estoient chascun jour tormenté pardurablement. Lors commencha sains Pous a plorer, et demanda a l'angele qui cil estoient qui estoient plongiéz jusques as genous. "Ce sunt," fist li angeles, "cil qui s'entremetent de mauvaisez paroles ; et quant il sont issu del iglise si detraient lour voisins. Li autre qui sont plongiéz jusques au nombrill, ce sont li luxurious qui onques ne firent penitance jusques a la mort. Cil qui sont plongiés jusquez as levres, ce sont cil qui plai(75ᵛ)dent en l'iglise et n'en escoutent pas la parole Damedieu. Cil qui sont plongiés jusques as sourcieux, ce sunt cil qui s'en esjoissent des maus a lour proismes." Sainz Pous dist : "Trop sunt chaitif cil qui sont appareilliés a souffrir si grant paine !" Il vit aprés un autre lieu tout plain d'omes et de femes qui manjoient lour langues. Si demanda sains Pous que li estoient. Li angeles respondi : "Ce sunt li usurier qui prestent lour deniers a usure et nen ont nule merci des povres ; et pour ce sunt il en cele paine." Il vit un autre lieu ou il avoit toutes manieres de paines. Si i avoit pucelles noires qui avoient vestu noires robes faites de poudre et de souffre et de fu, et dragons et serpens qui estoient entour leur cors et leur cous ; et .iiii. deables estoient entour eles qui avoient cornes de feu. Si les blasmoient et disoient : "Reconoissiez le fill Dieu qui ra[76ʳ] chata le monde par son sanc !" Sainz Pous demanda qui eles estoient, et li angeles li dist : "Ce sunt celes qui n'ont pas gardé chasteté en lour mariages, et celes qui ont estranglés lour enfans et les ont doné a mangier as pourceaus et as chienz et les ont noiés, et si n'en ont fait point de penitance." Et aprés il vit homes et femes sour le chanel d'une eve, et devant eaus avoit molt de fruis, mais l'on en lour laissoit pas prendre. "Ce sunt," fist li angeles, "cil qui brisent lour geunes et manjuent ains que tans en soit." Aprés il vit homes et femes en un lieu plain de glace et de feu, si que li feus les brusloit d'une part et la glace les engeloit d'autre part. "Ce sunt," dist li angeles, "cil qui ont nuisi et maufait as orphelins et as veves." Sains Pous plora et dist : "Las, las peecheours ! Pourquoi furent il onques nés ?" Li angeles li dist : "Pourquoi pleures tu sour le

humain lignage ? En[76ᵛ]core n'as tu pas les greignours paines
d'enfer veu." Lors li monstra il un puis qui estoit seelés de
.vii. seaus, se li dist : "Estez un poi loins si que tu puissez
souffrir la puour." Doncques fu overte la bouche del puis ; si
en eissi une si tres grant puour qui sourmonta toutes les autres
paines. Li angelez dist a saint Pou : "Se aucuns est mis en
cest puis, jamais ramenbrance n'en sera faite de lui devant
Damedieu." Sains Pous dist : "Qui sont cil qui i sont mis ?"—
"Ce sont," fist li angeles, "cil qui ne croient pas que Ihesu
Crist ven isten terre pour le monde sauver, ne que il nasquist de
la virge sainte Marie, et cil qui ne sont pas baptiziés ne com-
muniés del cors et dou sanc nostre seignour Ihesu Crist."
Saint Pous vit en un autre lieu homes et femes, et vers et serpens
qui les manjoient. Et les armes estoient les unes sour les autres
autresi comme les berbis sont el cloit. Et li pui estoit parfont
autresi com[77ʳ]me de la terre jusques au ciel. Si les oï gemir et
plorer autresi comme ce fust tounoires. Il regarda entre le ciel
et la terre, si vit l'ame d'un peecheour qui usloit entre .vii.
deablez qui cel jour l'avoient trait del cors. Et li angeles
Damedieu s'en escrioient contre lui et distrent : "Lasse, lasse,
chaitive arme ! Que as tu fait en terre ?" Il distrent li uns a
l'autre : "regarde ceste chaitive arme, comment ele a despis le
commandement Dieu en terre !" L'arme lut sa chartre en quoi
si pechié estoient escritez, et ele meisme se juja ; et li deable la
pristrent, si la mistrent el plus parfondes tenebres, ou il n'avoit
se plour nom et escroissemens des dens et grant uslement en
enfer. Li angeles dist a saint Pou : "Crois tu bien que li home
recevront selonc ce que il auroit fait en terre." En cele hore
meisme pristrent li angele une arme juste si comme ele en eissi
del cors et le aporterent au ciel. Et [77ᵛ] sains Pous oï la vois de
mil millie rs d'angeles qui s'en leechoient pour lui et disoient :
"Arme liee et bieneuree, enleesce toi ! Tu es hui bieneuree
pour ce que tu as fait la volenté Damedieu." Lors distrent li
angele : "Levez la devant Dieu !" Il la leverent, et ele lut sez
bones oevres ; et aprés sains Michieux la porta en paradis, ou
tuit li saint estoient en grant leesce. Lors firent tuit li saint grant
joie de l'arme juste. Se i out autresi grant noise comme se li
cieus et la terre fussent commeu. Lors s'en escrierent li peecheour qui estoient en enfer et distrent : "Michieux archangeles,

aies merci de nous ; et tu sainz Pous, ami Dieu, prie Dieu pour
nous ! Nous savons bien que par tes orisons a Dieus eu merci de
ceaus qui encor sont en terre." Li angeles lour dist : "Ore
plores, et je plorrai pour vous, et li angele qui sont o moi, et
sainz Pous nostre amis pour savoir se Dieux auroit merci de
vous tant [78ʳ] que il vous donast aucun remede." Quant cil
qui estoient en paine oïrent ce, il s'en escrierent tuit a une vois,
et sainz Michieus li archangeles, et saint Pous, et mil milliers
d'angeles ; et li cris fu oïz jusques el ciel. Lors vit saint Pous
le ciel mouvoir soudainement, et li filz Dieu descendi del ciel,
qui avoit une coroune d'or en son chief. Et les armes qui
estoient en enfer s'en escrierent et distrent : "Aies merci de
nous, li filz Dieu le haut !" Et la vois au fill Dieu fu oïe par
tous les lieus d'enfer, qui dist : "Quel bien avez vos fait ?
Pourquoi me demandés vous repos ? Je fui crucefiés pour vous
et ferus d'une lance et a clous fichiés. Vous me donastes a
boivre aisil et fiel mellé ensemble. Je vouz morir pour vous si
que vous vesquisiez o moi ; et vous fustes menchoingnier et
larrons et avers et enviouz et orgueillous et maudisant, ne ne
feistes onques bien ne geune [78ᵛ] ne penitance ne aumosne :
ainz fustez menchoingier et feistes toz les maus en vostre vie."
Aprés ce se laissierent chaoir sains Michieus et sains Pous et
mil milliers d'angeles devant le fill Dieu, et li requistrent que
tuit cil qui estoient en enfer eussent ropos au diemenche. Lors
dist Dieus : "Pour Michiel et pour Pol et pour mes angeles,
et meisment pour ma bonté, je vous doins repos a touz les
samedis none jusques au lundi prime." Et li portiers d'enfer
qui a nom Zeberus leva son chief sor toutes les paines d'enfer
et fu molt correchiés : et tuit cil qui estoient en enfer firent
joie et s'en escrierent tuit a une vois : "Li filz Dieu, beneois
soies tu qui nous a doné remede d'un jour et de .ii. nuis que
nos nen avons pas deservi. Mieus noz vaut cist remedes que
tous li tans que nous fumes seur terre ne fist onques." Qui
gardera le saint jour del diemenche, il aura [79ʳ] part o Dieu et o
ses sains. Sains Pous demanda a l'angele : "Quantes paines a
il en enfer ?" Li angelez li respondi : ".C. et xliiii mile ; et si
.c. home avoient commenchié a parler des le commenchement
du monde et chascuns de eaus eust .iiii. langues de fer, si ne
porroient il pas raconter ne nombrer les paines d'enfer." Nous

qui oions ces maus, convertissons nous a nostre seignour Ihesu Crist, si que nous vivons o lui et regnons par touz siecles. Amen.

NOTE

1. A small area of this folio is damaged by rubbing. I have not sought to complete the text or, here or elsewhere, to correct scribal errors. Illuminated capitals are italicised.

THE DESCENT EPISODE
from the
HISTOIRE DE CHARLES MARTEL ET DE SES SUCCESSEURS
(Bibliothèque Royale de Belgique, MS 6, fols. 289–97)[1]

The *Histoire de Charles Martel* may have been compiled for Philippe le Bon of Burgundy; for at about the time when, eighteen years after its compilation, David Aubert made the existing copy in fine *bâtarde bourguignonne* script on Philippe's orders, we find him attesting that "Philippe duc de Bourgogne a dès longtemps accoustumé de journellement faire devant lui lire les anciennes histoires".[2] Perhaps the order was of long standing and other matters had been found more pressing for the attention of the hard-working David; or perhaps this particular "histoire" had only just come to Philippe's notice.

David Aubert, a native of Hesdin in Artois, was the chief copyist to Philippe le Bon and Charles le Téméraire, a position earned by his skilled and at the same time prolific craftsmanship. In this case his work is complemented by a series of miniatures by a capable, if not outstanding, artist, Loyset Liédet.

In the earlier part of MS 6 we learn of Charles Martel's youth and his marriage with Marsebille, daughter of King Theodorus of France. But he had a son, Archefer, by the fair Sagramoire, whose father was King Menelaus of Ammarie; and he had to conquer this errant son in battle in order to force him to take the Sacrament. Later, both Sagramoire and Marsebille were burned to death by the Tartar king, whereupon Charles branded Archefer with treachery in the matter of Marsebille's death and imprisoned him. He was released with the strict injunction to go to Hell on an ambassadorial errand to his Satanic majesty.

Journeying thither, he was retained for a time in the service of
King Grimault of Sathalie and while with him showed his
prowess by vanquishing not only King Gloriant of Cyprus and
another pagan king, Agoulant, but also Sorbrin, the formidable
magician. In Cyprus his toils were to a large measure rewarded
by the favours shown him by the much sought-after Rose, "la
belle". Finally he took leave of the subjected kings, saying :

> "Et au regard de moy, je m'en iray en enfer faire aux deables
> ung message depar luy [Charles Martel], a celle fin qu'ilz luy
> facent hommage, et que de luy ilz tiengnent leur mansion ;
> car lors que de luy je partis, je luy encouvenençay de ce faire,
> et de luy en reporter braves et bonnes enseignes ; pourquoy
> j'ay moult grant desir de tout ce accomplir. Et vous, sire
> Grimault, je vous prie que me laissiés vostre enchanteur
> Corniquant, car de luy j'ay ung petit a besongnier." Que
> vous diroie je ? Chascun des princes luy accorda sa requeste,
> et Grimault luy bailla son enchanteur Corniquant et s'en
> party d'illec a ytant et retourna en son royaulme des Sathalie.
> Si se taise a tant l'istoire de luy et de ses hommes, pour parler
> de Archefer et du voyage qu'il fist en la maison noire d'enfer.
> (fol. 289ʳ)

Thus we are led into the episode describing the descents of
Archefer and of his father, Charles Martel, into the infernal
regions.

[289ʳ] Comment Archefer ala en enfer, par la science que il
aprist de Corniquant l'enchanteur, et par la lettre qu'il avoit
par avant de Sorbrin le maistre enchanteur du roy Gloriant de
Chyppre qu'il avoit occis en champ cloz devant la cité de
Bonyvent en Puille.³

[289ᵛ] L'istoire racompte que quant le roy Grymault fut party
de Bonyvent pour retourner vers son royaulme de Sathalie⁴
et qu'il eust promis au roy Archefer de tenir son royaulme du
roy Charles Martel, Archefer demoura en Bonyvent avecques
Corniquant l'enchanteur que le roy Grimault luy avoit baillié
pour s'en aydier en son voiage. Et de luy s'acointa tellement
que grant amour se nourry entre eulx deux, tant que l'enchan-

teur fut moult au commandement du gentil Archefer, si que il luy dist ung jour : "Certes Corniquant mon bel amy, il m'est prins voulenté de toy descouvrir mes secrets. Si est bien vray que j'ay ung voyage a faire quy m'est moult difficille et pesant sans ton ayde et ta science, qu'il me couvient de ton bon gré sçavoir, veoir, et experimenter. Si te prie que de tout ce que je te requerray tu ne me vueilles faillir. Car en enfer me couvient aler, parler a Lucifer, Burgibus, et a Neron. Et si me fault rapporter a mon pere le roy Charles Martel de France vrayes enseignes, comment je auray fait le voiage, ou estre a tousjours mais bagny de son royaulme et de sa compaignie." Adont luy respondy l'enchanteur : "Sire, sachiés que ce n'est pas une chose que l'en puist faire de legier que ung tel voyage, sans grant enseignement, advertissement, et sans tres grant maistrise. Mais bien est aisié a faire pour ung homme comme moy, quy y sçay les voyes, les destours, et les droits chemins aussi bien comme vous [290ʳ] le sçauriés de Paris a Saint Denis, ou vous ne pourriés faillir. Pour tant se c'est vostre plaisir, je iray pour vous et si vous rapporteray response partinente a la demande que vouldrés que je face."—"Corniquant, beausire, ainsi ne seroie je pas loyaulment acquitté ; car il me couvient faire le voiage en propre personne, comme je feray puis que je l'ay entreprins, et deusse je ton mestier et ta science aprendre. Si te prie que nullement tu ne me failles a ce besoing, et que de tes habillitez tu me vueilles icy moustrer."

*A*dont Corniquant l'enchanteur, oyant Archefer quy de ses habillitez vouloit lors veoir jouer, et l'art de magique et de nigromancie sçavoir et aprendre, le regarda pour tant qu'il estoit noble homme et grant seigneur. Si luy respondy lors : "En verité, sire, ce n'est pas une chose partinente de sçavoir a ung tel homme comme vous estes les ars de thoulette et la science de magique, que les deables composerent et ordonnerent jadis, pour abuser et decepvoir les hommes. Si ne vous en entremettez ja, se croire me voulez."—"Certes, Corniquant," respondy Archefer, "il m'en fault entremettre, et pour tant ay je tresgrant besoing de le sçavoir. Si te prie de rechief que tu me moustres de tes habillitez, et je te moustreray de ceulx que me enseigna Sorbrin, lors qu'il estoit sur le champ, avant que je luy ostasse la vie, par luy meismes. Car il ne voult lors nullement que je luy respitasse la vie, pour tant qu'il me declaira comment le deable luy avoit dit qu'il devoit mourir par mes [290^v] mains." Et lors que Corniquant entendy le roy Archefer, quy des sciences sçavoir par nigromancie venans de Sorbrin l'enchanteur luy parla, il desira d'en veoir aucunes experiences; si luy couvenença qu'il joueroit. Adont Corniquant ordonna son charme par Ebron son maistre quy la science luy avoit aprinse, et ordonna ung conjurement par lequel il fist comme il sembla a Archefer venir une tour haulte et bien garitee, ou gens d'armes estoient prestz et armez pour deffendre la tour, se l'en la venoit par adventure assaillir. Si la regarda moult Archefer, lequel par la science de Sorbrin conjura le deable qui Sorbrin avoit gouverné et apris en son temps; lequel en faisant son charme fist illecques devant celle tour venir gens d'armes lesquelz assaillirent si asprement que la tour fut prise et versee par terre veant tout ce Corniquant, quy dilligamment la regarda et bien perceu que il en sçavoit assez pour en ouvrer devant roys, princes, et grans seigneurs.

Quant le roy Archefer eust desfait le charme que Corniquant avoit fait, il en recommença ung autre, et fist son conjurement par le maistre de l'enchanteur Sorbrin; et fist apparoir en la place ung grant four a deux gueules, lequel a son advis ardoit devant et derriere a si tresgrans brandons qu'il sembloit que tout deust ardoir a l'environ. Si le regarda lors Corniquant, quy moult en fut esbahy et dist: "En verité, sire Archefer, encontre vous je ne feroie riens. Que mauldit soit celluy quy [291^r] tant vous en a moustré. Et vous meismes je seroie tost conseillié de mauldire, quant vous l'avez apris et si bien retenu, se vous n'en eussiés grandement a besongnier. Si accorde d'aler avecques vous en enfer non mie comme maistre. Car bien y sçauriés aler sans moy se c'estoit vostre plaisir. Mais comme vostre vallet je vous y compaigneray, sans avoir paour que deable quel qu'il soit me face mal, ennuy, ne destourbier." A tant se sont destournez les deux enchanteurs, et se sont retrais en ung lieu ou nulz ne les puelt veoir ne ouyr, pour faire leur charme, que Corniquant commença. Car il sçavoit trop plus que Archefer, quy ancoires ne faisoit que commencier a entrer en feste. E d'une espee qu'il tenoit fist entour luy ung parc, et le croisat Puis se mist en celluy parc et commanda a Archefer meismes.

que il y entrast comme luy. Et lors que tous deux y furent
entrez, l'enchanteur maistre Corniquant fist ung conjurement tel qu'en ung moment vint celle part ung deable infernal,
lequel luy demanda qu'il vouloit. Et il luy respondy : "Autres-
fois," dist Corniquant, "m'as tu servy, et ancoires fault il que
tu me serves. Car avecques toy me couvient en enfer aler
aveuc Archefer quy cy est, lequel voeult a Lucifer parler. Si te
commande que tous deux nous y portes le plus doulcement que
faire tu pourras. Et lors que nous aurons nostre besongne faitte
et achiefvee, tu nous rapportes pareillement sans aucun mal ne
douleur avoir, comment que ce soit."
[291ᵛ] Adont le deable quy la estoit venu respondy et dist :
"Mal feu puist ton corps bruir et en cendre mettre, Corniquant, car trop m'as donné de paine et traveil, et donnes
ancoires, dont cy aprés ton ame aura a respondre en enfer.
Saulte hors de ce parc que tu as croisié, et je feray ton commandement." Alors Corniquant prist Archefer par la main,
puis le mena hors du parc. Si les prist tous deux le deable, et les
emporta par l'air entre les vens, par dessus les montaignes, par
dessus terres, par dessus bois, par dessus rivieres, par dessus la
mer, et par dessus villes, chasteaulx, bourgs, et citez, jusques
aux portes d'enfer, ou il les descendy le plus doulcement que il
peust, et ainsi qu'il luy estoit commandé. Et quant il les eust
la descendus, il entra dedens, et s'en ala de prime face vers
Lucifer, qu'il salua ; et luy dist que jusques aux portes d'enfer
il avoit apporté deux hommes quy vouloient parler a luy.
Adont Lucifer jetta ung bruit si grant que plainement l'ouïrent
tous les deables lesquelz le compaignerent comme leur roy. Et
lors qu'ilz furent venus a la porte, et que Archefer les vist, il
parla haultement, disant : "Faulz ennemis del humaine lignie
que Jhesus par sa passion vainquy, par sa mort, et par sa
resurrection, je suis icy envoié depar le roy Charles Martel mon
pere, lequel comme le roy souverain sur tous autres roys du
monde vous mande que de luy vous tenez ceste mansion tene-
breuse, et que luy en faciés hommage. Et si luy envoiés treu tel
qu'il puist ou doye de vous estre [292ʳ] contens, et que il soit
acertené que j'aye mon message fait, ainsi comme je luy ay
promis du faire."
Merveilleusement fist Lucifer laide chiere lors qu'il eust

entendu celluy quy demandoit servage sur ceulx d'enfer.
Adont il s'escria haultement et dist : "Comment beausseigneurs, depar tous les deables, veult ung homme mortel demander treuage sur nostre maison, ou oncques homme n'entra par
force que ung ?"⁵—"Ouy certes, sire Lucifer," ce respondy ung
autre deable quy la vint vollant de l'air : "assamblez vostre
conseil, et je vous diray que c'est de Charles Martel. Car tout
incontinent je viens de France, dont je vous diray telles nouvelles que hommage luy ferez voirement, pour tant que a luy
appartient mieulx que a nul autre quy regne pour le jour d'huy."
Adont Lucifer assambla les dampnez en son consistoire, et le
tint son parlement ; mais en ce tandis, Archefer impetra ung
congié du prince de tenebres, Lucifer, pour aler veoir la maison
et les paines que les ames y souffroient. Si luy fut accordé par
Sathan, quy procureur et gouverneur des enfers estoit. Alors
Archefer entra dedens enfer et vist les tourmens que les
dampnez y souffroient, les lieux noirs, obscurs, et parfons. Et
en autres lieux il ouy les plaintifz que les ames faisoient moult
piteusement, voire en recepvant divers tourmens, de feu ardant,
d'eaue froide, de gellees, de glaces, de souffre puant, de couleu-
vres, et de diverses bestes, quy les tourmentoient en maintes
manieres. Et si avant passa, Corniquant aprés luy, que il vist
la royne [292ᵛ] sa mere en tourment merveilleuz. Car comme
tres douloureuse elle s'escria moult haultement, disant : "Ha a
mon chier enfant, viens a moy et tu verras la grant douleur ou
mon corps est tourmenté pour les terribles et enormes pechiés
que j'ay contre le commandement de Dieu commis, moy estant
ou monde."

Moult fut le roy Archefer esbahy, quant il voy l'ame de sa
mere ainsi tourmentee, voire en feu ardant. Elle estoit rouge
comme charbon vif et embrasé ; et sur son chief elle avoit une
couronne de fer chault, quy la teste luy ardoit sans estaindre.
Puis estoit chainte d'un grant carquant rouge et embrasé, quy
si grant douleur luy faisoit sentir que merveilles. Et au long de
son corps luy couroit telle la flambe quy de douleur la faisoit
esragier. Et d'elle se vouloit approchier Archefer, lors que
Corniquant l'en destourna, disant : "Sire, gardez vous d'aler
celle part, car trop y fait perilleux pour le feu ; se lequel vous
avoit tant fust peu attouchié, jamais par nul sens vous n'en

seriés guary ne descombré." Adont se retray Archefer, et
demanda a sa mere se rien estoit ou monde possible parquoy
l'en la peust allegier de celluy tourment, ou l'en de tous poins
delivrer. Et elle respondy : "Nanil certes, beau tresdoulz
filz, et si meurs icy toute vifve en langueur infinie ; touteffois
je ne puis morir, et si languis incessamment en une inestimable
douleur. Mais pour mes tourmens allegier, fay moy dire
messes tous les jours, jusques a sept ans, quy me seront plus de
cent mil [293^r] ans d'allegement des peynes de l'autre monde.
Et saches que tout ce me vient et procede pour la tres grant
trahison que toy et moy avons naguaires pourchassee a l'encontre de Marsebille, dont tu atens autel payement et guerredon
comme j'ay, se tu ne mets brief et bon remede a ton fait."

Moult fut dolant et non sans cause le tres vaillant chevallier
lors que il entendy sa mere quy d'amendement faire luy parla.
Adont il luy demanda par quelle maniere il pourroit estre
purgié de celluy meffait. Et elle luy resondy que par trois choses
il en povoit de tous poins estre nettoyé et deschargié, se a ce
faire il vouloit dilligamment vacquier et entendre, dont la
premiere et la principale estoit confession, la seconde repentance, et la tierce satisfation, quy toutes trois sont entendues
penitance, par laquelle ung pecheur se puelt nettoier et purgier
d'un pechié combien grant qu'il soit avecques bonne devotion
et bon vouloir. "Et ainchois que tu faces toutes ces choses, il te
fault ton pechié plourer par grant contrition, et promettre de
non y plus rencheoir." Adont Archefer ploura de pitié, et
promist a sa mere qu'il la secourroit tout le mieulx que possible
luy seroit, ce dont elle luy requist moult chierement. Alors il
souvint a Archefer de Marsebille, pourquoy il demanda a sa
mere ou elle estoit, laquelle luy respondy et dist : "Beau filz,
ceans a plusieurs mansions, mais je ne la sache en nesune, et
penseroie qu'elle seroit [293^v] plus tost en purgatoire que ceans.
Car se elle estoit es tourmens orribles comme je suis, je ouroie
ses plaintes et clameurs de fois a autre." Et en parlant a
Archefer sentoit Sagramoire tant de maulx et de terribles
pointures que incessamment elle se remuoit par force de douleur,
et si ne se bougoit d'une place. Fin de compte, Archefer party
d'illec ; car trop doubtoit la longue demouree, et non sans cause.
Mais a son departement, sa mere jetta ung cry si tres orrible

que toute la mansion d'enfer en fist retentir. Atant Archefer
revint devers celluy deable quy celle part l'avoit apporté, et les
autres quy ancoires tenoient leur parlement sur le fait du roy
Charles Martel, et leur dist que temps estoit de s'en retourner,
mais que il eust sa response pour son acquit et descharge.

Adont Luciffer le grant, quy ses compaignons avoit appellez
a conseil, demanda en general quelle response l'en donroit au
messagier de Charles Martel, et quelz homs c'estoit tant oultra-
geux comme d'avoir sur eulz envoié treuage demander. Adont
celluy deable quy de nouvel estoit venu de France leur respondy,
et dist : "Beausseigneurs, ne soiés de ceste besongne esbahis ;
et envoiés seurement a Charles Martel ung present. Car a son
entreprinse il finera en brief temps si tres grant nombre de gens
que il couvendra accroistre nostre enfer pour les y bouter. Et
sachiés que durant son regne il aura tant et de si merveilleuses
guerres, que oncques roy en France n'en eust tant comme il
aura." Alors Lucifer parla [294ʳ] a Archefer, et luy dist :
"Saches, Archefer, que a Charles Martel nous ne voulons que
paix et amour. Et, comme tu luy diras, nous voulons franchement tenir de luy. Et a celle fin qu'il croie comment tu as fait
ton message, nous luy envoierons pour ceste fois ung destrier
grant et puissant en signe que c'est le plus vaillant chevallier
du monde. Et quant il sera sur celluy destrier monté, saches
que ja de l'esperon picquier ne le couvendra. Car il sera en ung
moment la ou il le vouldra souhaidier. Et oultre plus, tu luy
menras deux bracques, pour chasser et prendre tout ce qu'il
desirra avoir. Et bien luy diras que la court d'enfer les luy fait
presenter par toy en signe de seignourie et de hommage, et
non autrement."

Incontinent que l'ennemy Lucifer eust parlé comme dit est et
que Archefer eust dit qu'il fera le message, vint illec ung deable
quy mena ung grant destrier noir pommelé, sur lequel Archefer
monta de legier. Puis en arriva ung autre quy luy bailla deux
bracques tous noirs en une lesse, et il les receu. Puis dist a
Corniquant que il montast derriere luy, et il y sailly legierement.
Et quant tous deux furent montez, ilz demanderent quelle ilz la
feroient, et comment ilz se maintendroient. Surquoy Corniquant respondy : "Sire, je vous tiens assez recors comment
vous avez promis a Rose la belle et noble royne que vers elle

retourneriés, et que vous la menrez en France. Si seroit grant
reproche se par nulle voye vous luy failliés de promesse. Et
pour [294ᵛ] tant il nous est mestier de aler en la cité de Bonyvent.
Adont dist Archefer : "Certes Corniquant mon bon et leal amy,
vous ne dittes que toute raison. Car a la verité je luy promis
que a mon retour je luy menroie. Et bien luy vueil ma promesse
tenir. Si nous souhaide en sa chambre, ou en quelque lieu
qu'elle sera." Si s'en party le cheval aussi tost que il eust dit le
mot. Et tout ainsi comme ilz avoient estez portez en enfer
furent ilz rapportez en Bonyvent, la ou estoit Rose la noble
royne, laquelle se merveilla moult dont ilz estoient venuz celle
part si soubdainement. Lors elle leur demanda dont ilz venoient,
et il respondy que deables les avoient illec apportez. Si se taist
a tant ung petit l'istoire de celle matiere pour racompter comment le roy Charles Martel fut porté en enfer, comment le roy
Archefer de Ammarie⁶ retourna vers son pere Charles Martel, et
comment Archefer luy presenta depar Lucifer le grant noir
cheval, quy le porta aux enfers.

    L'istoire racompte que quant le roy Archefer et Corniquant
l'enchanteur furent en Bonyvent arrivez, et qu'ilz se retrouverent
avecques Rose la belle royne, Archefer luy dist qu'il vouldroit
brief retourner par devers le roy Charles Martel son pere, et
que il avoit esté en enfer parler a Lucifer, et que avecques luy il
avoit besongnié de ce pourquoy il y estoit alé. "En verité,
madame," dist Archefer a la royne Rose, "je fusse tout d'une
voye alé en France n'eust esté que promis vous avoie de retourner pardeça. Et pour [295ʳ] tant advisez lequel vous amez
le mieulx—ou vous en venir comme moy, ou que je retourne
icy vers vous lors que je auray le roy mon pere contenté de la
couvenence que je luy ay faitte." Et quant la belle vey que elle
avoit le chois de demourer ou de aler avecques son amy, elle
luy dist moult courtoisement : "Sire Archefer, en vous je ne
treuve que toute loyaulté. Et pour ce que vostre promesse
avez si vaillamment tenue, je suis tresbien contente de m'en aler
avecques vous, pour tant que trop mal me feroit de laissier
vostre compaignie." Si se reposerent celle vespree, et firent
tous ensemble bonne chiere de boire et de mengier. Mais
incontinent que la nuit fut venue, la belle royne Rose appresta
son tresor portatif, puis se charga Archefer en la selle du cheval

noir, et mist la royne devant luy et Corniquant l'enchanteur
derriere et le tresor dessus. Et quant il tint les deux bracques
par la lesse, il dist : "Je me souhaide ou palais ouquel est pour
le present le roy Charles Martel mon pere." Atant sans plus
arrester, le deable les esleva en l'air tous trois, et en ung soubit
il les mist en la salle du palais de Ammarie, ou ancoires estoient
aucuns des gentilz hommes quy pas ne avoient desemparé ne
alez couchier ; lesquelz cogneurent legierement le preu Archefer, et tant furent esbahis que plus ne povoient de le veoir illec
a celle heure.

Le noble roy Charles Martel estoit en sa chambre et a celle
heure se devalloit en son lit, lors que ung sien chambellan vint
hurter [295ᵛ] a l'huys. Et quant il fut dedens, il ala jusques a
son lit, et luy dist : "Sire, il seroit besoing de vous ung petit
relever, et habillier pour venir jusques en salle. Car la est le roy
Archefer vostre filz venu, lequel comme j'entens est revenu
d'enfer et vous apporte nouvelles de Lucifer et de ses menistres."
Adont le roy Charles se sourdy, cuidant que son chambellan se
gabast, quant il luy asseura et dist de rechief que certainement
il l'avoit veu et que il estoit retourné. Lors Charles Martel
oyant ce que dit est se chaussa et vesty ; et quoy faisant il
menassoit fort Archefer, disant que jamais n'auroit son voiage
si tost fait, et que grandement se sçauroit excuser se mourir ne
le faisoit pour l'offense qu'il avoit commise touchant la mort de
la royne Marsebille que jamais ne luy pardonneroit, comme il
disoit. Atant vint le roy Charles Martel en salle, ou il perceu le
roy son filz, quy le salua, puis luy dist qu'il venoit de acquiter sa
promesse, et que il avoit esté en enfer. Lors le roy Charles
Martel le regarda par si grant despit que merveilles, puis luy
dist : "Archefer, Archefer, tu te gabes de moy quy me veulz
faire entendre que tu viens d'enfer. Saches que je ne t'en croy
pas, et d'autre part tu es trop mal adrechié pour le me faire
entendre, et soies tout certain que je te feray pendre et estrangler
puis que je tiens en ma subgection. Car tu m'avoies promis a ton
partement que d'enfer tu me rapporteroies certaines nouvelles
et enseignes telles que de toy je devroie estre content, par l'ac-
cord quy estoit fait d'entre toy et moy." Adont luy respondy le
roy Archefer, et dist :

[296ʳ] "Chier sire, vous povez tresbien penser que jamais par

devers vous ne fusse retourné se je n'eusse accomply ce que je
vous avoie promis a mon partement. Et pour tant plaise vous
sçavoir que j'ay en enfer esté, et si ay fait vostre message au
grant prince de tenebres Lucifer, a Sathan, a Ebrom, a Noiron,
a Caym, a Burgibus,[7] et a tant d'autres deables que merveilles.
Et leur ay sommé qu'ilz vous feissent hommage de leur mansion
infernale, laquelle n'est pas desgarnie. Surquoy ilz me ont
respondu que a vous ilz ne voeulent point de guerre. Ainchois
ilz me ont fait la reverence; et en signe de bon devoir et pour
le treuage que depar vous je leur ay demandé, ilz vous envoient
cestuy cheval, sur lequel vous povez monter se bon vous semble.
Et se croire ne me voulez que je y aye esté, il vous y portera se
c'est vostre bon plaisir, et vous la venu en pourrez la verité
sçavoir. Mais toutesfoiz faittes mon vallet monter derriere vous,
pour tant qu'il scet comment en ung tel voyage il se fault con-
duire. Et se vous ne trouvez que j'aye vostre messaige souffissam-
ment fait et accomply, prenez de mon corps telle pugnition que
bon vous semblera."

Adont le roy Charles Martel sans plus mot dire monta sur le
cheval noir que Archefer luy avoit presenté depar Sathan,
comme dit est. Et Corniquant l'enchanteur monta derriere luy
moult habillement, lequel dist si bas que de homme nul ne fut
entendu: "Je me souhaide aux portes d'enffer, dont nous
sommes naguaires partis." Atant le cheval noir se [296ᵛ] party
et les porta tous deux jusques devant les portes d'enfer, ou
Archefer avoit esté en celle journee. Si fut lors Charles Martel
tant esbahy que se n'eust esté Corniquant quy avecques luy
estoit alé par le conseil de Archefer, a grant peine en fust il
jamais en bon sens retourné. Mais Corniquant l'enchanteur luy
aprist et enseigna ce qu'il avoit a faire. Si dist lors Charles
Martel en son courage que son filz Archefer estoit moult hardy
et vaillant quant ung si dangereuz voyage il avoit franchement
entrepris. Il regarda et escouta moult songneusement entour
luy, et devant et derriere. Si ouoit a tous costez fouldres, ton-
noirres, et tempestes, habais, et ullemens de deables, voire si
merveilleuz et quy si terrible noise et bruit demenoient, que en
peu d'heure il en eust esté tout estonné et hors de sa memoire.
Puis veoit les grans fumees sentans le souffre, tant hideuses et
puantes a sentir que longuement il n'y eust peu arrester. Et

lors vindrent illecques au hannissement du cheval surquoy il
estoit monté, quy fut grant et hideux comme chascun puelt
assez croire, Lucifer le grant prince de tenebres, Ebrom,
Burgibus, Aggrapart, Satham, Caym, Judas, et Noiron;
lesquelz incontinent qu'il les vey venir celle part, se par avant il
avoit eu grant paour que ancoires l'eust il trop plus grande sans
nulle comparoison. Premierement parla lors le prince Lucifer,
et dist : "Saches, Charles Martel, que moult a esté preu et
vaillant ton filz Archefer quant pour toy complaire il est venu
icy devers nous faire aucuns [297ʳ] messages. Et toy, je te tiens
estre homme garny d'un hault courage quant tu nous as envoié
demander treu, et que nous te feissons hommage. Or nous dy
francement se ce a esté depar toy qu'il y est venu, ou se ce fut de
son propre motif."—"Par moy fut ce voirement, et par mon
commandement, faulx ennemy d'enfer," dist lors Charles
Martel. "Car puis que tous princes du monde vifvans me font
hommage, est bien raison que le me faittes, se a moy ne voulez
avoir guerre." Adont luy respondy Lucifer : "Ne vous tour-
blez en nulle maniere Charles Martel, car a vous nous ne voulons
ne guerre ne tensson, pour tant que vous estes le plus preu quy
nasquist ne regnast depuis le temps que Dieu descendy ça bas,
et que il despoulla nostre mansion, si que il en emporta ce que
bon luy sembla. Mais elle sera par vous et par voz fais remplye
et garnie plus qu'elle ne fut jamais. Et desja en avez grant
commencement. Si avons a vous obey et fait hommage, ce que
nous faisons de rechief." Et de fait ilz se misrent a genoulz et
enclinerent devant luy, tellement que Charles Martel parla et
dist qu'il souffissoit assez. Et ce fait, Corniquant l'enchanteur
fist ung souhait. Car plus ne vouloit sejourner celle part, et non
faisoit Charles Martel, quy avoit telle paour que plus ne povoit.
Atant le cheval noir chargié comme dit est se mist au retour
parmy l'air en fendant tous vens, tellement qu'en ung soubit il
se retrouva en la salle du palais de Ammarie dont ilz estoient
naguaires partis, et ou estoient ancoires Archefer et Rose la
noble et belle dame, accompaigniés [297ᵛ] de plusieurs nobles
hommes, lesquelz avoient moult grant merveille de ce qu'ilz
veoient advenir. Mais tant estoit Charles Martel mal asseuré
que oncques ne fut son cuer joyeulz jusques a ce qu'il se retrouva
du noir cheval descendu et despeschié.

*C*omme entendre povez fut le noble roy Charles Martel trop plus asseuré que devant lors qu'il se vist du grant noir cheval despeschié, et bien dist en son courage que jamais n'y remontera. Lors luy demanderent les barons dont il venoit, et il leur respondy que il venoit d'enffer, ou son filz Archefer avoit fait le voyage avant luy. Adont le roy Charles Martel, voyant le grant peril et dangier en quoy son filz Archefer s'estoit mis pour avoir pardon du roy son pere pour l'offense qu'il avoit commise, luy pardonna son maltalent en la presence de ses princes et barons, quy moult en furent joyeulx. Et luy fist espouser la royne Rose.

Unfortunately, that is not quite the end of the tale. Charles Martel departed for France, leaving Archefer and his queen in Ammarie.

Et par ainsi le noble prince Archefer demoura ou royaulme de Ammarie, ouquel, si comme racompte l'istoire, il ne vesquy depuis que deux ans aprés le partement du roy Charles Martel son pere, quy de sa mort fut si dolant que plus ne povoit, lors que les nouvelles luy en furent apportees. (fol. 298ʳ)

NOTES

1. The old foliation is 285–93. This episode is mentioned by F. Bar (*Les Routes de l'Autre Monde*, p. 121). General studies of the *Histoire* have been made by Paul Meyer (*Girart de Roussillon. Chanson de geste traduite pour la première fois* [Paris, 1884]), Gaston Paris (*Orson de Beauvais, chanson de geste du XIIᵉ siècle* [Paris, 1899], pp. lxiii–lxvi), and G. Doutrepont (*La Littérature française à la cour des ducs de Bourgogne* [Paris, 1909]; and *Les Mises en prose des épopées et des romans chevaleresques du XIVᵉ au XVIᵉ siècle* [Brussels, 1939], where further references will be found). The manuscript's miniatures are reproduced in J. Van den Gheyn, *Histoire de Charles Martel. Reproduction de 102 miniatures de Loyset Liédet (1470)* (Brussels, 1910).
2. In his prologue to the *Croniques abregiés* . . . (see Doutrepont, *La Littérature française* . . . , pp. 16–17).
3. On fol. 282ᵛ we read of "Bonyvent en Chyppre". Benevento is actually in Campania.
4. Perhaps Satallieh, a town in Asia Minor (Adalia), where Louis VII was beaten by the Saracens in 1148.
5. I.e. Christ.
6. Probably the Spanish province of Almeria.
7. Nero and Cain often appeared, as here, with more conventional Old Testament devils.

APPENDIX III

TABLE OF CONTENTS
of
REGNAULD LE QUEUX'S
BARATRE INFERNAL
(Paris, Bibliothèque Nationale, MS fr. 450)

The rubrics of the Prologue are given on fols. 101^v–102^r as follows:

estat, et vye, Seigneur de l'Hommee, maistre
Jehan Pastureau.   xii
Passees les rubrices encores audict celebre com-
paignon.   xviii
Retour final faisant ledict le Queux a sondict amy,
lesdictes rubrices passees, le advisant de son tel
quel savoir, intelligence, et povoir des fatiga-
cions et paines tartarees, comme cy apprés en
entend plus graffiquier.   xxiii

The remaining rubrics are given on fols. 13ʳ–19ᵛ :

S'ensuyvent les rebruches du premier livre du
Baratre Infernal. Et premiers :
Preface en la description du baratre infernal, selon
que prennent et entendent les gentilz et payens.
Au foeullet   xxiiii
Six honneurs que Dieu a donnetz a l'homme dont
il en veult recougnoissance. Au fol.   xxv
Seconde preface, ou l'acteur sousmect auctorisier
ou deprimer son excogité labour a maistre
Jehan Meschineau, a Monseigneur de Gaucourt,
et a maistre Jehan Gaudete.   xxvi
Quel an cest oeuvre fut entrepriz.   xxviii
Argument dudict *Baratre* en cent predicatz.   eodem folio
Partition en deux livres : alleguetz pour le
premier pluiseurs poetes, hystoriens, et
orateurs ; pour le second, saincts docteurs
philosophes, et personages morelz de toutes
sectes.   xxix
Narration premiere pour la partie poetique.   xxx
Contre ceulx la qui contempnent les poetes et
leurs figments.
Quelle poeterie soit digne de recoeul, et de estre
notee et ouye pour fructueuse.   xxxi
Entree expediente selon le premier partitif et
procés dudict *Baratre* intenté.   xxxii
Des fleuves infernaulz en general.
Du fleuve de Acheron selon le dire excogité et
cause des anciens.   xxxiii

VH L

BIBLIOGRAPHY

ADAM DE ROS. *La Vision de saint Paul.* Ed. A. F. Ozanam in *Dante et la philosophie catholique du treizième siècle,* Paris, 1839; L. E. Kastner in *Zeitschrift für französische Sprache und Literatur* 29 (1906), pp. 274–90.

Aislingthi Adhamnáin. Ed. with translation by J. Vendryès in *Revue Celtique* XXX (1909), pp. 349–83.

AMBROISE, G. *Les Moines du moyen âge,* Paris, 1946.

APPEL, C. *Provenzalische Chrestomathie,* 6th edn., Leipzig, 1930.

ARBOIS DE JUBAINVILLE, H. D'. *L'Épopée celtique en Irlande,* Vol. I, Paris, 1892.

ASHE, GEOFFREY. *Land to the West,* London, 1962.

ASÍN PALACIOS, M. *Islam and the Divine Comedy,* London, 1926. This is an abridged translation by H. Sutherland of *La Escatología musulmana en la Divina Comedia,* Madrid, 1919.

Aucassin et Nicolete. Ed. F. W. Bourdillon, Manchester, 1930.

AURACHER, T. "Der Brandan der Arsenalhandschrift BLF 283" *Zeitschrift für Romanische Philologie* 2 (1878), pp. 438–57.

BAADER, HORST. *Die Lais,* Frankfurt am Main, 1966.

BADCOCK, F. J. *The History of the Creeds,* 2nd edn., London, 1938.

BAR, F. *Les Routes de l'Autre Monde,* Paris, 1946.

BARBAZAN, E. & MÉON, D. M. *Fabliaux et contes,* Vol. IV, Paris, 1808.

BARTSCH, K. *Denkmäler der provenzalischen Literatur,* Stuttgart, 1856.

Bauduin de Sebourc IIIᵉ roy de Jhérusalem. Ed. L. N. Boca (but published anonymously), Valenciennes, 1841.

BAUM, RICHARD. *Recherches sur les œuvres attribuées à Marie de France,* Heidelberg, 1968.

BECKER, E. J. *A Contribution to the Comparative Study of the Medieval Visions of Heaven and Hell, with Special Reference to the Middle English Versions,* Baltimore, 1899.

BECKER, W. "Die Sage von der Höllenfahrt Christi in der altfranzösischen Literatur", *Romanische Forschungen* 32 (1913), pp. 897–972.

BEDE. *Historia Ecclesiastica.* Ed. with translation by J. E. King in *Baedae opera historica,* 2 vols., London, 1930.

BÉDIER, J. "Fragment d'un ancien mystère", *Romania* XXIV (1895), pp. 86–94.

BENEDEIT. *The Anglo-Norman Voyage of St Brendan by Benedeit, a poem of the early twelfth century.* Ed. E. G. R. Waters, Oxford, 1928.

BENNETT, R. F. *The Early Dominicans,* Cambridge, 1937.

BEROL. *Le Purgatoire de saint Patrice par Berol.* Ed. Marianne Mörner, Lund, 1917.

BONNARD, J. *Les Traductions de la Bible en vers français au Moyen Âge,* Paris, 1884.

The Book of Enoch. Translated by R. H. Charles, London, 1917.

BOSSUAT, R. *Manuel bibliographique de la littérature française du moyen âge,* Melun, 1951.

BOSWELL, C. S. *An Irish Precursor of Dante. A Study on the Vision of Heaven and Hell ascribed to the eighth-century Irish Saint Adamnán with a trans-ation of the Irish text*, London, 1908.

BOUQUET, DOM. M. *Recueil des historiens des Gaules et de la France*, Vol. III, Paris, 1869.

BRANDES, H. *Visio S. Pauli. Ein Beitrag zur Visionslitteratur, mit einem deutschen u. zwei lateinischen Texten*, Halle, 1885.

BRANDON, S. G. F. 1962. *Man and his Destiny in the Great Religions*, Manchester.

—— 1967. *The Judgment of the Dead*, London.

BRUNEL, C. "Sur la version provençale du voyage de Raimon de Perillos au Purgatoire de Saint Patrice", *Estudios dedicados a Menéndez Pidal*, Vol. VI (Madrid, 1956), pp. 3–21.

BUTLER, PIERCE. *Legenda Aurea—Légende Dorée—Golden Legend*, Baltimore, 1899.

CABROL, F. & LECLERCQ, H. *Dictionnaire d'archéologie chrétienne*, Vol. XII, Paris, 1936.

CAUZONS, TH. DE. *La Magie et la sorcellerie en France*, 4 vols., Paris, n.d.

CERULLI, E. *Il "Libro della Scala" e la questione delle fonti arabo-spagnole della Divina Commedia*, Vatican, 1949.

CHAMARD, H. *Les Origines de la poésie française de la Renaissance*, Paris, 1920.

CHAMBERS, E. K. *The Mediaeval Stage*, 2 vols., Oxford, 1903.

CHAMPION, P. *Histoire poétique du XVᵉ siècle*, Paris, 1923.

La Chanson de Roland. Ed. J. Bédier, éd. définitive, Paris, 1937.

CHAYTOR, H. J. *From Script to Print*, Cambridge, 1945.

CHRÉTIEN. *Guillaume d'Angleterre*. Ed. M. Wilmotte, Paris, 1927.

CHRÉTIEN DE TROYES. *Le Chevalier de la Charrete.* Ed. Mario Roques, Paris (CFMÂ), 1958.

—— *Le Roman de Perceval ou le Conte du Graal.* Ed. A. Hilka, Halle, 1932; William Roach, Genève-Lille (TLF), 1956.

La Chronique des quatre premiers Valois. Ed. S. Luce, Paris, 1862.

CLORAN, T. *The Dialogues of Gregory the Great, translated into Anglo-Norman French by Angier*, Strasbourg, 1901.

COHEN, G. 1926. *Histoire de la mise en scène dans le théâtre religieux du moyen âge*, Paris.

—— 1928. *Le Théâtre en France au moyen âge*, new edn., Paris, 1948.

—— 1949. *Histoire de la chevalerie en France au moyen âge*, Paris.

COMPARETTI, D. *Virgilio nel medio evo*, new edn., 2 vols., Florence, 1937.

Le Compost et Kalendrier des Bergers. Reproduction en fac-simile de l'édition de Guy Marchant (Paris, 1493). Introduction par Pierre Champion, Paris, 1927.

COULTON, G. G. *Five Centuries of Religion*, 4 vols., Cambridge, 1923–50.

Le Couronnement de Louis, chanson de geste du XIIᵉ siècle. Ed. E. Langlois, Paris (CFMÂ), 1925.

COWPER, B. H. *The Apocryphal Gospels*, London, 1867.

CROSLAND, JESSIE. "*Eneas* and the *Aeneid*", *Modern Language Review* XXIX (1934), pp. 282–90.

CURTIUS, E. R. "Zur Literarästhetik des Mittelalters, II", *Zeitschrift für Romanische Philologie* 58 (1938), pp. 129–232.

DAMON, S. F. "Marie de France Psychologist of Courtly Love", *Publications of the Modern Language Association of America* 44 (1929), pp. 968–96.

DANDO, M. *The Conception of Hell, Purgatory and Paradise in Medieval Provençal Literature*, unpublished London Ph.D. thesis, 1965.

DE GOEJE, M. J. *La Légende de saint Brandan*, Leiden, 1890.

DELEHAYE, H. "Le Pèlerinage de Laurent de Pászthó au Purgatoire de s. Patrice", *Analecta Bollandiana* 27 (1908), pp. 35–60.

DELEPIERRE, O. *L'Enfer décrit par ceux qui l'ont vu. Essai philosophique et littéraire (Miscellanies of the Philobiblon Society* VIII *&* IX), London, 1863–6.

DESONAY, F. *Antoine de la Sale, aventureux et pédagogue*, Liége *&* Paris, 1940.

Li Dialoge Grégoire lo Pape: Altfranzösische Übersetzung des XII. Jahrhunderts, mit dem lateinischen Original. Ed. W. Foerster, Halle *&* Paris, 1876.

Dictionnaire de théologie catholique. Ed. A. Vacant, E. Mangenot *&* É. Amann, Paris, 1909–50.

DIELS, H. "Himmels- und Höllenfahrten von Homer bis Dante", *Neue Jahrbücher für das klassische Altertum, Geschichte und deutsche Literatur* 49 (1922), pp. 239 ff.

DOUTREPONT, G. 1909. *La Littérature française à la cour des ducs de Bourgogne*, Paris.

—— 1939. *Les Mises en prose des épopées et des romans chevaleresques du XIVe au XVIe siècle*, Brussels.

ECKLEBEN, S. *Die älteste Schilderung vom Fegefeuer des heil. Patricius*, Halle, 1885.

Eneas, roman du XIIe siècle. Ed. J. J. Salverda de Grave, Paris (CFMÂ), 2 vols., 1925–9.

ESPOSITO, M. "Sur la *Navigatio Sancti Brendani* et sur ses versions italiennes", *Romania* LXIV (1938), pp. 328–46.

FARAL, E. 1910. *Les Jongleurs en France au moyen âge*, Paris.

—— 1913. *Recherches sur les sources latines des contes et romans courtois du moyen âge*, Paris.

—— 1923. *Les Arts Poétiques du XIIe et du XIIIe siècle*, Paris.

—— 1934. *Le Manuscrit 19152 du fonds français de la Bibliothèque Nationale*, Paris.

—— 1962. "Guillaume de Digulleville, moine de Chaalis", *Histoire littéraire de la France* 39, pp. 1–132.

FÉLICE, PH. DE. *L'Autre Monde: mythes et légendes. Le Purgatoire de saint Patrice*, Paris, 1906.

FIELDING, W. J. *Strange Superstitions and Magical Practices*, Philadelphia, 1945.

FLICHE, A., MARTIN, V., DUROSELLE, J. B.*&* JARRY, E. *Histoire de l'Église depuis les origines jusqu'à nos jours*: Vol. 9, *Du premier Concile du Latran à l'avènement d'Innocent III*, Part ii by R. Foreville *&* J. Rousset de Pina, Paris, 1953; Vol. 10, *La Chrétienté romaine* by A. Fliche, C. Thouzellier *&* Y. Azais, Paris, 1950.

FOSTER, F. A. *The Northern Passion*: Vol. II, *French Text, Variants and Fragments, etc.*, London (EETS), 1916.

FRANK, GRACE. *The Medieval French Drama*, Oxford, 1954.

FRAPPIER, J. "Châtiments infernaux et peur du diable, d'après quelques textes français du XIIIe et du XIVe siècle", *Cahiers de l'Association Internationale des Études Françaises*, No. 3–4–5 (July 1953), pp. 90–1.

FRITZSCHE, C. "Die lateinischen Visionen des Mittelalters bis zur Mitte des 12. Jahrhunderts", *Romanische Forschungen* 2 (1886), pp. 247–79, and 3 (1887), pp. 337–69.

FROISSART, JEAN. Œuvres complètes. Ed. Kervyn de Lettenhove, Vol. XV. Brussels, 1871.

GALPIN, S. L. "On the Sources of Guillaume de Deguileville's Pèlerinage de l'Âme", Publications of the Modern Language Association of America 25.ii (1910), pp. 275–308.

GARINET, J. Histoire de la magie en France, depuis le commencement de la monarchie jusqu'à nos jours, Paris, 1818.

GAUTIER DE COINCY. Les Miracles de la sainte Vierge. Ed. Abbé A. Poquet, Paris, 1857.

GEISTER, O. Die Teufelszenen in der Passion von Arras und der Vengeance Jhesucrist : ein Beitrag zur Verfasserfrage, Greifswald, 1914.

GILDEA, Sister M. Expressions of Religious Thought and Feeling in the "Chansons de Geste", Washington, 1943.

GLUTZ, R. Miracles de Notre Dame par personnages, Berlin, 1954.

GOSSOUIN DE METZ. L'Image du Monde de Maître Gossouin. Ed. O. H. Prior, Laus anne & Paris, 1913.

GRAF, A. 1878,. "Di un poema inedito di Carlo Martello e di Ugo Conte, d'A lvernia", Giornale di Filologia Romanza 1, pp. 92–110.

—— 1892. Miti, Leggende e Superstizione del Medio Evo, 2 vols., Turin.

—— 1931. The Story of the Devil. Translated by E. N. Stone, London.

GRÉBAN, ARNOUL. Le Mystère de la Passion. Ed. G. Paris & G. Raynaud, Paris, 1878.

GREGORY, SAINT. The Dialogues. Translated by E. G. Gardner, London, 1911.

GRÖBER, G. Grundriss der romanischen Philologie, Vol. II.2, Strasbourg, 1902.

GUI DE CAMBRAI. Barlaham und Josaphas. Ed. C. Appel, Halle, 1907.

GUILLAUME DE DEGUILEVILLE. Le Pèlerinage de l'Âme. Ed. J. J. Stürzinger, London, 1895.

GUILLAUME DE LORRIS & JEAN DE MEUN. Le Roman de la Rose. Ed. E. Langlois, Paris (SATF), 1914–24.

GUILLAUME DE MACHAUT. Œuvres. Ed. E. Hoepffner, 3 vols., Paris (SATF), 1908–21.

GUY, H. Histoire de la poésie française au XVIe siècle : Vol. I, L'École des Rhétoriqueurs, Paris, 1910.

HASSELMANN, F. Ueber die Quellen der Chronique Rimée von Philipp Mousket, Göttingen, 1916.

HASTINGS, J. Encyclopaedia of Religion and Ethics, Vol. IV, New York, 1911.

HETTO (HEITO). Visio Wettini. In Monumenta Germaniae Historica : Poetarum Latinorum Medii Aevi, ed. E. Dümmler, Vol. II, Berlin, 1884.

HILKA, A. Drei Erzählungen aus dem didaktischen Epos "L'Image du Monde" (Brendanus—Natura—Secundus), Halle, 1928.

HOLMES, U. T. A History of Old French Literature from the Origins to 1300, New York, 1948.

HUGHES, ROBERT. Heaven and Hell in Western Art, London, 1968.

Huon de Bordeaux. Ed. Pierre Ruelle, Brussels & Paris, 1960.

HUON DE MÉRY. Li Tournoiemenz Antecrist. Ed. G. Wimmer, Marburg, 1888.

L'Image du Monde : poème inédit du milieu du XIIIe siècle. Ed. C. Fant, Uppsala, 1886.

JACOBUS A VORAGINE. Legenda Aurea. Ed. Th. Graesse, 2nd edn., Leipzig, 1850.

JAMES, E. O. 1938. *Comparative Religion: An Introductory and Historical Study*, London.

—— 1957. *Prehistoric Religion*, London.

JAMES, M. R. 1893. *Apocrypha anecdota*, Cambridge.

—— 1924. *The Apocryphal New Testament*, 5th impression, corrected, 1953.

JAUSS, H. R. "Form und Auffassu ng der Allegorie in der Tradition der *Psychomachia*", in *Medium Ævum Vivum: Festschrift für Walther Bulst*, Heidelberg, 1960, pp. 179–206.

JEANROY, A. "Le Théâtre religieux en langue française jusqu'à la fin du XIVe siècle", *Histoire littéraire de la France* 39 (1959), pp. 1–91.

JEHAN DE LE MOTE. *La Voie d'Enfer et de Paradis*. Ed. Sister M. A. Pety, Washington, 1940.

JEVONS, F. B. *An Introduction to the History of Religion*, London, 1896.

JOHNSTON, R. C. & OWEN, D. D. R. *Fabliaux*, Oxford, 1957.

JOINVILLE, JEAN, SIRE DE. *Histoire de saint Louis, Credo et Lettre à Louis X*. Ed. Natalis de Wailly, Paris, 1874.

JUBINAL, A. 1835. *Jongleurs et trouvères*, Paris.

—— 1836. *La Légende latine de s. Brandaines*, Paris.

—— 1837. *Mystères inédits du quinzième siècle*, Paris.

—— 1842. *Nouveau recueil de contes, dits, fabliaux et autres pièces inédites des XIIIe, XIVe, et XVe siècles*, Vol. II, Paris.

KASTNER, L. E. "Les Versions françaises inédites de la Descente de saint Paul en Enfer", *Revue des Langues Romanes* 48 (1905), pp. 385–95, and 49 (1906), pp. 49–62, 321–51, 427–49.

KENNEY, JAMES F. *The Sources for the Early History of Ireland: Ecclesiastical* (1966 reprint), Irish U.P. & Columbia U.P., 1968.

KLAPPER, J. *Exempla aus Handschriften des Mittlealters*, Heidelberg, 1911.

KNOWLES, CHRISTINE. "Jean de Vignay: Un traducteur du XIVe siècle", *Romania* LXXV (1954), pp. 353–77.

KNOWLES, D. 1941. *The Monastic Orders in England*, Cambridge.

—— 1948. *The Religious Orders in England*, Cambridge.

KÖLBING, E. "Zwei mittelenglische Bearbeitungen der Sage von St. Patrik's Purgatorium", *Englische Studien* I (1877), pp. 57–121.

KOLVE, A. *The Play Called Corpus Christi*, London, 1966.

KOSCHWITZ, E. *Les plus anciens monuments de la langue française: Textes critiques et glossaire*, Leipzig, 1902; *Textes diplomatiques*, 6th edn., Leipzig, 1902.

KRAPP, G. P. *The Legend of St Patrick's Purgatory: Its Later Literary History*, Baltimore, 1900.

KROLL, J. *Gott und Hölle: der Mythos vom Descensuskampfe*, Leipzig & Berlin, 1932.

KUHN, E. "Barlaam und Joasaph", *Abhandlungen der k. bayer. Akademie der Wissenschaften,* I Kl., XX Bd., 1 Abt., Munich, 1893.

LABANDE, E. R. *Étude sur "Baudouin de Sebourc"*, Paris, 1940.

LANGLOIS, CH.-V. 1921. "Gefroi des Nés ou des Paris, traducteur et publiciste", *Histoire littérarie de la France* 35, pp. 324–48.

—— 1926. *La Vie en France au moyen âge de la fin du XIIe au milieu du XIVe siècle*: Vol. II, ... *d'après des moralistes du temps*; 1928, Vol. IV, *La Vie spirituelle*, Paris.

LA SALE, ANTOINE DE. *Œuvres complètes*: Vol. I, *La Salade*. Ed. F. Desonay, Liège & Paris, 1935.

—— *Le Paradis de la reine Sibylle*. Ed. F. Desonay, Paris, 1930.

LEBÈGUE, R. "Le Diable dans l'ancien théâtre religieux", *Cahiers de l'Association Internationale des Études Françaises*, No. 3-4-5 (July 1953), pp. 97-105.

LECKY, W. E. H. *History of European Morals from Augustus to Charlemagne*, Vol. II (3rd edn.), London, 1877.

LECOY, F. "Le *Chronicon Novaliciense* et les 'légendes épiques'", *Romania* LXVII (1942-3), pp. 1-52.

LEFÈVRE, YVES. *L'Elucidarium et les Lucidaires*, Paris, 1954.

LEGGE, M. DOMINICA. 1950. *Anglo-Norman in the Cloisters*, Edinburgh.

—— 1963. *Anglo-Norman Literature and its Background*, Oxford.

LEHMANN, PAUL. *Die Parodie im Mittelalter*, Munich, 1922.

LESLIE, S. *St Patrick's Purgatory. A Record from History and Literature*, London, 1932.

LÉVY, I. "La Légende de l'ange et de l'hermite dans les écrits juifs", *Revue des Études juives* 8 (1884), pp. 64-73.

LEWIS, C. S. *The Allegory of Love : A Study in Medieval Tradition*, Oxford, 1936.

LIPSIUS, R. A. *Die Pilatus-Acten kritisch untersucht*, 2nd edn., Kiel, 1886.

Le Livre du Chevalier de la Tour Landry. Ed. A. de Montaiglon, Paris, 1854.

Le Livre de la Passion, poème narratif du XIVᵉ siècle. Ed. Grace Frank, Paris (CFMÂ), 1930.

LOCKE, F. W. "A New Date for the Composition of the *Tractatus de Purgatorio Sancti Patricii*", *Speculum* XL (1965), pp. 641-6.

LODS, A. *De Quelques récits de voyage au pays des morts*, Mâcon, 1940.

LOTE, G. *La Vie et l'œuvre de François Rabelais*, Paris & Aix-en-Provence, 1938.

MAAS, P. M. *Étude sur les sources de la Passion du Palatinus*, Tiel, 1942.

Le Manuel des péchés. Ed. F. J. Furnivall (*Willame of Wadington, Manuel ...*), London, 1862; E. J. Arnould, Paris, 1940.

MARIE DE FRANCE. *L'Espurgatoire de saint Patrice*. Ed. T. A. Jenkins, Philadelphia, 1894 (2nd edn. in *The Decennial Publications of the University of Chicago*, VII, 1903); K. Warnke (*Das Buch vom Espurgatoire ...*), Halle, 1938.

—— *Lais*. Ed. A. Ewert, Oxford, 1944.

MEIDEN, WALTER. *La Descente de Saint-Paul en enfer*, unpublished thesis (see *Abstracts of Doctoral Dissertations*, No. 50, Ohio State U.P., 1946).

—— 1954. "Versions of the *Descente de Saint-Paul*", *Romance Philology* VIII (1954), pp. 92-5.

Mélanges d'histoire du théâtre du moyen-âge et de la Renaissance offerts à Gustave Cohen, Paris, 1950.

Merlin, roman en prose du XIIIᵉ siècle. Ed. G. Paris & J. Ulrich, Paris (SATF), 1886.

MEYER, K. & NUTT, A. *The Voyage of Bran Son of Febal to the Land of the Living, with an Essay upon the Irish Vision of the Happy Otherworld and the Celtic Doctrine of Rebirth*, London, 1895.

MEYER, PAUL. 1871. *Documents manuscrits de l'ancienne littérature de la France conservés dans les bibliothèques de la Grande-Bretagne*, Paris.

—— 1877. "Notice sur un MS bourguignon ...", *Romania* VI, pp. 1-46.

—— 1880. "Ancienne traduction française en vers du Pater et du Credo", *Bulletin de la Société des anciens textes français*, 6ᵉ année, pp. 38-40.

—— 1884. *Girart de Roussillon. Chanson de geste traduite pour la première fois*, Paris.

MEYER, PAUL. 1887. "Notice du MS de l'Arsenal 5201", "Notice du MS 1137 de Grenoble", "Notice sur un manuscrit interpolé de la *Conception de Wace*", *Romania* XVI, pp. 24–72, 214–31, 232–47.

—— 1895. "La Descente de saint Paul en Enfer, poème français composé en Angleterre", *Romania* XXIV, pp. 357–75.

—— 1896. "Les anciens traducteurs français de Végèce et en particulier Jean de Vignai", *Romania* XXV, 401–8; "Notice sur le manuscrit fr. 24862 . . .", *Notices et extraits des manuscrits de la Bibliothèque Nationale*, 35.i, pp. 131–68.

—— 1898. "Versions provençales d'Évangiles apocryphes", *Histoire littéraire de la France* 32, pp. 102–6.

—— 1902. "Satire en vers rythmiques sur la légende de saint Brendan", *Romania* XXXI, pp. 376–9.

—— 1906. "Légendes hagiographiques en français", *Histoire littéraire de la France* 33, pp. 328–458.

—— 1909. "Notice sur la 'Bible des Sept Etats du Monde' de Geufroi de Paris", *Notices et extraits . . .*, 39.i, pp. 255–322.

MIGNE, J. P. *Patrologiae Cursus Completus. Series Latina*, Paris, 1844.

MIQUEL Y PLANAS, M. *Llegendas de l'altra vida*, Barcelona, 1914.

Miracles de Nostre Dame. Ed. G. Paris & U. Robert, Vol. II, Paris (SATF), 1877.

MONNIER, JEAN. *La Descente aux enfers*, Paris, 1904.

MONTAIGLON, A. DE & RAYNAUD, G. *Recueil général et complet des fabliaux des XIIIᵉ et XIVᵉ siècles*, 6 vols., Paris, 1872–90.

MOORMAN, J. R. H. *Church Life in England in the Thirteenth Century*, Cambridge, 1945.

MOREL, C. *Les plus anciennes traductions françaises de la Divine Comédie*, Paris, 1897.

MOSS, ROSALIND. *The Life after Death in Oceania and the Malay Archipelago*, Oxford, 1925.

La Mule sans frein. Ed. R. T. Hill, Baltimore, 1911; B. Orlowski (as *La Damoisele à la mule*), Paris, 1911.

MUSSAFIA, A. *Sulla Visione di Tundalo*, Vienna, 1871 (first published in *Sitzungsberichte der Phil.-Hist Classe der Kais. Ak. der Wiss.* 67, Vienna, 1871).

Le Mystère d'Adam. Ed. P. Studer, Manchester, 1918; P. Aebischer, Geneva & Paris (TLF), 1963.

Le Mystère de la Passion. Texte du MS 697 de la Bibliothèque d'Arras. Ed. J. M. Richard, Paris, 1893.

Mystères provençaux du quinzième siècle. Ed. A. Jeanroy & H. Teulié, Toulouse, 1893.

NOTHOMB, J. "La Date de la Chronique Rimée de Philippe Mousket", *Revue belge de Philologie et d'Histoire* 4 (1925), pp. 77–89.

Orson de Beauvais, chanson de geste du XIIᵉ siècle. Ed. Gaston Paris, Paris (SATF), 1899.

Ovide moralisé, poème du commencement du quatorzième siècle. Ed. C. De Boer, 5 vols., Amsterdam, 1915–36.

OWEN, D. D. R. 1953. "The Principal Source of *Huon de Bordeaux*", *French Studies* VII, pp. 129–39.

—— 1955. "The Element of Parody in *Saint Pierre et le Jongleur*", *French Studies* IX, pp. 60–63.

OWEN, D.D.R. 1958. "The *Vision of St Paul*: The French and Provençal Versions and their Sources", *Romance Philology* XII, pp. 33–51.

—— 1966. "Païen de Maisières—A Joke That Went Wrong", *Forum for Modern Language Studies* II, pp. 192–6.

—— 1968. *The Evolution of the Grail Legend*, Edinburgh & London.

—— 1970. "Profanity and its Purpose in Chrétien's *Cligés* and *Lancelot*", *Forum for Modern Language Studies* VI, pp. 37–48 (reprinted in *Arthurian Romance: Seven Essays*, ed. D. D. R. Owen, Scottish Academic Press, 1970).

OWST, G. R. *Literature and Pulpit in Medieval England*, Cambridge, 1933.

The Oxford Dictionary of the Christian Church, ed. F. L. Cross, London (O.U.P.), 1958.

OZANAM, A. F. *Dante et la philosophie catholique du treizième siècle*, Paris, 1839.

PARÉ, G., BRUNET, A. & TREMBLAY, P. *La Renaissance du XIIᵉ siècle: les écoles et l'enseignement*, Paris & Ottawa, 1933.

PARFAICT brothers. *Histoire du théâtre françois*, Vols. I & II, Paris, 1734.

PARIS, GASTON. 1885. "Chrétien Legouais et autres traducteurs ou imitateurs d'Ovide", *Histoire littéraire de la France*, pp. 455–525.

—— 1903. *Légendes du moyen âge*, Paris.

PARIS, GASTON & BOS, A. *Trois versions rimées de l'Évangile de Nicodème par Chrétien, André de Coutances, et un anonyme*, Paris (SATF), 1885.

PARIS, PAULIN. "Baudouin de Sebourg", *Histoire littéraire de la France* 25 (1869), pp. 537–93.

La Passion d'Autun. Ed. Grace Frank, Paris (SATF), 1934.

La Passion du Christ. Ed. Gaston Paris in *Romania* II (1873), pp. 295–314.

La Passion du Palatinus, mystère du XIVᵉ siècle. Ed. Grace Frank, Paris (CFMÂ), 1922.

La Passion provençale du manuscrit Didot. Mystère du XIVᵉ siècle. Ed. W. P. Shepard, Paris (SATF), 1928.

PATCH, H. R. *The Other World, According to Descriptions in Medieval Literature*, Harvard U.P., 1950.

PAUPHILET, A. 1929. "Eneas et Énée", *Romania* LV, pp. 195–213.

—— 1950. *Le Legs du moyen âge*, Melun.

PERMAN, R. C. D. "Henri d'Arci: The Shorter Works", in *Studies in Medieval French Presented to Alfred Ewert*, Oxford, 1961.

PETIT DE JULLEVILLE, L. *Les Mystères*, Paris, 1880.

PFUHL, E. *Die weitere Fassung der altfranzösischen Dichtung in achtsilbigen Reimpaaren über Christi Höllenfahrt und Auferstehung*, Greifswald, 1909.

PHILIPPE MOUSKES. *La Chronique rimée*. Ed. Baron de Reiffenberg, 2 vols., Brussels, 1836–8 (Suppl. 1845).

PINCHBECK, C. "Three Old French Verse Sermons", *Medium Ævum* XXIII (1954), pp. 1–30.

PLUTARCH. *Moralia*. Ed. with translation by Ph. H. De Lacy & B. Einarson, Vol. VII, London & Cambridge (Mass.), 1959.

PRIOR, O. H. "Remarques sur l'anglo-noramnd", *Romania* XLIX (1923), pp. 161–85.

Pseudo-Turpin Chronicle. Ed. C. Meredith-Jones (*Historia Karoli Magni et Rotholandi ou Chronique du Pseudo-Turpin*), Paris, 1936.

Le Purgatoire de saint Patrice des MSS Harl. 273, et fonds fr. 2198. Ed. J. Vising, Gothenburg, 1916.

Le Purgatoire de saint Patrice du manuscrit de la Bibl. Nat. fds. fr. 25545. Ed. Marianne Mörner, Lund, 1920.

Li Purgatoire de saint Patrice. Ed. P. Tarbé, Rheims, 1842.

QUASTEN, JOHANNES. *Patrology*, Vol. I, Utrecht, 1950.

RABELAIS, FRANÇOIS. *Œuvres.* Ed. A. Lefranc, Vol. I, Paris, 1912.

RAOUL DE HOUDENC. *Le Songe d'Enfer suivi de la Voie de Paradis, poèmes du XIIIe siècle.* Ed. P. Lebesgue, La Rochelle & Paris, 1908.

REID, T. B. W. *Twelve Fabliaux*, Manchester, 1958.

RENAUT DE BEAUJEU. *Le Bel Inconnu.* Ed. G. P. Williams, Paris (CFMÂ), 1929.

RÉNIER, R. *La Discesa di Ugo d'Alvernia all'inferno secondo il codice franco-italiano della Nazionale di Torino*, Bologna, 1883.

RIQUER, M. DE. *Història de la literatura catalana*, Vol. II, Barcelona, 1964.

RITTER, E. "Notice du MS 179bis de la Bibliothèque de Genève", *Bulletin de la Société des anciens textes français*, 3e année (1877), pp. 85 ff.

Le Roman de Flamenca. Ed. P. Meyer, 2nd edn., Paris, 1901.

Le Roman de la Rose ou de Guillaume de Dole. Ed. G. Servois, Paris (SATF), 1893.

Le Roman de l'estoire dou Graal. Ed. W. A. Nitze, Paris (CFMÂ), 1927.

Le Roman de Renart. Première Branche. Ed. Mario Roques, Paris (CFMÂ), 1948.

Le Roman de Thèbes. Ed. L. Constans, 2 vols., Paris (SATF), 1890.

Le Romanz de saint Fanuel et de sainte Anne. Ed. C. Chabaneau, Paris, 1889.

ROY, E. "Le Mystère de la Passion en France du XIVe au XVIe siècle", *Revue Bourguignonne* 13 (1903), § 3–4, and 14 (1904), § 3–4.

RÜEGG, AUGUST. *Die Jenseitsvorstellungen vor Dante und die übrigen Voraussetzungen der "Divina Commedia"*, 2 vols., Einsiedeln/Köln, 1945.

RUTEBEUF. *Œuvres complètes.* Ed. E. Faral & Julia Bastin, Vol. II, Paris, 1960.

—— *Miracle de Théophile.* Ed. Grace Frank, Paris (CFMÂ), 2nd edn., 1949.

SCHIRMER, G. *Zur Brendanus-Legende*, Leipzig, 1888.

SCHÖNBACH, A. E. "Nachträge zur Legende vom Erzbischof Udo von Magdeburg", *Sitzungsberichte der Ak. der Wiss. in Wien (Ph.-hist. Kl.)* 145 (1903), Abh. VI, pp. 78–91.

SCHULZE, A. "Zur Brendanlegende", *Zeitschrift für Romanische Philologie* 30 (1906), pp. 257–79.

SCHWAN, E. "La Vie des anciens Pères", *Romania* XIII (1884), pp. 233–63.

La Seinte Resureccion. Ed. J. G. Wright (*La Résurrection du Sauveur, fragment d'un jeu*), Paris (CFMÂ), 1931; T. A. Jenkins, J. M. Manly, M. K. Pope & J. G. Wright, Oxford (ANTS), 1943.

SEYMOUR, ST. JOHN D. *Irish Visions of the Other World*, London, 1930.

SEZNEC, J. *La Survivance des dieux antiques*, London, 1940.

SIEGMUND, ALBERT. *Die Überlieferung der griechischen christlichen Literatur*, München, 1949.

SILVERSTEIN, H. T. 1933. "The Source of a Provençal Version of the Vision of St Paul", *Speculum* VIII (1933), pp. 353–8.

—— 1935. *Visio Sancti Pauli: The History of the Apocalypse in Latin, together with nine texts*, London.

—— 1960. "The Vision of St Paul: New Links and Patterns in the Western Tradition", *Archives d'histoire doctrinale et littéraire du moyen âge*, Paris, 34e année, pp. 199–248.

SIMUND DE FREINE. *Œuvres*. Ed. J. F. Matzke, Paris, 1909.

SINCLAIR, K. V. "Anglo-Norman Studies: The Last Twenty Years", *Australian Journal of French Studies* II (1965), pp. 113–55, 225–78.

SPARGO, J. W. *Virgil the Necromancer*, Cambridge, Mass., 1934.

SPENCE, L. *The Magic Arts in Celtic Britain*, London, 1945.

Le "Sponsus". Ed. L.-P. Thomas, Paris, 1951.

STENGEL, E. 1897. *Philologischer Kommentar zu der französischen Übertragung von Dantes Inferno in der Hs. L.III.17 der Turiner Universitätsbibliothek*, Paris.

—— 1908. *Huon's aus Auvergne Höllenfahrt, nach der Berliner und Paduaner Hs.*, Greifswald.

—— 1911. "Karl Martel's Entführung in die Hölle und Wilhelm Capets Wahl zu seinem Nachfolger. Stelle aus der Chanson von Huon d'Auvergne nach der Berliner Hs.", in *Studi letterari e linguistici dedicati a Pio Rajna*, Milan, pp. 873–91.

—— 1912. *Huons aus Auvergne Suche nach dem Hölleneingang*, Greifswald.

STOKES, WHITLEY. "The Voyage of Mael Duin", *Revue Celtique* 9 (1888), pp. 447–95, and 10 (1889), pp. 50–95.

STONE, L. W. "Old French Translations of the *De Consolatione Philosophiae* of Boethius: some unnoticed manuscripts", *Medium Ævum* VI (1937), pp. 21–30.

SUCHIER, H. 1875. "Brandans Seefahrt", *Romanische Studien* I, pp. 553–88.

—— 1883. *Denkmäler provenzalischer Literatur und Sprache*, Vol. I, Halle.

THEBEN, H. *Die altfranzösische Achtsilbnerredaktion der "Passion"*, Greifswald, 1909.

THOMAS, A. 1892. "Le Théâtre à Paris et aux environs à la fin du quatorzième siècle", *Romania* XXI, pp. 606–11.

—— 1938. "Traductions françaises de la *Consolatio philosophiae* de Boèce", *Histoire littéraire de la France* 37, pp. 419–70.

TISCHENDORF, C. *Evangelia Apocrypha*, Leipzig, 1853.

TOBLER, A. "Die Berliner Handschrift des *Huon d'Auvergne*", in *Sitzungsberichte der Kön. Preuss. Ak. der Wiss. zu Berlin*, 29th May 1884, pp. 605–20.

Le Tournoiement d'Enfer. Ed. A. Långfors in *Romania* XLIV (1915–17), pp. 511–58.

TYLOR, E. B. *Primitive Culture*, 2 vols., London, 4th edn., 1903.

VAN DEN GHEYN, J. *Histoire de Charles Martel. Reproduction de 102 miniatures de Loyset Liédet (1470)*, Brussels, 1910.

VAN DER ZANDEN, C. M. *Étude sur le Purgatoire de saint Patrice, accompagnée du texte Latin d'Utrecht et du texte anglo-normand de Cambridge*, Amsterdam, 1927.

VAN GENNEP, A. *Les Rites de passage*, Paris, 1909.

VAN OS, A. B. *Religious Visions: The Development of the Eschatological Elements in Mediaeval English Religious Literature*, Amsterdam, 1932.

Li Ver del Juïse. Ed. H. von Feilitzen, Uppsala, 1883.

VERDEYEN, R. & ENDEPOLS, J. *Tondalus' Visioen en St. Patricius' Vagevuur*, Iᵉ Deel, Ghent & The Hague, 1914.

VILLON, FRANÇOIS. *Œuvres*. Ed. A. Longnon & L. Foulet, Paris (CFMÀ), 4th edn., 1932.

VISING, J. *Anglo-Norman Language and Literature*, London, 1923.

Vision of Alberic. In *Bibliotheca Casinensis*, Vol. V.i, Monte Cassino, 1894, pp. 191–206.

Visio Tnugdali. Ed. O. Schade, Halle, 1869; A. Wagner (*Visio Tnugdali : lateinisch und altdeutsch*), Erlangen, 1882.

La Vision de Tondale (Tnugdal) : Textes français, anglo-normand et irlandais, Paris, 1907.

VOIGT, M. *Beiträge zur Geschichte der Visionenliteratur im Mittelalter, I : Visio Lazari*, Leipzig, 1924.

Les Voyages merveilleux de saint Brendan à la recherche du Paradis Terrestre : légende en vers du XIIe siècle. Ed. Francisque Michel, Paris, 1878.

Voyage au Purgatoire de St Patrice, Visions de Tindal et de St Paul, textes languedociens du quinzième siècle. Ed. A. Jeanroy & A. Vignaux, Toulouse, 1903.

The Vulgate Version of the Arthurian Romances, Vol. I, *L'Estoire del saint Graal.* Ed. H. O. Sommer, Washington, 1909.

WADDELL, HELEN. 1952. *Mediaeval Latin Lyrics*, Penguin Books.

—— 1954. *The Wandering Scholars.* Penguin Books.

WAHLUND, C. 1900. *Die altfranzösische Prosaübersetzung von Brendans Meerfahrt, nach der Pariser Handschrift Nat. Bibl. fr. 1553*, Uppsala.

— 1901. "Eine altprovenzalische Prosaübersetzung von Brendans Meerfahrt", in *Festgabe für W. Foerster*, Halle, 1901, pp. 129 ff.

WALBERG, E. *Quelques aspects de la littérature anglo-normande*, Paris, 1936.

WALTERS-GEHRIG, M. *Trois fabliaux : Saint Pierre et le jongleur, De Haimet et de Barat et Travers, Estula* (Beihefte zur *Zeitschrift für Romanische Philologie* 102), Tübingen, 1961.

WARD, H. L. D. *Catalogue of Romances in the Department of Manuscripts in the British Museum*, Vol. II, London, 1893.

WATMOUGH, J. R. *Orphism*, Cambridge, 1934.

WEBER, A. "Zu den Legenden der 'Vie des peres'", *Zeitschrift für Romanische Philologie* I (1877), pp. 357–65.

WELTER, J. T. *L'Exemplum dans la littérature religieuse et didactique du moyen âge*, Paris, 1927.

WIECK, H. *Die Teufel auf der mittelalterlichen Mysterienbühne Frankreichs*, Leipzig, 1887.

WIESE, L. *Die Sprache der Dialoge des Papstes Gregor mit einem Abhang : Sermo de Sapientia und Moralium in Job fragmenta*, Halle, 1900.

WRIGHT, T. *St Patrick's Purgatory*, London, 1844.

WÜLCKER, R. P. *Das Evangelium Nicodemi in der abendländischen Literatur*, Paderborn, 1872.

YOUNG, K. *The Drama of the Medieval Church*, 2 vols., Oxford, 1933.

ZIMMER, H. "Keltische Beiträge II. Brendans Meerfahrt", *Zeitschrift für deutsches Alterthum und deutsche Litteratur* 33 (1889), pp. 129–220, 257–338.

ZUMTHOR, P. *Histoire littéraire de la France médiévale*, Paris, 1954.

INDEX

The listing of proper names is selective, e.g. modern scholars are not included nor are some historical or fictional characters of marginal interest to the main subject-matter. Pages containing extended summaries and transcriptions of texts are shown in heavy type.